T0301345

Treasury Finance and Development Banking

Treasury Finance and Development Banking

A Guide to Credit, Debt, and Risk

Biagio Mazzi

WILEY

Library of Congress Cataloging-in-Publication Data:

ISBN 978-1-118-72912-0 (Hardcover)
ISBN 978-1-118-72942-7 (ebk)
ISBN 978-1-118-72936-6 (ebk)

Printed in the United States of America

10 9 8 7 6 5 4 3 2 1

To Eglantine, Edmondo, Albertine, and Leopoldo

Contents

List of Figures

List of Tables

Acknowledgments

The topic of this book is treasury finance, but the way it is written tries to reflect a broader view and an approach to finance in general, which I have built throughout my career and for which I am indebted to many people.

Tal Sandhu, whom I worked with at Banca Caboto and Morgan Stanley, took a chance on a green PhD graduate and taught me to look at finance in terms of fundamentals: one should always start from first principles, and often risk neutrality is just plain common sense. He has the same traits as the great experimental physicists I had worked with in my previous career: when one truly understands a subject, no amount of obscure math can get in the way. Stefano Boschian Pest, also a colleague from Banca Caboto and Morgan Stanley, shares the same worldview and many of the issues treated in this book can be traced back to questions and problems we have asked ourselves in the past.

At the Word Bank I need to thank Christopher Vallyeason: some key discussions we have had on the topics of funding and nonprofit banking have helped greatly to shape my understanding. In this book I try to paint a picture (albeit an often simplified one) of how an entire banking operation works: I owe part of the success of this attempt to him (while I reserve the full blame in case of failure). Also at the World Bank I need to thank Carlo Segni and Tenzing Sharchok for some very useful discussions on the dynamics of the search, particularly when option driven, for lower borrowing costs; George Richardson for explaining to me some important points on funding in Emerging Markets and non-deliverable currencies. Finally, I need to thank Dirk Bangert for a few extremely interesting conversations on credit modeling.

I need to thank at John Wiley & Sons the editorial team and, in particular, Susan McDermott, Jennifer MacDonald, and Tiffany Charbonier: their enthusiasm and help were crucial to the publishing of this book.

Finally I would like to thank my wife, Eglantine, for putting up with me during the writing of this book. As Tom W. Körner would say, though, the last six words seem unnecessarily limiting.

Introduction

I.1 TREASURY, FUNDING, AND THE REASONS BEHIND THIS BOOK

Any economic activity, or practically any activity for that matter, needs to be funded somehow. The parallel between these funds, or cash, and the blood in an organism has been abused at great length but it remains a powerful one. While we are used to the idea of corporations or governments raising cash for investments, we are less familiar with the idea of financial institutions doing the same. When we study finance, and in particular the derivatives world, we often assume that the money used for these transactions is basically already there. This of course is not the case since financial institutions need to raise the liquidity they subsequently use to finance derivatives transactions. At the center of the operation of raising funds is the treasury, a specific desk or unit in an investment bank or a separate division in the case of a corporation.

Funding, through the action of borrowing, is intimately connected to the concept of credit and since the financial crisis of 2007 to 2009, credit has been a central topic in any financial discussion. When discussing financial theory at a more or less quantitative level, the cost of funding has never entered as a deciding factor. Now (as it is elegantly described by Piterbarg [70]) this can no longer hold true.

There is a fair amount of literature covering treasury operations, but none that addresses the need of understanding at the same time the role of a treasury desk and its impact on the valuation of financial instruments. The works by Bragg [16] or Cooper [28] or Horcher [47] are very specific to the operational aspects of a treasury and deal in great detail with its practical aspects. Of similar practical nature is the work of Jeffrey [54] where the role of treasury is seen through its corporate goals. In these books we see how a treasury can either participate in the corporate growth of an institution or how an institution can deal with specific challenges such as cash and debt management or currency risk. Of the literature that does focus on valuation issues of the risk-neutral type one might encounter on a trading desk, there is work by Kitter [58] with a good analysis, for example, of interest rate curve construction which, because of age, does not include the crucial developments that have taken place during the first decade of the twenty-first century. Banks' work [7] is another text that, while very similar in spirit to the present one, unfortunately lacks a very topical update on the recent financial crisis. Oricchio's work [67] is close to our goals but, focusing on highly illiquid credit, his treatment straddles the boundaries of risk neutrality within which we shall always try to remain.

What exactly are our goals? Who is the ideal reader of this book? While, as we said, treasuries are present in all corporations (and sovereign entities), we shall be focusing mainly on treasuries within financial institutions. We are going to show how the role of funding is crucial for these institutions and how it affects the way all activities are seen and transactions priced. Most important we shall highlight how focusing on the cost of funding introduces specific risk management considerations. Moreover we shall offer a special focus on the role of funding when it comes to development banking. The ideal reader of this book is the practitioner with experience in fixed income or another asset class, new to treasury and to concepts such as funding, asset swaps, or loan pricing. Of course, because of the special focus on development banking, the ideal reader might be a practitioner in an institution applying the tools of investment banking toward development goals. A basic knowledge of concepts such as optionality and types of options is assumed; while they will be briefly introduced again, a knowledge of simple fixed income concepts such as accrual or forward rates would be preferable. Except for the fairly brief one on the prepayment options of loans, no discussion will involve stochastic formalism: a solid grasp on financial modeling in the strict sense is not needed, any knowledge of it, however, can only be beneficial. To summarize as only a head hunter could, the ideal reader would be someone that, at some point in his or her career, has read and understood a substantial amount of Hull.[1]

Particularly since the issue of funding is so crucial to the functioning of any entity and in particular a financial institution, the approach has been to look at problems in terms of fundamentals: the mathematical tone of the book is kept at a minimum precisely because questions and answers have been based on fundamentally practical problems. Formalism has been modified in a way to suit the problems at hand sometimes, particularly when discussing the discounted value of bonds, with a twist that hopefully will add clarity rather than confusion. The same way mathematical physics needs to follow the logical laws of nature, finance, once we allow for the

---

[1]Meaning, of course, John Hull's *Options, Futures, and Other Derivatives*.

complexity of the instruments on which it is built, needs to follow very sensible rules based on profit, choice, and uncertainty. It is by this type of common sense that we describe the world of debt: as we shall see, all sorts of formulas can be written to value and describe the price of a bond; however, at the end it is just a number that rises and falls according to the investors' interest.

Next to mathematical simplicity, we have striven for brevity. This book is intended as a tale of credit. We shall discuss how it is a tool for the practitioner to see credit in terms of spread, and how the markets, through different phenomena, affect those spreads. In the belief that once the basic understanding is obtained—there is no better way to learn than through action— the size and scope of this book have been kept within the boundaries of this purpose. We have relied heavily on actual market data literally snapped from brokers' screens to show how to proceed with individual learning. A goal we hope to have achieved with this book is to show where to look and how to extract knowledge. Once this is achieved, there are few things as valuable as a few hours spent browsing Reuters (or an equivalent market data repository).

I.2 FUNDING ISSUES AS CREDIT AND PRICING ISSUES

As we show in Chapter 6, a treasury desk faces no hedging needs: if it is a desk within a financial institution the risk remains within the firm; if it is the treasury of a development institution or a corporation, the risk is outsourced. In any case it does not remain with the treasury itself. Because of this it has specific risk and valuation issues which it is our intent to prepare the reader for.

Not surprisingly for a book centered around debt, credit will be the paramount issue and we shall strive to show how as an issue it appears almost everywhere. Its first appearance is in the realm of curve construction, the fundamental process by which we generate forward floating rates and calculate their present values. The pricing of financial instruments, swaps in particular, have been subject to profound changes due to the interpretation and perception of the credit risk involved: from the different risk incurred by financial institutions borrowing in different currencies, to the different credit risk inherent in rates of different maturities, to finally the different credit risk linked to the posting or not posting of collateral. The classical theory of swap pricing (see Duffie and Singleton [32]) considered the credit risk of a swap to be the same as the interbank credit when in practice, due to collateral posting, it was the same as the overnight rate. These details appear small in a normal environment but assume great proportions in a turbulent market. Moreover, with the increasing disappearance of complex exotic structures and the focusing on vanilla ones, the small details will become even more important. Curve construction and in particular discounting plays an exact role in our discussion because, as we introduced previously, a treasury operation does not carry out hedging. A correct discounting of an instrument is essential to arrive at what constitutes the *raison d'être* of a treasury operation, the funding level.

In a debt-raising operation the funding level is the measure of everything. After showing how this level is essentially an asset swap spread, we will position it at the center of our discussion. Our goal will be to place in the reader's hands an imaginary rope representing the funding level of some imaginary entity of which the reader is the treasurer. Once in possession of the rope, the reader will learn what makes this rope move, what in the financial world pulls at its extremities or shifts it. Bond pricing will be seen almost entirely in terms of discounting and, with the risk of confusing the reader, the issue will be stressed to the point of introducing a quantity $\widetilde{D}_i$ representing the credit correction to the money market discount factor. This will be to show that this appendix to the risk-free discount factor is what moves, through the prism of the asset swap, the funding level on the other side. To remain with the image of the rope, we shall try to show how, while always representing credit risk, there are many, often parallel, curves that take different meanings. CDS spreads, yields, benchmarks, and the asset swap spread itself can be related to each other or differ by little, but they can also mean and imply different types of credit risks.

The understanding of the difference between the various representations of credit risk can only come from an understanding of credit as a modeling of default; because our focus is always the valuation of financial instruments in the context of trading, our modeling will be risk neutral and centered around the concept of credit default swaps. Although it might seem like a detour, an introduction to the basics of credit modeling is fundamental to understanding the relationship between the market data, the CDS spread, and the concept of survival probability. We have tried to present it in a way that makes the latter appear as a risky discount factor, the appendix to the riskless discount factor we mentioned previously.

Our goal is therefore to make the reader comfortable with the concept of credit risk and the idea of its representation as a spread. Once we do so, we can show what else can be seen to affect this spread from liquidity issues to leverage (Schwarz [75], Adrian and Shin [2], and Acharya and Pedersen [1]). It is partly with this intent that we touch upon emerging markets, markets that in their simplicity allow us to identify with ease individual factors. A simple example would be the bid-offer spreads: large or small spreads appear in every market; however, in developed markets many factors can drive their size. In emerging markets one can, most of the time, see a simple correlation between maturity, credit standing of the country and/or region, and bid-offer spread size—the mark of liquidity. We can simply offer an introduction without straying too much from our path: hopefully with it the reader can continue in the discovery of this fascinating topic.

I.3 TREASURY FINANCE AND DEVELOPMENT BANKING

The core of this book has two sides, debt management and development banking. The focus on development is not only for its own sake, but particularly because development banking, as an example of a simple banking activity that nonetheless maintains all the essential characteristics, allows the reader to understand concepts which apply to all banking but are easier to see in a simpler situation. Development banking will be introduced and then presented mainly through specific and yet theoretical financial examples. In the chapter on emerging markets we look at a few case studies in which we relate financial activity to realistic and practical development projects.

The type of development banking we are going to discuss is the one that uses the tools of investment banking—borrowing and lending—with the goal of assisting countries or institutions that would struggle to obtain the same type of assistance in the financial markets. Although the tools are the same, there are many differences that are important to stress. Earlier we mentioned the prism of the asset swap as the nexus between risky discounting and funding level. We will portray development banking as the prism through which to view credit going from the financial markets—open to everyone—to the bespoke lending (developed) markets where only development institutions dare to venture. A development bank, by lending at a level which is essentially (minus costs of operation) the one at which it can borrow, acts as a sort of transformer, enabling risky borrowers to access liquidity at rates they could never otherwise obtain. Throughout the book we stress the technical and formal elements differentiating the two types of banking (with the assumption that, unless stated otherwise, things are identical). At first one might be surprised that both types of institutions, only as far as borrowing is concerned of course, are not very different; however, when differences will appear (for example, in the case of the prepayment option in loans or the passing on of the institution's borrowing costs to the subsequent borrower) they will be as startling.

The development banking world is particularly interesting because it straddles the separation between a financial institution and a sovereign entity. A development institution borrows, lends, and invests more or less like a traditional bank, yet it has some of the constraints and limitations of a sovereign entity. The instruments used for investments are fairly simple—they do not borrow to fund financial investment, they do not seek exposure to exotic financial risks, and so on. Moreover, a development institution, or at least those that are known as supranational, has constraints that go beyond those of a sovereign entity, exemplified, as we shall see, in the view that a development institution can be seen as a credit cooperative.

In the volatile times following the 2007 to 2009 financial crisis it is particularly difficult to forecast the direction of finance. It is clear that a few issues seem to gain in importance and will likely remain in focus for a long time. Credit will probably never leave the center of any financial consideration; sovereign debt will be treated with more interest going forward; financial transactions will probably move toward plainer structures; the developing world with its mixture of need and growth will play a larger role in the financial world. Development banking, and we shall try to treat it in a way that will make this clearer, sits at the intersection of all these issues in the sense that each one of these can be illustrated and better understood if seen in the context of banking with the goal of development.

I.4 THE STRUCTURE OF THE BOOK

As we said, this book is structured in an attempt to build the foundations of a clear understanding of the role of a treasury within a financial institution, the special functions of a development institution, and the specific risks that are associated with funding and managing debt.

In Chapter 1 we offer an introductory view to banking, development banking, and the role of the treasury within a financial institution. We present the fundamental activities of banking as lending (Section 1.2), borrowing (Section 1.3), and investing (Section 1.4). In Section 1.5 we offer a brief picture of how a financial institution is structured and in particular where the treasury is placed. In Section 1.6 we introduce development banking.

In Chapter 2 we discuss what can be considered the single most important problem in fixed income, curve construction. No attempt to value a financial instrument can be considered serious without a careful construction of its discount and index curves. In Section 2.1 we lay the foundation for the problem and in Section 2.2 we describe the instruments available in the market to construct a curve. In Section 2.3 we discuss the fairly recent development of the simultaneous use of multiple instruments to build a curve. The even more recent use of overnight index swaps to discount cash flows is approached in Section 2.4, where it is inserted in the historical evolution of the perception of credit risk when valuing derivatives. We conclude the chapter with Section 2.5, the first numerical example section, in which we lead the reader through the bootstrapping of an interest rate curve. Like the other numerical sections that will follow, the examples will be limited only to those calculations that the reader could then independently replicate on, say, a spreadsheet or in a simple VBA piece of code, such as the one presented on the web site.

Chapter 3 is dedicated to credit. Given the fact that a treasury's main activity is raising debt, credit is central to it, and this chapter attempts to understand its fundamental concepts. In Section 3.1 we describe what characterizes credit as an asset class and what its main underlyings are. We end by introducing credit default swaps (CDS) upon whose risk neutral definition of survival we shall base further credit considerations. In Section 3.2 we show the three main approaches to credit modeling and we settle on the preferred choice, for our purpose, of intensity based model. We conclude the section with a useful and rigorous toolkit for obtaining survival probabilities from CDS spreads. In Section 3.3 we discuss the fair value of loans and we dedicate a considerable space to issues specific to development banking. In Section 3.4 we conclude the chapter with the numerical example of pricing the same loan issued by a development institution to four different borrowers.

As introduced earlier, the reasons for the focus on emerging markets in Chapter 4 are twofold. As a text dedicating considerable attention to development banking, it is important to discuss the regions and the markets where this takes place. At the same time, under a financial point of view, emerging markets offer an invaluable example of phenomena such as liquidity and capital control. After attempting a definition of the essentially nebulous concept of emerging markets in Section 4.1, we touch upon the financial characteristics typical of these markets such as liquidity, capital control, and credit risk in Section 4.2. We continue with Section 4.3

where we see the role played by emerging markets in development banking (or vice versa). In Section 4.4 we present two case studies of realistic projects involving the action of a development institution in an emerging market.

Chapter 5 is dedicated to the most important instrument we deal with and the essence of debt: bonds. In Sections 5.1 and 5.2 we introduce the idea of bonds and the essential concepts associated with it, such as par, duration, and—the most fundamental of all—yield. In Section 5.3 we discuss the credit element of bond and we understand how to express it through proxies such as asset swap spread and how to view it in terms of CDS spreads. We continue in Section 5.4 with a look at how to price illiquid and/or distressed debt (using as an example in Section 5.4.2 the default of Greece); on this particular topic in Section 5.5 we try to estimate the numerical value of a coupon of a real emerging market entity.

In Chapter 6, after having built the necessary knowledge, we finally approach the topic of treasury. In Section 6.1 we return to the all-important concept of asset swap and we discuss how funding is essentially seen through it. In Section 6.2 we discuss what it means to search for ever-smaller funding cost, the main role of a treasury desk, and what it entails in terms of risk and valuation. In Section 6.3 we look at how a development institution differs from a normal investment bank. In Section 6.4 we revisit the concept of benchmark in the context of a development bank's borrowing and investment strategies.

In Chapter 7 we analyze some of the risk and challenges facing treasury operations, irrespective of whether it is within a development institution or a desk within an investment bank. In Section 7.1 we return to the concept of leverage and see it in terms of capital requirements. In Section 7.2 we discuss what replication and hedging means in terms of pricing and what it means to price a financial instrument when no hedging or static hedging is carried out. We continue the chapter with a view on risk management. First, in Section 7.3 we discuss the management of risk associated with financial variables. In Section 7.3.1 we look at interest rate and FX risk and its management through static hedging. In Section 7.3.2 mentions briefly the explicit treatment of credit risk. We continue in Section 7.4 with a look at the different types of funding risk that are typical of the situation where a pool of debt and loans needs to be managed. In Sections 7.4.3 and 7.4.5 we offer two numerical examples of estimating refinancing and reset risk in a loan/debt portfolio.

We finish the book with Chapter 8 where we draw some conclusions from our discussion. We stress how credit is present in any corner of the financial landscape, and finally, as a way of putting everything together, we imagine we are setting up a treasury operation and we recap what the fundamental steps would be.

A few interesting topics, which would have nonetheless disrupted the flow of the main text, have been presented in a series of appendices. Finally, in the chapter, About the Web Site, we direct the reader to a web site where we offer some implementations of numerical techniques presented in the preceding chapters.

Treasury Finance and Development Banking

CHAPTER 1

An Introductory View to Banking, Development Banking, and Treasury

We have mentioned that our focus is going to be any treasury activity carried out by a traditional financial institution, a development bank, a corporation, or a government. When discussing the issuance of debt we will indeed draw examples from all four types of entities listed; however, when the objective will be a deeper understanding of several concatenated activities, we shall focus on the former two types of institution: investment banks and development banks. Furthermore, our view will narrow toward development banking not only because it is a special concern of ours but also because, in its simpler type of financial activity, it offers an opportunity to isolate clearly the different functions of a bank. A development institution that uses the tools of investment banking (we shall see in Section 1.6.1 that some do not) offers the simplest type of banking activity, a type made up of instruments upon which traditional investment banks have built increasingly more sophisticated ones; the higher level of sophistication, in our situation, does not translate necessarily to a better understanding.

In this chapter we shall introduce the fundamental activities of a financial institution as lending, borrowing, investing, and asset liability management (ALM); we shall try to present them in this order so as to follow the business line that goes from the client's need for a loan, through the bank's need to fund the loan, and then invest the income generated and hedge the potential risks. We shall then conclude with a sketch of the structure of a typical financial institution and a definition of the type of development bank we shall be dealing with.

1.1 A REPRESENTATION OF THE CAPITAL FLOW IN A FINANCIAL INSTITUTION

Before offering an introduction to fundamental banking activities, let us focus on a schematic representation of the flow of capital within a financial institution. As we have said before, we shall use a development institution as an example, since it encapsulates at least the fundamental aspects of banking plus a few additional features.

In Figure 1.1 we show the capital inflow and outflow to the treasury of a development institution. In Section 1.6 we describe which type of institutions obtain their funds in which particular way, but here we attempt to describe in a general way how development institutions obtain their funds and what they do with them.

A development institution, like many institutions, has shareholders who have brought a certain initial amount of equity to the institution and own a share of it. The sum of all these contributions constitutes the majority of the institution's equity. Additionally, and this is peculiar to development organizations, there are donors' contributions. These contributions can be made either by the shareholders themselves or by other entities; they can

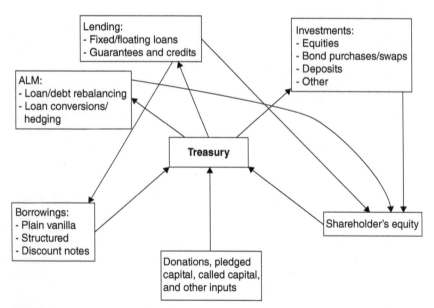

FIGURE 1.1   A schematic representation of the inflow and outflow of capital to the treasury of a development institution.

actually be given to the institution or they can be *pledged*, meaning that they remain with the donor until the institution asks for it. These contributions can be offered or, when coming from the shareholders, they can be requested by the collection of shareholders.

An additional inflow of capital, and the main topic of this book, is debt. In Section 1.3 we introduce how borrowing fits within the general activity of an institution and define the varieties of those instruments. Throughout the rest of the book we describe how debt is priced.

The main outflow, and the reason for being a development institution or a commercial bank, is lending. In Section 1.2 we introduce how lending takes place in relation to clients' needs. Income generated by loans is used to repay the debt; any additional return flows into the institution's equity.

The role played by the investment unit of a development institution will be introduced at a general level in Section 1.4 and in more detail in Section 6.4.2. Its main mandate is essentially to prevent depreciation in the institution's equity and to provide emergency liquidity to its lending unit. Investments' returns flow back into the institution's equity.

Finally, the institution's capital is also used for asset liability management, which will be introduced in Section 1.4 at a general level and then in detail in Chapter 7. Its main mandate is to balance debt and income and to hedge high-level exposures. It is an activity that should be more or less return neutral; however, any positive return would flow into the institution's equity.

Having sketched the general movement of capital within a development institution, we can now begin introducing its main activities in more detail before—in the subsequent chapters—getting into even greater detail by adopting more analytical tools.

1.2 LENDING

A bank is a firm whose core business is dealing with money itself. A bank exists and profits from making money available to others. To *make money available* is an intentionally vague expression because the ways banks *inject liquidity* (a favorite journalese expression meaning helping to increase the circulation of money) into the world are multiple and some are more direct than others. The simplest, and the one we shall focus on, is through lending money to whoever needs it (and, of course, qualifies for it).

A loan is the main instrument of lending and the one we shall discuss at length throughout the book. In Section 3.1.1 we give a rigorous definition of it, in Section 3.3.1 we discuss its valuation, and in Chapter 7 we discuss its relationship to debt. Here we are simply going to introduce a loan in the context of a description of the activity of a bank. If we allow for the statement that, irrespective of the sophistication of a banking activity, the business of a bank is lending, we can simply focus on loans, and for that matter the activity of a development bank is sufficient for our discussion. Any additional activity a traditional financial institution, such as an investment bank, carries out can be seen as built on this.

Who are the clients facing a development bank, the entities needing a loan? A typical client of a development institution is a sovereign or private entity most often associated with the developing world; such client would seek the help of a development bank because to do the same in the capital markets would be too expensive or downright impossible. The need for a loan can be associated with a more or less specific development project that the sovereign or corporate entity envisages to carry out. The term *development project* is vague but we can imagine it including building schools and hospitals, developing infrastructure and power sources, even developing a basic capital market. We can imagine it excluding unnecessarily the strengthening of armed forces or building infrastructures closely linked to the ruler or the ruling party (e.g., a road to the ruler's estate).

Not all projects benefit from the same type of loan, and the role of a development institution is to construct the lending instrument around the needs of the client. We now present some of the possible types of loans in the context of the type of project.

- **Loan versus credit or guarantee:** The first choice facing a development institution offering financial help to a borrower is whether this help should take the form of a loan, a credit, or a guarantee. A *loan* is an instrument where the repayment of the principal is linked to some market-driven variable; we leave this vague but it means that irrespective of whether the interest rate is fixed or floating (see the following), it is driven by some market considerations. A *credit* on the other hand is an instrument where the repayment is usually made of a nominal (small) rate. Finally, a *guarantee* is not an offer of funds but a guarantee to honor a promise made by a borrower that an investor will purchase a bond issued by some country with the understanding that, in case the borrowing country defaults, the development institution wil step in to honor the debt. In general, the wealthier the borrower, the more likely it will be offered a loan rather than the other two instruments. Another general rule is that the size of a credit or a guarantee is usually smaller than the size of a loan.
- **Bullet versus amortizing loans:** A project that might be more or less capital intensive and it might offer returns in a more or less gradual way. A way for the lending institution to accommodate the needs of the client is to issue a loan with a specific repayment profile.

A loan (we shall see this in more formal detail later) consists of a series of repayments of interest and principal, with the principal, as the name suggests, being the main component of the loan. Should the principal repayment prove to be difficult for the borrower, a solution is made available through a *bullet loan* in which the borrower throughout the life of the loan repays only the interest[1] and the principal is returned only at maturity. Let us imagine that the borrower needs the funds to build up the country's energy industry; these projects, ranging from dams to oil exploration, usually require a large initial investment, a long time to build, and then must produce a fairly regular source of income. During the build-up period it would be difficult for the borrower to repay the principal, therefore, in this situation, for example, a bullet loan would be ideal.

A lender is, however, hesitant to issue too many bullet loans. This will be treated more formally when dealing with the issue of credit, but it is easy to see how the further into the future we push the repayment of the main part of the loan, the more—particularly when dealing with countries and projects fraught with uncertainty—we place ourselves in a riskier situation. Because of this, the more standard form of loan is an *amortizing loan*, one where, at each interest paying date, the principal upon which the interest is calculated is partly repaid.

- **Fixed-versus floating-rate loans:** The interest repayments on a loan are a percentage amount that can be either the same at each repayment date (a *fixed-rate loan*) or variable, linked to some external parameter (a *floating-rate loan*). The choice of loan on the part of the borrower and the lender will be mainly driven by considerations linked to the financial markets of the currency in which the loan has been issued. The volatility of interest rates and the expected levels of inflation, all compounded by the length of the loan, will be deciding factors in the choice. Similar to the previous situation in which the choice was about which repayment profile, the choice of fixity in the interest repayments will be a balance between the borrower's needs and the lender's ability to deal with financial risk.

  Development banks are typically very risk averse and will usually try to convert both costs (from their own borrowing, which we shall see later) and income (from loans repayments) into an easy-to-interpret and manage cash stream. Fixed- and floating-rate loans offer the lender different risk profiles with typically a preference for floating-rate loans.[2]

---

[1]In the mortgage world, these type of mortgages are indeed known as interest only.
[2]To offer another comparison with the mortgage world, with the exception of the United States, fixed-rate mortgages tend to be less frequent than they used to be.

■ **The currency of the loan:** An important issue is the currency in which the loan is offered, important also because the currency will decide which interest rate regime will govern the loan (i.e., if the loan is in currency X, it will be X interest rates that both borrower and lender will examine in their decision for a floating- or fixed-rate loan).

The return on the investment the borrowing entity is hoping to obtain will drive, as it did in the previous cases, the choice of currency of the loan. We mentioned the example of oil extraction as a possible project: should the project be successful, the income generated will be in U.S. Dollars (USD) since oil is a global commodity priced in USD. The borrowing country will then be motivated to take a loan in USD. In the case, for example, of the construction of a dam to provide electricity to local customers (who are expected therefore to pay for consumption in local currency) the income generated will be in local currency and therefore the borrowing country would prefer the loan to be in local currency. We can easily see how from the borrower's point of view it would be desirable to match, currencywise, the income stream with the debt stream.

A similar and therefore symmetrical wish is on the lender's part. Development banks are usually financed (as we shall see in the following section) in strong currencies[3] and therefore would like to match the income they receive with the costs they face. A development bank would rather issue a USD loan than a local currency loan. Furthermore, a local currency loan is more subject to devaluation and/or inflation. An intuitive rule of thumb would be that anyone would rather receive income in a strong currency and pay debt in a weak one. As a consequence of this, local currency loans usually constitute a small, yet far from negligible portion of a loan portfolio.

The needs of a borrower are assessed at the moment of deciding the type and amount of loan. It is considered that the borrower will face certain costs throughout the life of the project, and the loan should be used to cover those costs. These costs, however, could change dramatically—driven by changes in the foreign exchange—after the issuance of the loan and this is because of a third currency other than the strong and the weak mentioned before (e.g., the borrower needs to purchase equipment in a third country). To manage this type of exposure there are also

---

[3]The definition of strong currency is not a precise one but it is usually intended to include USD, Euro (EUR), Japanese Yen (JPY), and sometimes British Pound (GBP) and Swiss Franc (CHF). In general, strong currencies are those currencies in which foreign reserves are held.

multi-currency loans that are issued, linked not to a single currency but to a basket of usually strong currency.

Here we have presented very briefly the type of choices facing a borrower and a lender when deciding which type of loan is best suited to the financing of a project. We now take on the point of view of the development institution and observe the different types of debt we can use to finance these loans.

1.3 BORROWING

The type of development institutions we are concerned with are those (we discuss them in more detail later) that use the tools of investment banking toward development, that is, they use their superior credit to borrow in the capital markets and then use the funds raised toward lending.

The debt profile of a development institution is one that should at the same time be in tune with its income profile (by income profile we mean the types of loans issued as discussed in the previous section) and capable of maximizing investors' needs. We shall discuss this at great length in the following chapters but, it is almost obvious, a bank should issue debt that can be considered as attractive as possible in the eyes of investors, otherwise not only will it be difficult to place, it will also be unduly onerous to serve.

In a way similar to the one adopted in the previous section we give a brief and informal description of the type of choices an institution has to make when it comes to funding through debt. The description is informal in that all mathematical and/or rigorous formalism is left for later parts of the book.

- **Currency of debt:** In the previous section we mentioned that any financial player tries to match the currency of its debt with the currency of its income. A development bank issues loans in at least a few strong currencies and, as we have seen, in some cases also in weak currencies. Assuming that for any institution there is only one mother currency, the other currencies, weak or strong, need to be obtained in order to be subsequently disbursed in the form of a loan. This could happen either by converting the institution's principal currency to the currency needed for the loan or, as in most cases, by issuing debt in that currency.

  Issuing debt in a specific currency not only has the advantage of matching the currency of a loan but also, as we shall see more formally in Section 6.2.1, has the advantage of exploiting investors' appetite for the institution's debt. Let us consider development bank ABC, which has a certain credit rating and is USD centered, meaning that its main currency of business is USD. Let us assume that in the United States there are other institutions similar to ABC, both in nature and in credit standing, but in Japan there are none. This absence results in a great interest on the part of Japanese investors for debt of ABC's kind. It would make sense for ABC to issue debt in Japanese Yen (JPY) since, all things considered, it would receive more favorable terms.[4] Now, ABC is in possession of a certain amount of JPY, which is not only needed for a loan, but results in an advantageous servicing of debt from its own point of view.

- **Profile and tenor of debt:** The careful balance between a bank's cost and income shall be treated rigorously in Chapter 7, however, it is quite intuitive to imagine that, the same way we would like to match the currency between debt and income, it would be ideal to try to match the tenor and general structure of our debt and our loans. As we shall see later, this turns out to be rather complicated.

  We mentioned in the previous section that bullet loans are extremely rare. It turns out that amortizing debt in the form of bonds with an amortizing principal profile is also rare. This means that there is an initial and fundamental mismatch in the principal profile of the debt issued by the institution and the income it receives in the form of loans. In Section 3.1.1 we shall attribute this difference principally to the fact that bonds tend to be securitized instruments as opposed to the overwhelming over-the-counter nature of loans. A second fundamental difference is driven by credit. It is almost a universal truth that borrowing over the short term is cheaper than borrowing over a longer one. Since, despite being not-for-profit organizations, development banks have some fixed costs and cannot operate at a loss, they are obliged to have a shorter average maturity for debt than for loans. This is what ensures, in principle, a small positive net income. However this also ensures that, as far as maturity and principal amortization are concerned, bonds and loans will never be matched and this can lead to serious risks.

- **Fixed or floating rate:** The choice, on the part of an institution, to issue fixed- or floating-rate debt is driven, like the one of currency, by a balance between the borrower's need and the investors' appetite. As in the case of a loan, a *fixed-rate bond* is one where the investor receives the same percentage amount of principal at regular intervals and a *floating-rate bond* is one where that amount is variable and is linked to some external parameter. Although, as we said, the tendency on the part of the lender (i.e., the bank) is to prefer the disbursement of floating-rate

---

[4]We shall give a formal definition of what "all things considered" means when discussing asset swap spreads when we shall also be able to understand formally what we grasp intuitively as to the meaning of "favorable terms."

loans, there could be situations in which, in response to great investors' interest in a fixed-rate bond, the bank is in the situation in which the fixed-rate nature of the loan matches the one of the bond.

■ **Vanilla or exotic:** A debt instrument can be anything in terms of complexity. It can be a bond paying a simple coupon (fixed or floating), it can be a coupon offering the payout of a simple option (a call or a put on a familiar[5] underlying), or it can be a coupon linked to the payout of an exotic option, that is, an option whose payout is complex and needs a serious computational effort in order to be priced. These payouts can include a combination of caps, floors, values linked to past performances (look-back features), spreads, and so forth. The reason behind the choice of more or less complexity, that is, more *vanilla* or more *exotic*, in the type of debt issued is linked to a search for more attractive funding levels. This will be explored in detail in Section 6.2.1.

■ **Debt managing tools:** We have mentioned quite a few times the concept of matching. Ideally a development bank would try to make sure that the nature (in terms of amortizing profile), currency, and fixity of rate of its debt is similar to the one of its income, that is, its loans. This, we have seen, is not always possible. We have also said that development banks are generally risk averse and prefer to be exposed to the smallest number of financial variables. A development bank would usually choose one currency and one type of rate and take them to be a measure of all things, so to speak. A U.S.-based development bank would, for example, choose USD to be its principal currency and a certain floating rate, for example, the LIBOR rate resetting every six months, to be its principal rate. (We have not defined the LIBOR rate yet, but for the rest of the chapter we shall simply treat it as some generic variable rate.) This means that all income and all debt that does not match the USD six-month LIBOR profile needs to be converted into it. A USD fixed-rate loan would need to be converted into a similar floating-rate loan, then the bank would seek to enter into a contract with some other party in which it pays the fixed rate received from the loan and receives a floating rate in return. A similar, if opposite, situation would be needed to convert a USD fixed-rate bond. The bank would enter into a contract paying a floating rate in USD and receiving the fixed-rate coupon in USD, which goes on to the investor. What applied to fixity also applies to currency. Should the loan be fixed (or floating) in, say, EUR, the bank would seek to enter

---

[5] By familiar we mean interest rate, equity, or FX: although the term familiar is not a standard one, even a simple option linked to credit or commodities would probably not be considered so simple.

into a contract in which it would pay another party the fixed (or floating) coupon in EUR it receives from the loan and it would obtain in return a floating payment in USD. A similar, if opposite, contract would be needed to convert a fixed (or floating) rate bond in EUR. These types of subsequent contracts are known as *swaps* and will be discussed at length later.

1.4   INVESTING AND ALM

The main source of income for a development bank is the revenues from its lending business. There is however usually, as in any normal financial institution, considerable investment activity taking place. In Section 7.1 we shall discuss where a development bank's funds come from and what percentage they constitute of the loan portfolio. Here we simply state that a bank is in possession of funds of its own that are independent of those raised through debt. We have seen in Section 1.1 that these funds can be made of equity and other assets or in the specific case of development institutions they can be donations or requested capital. We have also seen that these funds are also replenished by the net income (i.e, a profit, should there be one) given by the sum of the inflows from the loans and the outflows of the debt.

In a traditional financial institution these assets can be used to reward employees or shareholders (or partners) or can be used for other specific activities such as share buybacks. In a development institution, which of course is not for profit, they are mainly used as a buffer. These assets are held and nurtured not only to mitigate some of the institution's risks but also to provide a safety net in case a borrower should default on a bank's loan. In Section 7.1 we shall discuss the concept of capital requirement, but it is already quite easy to grasp that a situation where a large portion of a loan is funded through cash is less risky than one where the loan is almost completely funded through debt. A further requirement on the type of investment carried out with these funds, so that they can be used as a buffer, is that they need to provide *emergency liquidity*: they need to be invested in assets so liquid that, should there be the need to repair the damage caused by a defaulting borrower, they can be liquidated at a moment's notice. We shall see this in more detail in Section 6.4.2.

Some of these assets are also used by the fourth main activity of a development institution, which is asset-liability management (ALM), the activity that tries, using our previous term, to match in the best possible way loans and debt.

What are some of the activities carried out by the investment and ALM arm of a development institution? As we have stressed already quite a few times, a development institution is rather risk averse, therefore these activities are considerably less adventurous than those carried out by a similar *prop desk* in a traditional investment bank.

- **Currency risk management:** One could look at things philosophically and claim that currency risk is one of the most insidious because it makes us aware, particularly in our globalized world, that there is no such thing as an absolute frame of reference and everything is relative to something else, in this case, the rate of exchange between currencies. These types of considerations aside, a development bank, like any institution, is subject to currency risk and at the same time stands to gain from it.[6]

  A way to protect and/or gain from currency exposure is to either trade instruments—such as the one mentioned in the previous section where cash flows are linked to floating interest rates in different currencies—or simpler, purely currency-related instruments—such as one where cash amounts in different currencies fixed in the present are exchanged at future dates.

- **Interest rate risk management:** We shall later see, and understand, how a development bank's business is essentially a fixed-income business where interest rates play the dominant role. We have already seen how a development institution prefers to see everything in terms of one specific standard interest rate. To this end it would trade instruments converting any floating- or fixed-rate cash flow not conforming to its chosen standard into that standard rate. Later we shall learn that this standard rate, like similar other rates used in the market, is called a benchmark. This benchmark is also used to measure similar trades made by the investment arm of the institution to gain from exposure in the interest rate markets.

- **Inflation risk management:** Inflation is the great enemy of the creditor and the prudent. Any holder of substantial assets stands to lose from the eroding effect of inflation. Given that development institutions are, particularly when compared to traditional investment banks, considerably better funded than the average institution in terms of liquid assets, they would in principle stand to lose a great deal from the effect of inflation. To this end some of the investment energy of the bank goes toward purchasing protection against inflation. The simplest and least adventurous

---

[6]To be precise, a risk by definition is something one can stand to gain something from, however, in a risk-averse view, one tends to see risk as something dangerous-and therefore, here we choose to stress the profit opportunities next to it.

kind of protection is given by government bonds where the principal does not remain fixed but grows with inflation.

■ **Investment and liquidity creation:** The final high-level objective is the one of not letting the institution's equity depreciate (for reasons other than inflation) by investing it with a certain target in mind. The type of investments need to be of the most liquid kind so that they can be sold/unwound in order to provide an emergency buffer for the institution. These investments can be of the spot kind, such as buying and selling shares or foreign currency; they can involve placing deposits abroad and swapping the income into USD (or the native currency of the institution); they can involve purchasing different type of debt (sovereign, agency, corporate) and swapping it into the native currency; or they can involve investing in more exotic instruments, such as asset-backed securities (ABS), and swapping the income into the native currency of the institution. We shall revisit these in Section 6.4.2, however, it is already easy to see how different mixes with different proportions of each of the above result in different risk profiles.

After having given a very high-level description of what the fundamental activities of an investment bank and particularly a development bank are, let us try to paint a schematic structure of the internal organization of these institutions.

1.5 THE BASIC STRUCTURE OF A TRADITIONAL FINANCIAL INSTITUTION

Each financial institution has its own structure which can vary according to size, profitability, geographical location, and so on, however, we could try to sketch a skeleton structure that describes the average investment bank. Let us remind ourselves that our goal is to locate the treasury within an institution and therefore what matters to us particularly is the interaction between the treasury desk and the other parts of the bank. This is important because, as we will try to prove throughout this book, one cannot judge the value attached to a financial instrument without considering where the liquidity financing it comes from.

1.5.1 Private and Public Sides

The first crucial distinction is between a private, client-facing side and a public, market-facing side. The distinction is important under a legal point of view in the sense that the former deals with private and confidential information that the latter deals with information which is open to the general public. The two are separated by internal controls (the famed Chinese walls).

On the private side of an institution are all those units dealing with products tailor-made to suit the needs of a specific client. These could be mergers and acquisitions, flotations of companies including underwriting (the promise to buy a certain amount of issued assets); it could be leveraged buyouts in which a client company is helped to raise (a significant amount of) debt in order to acquire another company. It could also be lending, a topic close to our scope; lending might lead to loan syndication, which consists of taking a loan and parceling it out to other financial institutions. All these activities hinge on confidentiality since they rely on very sensitive information, information that should not be disclosed either to the general public or, even more crucially, to the rest of the institution. The profit generated by the private side of a bank is made of fees, either up front as in the case of advisory roles or in terms of spreads over some reference rate in the case of loans. The liquidity needed for these types of activities (for example, to underwrite a stock issuance) is usually greater than the profits generated, meaning that it must come from the public side of the bank.

On the public side there is what is sometimes described as the capital markets division, which is made up of the sales and trading desks. Information on this side is not confidential; it is public and open for everyone (with access to a broker's screen) to see. One could argue that it is in everyone's interest that the information is as open as possible: the liquidity we have praised in the previous sections is directly proportional to an open access to information. Since our focus is, at least as far as the valuation of financial instruments is concerned, on activities carried out on the public side of a financial institutions, we shall describe them in greater detail.

1.5.2　Sales and Trading Desks

Trading activity is usually divided by asset class: equity, commodities, and fixed income (which includes interest rates, credit, and foreign exchange). The type of trading can roughly be considered as belonging to one of three kinds: proprietary, meaning that it is carried out with the bank's money; on behalf of clients for those banks who are market makers (institutions offering a two-way price on selected financial instruments); or as a hedge of the bank's positions. Within each asset class (with some variations taking into account characteristics that are specific to a certain asset class) trading desks vary according to the complexity of the traded instruments. There are the cash desks, carrying out the simplest type of activity, which can be trading shares in equities or spot foreign exchange (FX) rates in FX, vanilla options desks, and exotic options desks,[7] On each desk there can be a mixture of trading for proprietary purposes or on behalf of clients. Almost all traders need to trade for hedging purposes since they need to mitigate the risk in their portfolios. Proprietary trading, as a consequence of the 2007 to 2009 financial crisis, is disappearing, particularly within those institutions that have accepted government intervention.

Sales desks facilitate the contact between clients and traders: a client who wants to do a simple but large transaction for hedging purposes (e.g., an exporter wanting to protect itself from all currency fluctuations) or an institution (e.g., a retail bank) wanting to offer its own clients a structured product, will contact a sales desk, which in turn will contact a trading desk. A sales commission goes to the sales desk and is a one-off percentage of the profit on the first day. The profit for the trader is calculated as a percentage of the profit of the trade throughout its life.

This different compensation structure is behind a trader's (irrespective of what the popular press might think) natural risk aversion compared to the salesperson's greater insouciance: a trade might be very costly to hedge over a long period but this has no effect, or only a small one, on the sales commission. The note on different compensations is key to understanding the difference in the alignment of interests. Not only will this be stressed when discussing the difference between a for-profit investment bank with a nonprofit development bank, but the fact that a trader has some future costs *throughout the dynamic life of a trade* is crucial toward asking the question, where do the funds come from?

When a trader decides to enter into any transaction, be it a swap, a forward, or the purchase of an option, when he needs to post collateral or pay margin calls, he needs ready available cash. Some of this cash comes from the treasury desk.

1.5.3 The Treasury Desk

Of the cash used by a financial institution, some might be the institution's own and some might be borrowed, the latter with the intent of having it yield more than it cost to borrow in the first place. In order to borrow, the

---

[7]Sometimes cash desks are called Delta 1 using their sensitivity to their underlying as their name (a certain move in the underlying corresponds to the same exact move in the value of the portfolio). A mathematically minded and slightly irreverent nomenclator would call cash desks Delta 1 Gamma 0; vanilla options desks Delta non 1, Gamma constant; and exotic options desks Delta non 1, Gamma non constant.

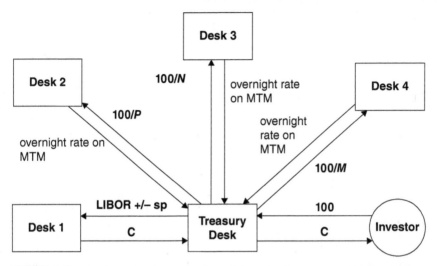

FIGURE 1.2   A schematic representation of the role of a treasury desk in relation to other trading desks. Desk 1 provides the coupon and the other desks receive the proceeds of the issuance. $100/M$, $100/N$, $100/P$ (with M, N, P some integers) are fractions of the original principal, 100, of the issuance.

institution issues bonds (which are often called *notes*) and this activity is carried out by the treasury.

The treasury desk, after deciding what type of notes investors are mainly going to be interested in, enters into a structure with a trading desk in which the following takes place: the investor pays the nominal value of the bond (100) to the treasury desk, the treasury desk receives the coupon of the bond from the trading desk and it pays it to the investor. In return the treasury desk pays the trading desk some floating rate (e.g., LIBOR) plus or minus a spread. At maturity the investor receives the initial principal (par value) of the bond.

In Figure 1.2 we have drawn a rough sketch of the situation. According to the type of note, the treasury desk would contact a specific trading desk. For example if the note is a simple fixed- or floating-rate note, Desk 1 in Figure 1.2 would be the vanilla interest rates desk. If the note is linked to a more complex payoff, Desk 1 would be the interest rates exotics desk. Should the note be linked to, say, an equity option, then Desk 1 would be an equity desk. Once the desk is chosen, the issuing of the note and swapping it with the desk takes place.

The institution, through the treasury desk, is now in possession of 100 units of cash. This can be used for the needs of the private side of the

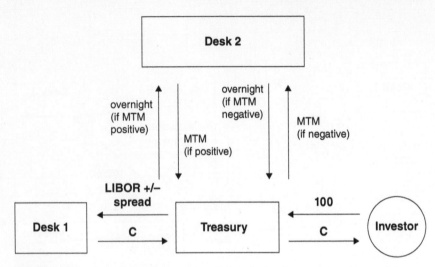

FIGURE 1.3 A more detailed version of the relation between treasury and any trading desk in need of funds.

bank (i.e, for lending purposes) or it can be allocated to the needs of the different trading desks. When a trader on, say, Desk 2 enters into a swap with a client, at the beginning of the trade there is no gain or loss for either party (we assume that the swap is entered at par). As the trade seasons, the mark to market (or MTM, i.e., the net value of the swap, which we shall discuss in Chapter 2) becomes either positive or negative for the trader. Should the MTM be negative, the trader needs to post collateral with the client, meaning that the trader needs cash. The treasury provides the cash (as shown in Figure 1.2) and the trader pays an overnight interest on this amount. If the MTM is positive, in which case the trader is owed by the client, the trader receives collateral from the client and he gives it to the treasury. The treasury, on this amount of cash (which it can use for general purposes), pays the trader an overnight rate, which in turn the trader passes to the client. In Figure 1.2 to avoid confusion we have not included the collateral going from the trader to the treasury: we have done so in Figure 1.3 where we show the two cases of MTM being either positive or negative.

Collateral management is a complicated process that is beyond our scope, however, we can easily see how changes in MTM for an institution are potentially dangerous in terms of liquidity. Although MTMs, as we shall see in Chapter 2, are netted for each counterparty at some high institutional level and therefore should be less volatile than individual ones, a change of sign from positive to negative can mean that an institution not only cannot count on that collateral for its needs, but it needs to find some cash to provide collateral. This is one of the manifestations of the funding risk we shall observe in Chapter 7. Hedge funds, which are by definition poorly funded (the investors' money is invested in order to obtain the highest return with the smallest up front), are masters of structuring trades so that the collateral needed is kept to a minimum.

1.6 DEVELOPMENT BANKING

1.6.1 The Different Types of Development Institutions

We have mentioned development banking a few times. It would be interesting now to give some historical perspective, some names, and specific business models.

The term *development* is fraught with ambiguities and even its intent, which should be straightforward, is often questioned—sometimes even violently.

After the end of World War II it was thought that the mandate of supranational organizations, which had proved ineffective after World War I to prevent the following one, should be strengthened with an economic activity geared toward reconstruction, development, and financial stability. At the Bretton Woods agreements of 1945 the International Monetary Fund (IMF) and the International Bank for Reconstruction and Development (IBRD) were created. Although the most important outcome of the meetings was probably the system of foreign currency exchanges (in practice a worldwide pegging system that lasted until 1971 when the United States stopped converting dollars into gold), as far as we are concerned the creation of the two institutions is crucial for us as it marks the beginning of development banking.

The IMF and the IBRD both lend only to sovereign entities, but they do so with two distinct missions: the IMF's objective is financial stability, the IBRD's objective is the reduction of poverty. When it comes to lending, providing funds is only half of their activity, the second half consists of offering advice. The IMF would offer a loan to a country and at the same time offer advisory services on how to straighten its finances;[8] the IBRD would offer a loan to a country with the idea of, say, building a road and it would also

---

[8]Since the receiving country cannot accept the loan without the advice, this is the controversial aspect of the IMF's mission.

send infrastructure specialists to advise the country on how best to invest the loan amount.

The crucial difference between the IMF and the IBRD, as far as the source of the money disbursed in the form of loans is concerned, is very important and represents roughly the two broad categories in which development institutions fall. The IMF lends money it obtained either through the shares sold to its member countries[9] or through donations. The IBRD, like any normal bank, funds its loans in small part through equity, but for the majority through debt. This means that the IBRD first needs to borrow in order to lend.

The different source of funds means that the lending is itself different: whereas the rate paid on IBRD loans is driven purely by the cost of funding the IBRD itself, the rate paid on IMF loans, since there is no real cost of funding to speak of, is based on other criteria.

Other development banks originated through the years. Belonging with the IBRD to the World Bank Group, the International Financial Corporation (IFC) lends to corporate entities and it falls in the category of institutions issuing debt; also part of the World Bank Group, the International Development Association (IDA) falls instead in the category of institutions funding loans through equity and donations. Founded in 1960 when most African countries gained independence, IDA only lends to the poorest countries while the IBRD lends to middle-income countries (apart from a few exceptions, countries do not receive loans from both institutions). IDA loans charge a very low interest rate. Falling in the category of debt-issuing institutions, one could mention the Asian Development Bank (ADB), the Inter-American Development Bank (IDB), the European Investment Bank (EIB) with connections to the European Union, and the European Bank for Reconstruction and Development (EBRD), founded in 1991 with a large focus on the countries of the former Soviet block.

The IBRD played a major role in the post-war reconstruction and some of the first loans went to France and a war-ravaged Japan. The marvel that is the Japanese high speed rail system was built in the 1960s using an IBRD loan (after which Japan stopped being a receiver of loans and instead, through its vast network of retail banks, became a great investor in IBRD bonds). Despite development institutions being often criticized (more or less soundly; see for example Weaver [83], Babb [5], or Peet [69]), an alternative to an institution with an excellent credit standing, great risk aversion,

---

[9]When member countries joined the IMF, they bought a form of share that corresponded to their respective voting power.

and governed by large consensus within what can be described as a credit cooperative has not yet been proposed.

1.6.2   The Structure of a Development Bank

Between the two types of development bank we have mentioned, the one lending donated funds or equity and the one lending borrowed funds, we shall concentrate on the latter, as it is in essence an institution using the tools of investment banking for the purpose of development. From here onward we will refer to this type of institution when we discuss a development bank or a development institution.

The private side of the institution is the one dealing with clients, in this case borrowers (sovereign or corporate). Staff at headquarters or at country offices would deal with borrowers so as to arrange specific loan disbursements with specific projects in mind. Once the loan has been disbursed to the borrower, specific advisers work with the borrower to put the loan to its best use. Should the loan be for a project involving, say, the construction of a road through an undeveloped area, experts in infrastructures (civil engineers and infrastructure economists) from the development institution would work closely with the locals to implement the project in the most efficient way. The goal would be to spread not only wealth but also knowledge. Advisory can also come in the form of financial knowledge. A development bank might share its debt management expertise with a borrower by helping improve its debt issuance or by helping to develop or build a financial market. (In Section 4.3.1 we shall see how the action of issuing debt on the part of a development institution in an emerging market currency is in itself a move toward developing a local financial market). The bank might also help a client manage its trade inventory, for example, by swapping bonds or entering into derivatives to mitigate a client's risk.

The public side of a development bank consists of the treasury.[10] The fundamental activities of banking we have mentioned in the previous sections are carried out by the treasury. The treasury ensures that the bank is adequately (and cheaply) funded to be able to serve its clients' needs. In Chapter 7 we shall see how borrowing and lending entail some very specific risks. Since a development bank (we shall also see later) does not hedge its positions, the treasury attends to the mitigation of these risks without carrying out the usual day-to-day hedging a trading desk in a normal investment

---

[10] This does not mean that the treasury's activity is limited to the public sphere. Some of the advisory mentioned above can be carried out by its staff.

bank would practice. The main function of a treasury desk would be similar to the one carried out by structurers in a for-profit investment bank: they would work closely with investors and market counterparts to structure a bond issuance in the way most likely to lead to a low funding cost. As we have mentioned in Section 1.4, a small component of the treasury manages the equity portfolio of the bank with a very conservative approach to risk.

CHAPTER 2

Curve Construction

In Chapter 1 we illustrated the structure of a financial institution and we gave a high-level introduction to the fundamental activities that an investment or development bank carries out. We shall now undertake the process of gaining a deeper understanding of what we have introduced.

We mentioned in the introduction that our two goals are an understanding of credit and how credit manifests itself through the valuation of financial instruments. The starting point must be the understanding of how to assess the present value of a future cash flow: this is crucial in pricing an instrument and it will also become apparent how this is closely linked to the concept of credit. In this chapter we will learn how to combine the information given by the rates markets into constructing an index curve to predict future cash flows and a discount curve to assess their present value.

As our prime focus is debt and therefore credit, we should view the exposition that follows as an incremental involvement of credit in the way we discount cash flows. To assess the present value of a future cash flow is, by admitting that a promise is worth less than the immediate possession, to pass an implicit judgment on credit. By gradually presenting the instruments that contribute to the construction of an interest rate curve from the simplest to the most complex, we will show how historically the market has become more and more sophisticated in the treatment of credit when building a discount curve. From including the impact of borrowing in different currencies, to the impact of rates with different tenors, to finally the inclusion of collateral, the market has let credit play an increasingly important role in refining the simple concept of the time value of money.

The concepts and tools learned in this chapter will result in the pricing of bonds presented in Chapter 5 as we will see that overall discounting is the main driver of a bond price.

2.1 WHAT DO WE MEAN BY CURVE CONSTRUCTION?

Assessing the present value (or discount) of a future cash flow is the single most important problem in fixed income; to generate correct index-linked future cash flows comes at a close second. By index-linked future cash flow we mean a cash flow linked to a rate $L_{S,T}$ setting at some future time S and paying at a time $T > S$. This cash flow, if applied to a unit principal, can be written as

$$L_{S,T} dt_{S,T} \tag{2.1}$$

where $dt_{S,T}$ is the day count fraction to assign the portion of L (which is quoted annually) to the correct accruing period[1] between S and T. Two questions arise here. First, what is the value of $L_{S,T}$ that I am expecting *to-day* with the information in my possession *today*? We stress the role played

---

[1] An important problem when dealing with interest rates is one of accrual since an interest rate is always a number that is valid within two moments in time *and it is quoted annually*. How do we actually count the time elapsed between the two points and therefore establish what portion of the interest rate has accrued?

Let us imagine that we have an interest rate $R = 5\%$ and this value is agreed between a borrower and a lender on March 10 on a sum of \$100,000. Over the entire period of one year, 5% is paid, that is, \$5,000. However, how do we calculate the fraction of that interest rate that is paid between any two points in time, for example, between August 4 and October 10? What is the fraction of one year that needs to be applied to the rate?

The answer is far from unique and it is based on literally counting the days between the two points in time, which is why it is often called *day count fraction*. The way we count the days is based on day count conventions and the borrower and the lender will agree on one at the beginning of the transaction.

Two common conventions are Act/360 and Act/365, which dictate that to obtain the fraction we count the actual number of days between the two points in time and divide by, respectively, 360 and 365 (which we have assumed to be the number of days in a year). In our example, the interest accrued between August 4 and October 10 amounts to \$930.56 using an Act/360 day count convention and \$917.81 using an Act/365 day count convention. Another type of convention, 30/360, dictates that every month brings to the calculation only 30 days even if the month in question has 31 (or fewer in the case of February); once we sum them, we divide them by 360. In our example, the accrued interest with a 30/360 convention is \$916.67.

There are many conventions (South American currencies have some of the strangest ones) that could apply to a time interval and, although very important in practice, they are mostly irrelevant to our subsequent discussion. Whenever we indicate a time interval (as $dt_{S,T}$ or dt_i or $T_i - T_{i-1}$, etc.) we shall always assume that the proper day count convention has been applied.

by the present: in all fair value and risk-neutral calculations of financial derivatives, we only expect to produce a price correct in the instant. Second, once I have established the value of the cash flow in the future, what is the value of that cash flow now? Because of the time value of money, calculating the present value of a future cash flow is a crucial way of comparing different cash flows in different context and/or currencies. We could see it as a way of normalizing all cash flows by their natural appreciation.

The two problems above are closely related but, perhaps counter-intuitively, the second one is more challenging. While certainly elegant, to see discounting as some sort of normalization is not immediately helpful in practice. If we look closely, however, it offers an important clue to the process. We are trying to normalize *all* cash flows, meaning that whatever calculation we intend to carry out needs to apply to our particular cash flow and to all cash flows of traded instruments in a selected financial landscape. The term *selected financial landscape* is willfully vague. Let us clarify it with a more specific example.

Let us call V the present value of equation 2.1 and let us write it as

$$V = D_T L_{S,T} dt_{S,T}$$

where D_T is the discount factor. Crucially, D_T is unknown to us. Let us now imagine that we are operating in a very primitive market where the only type of instruments actively traded are bonds that promise the investor a unit of principal at a future maturity. By coincidence there is one with maturity T, trading at a price P. If one unit of principal paid at time T is worth P now, then any other cash flow paid at time T will be worth the cash flow amount times P. This means that we have found the value of our discount factor, namely $D_T = P$. While this helps us in determining the value of the discount factor, it does not help us yet in determining the value of the floating cash flow. We have said that in our market there are only simple bonds: by another happy coincidence there is another one actively traded expiring at time S, from which we know immediately the value of the discount factor is D_S. By using a relationship

$$L_{S,T} = \frac{1}{dt_{S,T}} \left(\frac{D_S}{D_T} - 1 \right)$$

defining a forward rate,[2] we can easily find the value of our future cash flow and hence the value of V.

---

[2]The attentive reader must have recognized in the above equation the definition of LIBOR. Its absence, in name, from our primitive market is purely for illustration purposes.

In the preceding, we show the principles of *curve construction* (or *curve calibration*), the process by which we establish, using information provided by traded instruments, the values of future rate resets $L_{i,j}$ and at the same time a discount function D_t enabling us to assess their present value. These principles can be summed up in the following:

- We use *simultaneously* all the information available in the market, which we believe is relevant for our curve construction.
- Once we have constructed our curve, we should expect to be able to reprice *only* the instruments we have used.

At the moment, judging from our simple example, the terms stressed previously might seem puzzling: we shall see later how important they become when we embark on a real-world curve construction.

Since we have established that curve construction consists of building a set of functions that need to be calibrated to a set of market instruments, we now introduce what these market instruments are.

2.2 THE INSTRUMENTS AVAILABLE FOR CURVE CONSTRUCTION

The number of different fixed-income instruments one can trade in the market is enormous; however, allowing for variations on common characteristics, one can attempt to give a fairly complete picture. We will do so going from the simplest to the most complex instruments.

2.2.1 Discount Bonds and Cash Deposits

Discount bonds are the simplest of all instruments and do not need any calculation when used for constructing a curve. As shown in the previous example, these instruments offer a unit of principal at some future time: the bond price is the discount factor itself. Discount bonds are usually available in developed markets and for very short maturities (around three months). In Figure 2.1 we see an example of quotes of U.S. Treasury debt with the quotes for discount notes highlighted (boxed). The quote is given as the difference between 100 and the note's price. For example, we see that for the note expiring on March 21, 2013, the mid quote (the mid quote is obtained by average the bid quote and the offer quote) is 0.06, meaning that the discount factor for that maturity is 0.9994.

The market information given by a cash deposit is the rate r at which a cash deposit will grow from today up to time T. If we know that a unit of cash will grow, assuming linear compounding, to $1 + rT$ in a period of time

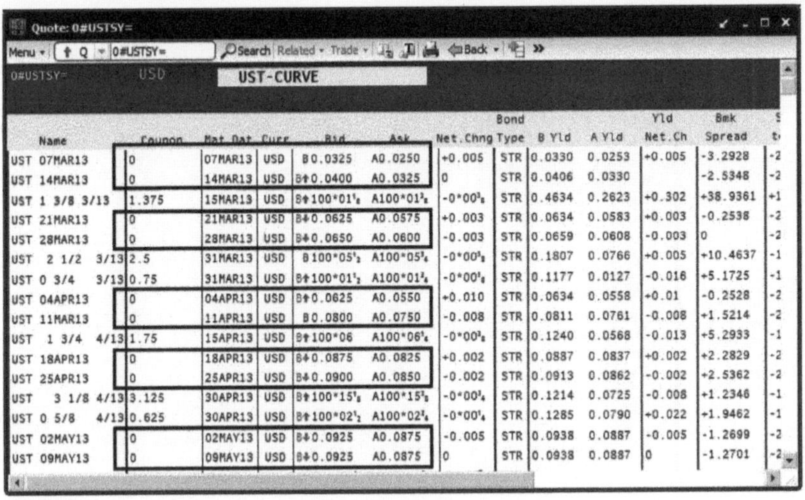

Name	Coupon	Mat Dat	Curr	Bid	Ask	Net.Chng	Bond Type	B Yld	A Yld	Yld Net.Ch	Bmk Spread	S t
UST 07MAR13	0	07MAR13	USD	B0.0325	A0.0250	+0.005	STR	0.0330	0.0253	+0.005	-3.2928	-2
UST 14MAR13	0	14MAR13	USD	B↑0.0400	A0.0325	0	STR	0.0406	0.0330		-2.5348	-2
UST 1 3/8 3/13	1.375	15MAR13	USD	B↑100*01⅛	A100*01⅜	-0*00⅜	STR	0.4634	0.2623	+0.302	+38.9361	+1
UST 21MAR13	0	21MAR13	USD	B↓0.0625	A0.0575	+0.003	STR	0.0634	0.0583	+0.003	-0.2538	-2
UST 28MAR13	0	28MAR13	USD	B↓0.0650	A0.0600	-0.003	STR	0.0659	0.0608	-0.003	0	-2
UST 2 1/2 3/13	2.5	31MAR13	USD	B100*05½	A100*05¾	-0*00⅜	STR	0.1807	0.0766	+0.005	+10.4637	-1
UST 0 3/4 3/13	0.75	31MAR13	USD	B↑100*01½	A100*01¾	-0*00⅛	STR	0.1177	0.0127	-0.016	+5.1725	-1
UST 04APR13	0	04APR13	USD	B↑0.0625	A0.0550	+0.010	STR	0.0634	0.0558	+0.01	-0.2528	-2
UST 11MAR13	0	11APR13	USD	B0.0800	A0.0750	-0.008	STR	0.0811	0.0761	-0.008	+1.5214	-2
UST 1 3/4 4/13	1.75	15APR13	USD	B↑100*06	A100*06¼	-0*00⅜	STR	0.1240	0.0568	-0.013	+5.2933	-1
UST 18APR13	0	18APR13	USD	B↓0.0875	A0.0825	+0.002	STR	0.0887	0.0837	+0.002	+2.2829	-2
UST 25APR13	0	25APR13	USD	B↓0.0900	A0.0850	-0.002	STR	0.0913	0.0862	-0.002	+2.5362	-2
UST 3 1/8 4/13	3.125	30APR13	USD	B↑100*15⅛	A100*15⅜	-0*00¾	STR	0.1214	0.0725	-0.008	+1.2346	-1
UST 0 5/8 4/13	0.625	30APR13	USD	B↑100*02½	A100*02¾	-0*00¼	STR	0.1285	0.0790	+0.022	+1.9462	-1
UST 02MAY13	0	02MAY13	USD	B↓0.0925	A0.0875	-0.005	STR	0.0938	0.0887	-0.005	-1.2699	-2
UST 09MAY13	0	09MAY13	USD	B↓0.0925	A0.0875	0	STR	0.0938	0.0887	0	-1.2701	-2

FIGURE 2.1 Quotes for U.S. Treasury notes as of March 1, 2013, with a few discount notes highlighted. *Source*: Thomson Reuters Eikon.

T, it must be that a unit of cash at time T that has grown at rate r must now be worth

$$D_T = \frac{1}{1 + rT} \tag{2.2}$$

our discount factor.[3] Cash deposits are available in all markets and are available only for short maturities (less than one year). In Figure 2.2 we see an example of quotes of deposits in Canadian Dollars.

[3]We remind the reader of the possible type of relations, depending on the compounding chosen, between a rate r_T and the corresponding discount factor D_T. With linear compounding we have

$$D_T = \frac{1}{1 + r_T T}$$

with annual compounding we have

$$D_T = \frac{1}{(1 + r_T)^T}$$

and with continuous compounding

$$D_T = \exp(-r_T T)$$

For short maturities the three values would be virtually identical.

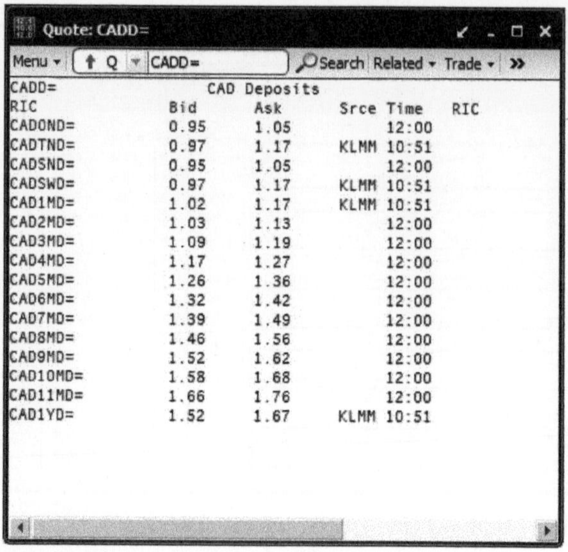

CADD= CAD Deposits

RIC	Bid	Ask	Srce	Time	RIC
CADOND=	0.95	1.05		12:00	
CADTND=	0.97	1.17	KLMM	10:51	
CADSND=	0.95	1.05		12:00	
CADSWD=	0.97	1.17	KLMM	10:51	
CAD1MD=	1.02	1.17	KLMM	10:51	
CAD2MD=	1.03	1.13		12:00	
CAD3MD=	1.09	1.19		12:00	
CAD4MD=	1.17	1.27		12:00	
CAD5MD=	1.26	1.36		12:00	
CAD6MD=	1.32	1.42		12:00	
CAD7MD=	1.39	1.49		12:00	
CAD8MD=	1.46	1.56		12:00	
CAD9MD=	1.52	1.62		12:00	
CAD10MD=	1.58	1.68		12:00	
CAD11MD=	1.66	1.76		12:00	
CAD1YD=	1.52	1.67	KLMM	10:51	

FIGURE 2.2 Quotes for Canadian Dollar cash deposits as of February 27, 2013. *Source*: Thomson Reuters Eikon.

2.2.2 Interest Rate Futures and Forward Rate Agreements

Forward rate agreements (FRAs) are the first derivatives we encounter and are traded contracts betting on the future settings of LIBOR. Since they are over-the-counter instruments, their characteristics are far from standard. The contract consists of an exchange at some time in the future between a cash flow fixed at that time in the future and a cash flow fixed on the day in which the contract is entered upon. FRAs are referred to as "the in x months for x months FRA." For example, the USD in three months for a six-month FRA would be a contract in which one party pays the six-month rate fixed in three months and the other party pays a rate fixed today. From the screenshot shown in Figure 2.3, the mid quote of that rate would be 0.457%. As we can also see from the same figure (which is in itself cropped from a bigger screen), the combinations of contract expirations and rate lengths are varied, at least for the major currencies.

Interest rate futures are similar to FRAs but are exchange traded. They are available only for the most developed currencies and are used for building the short end of the curve (less than one year). In the case of the U.S. Dollar, they are available up to 10 years and extremely liquid (hence the instrument

Quote TOPFRA											
⬜ ↑Q TOPFRA					FRA Majors			L2NKED DISPLMYS		MONEY	
	JPY	FRA		GBP	FRA		USD	FRA		EUR	FRA
1X4	0.18375	0.21375	09:35	1.039	1.059	10:50	0.496	0.536	10:50	1.06	1.08
2X5	0.18625	0.21625	09:35	0.999	1.019	10:50	0.459	0.499	10:50	0.950	1.000
3X6	0.19000	0.22000	09:35	0.972	0.992	10:50	0.4700	0.5100	10:50	0.92	0.94
4X7	0.19625	0.22625	09:35	0.950	0.970	10:50	0.482	0.522	10:50	0.87	0.89
5X8	0.20125	0.23125	09:35	0.932	0.952	10:50	0.495	0.535	10:50	0.83	0.85
6X9	0.20250	0.23250	09:35	0.925	0.940	10:49	0.503	0.543	10:50	0.82	0.84
7X10	0.20500	0.23500	09:35	0.906	0.926	10:50	0.511	0.551	10:50	0.81	0.83
8X11	0.20750	0.23750	09:35	0.898	0.918	10:50	0.531	0.551	10:50	0.80	0.82
9X12	0.20875	0.23875	09:35	0.900	0.920	10:49	0.537	0.557	10:50	0.80	0.84
12X15	0.21250	0.24250	09:35				0.548	0.567	10:50	0.791	0.841
1X7	0.32375	0.35375	09:35	1.325	1.345	10:50	0.710	0.750	10:50	1.33	1.37
2X8	0.32500	0.35500	09:35	1.277	1.297	10:50	0.687	0.727	10:50	1.23	1.25
3X9	0.32750	0.35750	09:35	1.246	1.266	10:50	0.688	0.708	10:50	1.18	1.20
4X10	0.33000	0.36000	09:35	1.218	1.238	10:50	0.687	0.727	10:50	1.14	1.16
5X11	0.33375	0.36375	09:35	1.191	1.211	10:50	0.687	0.727	10:50	1.108	1.128
6X12	0.33750	0.36750	09:35	1.130	1.150	01:36	0.688	0.728	10:50	1.09	1.11
12X18	0.35375	0.38375	09:35	1.303	1.323	08:40	0.716	0.736	20:50	1.027	1.077
18X24	0.36125	0.39125	09:35	1.174	1.194	10:50	0.704	0.744	10:50	1.070	1.150
1X10	0.6350	0.6550	04:35	1.416	1.436	10:50	0.773	0.813	10:45	1.52	1.54
2X11	0.6213	0.6413	05:05	1.395	1.415	10:50	0.748	0.788	10:45	1.43	1.45
3X12	0.6120	0.6320	05:05	1.380	1.400	10:50	0.734	0.774	10:50	1.379	1.399
2X14	0.76	0.77	04:51						:	1.492	1.512
3X15	0.77	0.78	04:51							1.492	1.512
6X18	0.6739	0.6939	05:05	1.551	1.571	10:50	0.966	0.986	10:50	1.458	1.478
9X21	0.83	0.84	04:51							1.556	1.576
12X24	0.5631	0.5831	05:10	1.567	1.587	10:50	0.972	1.012	10:50	1.39	1.42

FIGURE 2.3 A sample of quotes of forward rate agreements for major currencies. *Source*: Thomson Reuters Eikon.

of choice for constructing a curve) for the first few years, and are usually used for maturities up to five years. Being an exchange-traded contract, it has a standardized quotation. For example, for USD it is a derivative on the three-month U.S. rate and there are four maturities every year in March, June, September, and December. The contract expires on the same weekday (two business days before the third Wednesday of the month) of the relevant month (e.g., March).

Futures are hedging instruments used by investors to lock in a specific interest rate: this is captured in the notation where the future is quoted as the difference between 100 and the rate locked at the moment of purchase. If today a future contract is trading at 97 it means that an investor is able to fix the rate at 3% at the maturity of the contract. Let us stress that the fixing or locking of a specific interest rate only happens when the future is used as a hedging instrument, that is, only when it is used in conjunction with another financial instrument taking an opposite view on interest rates movements.

We said that futures and FRAs are similar instruments. One could actually claim (a claim that we shall not prove) that they are the same thing seen in two different probability measures. Because of this difference, if we want to use interest rate futures in the construction of a discount curve we need to take into account the so-called *convexity adjustment*. The value itself depends on the model we use, but in essence this means that if we see a quote of 97, we actually need to use $97 + c$, where c is the adjustment, before implying what the rate is that we expect to set at the maturity of the contract.

While it is perhaps early to discuss what type of instruments contribute to which of the two main aspects of curve construction (discounting and future rates generation), we can safely say that FRAs (and futures) are very important in the latter role: for some currencies, particularly the more liquid emerging markets currencies, they constitute the most liquid instruments in the six-month to one-year range.

2.2.3   FX Forwards

We have seen up to now only instruments in one specific currency: foreign exchange (FX) forwards are, as one would suspect, cross currency instruments. An FX forward is in practice an agreement to exchange, at some point *in the future*, fixed (*at the time* the contract is entered upon) amounts in two different currencies: at some point in the future one party is going to pay N units of currency X and the other party is going to pay M units of currency Y. This type of contract implies that an exchange rate between X and Y in the future is almost always different from the exchange rate today, the spot exchange rate.

FX forwards can be quoted in two ways, as premia, as shown in Figure 2.4a, or outright, as shown in Figure 2.4b. Let us define the spot rate as FX_t and the expected exchange rate at some point T in the future, the forward, as FWD_T. An FX forward quoted outright, defined as FWD_{OR}, is meant to be the expected[4] FX rate in the future itself, that is,

$$FWD_T = FWD_{OR}$$

An FX forward quoted as premium, defined as FWD_{PP}, is meant to represent the number of pips one has to add (or subtract) to the spot rate in order to obtain the exchange rate at time T, that is,

$$FWD_T = FX_t + \frac{FX_{PP}}{10,000}$$

The great majority of FX forwards quoted as premia need to be divided by $10,000$ however, since that number is driven by the number of significant

---

[4]One should not interpret the term *expected* as having probabilistic undertones. By expected forward foreign exchange rate, we mean the rate *implied* by the rates' differential. The rest of the chapter will describe the link between the foreign exchange and the interest rates in each currency.

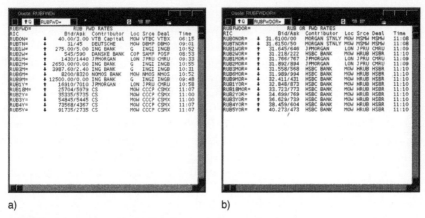

FIGURE 2.4 a) Russian Rubles FX forwards quoted in pips; b) Russian Rubles FX forwards quoted outright. *Source*: Thomson Reuters Eikon.

decimal places in the spot FX rate quote. For less liquid currencies we divide by other multiples of 10, usually smaller.[5]

How can FX forwards be used for curve construction? They are used through the application of the interest rate parity, which states that, *in principle*, for two currencies X and Y we must have

$$FWD_T^{X/Y} = FX_t^{X/Y} \frac{D_T^Y}{D_T^X}$$

where the FWD is quoted outright and where X/Y means the amount of X we obtain for one unit of Y and where, as before, D_T are the discount factors at time T (D_T^Y in currency Y and D_T^X in currency X). Unless otherwise specified, all spot and forward exchange rates are quoted versus USD. If we assume that the discount factors in USD are known, we can easily obtain the discount factor in the foreign currency. By setting $Y \equiv USD$ we have

$$D_T^X = \frac{FX_t^{X/USD}}{FWD_T^{X/USD}} D_T^{USD} \tag{2.3}$$

For those thinking that this seems a rather roundabout way of finding discount factors, the reply is that in many emerging countries the FX forward market is the first one to develop or the only one to offer a minimum of liquidity. There is no single reason why this is the case, but a few hypotheses

---

[5]For example, in the case of NGN, the Nigerian Naira, one needs to divide by 100.

can be formulated. Emerging economies face uncertainty in terms of credit and in terms of institutions. FX forwards are usually short dated, that is, one does not need to agree to a long contract in a risky environment, and they are very simple because they do not have some of the complexity of swaps agreements. Most importantly, FX forwards are fully collateralized in the sense that by exchanging principals simultaneously, the two parties essentially hold a collateral until maturity, and during the life of the trade only (and not always) pay margin calls, that is, amounts needed to correct the transaction should the realized FX rate at the expiration of the contract differ from the one expected at the beginning of the contract.

The attentive reader might have spotted two issues with this approach. The first is that, as we have stressed, interest rate parity works in principle and not always in practice. We shall address this when discussing currency basis swaps. The second is that we assume that the USD curve is known. Since, as we shall see later, there is no official way to construct a curve, two market participants—by building their respective USD curve in different ways—will necessarily obtain two different values for the discount factors in the foreign currency. This can be a very serious problem since, while most of the time the difference can be negligible (one hopes that two market participants agree fairly closely on such an important currency as USD), for some foreign currencies in some special cases it can lead to a large impact.

2.2.4 Interest Rate Swaps

We now reach a greater level still of complexity by introducing the interest rate swap, one of the most widely traded derivatives in the market. An interest rate swap is defined as

$$\sum_i C D_i dt_i = \sum_j L_j D_j dt_j \qquad (2.4)$$

where one party pays a fixed coupon C with a certain frequency and the other party pays, with a potentially different frequency, a floating rate L fixing at j; D_i are the discount factors and dt are the day count fractions, $dt_i = T_i - T_{i-1}$. Up to now we have used the term floating rate: from now on we will use it, unless too inappropriate, interchangeably with the term LIBOR. A LIBOR (London Interbank Offer Rate) is an interest rate representing the rate at which investment banks agree to lend to each other: it is set in London every day. Most liquid currencies have a LIBOR of at least one maturity (e.g., six months); the most liquid currencies such as USD and EUR

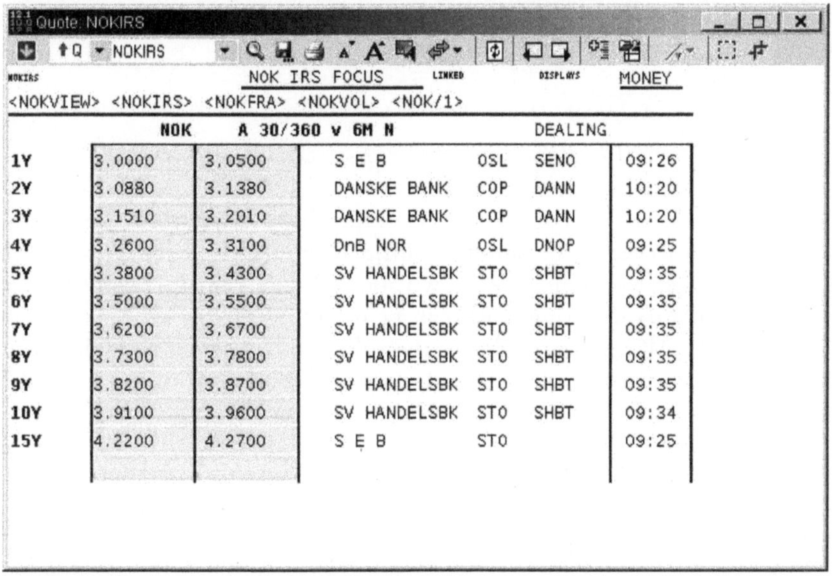

Quote: NOKIRS

NOKIRS NOK IRS FOCUS LINKED DISPLAYS MONEY

<NOKVIEW> <NOKIRS> <NOKFRA> <NOKVOL> <NOK/1>

	NOK	A 30/360 v 6M N			DEALING	
1Y	3.0000	3.0500	S E B	OSL	SENO	09:26
2Y	3.0880	3.1380	DANSKE BANK	COP	DANN	10:20
3Y	3.1510	3.2010	DANSKE BANK	COP	DANN	10:20
4Y	3.2600	3.3100	DnB NOR	OSL	DNOP	09:25
5Y	3.3800	3.4300	SV HANDELSBK	STO	SHBT	09:35
6Y	3.5000	3.5500	SV HANDELSBK	STO	SHBT	09:35
7Y	3.6200	3.6700	SV HANDELSBK	STO	SHBT	09:35
8Y	3.7300	3.7800	SV HANDELSBK	STO	SHBT	09:35
9Y	3.8200	3.8700	SV HANDELSBK	STO	SHBT	09:35
10Y	3.9100	3.9600	SV HANDELSBK	STO	SHBT	09:34
15Y	4.2200	4.2700	S E B	STO		09:25

FIGURE 2.5 Norwegian Krone interest rate swap quotes. *Source*: Thomson Reuters Eikon.

have several LIBORs. Market practitioners tend to perpetrate (when speaking, not when trading) an imprecision by defining LIBOR as any rate that is the most important rate of choice for banks in a certain currency to lend to each other. In reality it will have a different, if similar, name: for example EUR has two rates, the EUR-LIBOR set in London and the EURIBOR set in Frankfurt; Australian Dollar (AUD) has an AUD-LIBOR set in London and a more liquid one set in Sydney. When speaking, a practitioner will often call all these LIBOR and say that a swap pays a floating LIBOR. We shall follow this practice. In Figure 2.5 we see quotes for interest rate swaps in Norwegian Krone (NOK): what is quoted is the fixed coupon C. Swaps are quoted at *par*, meaning that the value of C quoted is the one that will make, at the moment of entering the contract, both sides of Equation 2.4 equal.

With interest rate swaps, we now start to see a level of complexity absent from the previous instruments. This complexity easily turns into a considerable computational challenge. Let us illustrate this with an example. Let us imagine that we want to build a NOK curve for maturities up to two years and we have at our disposal a six-month cash deposit R_6, a six-month in six-months FRA $L_{6,6}$, and a two-year interest rate swap where, as one can read from Figure 2.5, the fixed rate C is paid annually and the floating rate semiannually.

Let us first write the interest rate swap, with times given in months, in full.

$$\begin{aligned}
CD_{12}T_{12} + CD_{24}\left(T_{24} - T_{12}\right) = L_{0,6}D_6T_6 + L_{6,6}D_{12}\left(T_{12} - T_6\right) \\
+ L_{12,6}D_{18}\left(T_{18} - T_{12}\right) + L_{18,6}D_{24}\left(T_{24} - T_{18}\right)
\end{aligned} \tag{2.5}$$

At first it seems that apart from C in the above equation we have eight unknowns; however, things simplify a little. First of all, $L_{0,6}$ is the six-month rate starting today so it must be known and we can say (in our simple world) that it is equal to R_6. Second, D_6 can be found also from R_6, as shown in Equation 2.2. Third, we also know the value of $L_{6,6}$, given from the FRA. Finally, D_{12} can also be obtained easily using a second iteration[6] on Equation 2.2, mainly

$$D_{12} = \frac{1}{(1 + R_6 T_6)\left[1 + L_{6,6}\left(T_{12} - T_6\right)\right]}$$

We are now left with four unknowns: the forward rates and discount factors beyond one year. In order to find them we need to use a solver, that is, a process that will try to fit two functions, $f_t(L)$ and D_t, so that they will generate, respectively, the forward rates L and discount factors D_T that will make the swap price at par. More and more often we shall try to call $f_t(L)$ the **index curve** and D_t the *discount curve*. (While the use of a solver would certainly be appropriate, in some simple situations, as we shall describe in the numerical example concluding this chapter, one can find simpler solutions based on assumptions and interpolations.)

We are starting to see what the two principles outlined in Section 2.1 might mean. All the information given above (deposit, FRAs, and interest rate swaps) needs to be used simultaneously and only that information will be repriced correctly. This second point is very important, and to stress it, let us imagine that although $L_{6,6}$ is traded in the market as an FRA, we chose to ignore it. After using the information given by the cash deposit, the solver needs to find $f_t(L)$ and D_t fitting six unknowns instead of four. One of these will be a $\widetilde{L_{6,6}}$, rate found after solving. Should we expect this rate to be equal to the rate $L_{6,6}$, quoted by the FRA? The answer should be a resounding no,

---

[6]This is based on the idea that if we invest a unit amount for a period T_2 at a rate R_2, this has to be equivalent to investing it for a period T_1 at a rate R_1 and then reinvesting it from T_1 to T_2 at a forward rate $L_{1,2}$, that is,

$$1 + R_2 T_2 = (1 + R_1 T_1)\left[1 + L_{1,2}\left(T_2 - T_1\right)\right] \tag{2.6}$$

and to expect otherwise, a rather common mistake is to forget that in any calibration process if one wants a definite output this has to also be an input.

With the second principle of curve construction being so important, let us elaborate further by again using our simple example. We are all familiar with the concept and requirement of an arbitrage-free framework: when modeling finance in a risk-neutral framework we assume that it is impossible to make a riskless profit. This means that the same instrument cannot have two different prices. This leads to a safe assumption that two different instruments implying the same financial quantity cannot have two different prices, which in turn results in the requirement that our discount and index curves should be unique. Even in our brief review of financial instruments we have seen that many of these overlap in time, from which we can ask is it possible that two different instruments being used to calibrate the same portion of the discount and/or index curve could lead to two different results? The answer is sadly yes. One would think that all instruments fit in properly, but it is not the case.[7] Computationally this means that there could be situations where there is an information glut and the calculation would fail. Let us imagine that in our simple world a further piece of information is available, the one-year *NOK/USD* FX forward. We know that from it we can derive the 12-month discount factor, however, we already have the 12-month discount factor. In practice we are asking

$$\frac{FX_t^{NOK/USD}}{FWD_{12}^{NOK/USD}} D_{12}^{USD} \stackrel{?}{=} \frac{1}{(1 + R_6 T_6)\left[1 + L_{6,6}\left(T_{12} - T_6\right)\right]}$$

and the answer is, not necessarily. In this case, not only because we cannot always expect two different instruments to imply the same financial information but also because, in the specific case of FX forwards, we have seen that the outcome relies on the assumption of the USD curve construction. In the presence of overspecification, a curve construction process will fail, so what should one do? One should choose one or the other instrument and be ready to accept that the outcome is a framework potentially unable to price the excluded one. The choice could be based on liquidity: the more liquid

---

[7]However, before jumping to the conclusion that the world is full of arbitrage, I would like to quote an old hand at Morgan Stanley who used to say, if you think there is arbitrage, show me the money. Most of the situations where one thinks there is arbitrage to exploit, when one goes through the trouble of exploiting it, there is no profit at all since it will have been eaten away by transaction costs, bid-offers, and so on.

instrument should be given preference. The choice could be based on portfolio affinity: if we trade a considerable amount of, say, FX forwards it would be more sensible to use those as input in our curve construction process. The choice could also be based on operational issues. While this example is simple, there could be cases in which we need to exclude instruments simply because we are not able to process the information they give us.

A final point is one about consistency: within an institution, curves should be constructed in the same way to avoid internal arbitrage. Let us imagine that within an institution a group trades mainly FX forwards and another trades mainly cash deposits. By applying the suggestions above and ignoring consistency, each will choose a different input in their calibration process, meaning that to each, a cash flow in six months will have a different present value.

2.2.5 Basis Swaps

What is a basis? A basis is a beautiful financial concept that is used to apply a numerical value (and therefore being able to trade it) to a discrepancy or to what at first can seem an anomaly. As far as curve construction is concerned, a basis is extremely important as it appears to indicate where two floating rates, which we would have assumed are equal, are in fact different. Within the same currency, a basis is traded through tenor basis swaps and between two currencies through (cross) currency basis swaps.

2.2.5.1 Tenor Basis Swaps A tenor basis swap can be defined as an exchange between a longer rate and a shorter rate plus a basis b_T, that is,

$$\sum_i \left(L_i^{XM} + b_T\right) D_i dt_i = \sum_j L_j^{YM} D_j dt_j \tag{2.7}$$

where the rate L^{YM} accrues over a number of months Y multiple of X, the number of months over which the rate L^{XM} accrues.

At the origin of tenor basis swaps—a reason for which they have become more and more common lately—is an issue of credit. In a safe environment it should be irrelevant whether we choose to borrow a certain amount over a period of, say, six months or we choose to compound it in two three-month periods. The rate we should be charged should be the same. In a less-safe environment this is no longer the case: the longer term is riskier for the lender and therefore the borrower is charged a higher rate. In liquid currencies there are several types of tenor basis swaps available, as shown in Figure 2.6 (which shows only a subsection of the USD ones): the swap is quoted, as we did in Equation 2.7, by putting the basis on top of the rate

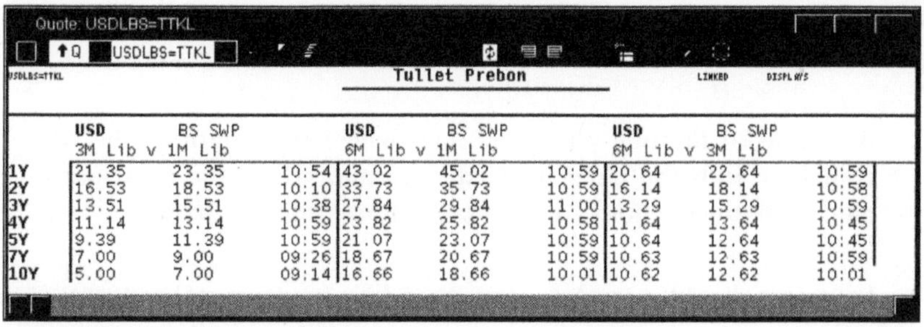
Quote: USDLBS=TTKL

USDLBS=TTKL

Tullet Prebon

	USD 3M Lib v 1M Lib	BS SWP		USD 6M Lib v 1M Lib	BS SWP		USD 6M Lib v 3M Lib	BS SWP	
1Y	21.35	23.35	10:54	43.02	45.02	10:59	20.64	22.64	10:59
2Y	16.53	18.53	10:10	33.73	35.73	10:59	16.14	18.14	10:58
3Y	13.51	15.51	10:38	27.84	29.84	11:00	13.29	15.29	10:59
4Y	11.14	13.14	10:59	23.82	25.82	10:58	11.64	13.64	10:45
5Y	9.39	11.39	10:59	21.07	23.07	10:59	10.64	12.64	10:45
7Y	7.00	9.00	09:26	18.67	20.67	10:59	10.63	12.63	10:59
10Y	5.00	7.00	09:14	16.66	18.66	10:01	10.62	12.62	10:01

FIGURE 2.6 A few examples of quotes for common USD tenor basis swaps. *Source*: Thomson Reuters Eikon.

with shorter maturity. In Figure 2.6, for example, we see quotes for swaps exchanging USD three-month LIBOR flat versus USD one-month LIBOR plus basis; USD six-month LIBOR flat versus USD three-month LIBOR plus basis; and finally, in the third column, USD six-month LIBOR flat versus USD one-month LIBOR plus basis. One can check that, as it should be, the average between the bid and offer (the mid) in the second column should be the sum of the mids in the first and second column. In other words it should be the same to swap, in one step, a one-month rate for a six-month rate or, in two steps, to swap a one-month rate for a three-month rate and then a three-month rate for a six-month rate.

2.2.5.2 Cross Currency Basis Swaps Cross currency basis swaps, like the tenor kind, also highlight the difference between two floating rates, but they do so with rates of two difference currencies. Although simple in principle they raise a lot of questions and not everyone agrees about the answers.

A cross currency basis swap is defined as an exchange between the floating rate of one currency (usually USD but sometimes EUR) without basis (flat) and the floating rate plus basis b_C of another currency. Also, crucially, the two parties exchange the principals at the beginning and at time T at the end of the transaction.[8] We can write this as

$$N^Y\left\{-1+\sum_i\left(L_i^Y+b_C\right)D_i^Y dt_i+D_T^Y\right\}=N^X\left\{-1+\sum_i L_i^X D_i^X dt_i+D_T^X\right\} \tag{2.8}$$

[8]There are also rarer cases in which the principal is exchanged at intermediate stages of the swap's life at an exchange rate fixed at the moment of each initial exchange. These types of swaps can be seen as a series of forward starting, standard currency basis swaps.

where N is the principal amount. Let us try to understand the concept of principal exchange. Before doing so let us state a very important fact:

A stream of floating payments (leg) where the length of the rate coincides with the payment frequency and where the principal is paid at maturity should always price more or less at par.

Let us try to understand this simple and yet fundamental concept (about which more or less volumes could be written). First of all, *to price at par*, which we introduced in Section 2.2.4, means here the same as it did previously: it means that there is no gain for either side. When there are two legs, that is, two sides as in a swap, it means that both legs are worth the same; when there is only one leg it means that it is worth 0. (To be more precise, 0 or 1 (or 100), depending on whether we consider the principal itself.) A simple way to illustrate this is by using some of the tools and instruments previously shown.

Let us imagine that we have a floating leg that pays once in six months and a second time plus principal in one year. We know, and we consider these the only instruments traded in the market, the six-month cash deposit R_6 and the six-month rate setting in six months $L_{6,6}$. The present value of our floating leg will be given by

$$V = R_6 T_6 D_6 + [1 + L_{6,6} (T_{12} - T_6)] D_{12}$$

We have already found in Section 2.2.4 the values of D_6 and D_{12}, so by substituting we obtain

$$V = \frac{R_6 T_6}{1 + R_6 T_6} + \frac{[1 + L_{6,6} (T_{12} - T_6)]}{(1 + R_6 T_6) [1 + L_{6,6} (T_{12} - T_6)]} \tag{2.9}$$

which, after simplification, leads to $V = 1$, that is, par. The above can be obviously extended to any maturity, provided that we pay every six months a rate of type $L_{i,6}$ and that we pay the principal at maturity. Since we have made no mention of currency we must assume the above to be true for any currency.

If we now return to the definition of cross currency basis swap we begin to understand the role of the principal exchange. It is a way of saying: "Let us set the stage for the accepted situation, that is, that a floating leg should price at par in any currency, at which point we introduce the basis to show that this is not always the case." This also follows our first definition of basis as a way of trading an anomaly, in this case the anomaly on the intuitive idea that a floating leg should price at par.[9]

There is no single accepted reason for this anomaly and this anomaly has not always been acknowledged. Before 2005, even sophisticated market participants accepted the idea that all floating legs should price at par. The next section, dedicated to constructing curves with multiple inputs, will try to shed some light on the issues involved in the use of currency basis swaps.

2.3 USING MULTIPLE INSTRUMENTS TO BUILD A CURVE

We introduced in the previous section the importance of basis swaps. We explained the introduction of the tenor basis swap as a way of literally putting a price, in an uncertain environment, on the inherent riskiness of lending for a longer period. It is a principle fairly easy to accept. The introduction of the currency basis swap is also in nature linked to credit, but it is considerably more complex.

First of all let us state the obvious: a cross currency basis swap is a trade with two currencies. This means that there is an FX element involved and when this happens we lose the idea of an absolute frame of reference—everything can be seen in two ways. What is there to be seen? We will show in great detail when explaining the role of the treasury desk within a financial institution, that the activity of an investment bank can be summed as borrowing short term and lending long term. Instead of lending, there can be other forms of trading, but the principle is that the money an investment bank uses needs to be borrowed somehow. Being global institutions, investment banks can choose to borrow (or fund themselves) in their native currencies (USD for American banks, EUR for European, etc.) or in other currencies abroad. The level at which one borrows and the discounting one applies to a future cash flow are strictly linked: the way we see now a payment in the future has to be the same way we see the money we have to repay ourselves at the same moment in the future.

Borrowing rates have everything to do with the perception the lender has of the borrower. This means that shifting perceptions have a direct influence on the way we discount. As we have previously mentioned, before

---

[9]While this is true mathematically and it is useful in our subsequent discussion, a trader would not see the principal exchange in the same light. The principal exchange is primarily seen as a way of eliminating currency risk from the trade and simply concentrating on the interest rate sensitivity linked to the floating rate payments.

2005 (the date is very approximate; for a good description of the changing environment, see Piterbarg [70] and Johannes and Sundaresan [55]) a, say, U.S.-based institution would borrow funds in EUR paying EUR LIBORs (or very close to it) and hence would believe that a floating leg in EUR would price at par. The only instrument needed (assuming the short end of the curve is taken care of with deposits and/or interest rate futures) to fit its index function $f_t\left(L^{EUR}\right)$ and discount function D_t^{EUR} would be an interest rate swap of the form

$$\sum_i CD_i^{EUR}dt_i = \sum_j L_j^{EUR} D_j^{EUR}dt_j \qquad (2.10)$$

The market then changed and perceptions shifted. The market wondered whether it is true that all institutions can borrow EUR at the same level, or any other currency for the matter. A currency basis gives a numerical value to this: the market believes that not everyone should be able to borrow currency X at the same level. The basis gives a level of this belief and institutions are then charged different rates. This is one of those situations where it is difficult to distinguish the cause from the effect. Was it the difficulty of financial institutions to borrow abroad that caused the market to doubt their ability, or was it the market's doubt which caused their inability? In, say, 2001 a U.S.-based institution would have borrowed, for 10 years, Euro paying EUR LIBOR basically flat or Japanese Yen paying JPY LIBOR basically flat. Now, looking at Figure 2.7, it would pay, respectively, EUR LIBOR minus 37.25 basis points (mid level) and JPY LIBOR minus 64.75 basis points. Now the same institution cannot construct its EUR curve simply using Equation 2.10, the currency basis information needs to be applied. Equation 2.10 needs to be combined with

$$N^{EUR}\left\{-1 + \sum_i \left(L_i^{EUR} + c_B\right) D_i^{EUR}dt_i + D_T^{EUR}\right\} =$$
$$N^{USD}\left\{-1 + \sum_i L_i^{USD} D_i^{USD}dt_i + D_T^{USD}\right\} \qquad (2.11)$$

Equations 2.10 and 2.11 need to be solved simultaneously, which is not an easy task if we consider how many terms each summation sign could be expanded to (let us imagine, for example, a 40-year swap paying every three months). Not only a numerical solver is needed but a further consideration can simplify things considerably. From Figure 2.7 we noticed that all currency basis are quoted against a USD LIBOR leg flat. This is

```
Quote:ICAB1
  ↑Q  ICAB1                                    ⊞ ≡ ≣
15:37 17JAN12   ICAP                           UK69580            ICAB1
Basis Swaps - All currencies vs. 3m USD LIBOR - Also see <ICAB2>
      REC/PAY      REC/PAY      REC/PAY      REC/PAY      REC/PAY
      EUR          GBP          JPY          CHF          SEK
1 Yr -72.75/-77.75 -03.25/-13.25 -25.25/-33.25 -26.50/-36.50 -25.00/-31.00
2 Yr -67.00/-72.00 -00.75/-05.75 -45.50/-53.50 -40.00/-46.00 -14.50/-20.50
3 Yr -61.50/-66.50 +01.00/-04.00 -60.75/-68.75 -45.00/-51.00 -07.00/-13.00
4 Yr -56.75/-61.75 -00.25/-05.25 -70.50/-78.50 -50.00/-56.00 -03.00/-09.00
5 Yr -52.50/-57.50 -01.50/-06.50 -75.75/-83.75 -54.00/-60.00 +01.50/-04.50
7 Yr -44.00/-49.00 -06.00/-11.00 -74.00/-82.00 -54.00/-60.00 +09.50/+03.50
10Yr (-34.75/-39.75) -10.00/-15.00 (-60.75/-68.75) -52.00/-58.00 +16.00/+10.00
15Yr -22.75/-27.75 -13.25/-18.25 -41.25/-49.25 -47.00/-53.00 +24.50/+18.50
20Yr -15.75/-20.75 -11.75/-16.75 -24.75/-33.75 -45.50/-51.50 +33.50/+27.50
30Yr -7.250/-12.25 +00.50/-04.50 -06.75/-14.75 -45.00/-51.00 +39.00/+33.00
40Yr -3.250/-8.250 +06.50/+01.50                 DKK          NOK
50Yr -0.750/-5.750 +09.50/+04.50       1Yr -80.00/-90.00 -67.00/-77.00
                                       2Yr -72.50/-82.50 -52.50/-62.50
**FOR OIS BASIS <ICAB5>**              3Yr -66.00/-76.00 -43.00/-53.00
                                       4Yr -62.00/-72.00 -36.00/-46.00
                                       5Yr -59.00/-69.00 -32.00/-42.00
** Call Brendan McVeigh,               7Yr -49.50/-59.50 -24.50/-34.50
Marcus Kemp or Simon Payne            10Yr -38.00/-48.00 -22.00/-32.00
on +44(0)207 532 3660 **              15Yr -26.00/-36.00 -20.50/-30.50
                                      20Yr -19.00/-29.00 -18.50/-28.50
                                      30Yr -10.00/-20.00 -16.50/-26.50
```

FIGURE 2.7 A few examples of quotes for common cross currency basis swaps quoted as USD three-month flat versus foreign currency three-month rate plus basis. *Source*: Thomson Reuters Eikon.

probably because U.S.-based institutions are the largest market participants,[10] but in any case it means that the view is, in general, USD-centric. From this we can assume that at least in USD (and for a U.S. institution, as we shall discuss soon), a flat floating leg does indeed price at par. In an instant, this wipes out any USD-denominated variable from Equation 2.11 and we are left with having to solve simultaneously the following set of equations

$$\sum_i CD_i^{EUR} dt_i = \sum_j L_j^{EUR} D_j^{EUR} dt_j$$

$$N^{EUR} \left\{ -1 + \sum_i \left(L_i^{EUR} + c_B \right) D_i^{EUR} dt_i + D_T^{EUR} \right\} = 0 \quad (2.12)$$

What does the basis signify and why are they different from currency to currency? Theories abound on this point and few people agree, however, one

---

[10]Currency basis for some Eastern European currencies are quoted against EUR LIBOR flat and, in a bout of quirkiness, for Mexican and Chilean Pesos the swap is against USD but the basis is on the USD leg.

could see the basis as an indication of the average ease with which a U.S.-based institution can borrow in the currency of country X and/or the perception within country X of the creditworthiness of the average U.S.-based institution. A further question is, should an institution based in a country with currency X include the currency basis when constructing the discount curve for X? The question does not have a clear answer and there are many arguments about it. We believe (a very elegant point is made by Fujii et al. [41] and by Benhamou [11]) that they should not include the basis. The move toward collateralized discounting, however, which we shall introduce later, has rendered the argument almost irrelevant. It would be interesting to insert here an argument often raised by local currency traders[11] at the time of the move toward a curve construction including currency basis: I agree one should include the basis if one trades cross currency swaps (i.e., a trade in two frames of reference, so to speak), but if all my trading activity takes place in local currency, why should I include the basis? First of all, let us say that a trader will instinctively resist any move toward a different price resulting in a financial loss, particularly if driven by a reason obscure to him. The answer, and the goal of this chapter, is that one should try to take into consideration the wider activity of a financial institution (see for example Tuckman and Homè [80]). While it is true the pseudo-scientific argument that in the frame of reference of the local currency (which we have seen is the point of view of an institution in that country) there is no basis, the money the trader is using to fund the trade has come from a frame of reference where there is basis.

Another argument used against two different discounting (one with and one without currency basis according to the country of origin) is the following: the swap rate quoted, that is, actually traded, is one, how can there be two discounting? We should not forget that the swap rate is the starting point, not the arrival point. A swap rate of C means that one party agrees to pay C and the other to pay a series of floating rates. This is the only contractual agreement and the only thing that matters. Each party will then construct its discount function accordingly and both will price the swap correctly. Of course, as we shall see in the next sections, what is true at inception, when the swap is at par, is not true when the swap seasons. Later in the life of the trade the two parties—the one using the currency basis and the one not using it—will disagree on the price of the swap, and this is another reason for the recent move away from LIBOR-driven discounting.

---

[11]Local currency, used particularly when it comes to very small and/or emerging market currencies, is another admittedly confusing way to say foreign currency.

It is probably important to mention here the current argument (see[12] Carver [27]) that the new advances in discounting are dangerously flirting with the idea of abandoning the concept of one price. We have mentioned earlier that a pillar, if not *the* pillar, of financial modeling in the risk-neutral framework is the fact that the same instrument cannot have two different prices, this of course is because it would lead to arbitrage. When trading a swap, is the existence of one price given by the uniqueness of the swap rate value (for example, the fixed rate C) or by the fact that both parties see the value of the swap as initially at par? In the past the two have almost always, and certainly at inception, coincided, but we should not forget that the former, the swap rate, is the traded quantity, while the latter is the fruit of an institution-dependent calculation, the act of implying discount factors from market quantities. Of course, the fact that two market participants see the present value of the same stream of cash flows in different ways is rather unsettling, and it is certainly cause for discussion. One should not, however, fear for risk neutrality as this is preserved by the fact that both agree that one should pay the other a fixed amount at specific intervals.

We have not offered quite the full picture yet. In Equation 2.12 we have been vague with the frequency of reset, but in reality, the EUR LIBOR in the interest rate swap resets every six months, whereas the EUR LIBOR in the cross currency basis swaps resets every three months. We know from the mere existence of a tenor basis swap in EUR that these two rates are not the same. The tenor basis information needs to be included in our simultaneous curve construction, so what we actually need to solve is

$$\sum_{n}^{1Y} C D_n^{EUR} dt_n = \sum_{j}^{6M} L_j^{EUR} D_j^{EUR} dt_j$$

$$-1 + \sum_{i}^{3M} \left(L_i^{EUR} + b_C \right) D_i^{EUR} dt_i + D_T^{EUR} = 0 \qquad (2.13)$$

$$\sum_{j}^{6M} L_j^{EUR} D_j^{EUR} dt_j = \sum_{i}^{3M} \left(L_i^{EUR} + b_T \right) D_i^{EUR} dt_i$$

Our solver will need to fit three functions now: the discount function D_t^{EUR} and two index functions, $f_t\left(L_{3M}^{EUR}\right)$ and $g_t(L_{6M}^{EUR})$.

From Equation 2.13 we can easily see how, whenever a new tenor basis swap appears featuring a combination between two rates of different length,

---

[12]This article is part of a wider debate that can be found in Laughton and Vaisbrot [60] and in Hull and White ([48] and [49])

it needs to be included in our curve construction and we will need to solve for an extra index curve. As an aside, solvers needed to fit multiple index and discount functions, which requires considerable computational sophistication that is not available to all institutions. The mathematical problem is the one of finding the (global) minima of a function with an extremely high number of dimensions: this problem, together with the one of finding the factors of a number, is known to be among the most challenging numerically.

We have said that Equation 2.13 can be expanded beyond three instruments to n-instruments. The final concept that needs to be addressed is the one of collateralized curve construction.

2.4 COLLATERALIZED CURVE CONSTRUCTION

We have shown in Section 2.3 how curve construction evolves with market trends. The latest step in this evolution is the inclusion of collateral posting in the curve construction calculations. In this section we shall present some of the key steps in the evolution of the perception of counterparty credit risk and what this implies in terms of actual calculations. We shall also ask ourselves, does this really make a difference? To answer this question we shall stress how one needs to differentiate between the price of an instrument at inception and during its remaining life. Finally, we shall touch upon the special case of AAA institutions, which is the case of many development banks.

2.4.1 The Evolution of the Perception of Counterparty Credit Risk

When discussing FX forwards we mentioned how they tend to be common in less developed markets for reasons of simplicity and risk. We also mentioned that the immediate exchange of cash was the reason for their perceived (and in practice real) safety. What strikes the practitioner arriving to fixed income by way of another asset class, such as equity or FX, is the fact that everything is seen over a long period, contracts tend to have long maturities and a concept like accrual, foreign in other asset classes, is king.[13] Fixed income is about promises of repayments, repayments that only materialize after a certain period of time. This is bound to bring forward issues of credit.

---

[13]I remember once a colleague saying, after taming a particularly tricky stream of accruals, "fixed income is all about dates."

A swap (we can keep this discussion general and imagine a trade such as the one shown in Equation 2.4, ignoring more specific types) is an exchange of payments between two parties. We said that at inception a swap is worth par, which means that neither side owes the other anything. As soon as the market moves the following day, particularly easy to see in Equation 2.4 since one side pays a fixed amount, this is no longer true. The swap will no longer have a zero value; it will have a positive value for one party and a negative value for the other: this is called the mark-to-market (MTM) of the swap. The MTM shows what the party that sees it as positive is owed by the other party. That amount is not owed immediately since the actual payment will take place only at some precise moment in the future (when the MTM will most likely have a different value), but the MTM is seen as the value of the trade should the trade be exited at that moment. To exit a trade, or unwind, is a voluntary operation agreed by both parties in which, after a set of transactions, the party owed the MTM is satisfied. Of course we can easily see where this argument is leading to, what happens in a non-voluntary situation, for example a default? The party that sees the MTM as positive is essentially exposed to the other party's credit risk. The solution to this problem has been the introduction in swap agreements (see ISDA 1994 [52] and ISDA 1999 [53]) of the standardization of collateral payment.[14] Every day the MTM of the swap is calculated and that amount is posted as collateral by the party that sees it as negative. The day after the MTM changes value, the amount of collateral will increase or decrease accordingly. Of course the MTM can change sign, which would turn the table on the party, which up to this point, was receiving the collateral. To avoid a continuous switching of sides over many trades, which would be operationally intensive, collateral is managed at a very high level, netting all positions between two counterparties and posting collateral only on that global MTM.[15] Collateral takes the form of cash or treasury notes, that is, the most liquid financial objects available.[16] We shall now look at what happens to the collateral posted.

2.4.1.1 Overnight Index Swaps

A financial institution is in possession of a certain amount of cash, some of which has been received as collateral. Due

---

[14]Mechanisms for collateral payments have existed at least since the late 1980s; however, the inclusion in ISDA agreements only took place in the 1990s.

[15]One has to be careful, however, that netting is far from a trivial exercise and that it is carried out within a clear legal framework.

[16]Sometimes securities are also posted but subject to a haircut, or discount, for fear that, in case of the default of the counterparty posting the collateral, they could depreciate faster than the receiver of the collateral is able to sell.

to its liquid nature, cash is most sensitive to the overnight rate, the rate used by institutions to lend to each other from one day to the next. Because of the low risk associated with overnight lending, the overnight rate is usually the lowest available rate. In order to manage overnight rate exposure, an instrument called the overnight index swap (OIS) was introduced. Practice dictates, as it does in the case of LIBOR, that when there is no currency specified after it, OIS is intended to mean a swap linked to the USD overnight rate: we shall use this practice and refer to the similar swaps in other currencies as either X OIS or give them their proper name if it exists (such as EONIA for EUR OIS). In an OIS,[17] one side pays a fixed coupon C (the OIS rate) at certain intervals and the other side pays the daily compounded overnight rate l, that is,

$$\sum_i C D_i dt_i = \sum_i \left[\prod_j \left(1 + l_j dt_j \right) \right] D_i dt_i \qquad (2.14)$$

where j is a daily counter. OIS are very useful because they allow the user to manage over a long period (OIS can have maturities of up to 40 years) a rate resetting almost continuously. For us they are very useful because, in this form, we can include overnight index swap rates in our curve construction calculations. Before doing so, however, let us try to understand a bit more why collateral is important when pricing swaps.

In Section 2.5.2 we said we believe that a floating leg with principal repayment at the end should price at par value. In Equation 2.9 we have briefly shown how, if one uses the floating rate to obtain the discount factors, this is the case. At that moment we did not mention any credit-related aspect, basically assuming that the process of discounting was inherently as risky as the process of rate generation. Since the floating rate was LIBOR, the discounting was done at the same level. With the introduction of the currency basis, which we have presented as a credit-driven quantity, we saw that already this was no longer true as we were not discounting anymore with the same rate used for the forward rates. Let us repeat why, under a credit point of view, the action of calculating the present value, that is, discounting, is closely related to the rate generation: a certain cash flow will grow from its present discounted value (the way we see things at the moment) to its actual value at the moment of payment at the same rate we are charged to borrow.

---

[17]It is common to hear the term *OIS swap*. Considering that the "S" in OIS already stands for swap, it seems redundant.

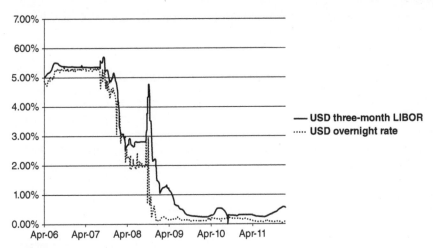

FIGURE 2.8 A plot highlighting the difference between the overnight rate and the three-month LIBOR over time before, during, and after the peak of the financial crisis.

The rate we are charged to borrow is driven by a perception of credit risk, hence discounting should be driven by the same perception.

If we look at Equation 2.4 and assume that we are in a world without any other type of swaps, we could be tempted to say that rate generation and discounting should be driven by LIBOR. This was indeed the classical theory of swap pricing where (see for example Duffie and Singleton [[32]) swap rates were seen as bond par rates of an issuer at LIBOR level of risk for the life of the trade. This, however, would ignore the role played by collateral. It is true that the cash payments are indexed to the LIBOR, but hasn't the presence of collateral eliminated the credit risk element? This is indeed the case, although it is a fact that has been overlooked for a long time leading to the inconsistency (see for example Tuckman [79]) in which a trade that is risk free and should have been discounted using risk-free rates, was discounted using a risky rate such as LIBOR. Why this is the case is very simple: for a long time it mattered very little. The spread between LIBOR and OIS rate, an indicator of the market's feeling toward credit risk (see Michaud and Upper [63]), had always been around few tens of basis points up to the 2007 to 2009 financial crisis. It is when the same spread went above 300 bps (see Figure 2.8) that practitioners started to seriously take into consideration a change in the methodology with which discount factors should be calculated.

We shall now see how discounting takes into account collateral in practice and how this consideration has evolved in time.

2.4.2 Discounting in the Presence of Collateral

A financial institution receiving collateral is expected to pay interest on the collateral amount to the financial institution posting the collateral. The rate paid is almost always the overnight interest rate. This means that if the cash matching the MTM of the swap grows at the risk-free rate, then the discounting (the inverse of growth) of the same swap should be done using the same rate.[18] OIS is the tool that allows us to imply this new discount function. Let us rewrite Equation 2.14 as

$$\sum_i C \widetilde{D}_i dt_i = \sum_i \left[\prod_j \left(1 + l_j dt_j\right) \right] \widetilde{D}_i dt_i \qquad (2.15)$$

where we write $\widetilde{D}_t$ to stress the discount function driven by the overnight rate. If we now wish to value a swap or use a swap to construct a set of LIBORs (let us first think of the single currency situation, but let us assume that we deal with rates of more than one length and therefore we need to find $f_t(L^{XM})$ and $f_t(L^{YM})$), we use, instead of Equations 2.4 and 2.7,

$$\sum_i C \widetilde{D}_i dt_i = \sum_j L_j \widetilde{D}_j dt_j$$
$$\sum_n \left(L_n^{XM} + b_T\right) \widetilde{D}_n dt_n = \sum_j L_j^{YM} \widetilde{D}_j dt_j \qquad (2.16)$$

in conjunction with Equation 2.15, which is needed for the discount factors. The above can be extended, similarly to Equation 2.13, should we need rates of additional lengths. Since the above applies to the single currency situation, what should we do in the presence of multiple currencies?

We see that now we are moving further and further away from the assumption that a floating leg should price at par since now, even more so than when we introduced the currency basis, we are using two completely different rates to generate the forward cash flows and to discount them. We are going to return to this point, but now we need to consider carefully what it

---

[18]We shall return to this, but this statement is far from being universally accepted (see for example Hull and White [48]).

means to price a swap at par (as opposed to a single leg). The real definition of a par swap is one where the net of both legs is zero; however, in the past this was informally extended to the requirement that each leg would be equal to par, that is, zero (or one depending on whether there was an initial payment of principal). Now the change in discounting forces us to go back to the initial and rigorous definition, as we can no longer expect each leg to price at par.

2.4.2.1 Collateral in a Foreign Currency

The problem of multiple currencies arises in two ways: first, we need to see what happens to the discount factors in the other currency if we are pricing a leg in a different currency,[19] and second, what happens when the collateral posted is in a foreign currency.

Imagine that, as a U.S.-based institution, we need to discount a stream of cash flows in EUR. Up to the introduction of collateralized curve construction we would have discounted it using information obtained from the currency basis swap market. We have seen that this reflected the cost of funding an institution in a foreign market. The information is expressed as a spread over LIBOR, that is, over a risky rate. With the introduction of collateral we turn toward different types of instruments. The first question is, in what currency is the collateral posted? We should not assume that the collateral is in EUR; it could be in either USD or EUR.[20] Over time the currencies and the ways in which collateral is posted become more and more numerous so that the different options below almost follow an evolution in time.

In the case that the collateral is posted in USD, one could convert each cash flow with the appropriate FX forward and then discount using the OIS-driven discount function. We could write this (showing only the EUR leg) as

$$\sum_i FWD_i L_i^{EUR} \widetilde{D_i^{USD}} dt_i + FWD_T \widetilde{D_T^{USD}} \tag{2.17}$$

where FWD_i is the FX forward rate at time T_i and the discount factors are the same as in Equation 2.15 (we have stressed the currency for absolute clarity). Someone might wonder whether the FX forward would not introduce an interest rate element that would make things murkier. To this very interesting point one would reply that, first of all, the interest rate component of an FX

---

[19]We keep it general so that the leg can either belong to an interest rate swap in a foreign currency or it can be the foreign leg in a cross currency swap.

[20]Technically, collateral can be posted in *any* currency and there are traders who actively search and profit from seeking the most attractive form of collateral (cheapest to deliver). Let us ignore, however, these more perverse situations.

forward is there only when we try to extract it. This cryptic, Schrödinger-like argument needs clarifying. First, when an FX trader is trading forwards, he is not thinking about interest rates. The fact that we can imply them is just a handy financial argument that works most of the time. The fact that we need to make assumptions about one of the two curves shows that the information never really comes out completely. Second, didn't we say that the sense of greater safety derived from the trading of FX forwards originated from the fact that they were fully collateralized, that is, the principals were exchanged at the beginning of the trade? This means that FX forwards were never meant to be proxies of LIBOR levels, instead they are particularly suited to the argument that we need to take into account the collateral posted. The interest rate intrinsic to the FX forward should be very close to an overnight rate and therefore it does not introduce murkiness into Equation 2.17.

With collateral being posted in different currencies, the above does not seem to be the ideal solution, which instead would be to use some form of swap indexing the overnight rate for EUR discounting. One cannot tell with certainty whether the appearance in the market of an OIS-type swap for currency X motivates institutions to post collateral in currency X or is the posting in that currency that gives birth to the trading in the overnight index swap as the two tend to appear together (see Andersen and Piterbarg [4] for a few interesting considerations on the proliferation of instruments used for collateralized discounting, and Fujii et al. [42] for a rigorous treatment of collateralized curve construction). With this tool at hand we can obtain discount factors of the form $\widetilde{D_t^{EUR}}$ and discount the EUR leg of a swap as

$$\sum_i L_i^{EUR} \widetilde{D_i^{EUR}} dt_i + \widetilde{D_T^{EUR}} \qquad (2.18)$$

Collateral is being posted in several (major) currencies nowadays, and operationally, since a certain collateral is linked to a certain counterparty, the tendency is to assume that that counterparty will always post, to collateralize a certain currency, the same currency (e.g., bank XYZ will always post EUR to collateralize Hungarian Florins trades). We shall now ask ourselves, does the change in methodology really matter?

2.4.3 Clearing, the Evolution of a Price, and the Impact of Discounting

When presenting the history behind the choice of OIS versus LIBOR discounting, we have shown that, because of the small spread between the two rates, the impact was very small. We shall now discuss whether, in general, discounting has a large impact on a swap price.

The life of a swap can be very long. This statement of the obvious is to stress that we need to view the evolution of the price of a swap and basically observe two situations, when the swap price is close to par and when it is not. (Borrowing the terminology of options, we can call a par swap an at-the-money [ATM] swap, and otherwise, when it is not close to par, an out-of-the-money [OTM] swap.)

In Table 2.1 we see the cash flows of two swaps, an at the money and an out of the money. The two swaps are identical in characteristics in that they both pay a fix rate annually and a floating rate semiannually. We assume that we have built our curve using a certain amount of market information from which we have obtained the discount factors given in the first column and the forward rates which are given in the, identical, third and fifth columns. We can see that the difference between the two swaps lies in the fixed rate: the ATM swap pays 3.2668% and the OTM swap pays 4.5%.

In finance as in science it is very important, when observing an effect, to be able to say whether it is large or small. An effective way of doing this is to make it dimensionless, to scale it by an accepted quantity. In finance we do so by comparing any impact to the bid-offer spread of the relevant market data. To test the impact of a shift in discount factor we are going to take four steps. First, we are going to shift the discount factor by a certain amount; for simplicity this is going to be an artificial shift but it could realistically

TABLE 2.1 Cash flows in a par swap (ATM) and in an out-of-the-money swap (OTM).

D_T	Zero rate equiv. (%)	ATM swap: fix CF (%)	ATM swap: floating CF (%)	OTM swap: fix CF (%)	OTM swap: floating CF (%)
0.9852	2.9780		3.0000		3.0000
0.9706	3.0249	3.2268	3.0500	4.5000	3.0500
0.9558	3.0734		3.1000		3.1000
0.9412	3.1221	3.2268	3.1500	4.5000	3.1500
0.9264	3.1727		3.2000		3.2000
0.9118	3.2253	3.2268	3.2500	4.5000	3.2500
0.8970	3.2762		3.3000		3.3000
0.8826	3.3251	3.2268	3.3200	4.5000	3.3200
0.8681	3.3718		3.3300		3.3300
0.8540	3.4170	3.2268	3.3500	4.5000	3.3500
	MTM (in %)		0.0		−5.80

correspond to, for example, a choice of instrument used to build the discount curve. Second, we are going to translate the discount factor into a zero rate. A zero rate has the same definition of cash deposit with the difference that it is not a traded instrument. We are doing this purely for illustration purposes. Almost everyone has more familiarity with the concept of rate expressed in percentages rather than as discount factor. Third, we are going to recalculate the swap price with the new discount factors and show the impact in the MTM. Finally, in order to gauge whether the impact is a large one, we are going to calculate the equivalent impact in the swap rate, that is, that shift in the swap rate that would have given the same impact in MTM. (By a very rough rule of thumb, this is given by the MTM impact divided by the length in years of the swap.)

The first and second steps are shown in Table 2.2. For simplicity the shifts (-0.02 and -0.03) are constant throughout the discount factor's curve, meaning that they will have a greater impact on a short dated discount factor than a longer dated one. This can be seen by the fact that the difference between the zero rates shown in the second and fourth columns of Table 2.2 and the second column of Table 2.1 is very large for the first cash flow and it tapers out.

In Table 2.3 we see that the impact of the first shift on the MTM is 0.20 bps for the ATM swap and 12.93 bps for the OTM swap. The ratio of 60 times greater is reflected in the equivalent swap rate impact, which is 0.05 bps for the ATM swap and 2.90 bps for the OTM one. Not surprisingly, for the second shift the impact is even greater with an MTM impact of 0.30 bps for the ATM swap and a 19.40 impact for the OTM swap. The impact on the swap rate is 0.30 bps for the ATM swap and 4.40 bps

TABLE 2.2 Shifts in discount factors and zero rate equivalent.

D_T 1st shift	Zero rate equiv. (%)	D_T 2nd shift	Zero rate equiv. (%)
0.9652	7.1501	0.9552	9.3017
0.9506	5.1896	0.9406	6.3064
0.9358	4.5587	0.9258	5.3255
0.9212	4.2747	0.9112	4.8700
0.9064	4.1234	0.8964	4.6147
0.8918	4.0430	0.8818	4.4667
0.8770	4.0015	0.8670	4.3766
0.8626	3.9816	0.8526	4.3215
0.8481	3.9747	0.8381	4.2869
0.8340	3.9783	0.8240	4.2692

TABLE 2.3 Impact of shifts in discount factors on MTM of ATM and OTM swaps.

	Impact on MTM of ATM swap (bps)	Impact on swap rate of ATM swap (bps)	Impact on MTM of OTM swap (bps)	Impact on swap rate of OTM swap (bps)
1st shift	0.20	0.05	12.93	2.90
2nd shift	0.30	0.07	19.40	4.40

for the OTM swap. To put the impact into context, the bid-offer spread on USD interest rate swaps is 3 bps. This shows how, at inception when a swap is at par,[21] the impact of discounting matters very little. It is when a swap is already in the middle of its life (exemplified here by a fixed rate very different from the par swap rate) that two discount factors have very different effects on the swap price. This is not difficult to understand: the forward rates shown in the fourth column of Table 2.1 are fairly close to each other (we call this a rather flat swap curve), the par swap rate paid as fix rate in the third column of the same table is also a number roughly of the same magnitude. This means that on both sides the numbers we are going to multiply the discount factors by are very close, reducing the impact of the discount factors themselves. The same cannot be said of an OTM swap.[22]

Let us now remind ourselves why two parties need to agree on the MTM of a swap. This is not for actual settlement reasons: payments are linked to the rate itself, which sets officially and about which there is no disagreement. It is for collateral purposes: according to the value of the MTM, the party that sees it as negative needs to post collateral to the other party. Different discounting choices lead to collateral disputes when two parties disagree on the MTM of the swaps. Collateral disputes are frequent and tiresome processes rendered even less clear by the fact that, because of the netting of positions we mentioned in Section 2.4.1, a party will argue with different degrees of forcefulness according to whether certain transactions will result in a net lower or higher MTM (the ideal situation being one of lower MTM, hence, less collateral to be posted).

---

[21]Of course one can trade swaps that start out of the money, but it is a more unusual situation, and here, would fall in the same category as an already existing swap.

[22]There is also the less common situation of a swap built on a set of forward rates increasing not as smoothly as in Table 2.1. That would be the case of a steepening swap curve and the impact falls in between the two cases presented here.

After the financial crisis there is a general wish to move simple swaps (the one we have seen would fall in that category) to exchanges (for an interesting description of the time line of the issue and how exchanges try to deal with it, see Whittall [84]). Exchange-traded derivatives, such as interest rate futures, are not only fully standardized contracts, they are also contracts whose price is published by an exchange, that is, there is an official price. Crucially this price is not only official on the day of entering the contract (this would not differ very much from what takes place already with a broker publishing such a price), but also throughout the life of the trade. This process is known as clearing where an exchange (acting as a clearinghouse) becomes a third party and arbiter to a transaction between two market participants. Essentially the two market participants would not be facing each other but instead would each have a position with the clearinghouse. The exchange-decides on an indisputable MTM and as a consequence it decides on the collateral that needs to be posted. This collateral would be in the form of margin calls, similar to other exchange-traded contracts such as futures. We immediately see that in this situation there is no more argument as to what is the correct choice of instruments to build a discount curve on, the hopefully intelligent choice made by the exchange becomes the correct choice. It is up to each of the two financial institutions facing the exchange in this swap triangle to value it in a manner similar to the exchange, in which case it would avoid seeing internal surprises, or value it differently and accept the fact that the value obtained internally could be dramatically different from the official one.

The move, challenging as it may be for all the parties involved (clearinghouses included), is very important. Since we have seen how curve construction is a challenging numerical process that may elude some of the less sophisticated firms, there was always the risk that some institutions could have built large positions marked incorrectly, which, at the moment of reckoning, could have led to potential catastrophes.

2.4.4 The Special Case of AAA-Rated Institutions

We will finish the discussion on curve construction with the special mention of AAA-rated institutions, a category to which many development institutions belong. It is not uncommon for AAA-rated institutions not to post collateral and not to pay interest on the collateral paid to them. This arrangement is often referred to as one way CSA (CSA stands for Credit Support Annex, which appeared in the ISDA 1994), in the sense that, unless both parties are AAA, the rules of collateral apply only to one of the two. In most cases they do not have access to central bank windows for borrowing.[23] What does that mean in terms of curve construction? This is a very interesting question, which at the time of writing is at a center of a discussion that involves not only the move of swaps toward clearinghouses, but also the implication of the Dodd-Frank Act (a piece of U.S. legislation whose goal is to bring transparency, stability, and, hopefully, safety to the financial world). For consistency with all that has been said above, the view should be that AAA-rated institutions should not move toward OIS discounting. We have said that the discounting choice for an institution should be driven by the borrowing level of the institution itself and the rate of growth of the collateral received and paid. All of these arguments point to remaining a LIBOR-driven discounting. Of course this view is only one side, let's call it the funding view, of the current debate on discounting (see Hull and White [48] and Morini and Prampolini [64] for the original point and the reference section for the subsequent ones in the debate). This debate concerns the so-called FVA, or the Funding Value Adjustment, that needs to be applied to discounting in order to take into account differences in funding levels between counterparties. The other side, let's call it risk-free view, of the debate claims that funding levels should not have any input at all and discounting should only be done on what the market deems to be the current risk-free rate. This is because the risk-neutral framework, by which we all still abide, requires derivatives to be discounted at a risk-free rate. This rate is certainly not LIBOR at the moment, and the rate that would qualify as risk free is indeed the OIS rate. This is slightly different from the way we introduced OIS. In fact, the risk-free view believes in using OIS but not because it is the rate at which collateral grows (the way we introduced it), but because it is a form of risk-free rate. The risk-free view would then hold that a AAA institution, like everyone else, irrespective of its collateral and/or funding situation, should discount using the OIS rate. (Incidentally, this would prepare such institution for a future move toward central clearing.) In this book we do not believe that collateral and funding should be ignored, because we try to follow an argument by which the widest possible view of an institution's activities should be considered when valuing financial instruments. Nonetheless, we admit that no easy solution exists to the debate we have just mentioned and both sides have made valid arguments. Let us, however,

---

[23]In the United States for example, the Fed Fund window is a borrowing facility that has always been opened to commercial banks and not to investment banks (hence the need of the latter to borrow at LIBOR). With the move to commercial bank status, on September 18, 2008, on the part of Morgan Stanley and Goldman Sachs, all investment banks now have access to the window. Note: The access is not for *all* activities; the majority of funding for an investment bank still comes from LIBOR-level borrowing.

move away from this debate and discuss an interesting side effect of the special situation in which a AAA institution finds itself.

We have seen how swap pricing is not a solitary activity but involves at least two parties, and now, with the move toward clearinghouses, three. What does the perfectly understandable decision on the part of AAA-rated institutions to remain with LIBOR-driven discounting entail in the wider financial system? Operationally speaking, a financial institution chooses the type of discounting according to the counterparty. Because each counterparty can post collateral in one of several currencies,[24] a financial institution's curve construction system needs to be able to assign to counterparty ABC a curve construction driven by an X OIS curve. The association of a certain AAA party to a LIBOR-driven curve construction would be just another pairing. As far as clearing is concerned, however, unless there will be a special provision to keep trades involving AAA institutions over the counter, that might be more of a problem for which at present there does not seem to be a clear answer.

Let us finish with a brief change of perspective and imagine we are facing a AAA institution. Let us imagine that we trade a fix for floating swap with principal N in a generic currency such that we define the present value of the fix leg

$$FIX_t = N \sum_i C D_i dt_i$$

and the present value of the floating leg

$$FL_t = N \sum_j L_j D_j dt_j$$

Let us imagine the situation in which we are receiving fix and paying floating, meaning that the MTM of the swap is for us given by

$$MTM_t = FIX_t - F L_t$$

If the MTM is negative, meaning we need to post collateral, we will be receiving nothing in the sense that no interest will be paid by our counterparty, the AAA institution, on that amount. Instead, we will be paying overnight rate l to borrow the collateral we need to post. Should the MTM

---

[24]Sometimes a party has the option to switch collateral currencies, creating interesting situations (see Whittall [84]).

be positive, we will be receiving LIBOR (not from the counterparty but from the fact that we will be in the position to lend it at LIBOR). In practice

$$L1_{MTM_t > 0} - l1_{MTM_t < 0} \qquad (2.19)$$

where 1_X is the unit function, equal to one if X is true and zero otherwise. Note that Equation 2.19 shows the situation at a specific moment in time. As we have said previously, collateral calculations are daily exercises, meaning that the above will be summed over a whole payment period. In Equation 2.19 we see a discontinuity, a function that goes in a nonsmooth way across a single point (or, one could say, a function that is nondifferentiable at the point $MTM_t = 0$). Whenever we see a situation like this, we know that there should be special hedging involved, in this case made even more special by the underlying itself. Banks trade CSA options to hedge structures like these arising from special collateral agreements (which we have defined previously as one-way CSAs).[25] We should note that the situation presented in Equation 2.19 is interesting because we have simultaneously two different exposures to LIBOR. This is particularly easy to see when it is in the money (i.e., $MTM_t > 0$): we are short LIBOR in the swap itself (if it decreases we pay less and therefore the MTM increases in our favor), but we are long LIBOR as far as the income we receive from investing the MTM amount itself.

The example above, although it might appear too specific for the general tone of the chapter, was mentioned nonetheless to show that one should try to take into consideration the biggest possible picture of the activities of an institution, from borrowing to hedging, in order to make the correct pricing choices.

2.5 NUMERICAL EXAMPLE: BOOTSTRAPPING AN INTEREST RATE CURVE

In order to put into practice what we have seen throughout this chapter, we shall give an example of what it means to bootstrap a simple interest rate swap curve. We shall show what can be accomplished in a so-called closed

---

[25]One needs to point out that it is not only AAA-rated institutions that do not post collateral. There are other entities, usually corporates, that might have agreements in which they do not pay collateral. The counterparty risk is then taken care of through Counterparty Value Adjustments (CVA), which we shall mention briefly in Section 7.3.2. We have reached the point where any discussion about discounting moves into explicit credit risk management. This is beyond the scope of this book and in particular beyond the scope of this chapter.

TABLE 2.4 Market inputs used to bootstrap the interest rate curve in our example.

Maturity	Instrument type	Instrument code	Market quote
1D	Deposit	1D	0.389 %
1W	Deposit	1W	0.444 %
1M	Deposit	1M	0.341 %
2M	Deposit	2M	0.351 %
3M	Deposit	3M	0.380 %
6M	Deposit	6M	0.560 %
9M	FRA	6M X 3M	0.650 %
12M	FRA	9M X 3M	0.670 %
2Y	Swap	2Y	0.630 %
3Y	Swap	3Y	0.810 %
4Y	Swap	4Y	1.030 %
5Y	Swap	5Y	1.240 %
7Y	Swap	7Y	1.670 %
10Y	Swap	10Y	1.850 %
15Y	Swap	15Y	1.960 %

form, without using a solver routine, and then discuss what the further steps might be.

Let us imagine that we have the market inputs shown in Table 2.4 at our disposal. In particular we have deposit rates, Forward Rate Agreements (FRA), and interest rate swaps. Deposit rates from one day up to six months, forward rate agreements each with three-month lengths starting in six months' time and nine months' time, respectively, and finally interest rate swaps for maturities from two years onward. We assume the date of the data is taken to be January 3, 2012.

2.5.1 The Short End of the Curve: Deposits and FRAs

Our initial objective is to find those discount factors D_t such that the market instruments used are priced correctly. As far as the deposits are concerned it is fairly simple. Using the fact that the deposit rate r_T is related to the discount factor D_T by

$$D_T = \frac{1}{(1 + r_D T)}$$

we can obtain the needed discount factors. (In the above we assume, as in Equation 2.2, linear compounding. We also assume, here and throughout this exercise as stated in the footnote in Section 2.1, that the correct day count convention has been applied when using the time variable T.) For example, using the overnight deposit we obtain, assuming an actual day count by which there are 366 days in the first year,

$$D_{1D} = \frac{1}{\left(1 + \frac{1}{366}0.00389\right)} = 0.99999$$

Similarly, using the weekly deposit, we obtain that

$$D_{1W} = \frac{1}{\left(1 + \frac{7}{366}0.00444\right)} = 0.99992$$

Since the date on which the data in Table 2.4 is assumed to have been collected is January 3, 2012, 31 days elapse in the first month and thus the discount factor corresponding to the one-month point will be given by

$$D_{1M} = \frac{1}{\left(1 + \frac{31}{366}0.00341\right)} = 0.99971$$

The remaining discount factors derived from deposits can be obtained in a similar fashion.

The information contained in the two FRAs can be used to find one discount factor each if we remind ourselves of the relation between floating rates and discount factors, namely that a forward rate $L_{i,j}$ contained in a FRA between T_i and T_j is given by

$$L_{i,j} = \frac{1}{T_j - T_i}\left(\frac{D_i}{D_j} - 1\right)$$

where $T_j - T_i$ is the time elapsed calculated according to the correct day count convention. If we take the first FRA we see that $L_{6M,9M} = 0.0065$, moreover we know, having calculated it from deposits, that the six-month discount factor is equal to 0.99722. Combining these two pieces of information to find the discount factors D_{9M} corresponding to the nine months, we have

$$D_{9M} = \frac{0.99723}{0.0065\frac{274-182}{366} + 1} = 0.99560$$

Similarly, using the discount factor obtained previously and the rate $L_{9M,12M} = 0.0067$ we have from the second FRA, we can obtain the one-year discount factor

$$D_{12M} = \frac{0.99560}{0.0067\frac{366-274}{366} + 1} = 0.99394$$

2.5.2 The Long End of the Curve: Interest Rate Swaps

We have used the information contained in all the deposits and the FRAs to build the short end of the curve. We are going to use interest rate swaps to build the remaining long end of the curve. We know that interest rate swaps are made of two legs, each made of a series of cash flows. In order to be able to solve one variable at a time, the goal of a closed-form methodology, we need to use an inductive process, one that uses knowledge recently built in order to solve for the variable at hand. This is also the definition of the term bootstrapping.

We know that a single currency fixed for floating swap with maturity T and paying a swap rate C_T is given by

$$C_T \sum_{i=1}^{T} D_i dt_i = \sum_{j=1}^{T} L_{j,j+1} D_j dt_j$$

where we have allowed for the two legs to have different payment frequencies. If we add a final payment of the entire principal on both sides, we can use the assumption that a floating leg with final principal payment is always equal to unity, and therefore

$$C_T \sum_{i=1}^{T} D_i dt_i + D_T = 1$$

The essence of a bootstrapping process is to check up to where we have data points, go one step further, and solve for that extra data point. We then repeat the process extending it by one point and consider the previous unknown as the last known data point. This means that in the above we assume that we know everything except from D_T, which we are trying to solve for. Since D_T appears twice, let us isolate it by writing the above in a slightly different form and a slightly different notation

$$C_{T_N} \sum_{i=1}^{T_{N-1}} D_i dt_i + C_{T_N} dt_N D_{T_N} + D_{T_N} = 1$$

$$D_{T_N} = \frac{1 - C_{T_N} \sum_{i=1}^{T_{N-1}} D_i dt_i}{1 + dt_N C_{T_N}}$$

(2.20)

where T_N indicates the time of the last cash flow, the one taking place at maturity, and T_{N-1} the one immediately preceding it. Let us now use an important piece of information, the fact that the frequency of the fixed leg in the swap is annual (the one of the floating leg is of no concern to us) and the accrual method is Act/Act, meaning that the time between two points as a fraction of one year is calculated by taking the actual number of days between those two points and dividing it by the actual number of days in that year. From this information we can see that $dt_i = 1 \ \forall \ i$. Since we know the discount factor for the first year, we need to use the information contained in the quote for the interest rate swap maturing in two years' time, that is,

$$D_{2Y} = \frac{1 - C_{2Y} D_{12M}}{1 + C_{2Y}}$$

which, using the actual values, becomes

$$D_{2Y} = \frac{1 - 0.0063 \cdot 0.99394}{1 + 0.0063} = 0.98752$$

Using the value for D_{2Y} we can now proceed with the next data point and solve for D_{3Y} using Equation 2.20. We need to calculate

$$D_{3Y} = \frac{1 - C_{3Y} (D_{12M} + D_{2Y})}{1 + C_{3Y}}$$

which becomes

$$D_{3Y} = \frac{1 - 0.0081 (0.99394 + 0.98752)}{1 + 0.0081} = 0.97604$$

For the following years the principle is the same, only with longer summations. Once we have found the discount factor corresponding to year five, we notice that the next point corresponds to year seven. Since we need to find the discount factor D_{6Y}, a reasonable approach is to assume that the market

TABLE 2.5 The output of the bootstrapping process: the discount factors, the zero rates (annually and continuously compounded), and the one-year forward rates.

Maturity	Discount factor	Zero rate (ann. comp.)	Zero rate (cont. comp.)	One-year forward rate
1D	0.99999	0.39 %	0.39 %	
1W	0.99992	0.44 %	0.44 %	
1M	0.99971	0.34 %	0.34 %	
2M	0.99943	0.35 %	0.35 %	
3M	0.99906	0.38 %	0.38 %	
6M	0.99723	0.56 %	0.56 %	
9M	0.99560	0.59 %	0.59 %	
12M	0.99394	0.61 %	0.61 %	0.65 %
2Y	0.98753	0.63 %	0.63 %	1.18 %
3Y	0.97607	0.81 %	0.81 %	1.71 %
4Y	0.95968	1.03 %	1.03 %	2.12 %
5Y	0.93981	1.25 %	1.24 %	2.59 %
6Y	0.91604	1.47 %	1.46 %	3.07 %
7Y	0.88879	1.70 %	1.68 %	2.19 %
8Y	0.86975	1.76 %	1.74 %	2.32 %
9Y	0.85002	1.82 %	1.80 %	2.46 %
10Y	0.82964	1.88 %	1.87 %	2.12 %
11Y	0.81241	1.91 %	1.89 %	2.17 %
12Y	0.79514	1.93 %	1.91 %	2.22 %
13Y	0.77786	1.95 %	1.93 %	2.27 %
14Y	0.76057	1.97 %	1.95 %	2.33 %
15Y	0.74328	2.00 %	1.98 %	

quote for year six, which we do not have, must be the linear interpolation between the quotes for year five and year seven, which we have. Thus

$$D_{6Y} = \frac{1 - \frac{1}{2}(C_{5Y} + C_{7Y})(D_{12M} + D_{2Y} + D_{3Y} + D_{4Y} + D_{5Y})}{1 + \frac{1}{2}(C_{5Y} + C_{7Y})}$$

The same approach applies to the other points where we do not have an actual market quote. Table 2.5 shows the discount factors obtained using the process above and also, as a reference, the corresponding zero rate obtained with annual or continuous compounding, which are also plotted in Figure 2.9a.

The advantage of this approach is that it is quite trivial to implement. It could also be extended to approximate, and let us stress the term approximate, the discount factors obtained in the presence of a cross currency basis.

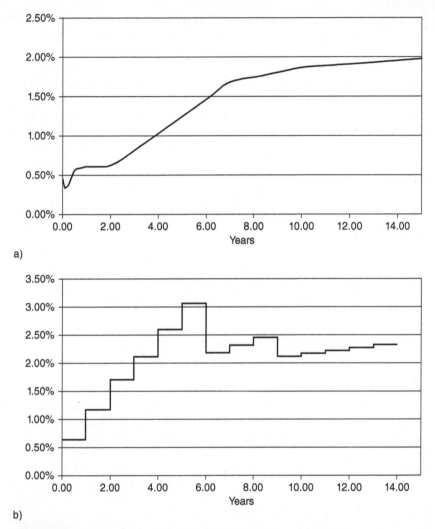

FIGURE 2.9 a) The zero rates of the bootstrapped curve; b) the one-year forward rates calculated from the bootstrapped discount factors.

We have seen in Section 2.2.5.2 that in some foreign currencies, if we want to calculate the discount factors, we need to include the information contained in a cross currency basis swap, a swap where, as shown in Equation 2.8, a flat floating (usually USD) leg is exchanged for a floating foreign leg plus some basis. Using the bootstrap process shown above we can approximate the foreign discount factors, and maintain the ease of calculation, by simply adding the basis onto the swap quote, that is, in Equation 2.20 have $C_T + b_C$ instead of C_T, where b_C is the cross currency basis.

Using the previous bootstrap methodology for cross currency basis swaps is an approximation, which nonetheless is considered sufficiently valid to be used by many commercially successful trade entry and management softwares. It is an approximation because it assumes that to put the basis onto the fixed leg of a swap is equivalent to adding it on to the floating leg of a swap. Purely in terms of values, if the swap is at par and the term structure of expected forward rates is more or less flat (let us remind ourselves that one can *very roughly* consider the fixed rate of a swap as the average of the expected forward floating rates), the resulting discount factors will be similar to the ones obtained by solving simultaneously Equations 2.10 and 2.11. Using the above process for currency basis swaps will fail completely, but not when applied to more exotic situations, such as the one presented by cross currency basis swaps in Mexican or Chilean Pesos (MXN and CLP respectively). In the case of MXN, the cross currency basis swap is not, as one would expect, an exchange of USD LIBOR flat for MXN LIBOR plus basis, but MXN LIBOR flat versus USD LIBOR plus basis

$$\sum_i L_i^{MXN} D_i^{MXN} dt_i = \sum \left(L_i^{USD} + b_C \right) D_i^{USD} dt_i$$

In the above we can immediately see how we cannot assume the USD leg to be equal to par (the point of view of a USD-centered institution, which we have always taken), the usual convenient way of eliminating D_i^{USD} from the equation and concentrating on solving for the discount factors of the currency under consideration. In the above we need to solve simultaneously for D_i^{MXN} and D_i^{USD} and this cannot be done in a closed form.

2.5.3   Interpolation and Extrapolation

In Table 2.4 we have shown the discount factors corresponding to some points in time for which we had market quotes and for some for which we have assumed market quotes. Since we are bound to need discount factors for all the points in between, how do we calculate them? There are many possible interpolation techniques. The simplest ones are linear interpolations of some kind that fall into two families, those that are linear in discount factors and those that are linear in rate.

If we need the discount factor D_k corresponding to the point in time t_k such that $t_i < t_k < t_{i+1}$, we can either interpolate linearly between discount factors and have

$$D_k = \left(1 - \frac{t_k - t_i}{t_{i+1} - t_i}\right) D_i + \frac{t_k - t_i}{t_{i+1} - t_i} D_{i+1}$$

or interpolate linearly between rates and have

$$D_k = \exp\left\{-t_k \left[\left(1 - \frac{t_k - t_i}{t_{i+1} - t_i}\right)\left(-\frac{1}{t_i}\ln D_i\right) + \frac{t_k - t_i}{t_{i+1} - t_i}\left(-\frac{1}{t_{i+1}}\ln D_{i+1}\right)\right]\right\}$$

where we have assumed continuous compounding of the zero rate. (Because of the way it is carried out, the above is sometimes called exponential interpolation.) Interpolation is important not only to discount cash flows that happen in between standard market point dates, but also for the generation of forward rates that, should we not interpolate, would look like the curve shown in Figure 2.9b. That curve, while correct, is of little use since it would lead to some very strange behavior when we go across one market point date and our rate jumps from two very different values.

To generate correct and smooth forward rates is crucial since an interest rate curve will be used for trading and hedging, where a correct index generation (let us remember what we said at the very beginning of this chapter about the two objectives of a curve construction process) is as important as a correct discounting. A solution to this problem is one where we combine bootstrapping and interpolation in one single process: this is what the most sophisticated curve construction systems do, but unfortunately, it cannot be done in a closed form. This is achieved by using cubic B-splines.

A cubic B-spline is a variation on the more general cubic spline (see de Boor [15] for a thorough treatment or Press et al. [72] for a more concise and yet clear introduction) and is a function $S(t)$ made of a collection of bases (hence the "B-" in B-splines) functions $s_1(t), s_2(t), \ldots, s_n(t)$ such that

$$S(t) = s_k(t) \quad \text{if } t_k < t < t_{k+1}$$
$$S(t) = 0 \quad \text{otherwise}$$

and where each base function is a third-degree polynomial

$$s_k(t) = a_k (t - t_k)^3 + b_k (t - t_k)^2 + c_k (t - t_k) + d_k$$

$S(t)$ will be used to interpolate a function $y(t)$ of which we have some data points $y_i(t)$ while satisfying the following conditions:

- $S(t)$ will interpolate all data points
- $S(t)$ will be continuous in the interval $[t_1, t_n]$
- both the first, $S'(t)$, and the second, $S''(t)$, derivatives of $S(t)$ will be continuous in the interval $[t_1, t_n]$

We can apply the spline interpolation to our situation if we imagine that $y(t)$ is the smooth index function $f(L_t)$ used to generate forward rates. This index function, which we defined at the very beginning of the chapter, is, for example, what we have called $f_t(L^{EUR})$ in Section 2.3 when discussing the curve construction of the EUR index curve. Of course, as we have shown when discussing tenor basis swaps, there is sometimes more than one index function (in the same section we mention $f_t(L_{3M}^{EUR})$ and $g_t(L_{6M}^{EUR})$), here for simplicity we assume that we are trying to solve for one generic index function. The nature of this function will be determined only by the data points chosen, the principle behind its construction is the same.

We assume that there are some coefficients f_k (ks represent the points in time we are trying to find rates for), such that our index function can be expressed as

$$f(L_t) = \sum_k f_k s_k(t)$$

In this framework, assuming continuous compounding, we would express the discount factors D_T as

$$D_T = \exp\left[-\sum_k \left(\sum_{t_n=0}^{T} s_k(t_n)dt_n \right) f_k \right] \tag{2.21}$$

and the forward rate $L_{i,j}$ would be expressed as

$$L_{i,j} = \frac{1}{T_j - T_i} \left\{ \frac{\exp\left[-\sum_k \left(\sum_{t_n=0}^{T_i} s_k(t_n)dt_n \right) f_k \right]}{\exp\left[-\sum_k \left(\sum_{t_n=0}^{T_j} s_k(t_n)dt_n \right) f_k \right]} - 1 \right\} \tag{2.22}$$

Let us assume that we have been given M market quotes (which could, for example, be made up of the FRAs and swap values shown in Table 2.4) with values $R_1, R_2, \ldots, R_M$. Let $\overline{R}_1, \overline{R}_2, \ldots, \overline{R}_M$ be the corresponding values found with our model, that is, using Equations 2.22 and 2.23. Our goal (see, for example, Waggoner [82]) is to minimize the expression

$$\sum_{i}^{M} \left(R_i - \overline{R}_i \right)^2 + \Lambda \qquad (2.23)$$

where the term Λ is a term added for extra smoothing, which can take several forms.[26]

The bootstrap-cum-interpolation outlined above cannot be done, of course, in a closed form but needs some solver routine such as the Levenberg-Marquardt algorithm (Press et al. [72]). There are pros and cons to the two methodologies outlined above. The B-spline methodology gives a smooth outcome and potentially can take as inputs overlapping instruments (which we do not have in Table 2.4 but could happen, for example, in the form of overlapping FRAs). The downsides are that it is not trivial to implement and it is also slower. Moreover, because of the conditions on continuity and differentiability, spline interpolations tend to be nonlocal, that is, the output value at one point depends on many neighboring points. In this respect the B-spline, with its requirement that the base function be zero outside a certain interval is a considerable improvement over the general cubic spline interpolation. Closed-form bootstrapping is simple and fast to implement and will perfectly reprice the inputs; moreover, it will be more local in its sensitivity to change in input points. The disadvantage is that it produces a less smooth outcome and it is less flexible in the way it takes its inputs (e.g., it cannot take overlapping data points).

The greatest advantage of the spline methodology is that it can be extended to multiple curves. In the example above, although we have not shown it, we have presented how a spline bootstrap-cum-interpolation would work, but we have done so with what essentially amounts to a single leg approach: swap rates were used only after assuming that one leg could be ignored because it was equal to par. We have seen, however, in Section 2.3 with the introduction of tenor basis swaps and in Section 2.4 with the introduction of OIS discounting, that to correctly construct a curve we need to be able to include not only more than one leg, but more than one swap at a time.

---

[26]When we have

$$\Lambda = \lambda \int_t f''(L_t)\, dt \qquad (2.24)$$

with λ being a positive constant and the integral being over the entire time span of our interest rate curve, Λ is called *Tikhonov regularizer*.

This is what the more sophisticated financial institutions do to construct index and discount curves and it hinges on using multidimensional solvers, solvers that minimize more than one variable at a time, that is, that (try to) find the global minimum of a function of several variables. The discussion of this is beyond the practical nature of this section, which was simply to offer the tools to bootstrap a curve and build a fairly general and accurate interest rate curve using nothing more than a spreadsheet.

In the chapter About the Web Site we provide the link to a spreadsheet where we offer an implementation in VBA of a simple bootstrapping process like the one shown in this chapter.

CHAPTER 3

Credit and the Fair Valuing of Loans

As we have reminded ourselves in the previous chapter, our prime focus is debt and therefore credit. We have seen how, when we discount a future cash flow, we are essentially using credit considerations implicit in interest-rate instruments. Here, we are going to consider credit explicitly. We are going to define what we mean by credit and what underlyings are used to capture it. Of all the possible ways to model credit we shall introduce a simple risk-neutral framework to assess survival probabilities. These will be used to value a loan, which, as we have said, is the fundamental tool of development banking.

3.1 CREDIT AS AN ASSET CLASS

Of all the asset classes, credit is arguably the most unusual. Whereas in other fields we deal with tangible objects—in equity, through shares, with the ownership of a company; in commodities with the ownership of something very real; in FX with the relative worth of money in different currencies—when it comes to credit we deal with something more elusive, we deal with the possibility of someone defaulting on a debt obligation. In this sense, if the interest rate is the asset class of borrowing, credit can be considered a by-product of it.

As pointed out by Schönbucher [74] in a great introduction to the topic, the most important characteristics of credit events (a term for default) is that they are rare, they can happen unexpectedly, and they do so with a magnitude unknown beforehand. Although we might not be familiar with the details of a bankruptcy, we can easily imagine it to be a process likely to be drawn out over a lengthy period of time and, despite the legal framework in place, not necessarily very clear.[1]

Since credit risk is the risk linked to payment default, in order for it to exist there needs to first be the promise of a payment: if there is no promise of payment there is no question of credit risk. The second question, not an easy one, is what constitutes default: is it the default on *one* payment, *any* payment, *all* payments? There are of course laws and agreements in place but, because of the rare and unexpected nature of the event itself, they might not be absolutely clear on all possible scenarios.[2] A great difference applies to the credit risk presented by corporate and sovereign entities: the former needs to abide by binding bankruptcy laws easily enforceable within a country or a treaty, the latter have on the surface looser restrictions, which are made in practice tighter by the markets (if they want to borrow again in the future). We will see how these differences apply in particular when it comes to development institutions, and we will see how the special form sovereign credit risk takes in the eyes of a development institution influences the way trades are priced.

Throughout this chapter and in even more detail when we will analyze the activity of a treasury desk, we will notice how credit is pervasive. The financial world is made of payments and promises of payment, to each one of them a credit risk is attached without exception. Credit touches upon the notion of trust and honoring of a promise. Although there is a framework to deal with the situation, when this is broken, there is still the sense that a credit event takes us into a region very close to the outer limits of what we consider civil society. Although in the everyday life of a practitioner this is something very far from his main concerns, when credit events occur, or we are very close to them, we experience a sense of unease and fear. This is probably one of the reasons, after all the technical ones, why a credit crisis such as the Great Recession is far more scarring than a crisis of another type (such as the tech bubble).

Credit, as we said above, is somehow a less tangible asset class than others. Within this asset class people have nonetheless managed to build a solid framework around the probability of default and create market instruments useful to protect us against it. Let us introduce what the underlying instruments of credit are and identify the derivatives used to hedge them.

---

[1]As of 2011, ten years later, the default of Argentina has not been dealt with completely [34].

[2]At the time of writing, the debate was still recent as to whether the voluntary acceptance by investors of the restructuring of Greece's debt would constitute a default.

3.1.1 The Underlyings

Although we will describe both of them in far greater detail later, let us introduce here, for the sake of understanding the basics of credit modeling, loans and bonds as the fundamental underlyings of credit.

A *loan* is a contract where a borrower repays an amount N over time. This usually involves repaying the principal itself and paying a (fixed or floating) interest with a certain frequency. The most common type of loan is the amortizing loan in which, at the same time the borrower pays the interest, he also repays a portion of the principal. As a consequence, the subsequent interest payment will be on the remaining principal. More precisely, the cash flow structure of a loan is given by

$$\sum_i [N_i\,(L_i + s)\,dt_i + (N_i - N_{i+1})]\tag{3.1}$$

where L_i is a LIBOR-like floating rate but it could as easily be a fixed-coupon C. The spread s is a value driven by the credit risk associated with the borrower. We have seen in Chapter 2 that while financial institutions lend to each other at LIBOR, the spread s is whatever financial institutions would charge a subsequent borrower[3] on top of that LIBOR. Note that here, as opposed to when we were dealing with curve construction in Chapter 2, we are not discussing, yet, the present value of a loan; we are simply describing its cash flow structure.

Loans are far from standardized instruments; there can be many variations (as anyone who has applied for a mortgage can attest) on the type of repayment profile, on grace periods, different spreads on top of the floating rate, and so on. However, Equation 3.1 represents a good general description. An interesting point to be made about loans is that, in general, they tend to be held as assets by the lender and they are not traded in some secondary market. An exception to this is the activity known as loan syndication by which the lender passes on the whole, or part, of the loan to other market participants for a profit. The activity, however, is fairly complicated and definitively over the counter and cannot be compared to the secondary market of, say, vanilla equity options.

A *bond* can be seen as either the opposite of a loan (whereas a loan is a lending instrument, a bond is a borrowing instrument) or as the securitized

---

[3]This subsequent borrower could be either an entity that is not a financial institution and therefore would have a borrowing level different from LIBOR or another financial institution which, since we have defined the LIBOR as an average, would have a borrowing level away from the mean.

version of a loan. An entity wishing to raise capital without relinquishing control of itself (which would happen by issuing shares) can do so by issuing a bond. From the start, this is not anymore a contract between two parties (as in the case of a loan), but immediately an exchange-traded instrument sold through an auction. The investor (which can be seen as a faceless lender) buys a bond and receives the promise of repayment of capital at the end and, in most cases, the promise of regular payments in between.

The bond can be subsequently and easily passed onto secondary investors, and these transactions, for the most liquid bonds, are as liquid as any equity stock. Because of the secondary activity requiring simplicity, particularly when it comes to knowing what amount is redeemable at the end, a bond is almost never amortizing. The simplest and most general form of the cash flow structure of a bond could written as

$$N \sum_i f_i dt_i + N \qquad (3.2)$$

where, again, N is the nominal amount and f_i is a function that can be a fixed coupon, a floating rate, or some more complicated function. An even simpler version is the case of zero coupon bond (similar to the discount bonds met in Section 2.2.1) in which the bond is made simply of the promise to repay the principal at the end.

A final point needs to be made when it comes to the payment of the principal before maturity, effectively putting an end to the transaction. This action is usually defined as prepaying when it comes to loans and calling/putting when it comes to bonds. A borrower would prepay a loan, an issuer would call the bond, and an investor would put the bond. Being that a loan is, in general, a transaction between two specific parties, it is almost impossible for the lender not to accept the principal should the borrower wish to prepay. This means that even if it is not explicitly stated (although it is almost always in the details of an agreement), a loan always has an embedded option of prepayment. Option is intended here in the financial sense of the word: the option holder has the possibility to make a decision based on some market information (e.g., finding a lower rate somewhere else), and the upside from this market information can be either zero or positive in a precise manner. As always, when there is an option there is some value for the option holder, which is why in the case of mortgages there is a charge for repaying the amount before maturity.[4] We shall see in Section 3.3 that on this aspect the case of development institutions is very different from the

---

[4]The charge can be explicitly expressed as a fee or included in a higher rate.

norm. When it comes to bonds, because of their securitized nature and active secondary market trading, there can be an option of prepaying on the part of the issuer (calling the note), or on the part of the investor (putting the note), but this option has to be stated explicitly and cannot be assumed.

We have shown the fundamental underlyings of credit. As we have stressed, with every promise of payment there is a credit risk associated with it. We are now going to discuss the main derivative instrument used to hedge against this risk.

3.1.2 Credit Default Swaps

Let us observe what happens in the case of a default. We have purchased a bond issued by ABC with unit principal paying a certain coupon and repaying the principal at maturity T. The bond issuer defaults (let us imagine that the event is clearly defined and accepted by all parties) and can no longer honor its obligation with respect to the bond we have purchased. Together with all the other creditors, we participate in the assessment of the assets of ABC to see what can be salvaged and distributed to us all according to the rules of liquidation. The fact that there is the chance of obtaining something at the end means that the bond after default is not worth zero, it is worth some value R. R is the *expected recovery rate* of the bond, the amount, as the name suggests, that can be assumed to be recovered from the default. The value of R is unknown in advance and there are many subtleties about it that we shall see later. Let us treat it, at the moment, simply as what we *expect* is left of the bond after default.

After purchasing the bond, in order to protect ourselves against the default of the issuer we decide to enter into a transaction with another counterparty, XYZ. In this contract, shown schematically in Figure 3.1, with

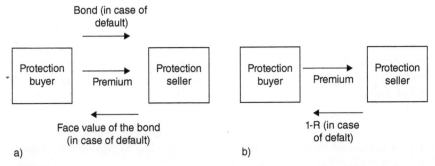

FIGURE 3.1 A schematic representation of a CDS contract with a) physical exchange of the bond and b) without.

the same maturity as the bond, we pay an annual premium to XYZ up to T. Should ABC default, traditionally we would have given, as shown in Figure 3.1a, the bond to XYZ in exchange for the nominal value of the bond, that is, the principal. This type of structure is called credit default swap or CDS. Nowadays (later, we are going to discuss the issue of leverage), since the outstanding principal of CDS contracts far exceeds the outstanding principal of the debt they are supposed to offer protection on, this is no longer feasible.[5] Instead, the value at which the debt trades after default is established through an auction mechanism and, as shown in Figure 3.1b, XYZ pays the difference between the nominal value of the debt and the traded value. The dynamics on how this value is obtained are beyond our scope, but the interested reader is directed toward Helwege et al. [46] where it is discussed in great detail with examples drawn from the financial crisis of 2007 to 2009. By entering into such a structure we are *buying protection* and XYZ is *selling protection*. The present value of a CDS structure can be written as

$$\sum_i CS_i D_i dt_i = (1 - R) \sum_j \left(S_{j-1} - S_j\right) D_j dt_j \qquad (3.3)$$

where C is the premium (or credit spread or CDS rate) and S_t is the *survival probability* at time t, the probability that ABC at time t has not defaulted yet. R is the recovery rate. Survival probability is the key concept of credit and we shall see that in this respect it resembles, in role, importance, and some of the characteristics, the concept of present value when dealing with interest rates. We shall discuss it at length later, but let us note a few things about Equation 3.3 first.

First of all, let us point out that we are considering here the traditional structure of a CDS agreement in which the protection buyer delivers the bonds upon default, that mathematically to say that in case of default we obtain $(1 - R)$ and to say that we exchange the bond for the principal with XYZ is identical. However, there is a subtle difference that should force us to remember that it is the latter that actually takes place. $(1 - R)$ is a quantity that depends on the value of R if that is what XYZ gave us. Immediately we would be asking the question, what is R? The physical exchange between bond and principal makes us indifferent[6] to the actual value of R. We are

---

[5]Otherwise we would be facing the paradox in which the value of debt *grows* after default because of the high demand of all those needing to borrow it in order to deliver it as part of the CDS agreement.

[6]In the case of physical exchange we are indifferent to the recovery rate R only if we buy a CDS to hedge our exposure to the credit of an issuer whose bond *we possess*.

indifferent as far as the protection offered by the CDS is concerned; however, we can easily see from Equation 3.3 (where, similarly to a swap rate, C is traded at that value making both sides equal) that the premium we are going to be charged by XYZ is indeed dependent on R. In practice R is not a traded quantity[7] and is treated as an assumed quantity. In a normal environment it is a constant value for all issuers of a certain kind (e.g., 30% for all American corporate issuers); however, when one in particular is in danger of default, the actual value used is refined to a more, supposedly, precise value. We shall see, when dealing with illiquid bonds in Section 5.4.1, how this takes place. As far as the recovery value is concerned we shall return to this when discussing the fair value of loans and the different role it plays for normal financial institutions and development banks.

A second point is that, while in the definition of bonds and loans given by Equations 3.2 and 3.1, we have not shown their present value; in the case of a CDS we had to. In Equation 3.3 we have a traded quantity C (we shall see later that the survival probability is an implied quantity) that can only be traded if both parties agree on the value of each leg: this can only happen if we calculate the present value of the transaction. In the case of a bond, the value of the coupon is decided by the issuer and is not agreed between issuer and investor, which is why we could present it without present value. Of course the issuer will decide a coupon value giving the bond a value close to par, and the investor will decide what price to pay for that bond, but the coupon value is not agreed by the two parties. This point might seem odd at this stage, but not being central to the discussion of credit we can leave its clarification to a later stage.

It is not difficult to see how the riskier the issuer is the higher the premium C is going to be. In Figure 3.2 we see a plot of the term structures of credit default swap rates for Germany, France, and Korea. For example we see that if we want to buy protection for five years against the default of the German Republic we need to pay an annual premium of 98 bps. Korea is considered riskier by the market and for the same type of protection we need to pay an annual coupon of 162 bps. France is considered riskier still and if we want to buy protection for five years against the default of the French government we need to pay a premium of 205 bps.

We shall view this in greater detail when discussing bond pricing, however, it is already easy to see how, in theory, the combination of the possession of a bond with the purchase of protection basically turns an exposure

---

If we simply bought the CDS naked, that is, without a link to the actual bond, then we are not indifferent to the value of R.

[7]There are recovery swaps trading the recovery itself but they are fairly rare.

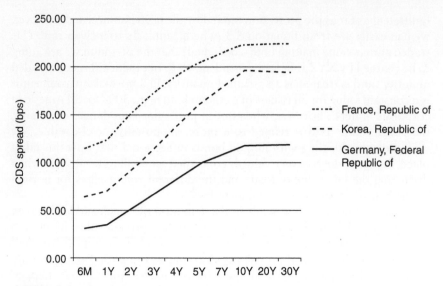

FIGURE 3.2 The credit default swap rate term structures for the republics of Germany, France, and Korea on January 18, 2012.

to credit risk into a risk-free situation. Before turning to a discussion of how this happens in practice through the concept of survival probability, let us end this section with a historical note centered around the combination of the possession we mentioned in the previous sentence.

CDSs were created to protect investors against the default of an issuer, meaning that if we purchase $100M worth of ABC bonds, we (should) only need to purchase $100M worth of protection. However, a CDS is a derivative instrument and, like all derivative instruments, it allows the owner to gain exposure to an underlying (in this case the credit risk of an issuer) without owning the underlying itself, a synthetic exposure. The same way we buy a CDS written on ABC's credit after having bought a bond issued by ABC, we could as easily buy the CDS on its own.[8]

Looking at Figure 3.2 we see that the five-year protection on France costs 205 bps. We sense that the market perception of the creditworthiness of France is deteriorating and *without* owning any French bond we purchase protection against France's default. In a week, the cost of protection against France's default has increased to, say, 225 bps, meaning that the 205 bps

---

[8]This type of operation is sometimes referred to as *naked* in the sense that we bare the hedging link between derivative and underlying.

we paid is now worth 20 bps more. We sell protection against France to someone else and we make a profit. In all this we have not even touched a French bond. Moreover, imagining that our feeling was very strong, there was nothing stopping us from doing this trade on a principal far greater than the total amount of all French debt,[9] that is, applying considerable leverage to our position. Doesn't this negate the principle of protection, which is not very different from the one of insurance? It does but, again, it is a problem affecting all derivatives in general.

A derivative allows the user to break the economic link grounded in the real world between the derivative (the function) and the underlying (the variable). This opens the door to a potentially excessive use of leverage, by entering into a derivative contract well in excess of the natural size of the trade. This natural size of the trade could be, for example, the market capitalization of a company we write an equity option on. If we buy protection against the default of a borrower, it could be the total amount of debt issued by the borrower.

Let us imagine that the principal of our trades was a great amount, say, $2BN (21 bps is a small number; if we want a large profit we need to multiply it by something large) and let us imagine that France defaults. On paper we should not worry: we are going to receive from one side the protection we need to pay on the other, but are we really sure of that? Some of these trades would be collateralized, but we have seen that some institutions do not pay collateral. The counterparty selling protection to us might in turn having bought it from someone else and so on until someone will have to find $(1 - R)$ of $2BN, which potentially could not be there.

3.2 A BRIEF OVERVIEW OF CREDIT MODELING

In the previous section we spoke at length of default, credit risk, and in Equation 3.2 we have introduced, albeit without much explanation, S_t, the survival probability at time t of a certain borrowing entity. Any model of credit must somehow try to estimate the value of this probability, either explicitly or in the form of a forecast of the default of the borrowing entity.

Credit models can be assigned to three broad families. We shall briefly mention all of them, but we will concentrate on the last one since it will be a useful introduction to the pricing of bonds shown in later chapters.

---

[9]This is a bit unrealistic when it comes to the debt of a large developed country, but not in the case of a corporation or a smaller state.

Structural models of credit can be traced to Merton's work (see Merton [62] or Hull et al. [51] for an interesting analysis) in the mid-1970s. In these types of models, as the name suggests, we look at the balance sheet structure of a company and we observe the debt amount owed at a time T and the assets of the company. We consider the company in default if the value of the assets falls below the promised debt amount. The equity of the company is seen as a (European) call option on the asset of the company with a strike given by the debt amount.

As soon as we mention a financial option we know that there must be an implied volatility associated with it, in this case linked to the risk-neutral probability of default. While elegant in its simplicity, this model is more suited to an estimate of default made by an economist rather than an assessment made in a trading environment (the situation in which we position ourselves). The inputs needed for the model are the value of the company assets and their volatility, two values that are far from clear. A way of implementing it is to assume that the market capitalization represents the company's assets, and its equity's instantaneous volatility represents its volatility. All the debt is mapped onto a single payment at time T. While simple, easy, and often able to reproduce information found in the market, this family of models is not as suited to our needs as other trading-based models.

Most of us are familiar with credit rating agencies. These agencies, of which there are many—over 90% of the market is dominated by three, Standard & Poor's, Moody's, and Fitch—observe the health of a company and issue a rating of its debt. An investor holding the company's debt should use the rating as an indication of the company's creditworthiness.

The ratings are made up of a combination of letters and numbers starting with AAA (for all three agencies) for the highest-rated bonds/institutions. The big distinction is between investment grade debt, that is, a debt that is worth considering as an investment and junk status debt where the name is descriptive enough. Note that junk status does not mean that the debt (or the company to be more precise) has defaulted;[10] it simply means that it is very risky. In the 1980s the trading of junk bonds showed that a lot of profit could be made out of them. The change in credit ratings is usually fairly slow (compared to the change in other financial data) because it should be the outcome of a thorough analysis on the part of the credit agencies.

Ratings are very important because they affect many things in a secondary way. We have seen in Section 2.4.4 that AAA-rated institutions have a special collateral regime. Since we have seen that collateral can take the

---

[10]Debt past default is not rated and is often referred to, somewhat euphemistically, as nonperforming.

form of cash or liquid instruments, institutions that do pay collateral can offer AAA-rated securities. Should the debt they have offered be downgraded, it does not qualify anymore and something else needs to be posted. (This is something that was feared when Standard & Poor's downgraded U.S. debt, but did not materialize.) Another example is investment on the part of institutions or portfolio/fund managers. Investment managers are given guidelines on the percentage of debt they can hold in each rating category.

Despite their acceptance by market participants, the role of rating agencies is not without critique, as was the case after the U.S. downgrade of 2011 (a downgraded entity is usually the first to complain) or after the financial crisis of 2007 to 2008 where it was revealed that many securities that proved to be worthless were rated AAA.

It seems natural to wonder whether credit ratings can be used to estimate the probability of default of a company. They can and this is undertaken through *credit rating* models. In these models (see Altman and Kao [3] and Lando and Skødeberg [59] for an interesting example of empirical data and implementation) the key concept is the one of transition and the probability associated with it, that is, the probability of the transition of the rating of a company from one value to another. This is visualized through a transition matrix with ratings on both dimensions: the highest values will be the diagonal ones, that is, the highest probability that a rating will not change; the next highest will be the near diagonal values, that is, the probability that a rating will go up or down by one notch; and finally low values will be given to the probability that a rating will jump across many rating grades.

Although these models can be integrated (see Schönbucher [73] and [74]) within a risk-neutral framework, they are not particularly suited to pricing derivatives, which is the focus of our attention since, let us stress again, we are concerned with the activities of a trading institution. The amount of information available, in terms of transition data, is enormous, but it is all historical and, while forward looking in nature (after all ratings are given to forecast future events), not suited to obtain implied quantities. To price an option we do not estimate the volatility of a stock from its time series but we use a volatility surface implied from traded option prices:[11] in a similar way rating transitions are historical data that cannot easily be used to price derivatives.

The third and final family is the one made of *spread-based* models. We will be concentrating on this one as it is the most suited to the pricing of

---

[11]Sometimes if implied volatilities are not available, historical ones are used, but it is done knowing that it violates the principles of risk neutrality.

derivative instruments and also because it is the one most suited to the understanding of someone familiar with the fixed-income world.

While structural models and credit rating models can reproduce observable results, this is not quite the same as the rigorous calibration someone familiar with risk-neutral pricing is used to. As shown in great detail by Brigo and Mercurio [19], in the spread-based framework an analogy between interest rate models and credit models can be taken very far.

The same way we have a variety of short rate models in fixed income, we have a set of *intensity models* in credit ranging from simpler Hull and White-like models to more complex models involving jump diffusion (see, for example, Brigo and Alfonsi [17] or Duffie et al. [33]). The same way we have forward rate models in fixed income, such as HJM or LMM, in credit we have forward credit spread models claiming to have a more immediate relation to the market (see, for example, Brigo and Morini [20] or Das and Sundaram [29]).

Between these two subfamilies we shall concentrate on the former as our needs are simpler than the majority of market participants. While it is important to obtain an understanding of wider credit issues, our immediate goals are the understanding of how credit affects a bond price (laying the foundation for the subsequent chapters dealing with bond pricing) and the discounting of the risky cash flows of a loan. More advanced topics, such as the pricing of exotic credit derivatives of, say, the range accrual type, which would benefit from a forward rate model, are beyond our scope.

3.2.1 Hazard Rates and a Spread-Based Modeling of Credit

Let us introduce the main elements of the spread-based framework for credit risk modeling. Although in this chapter's introduction we said that a default is not always a clear, linear, and transparent process, we assume that there is a precise moment in time τ when this takes place. From this we can define a survival indicator function $A(t)$

$$A(t) = \mathbf{1}_{\tau > t} = \begin{cases} 1 & \text{if } \tau > t \\ 0 & \text{if } \tau \leq t \end{cases} \tag{3.4}$$

telling us whether the entity is alive, that is, it has not defaulted, at time t. In the previous section we described bonds as coupon-bearing instruments, let us now discuss the simpler situation of a zero coupon bond, that is, the promise of a single payment at some point in the future. Let us define as

$B_t(T)$ the value at time t of a riskless, that is, default-free bond[12] paying a unit of principal at T. Let us also define as $\widetilde{B}_t(T)$ the price of a risky, that is, defaultable, bond at time t paying a unit of principal at time T.

No arbitrage (and common sense) dictates that we must have

$$B_t(T) \geq \widetilde{B}_t(T) \ \forall \ t < T \tag{3.5}$$

that is, the defaultable bond cannot be worth more, before maturity, than the riskless bond. At maturity we have, of course, $B_T(T) = \widetilde{B}_T(T) = 1$, since, by reaching maturity, the defaultable bond has by definition not defaulted.

Let us also assume that there is no recovery upon default, that is, the price of the defaultable bond is given by

$$A(t)\widetilde{B}_t(T) = \begin{cases} \widetilde{B}_t(T) & \text{if } \tau > t \\ 0 & \text{if } \tau \leq t \end{cases} \tag{3.6}$$

and that there is independence between riskless interest rates and default time, that is, no correlation between the riskless bond value $B_t(T)$ and τ.

We know from the assumptions behind all short rate models that the price of every contingent claim of unit principal is equal to the expected value of its discounted value, that is,

$$B_t(T) = \mathbf{E}\left[e^{-\int_t^T r_s ds}\right] \tag{3.7}$$

where r_t is the short risk-free interest rate. Since, in the case of a defaultable bond, the unit payment at maturity T happens only if $\tau > T$ (i.e., the default does not occur during the life of the bond), the risky bond value should be written as

$$\widetilde{B_t(T)} = \mathbf{E}\left[e^{-\int_t^T r_s ds} A(T)\right] \tag{3.8}$$

Since we have assumed independence between risk-free interest rates and default time, we can write the above as

$$\widetilde{B_t(T)} = \mathbf{E}\left[e^{-\int_t^T r_s ds}\right] \mathbf{E}\left[A(T)\right] \tag{3.9}$$

---

[12]A riskless bond, of course, does not really exist. We can choose to read this as either a bond of negligible risk or a bond for which we have chosen to ignore the credit risk.

or

$$\widetilde{B_t(T)} = B_t(T)\mathbf{E}\,[A(T)]$$

$$= B_t(T)S_{t,T} \tag{3.10}$$

where $S_{t,T}$ is the survival probability of the borrower at time T seen at time t. Since the survival probability is the ratio between the defaultable bond and the riskless bond

$$S_{t,T} = \frac{\widetilde{B_t(T)}}{B_t(T)} \tag{3.11}$$

we must have $S_t < 1$ for all $t < T$. We now introduce the fundamental concept of *hazard rate* $h(t, T)$ (which, when there is no confusion, we will simply define as h_t) as

$$h(t, T) = -\frac{1}{S_{t,T}}\frac{\partial S_{t,T}}{\partial T} \tag{3.12}$$

provided $\tau > t$. In a way more useful to us, we can express the relation between hazard rate and survival probability as

$$S_{t,T} = e^{-\int_t^T h_s\,ds} \tag{3.13}$$

so that immediately we recognize the similarities between hazard rate modeling and risk-free interest rate modeling. In this view any (see Brigo and Mercurio [19]) positive short rate model used for interest rates r can be used to model hazard rate h. Similarly to short rate models, where inputs are not taken directly from the market but need to be calibrated to the only available quantity (the bond price), hazard rates need calibration. The most important and common instruments used for calibration are CDSs and we shall illustrate in the next section how this takes place in practice.

Throughout the remainder of the book, unless otherwise stated, we shall simplify the notation and, taking the same approach we have taken for discount factors, assume that we are observing survival probabilities as of now ($t = 0$), meaning that we shall only write S_T instead of $S_{0,T}$.

3.2.2 The Bootstrapping of a Hazard Rate Curve

To explain how to calibrate hazard rates to CDS levels we shall follow closely O'Kane and Turnbull [65], to this day one of the clearest discussions on the topic.

We have defined a credit default swap as a contract in which one side pays a premium in the form of a coupon with a certain frequency up to a default (*premium leg*) and the other side, in case of default, exchanges the principal for the recovery value (i.e., it pays $(1 - R)$ and we call this the *recovery leg*).

The premium leg is defined as

$$C \sum_i D_i S_i dt_i$$

where D_i is the discount factor at time T_i, S_i is the survival probability at time T_i, and $dt_i = T_i - T_{i-1}$. As far as the premium leg is concerned we need to know whether, in case of default, the party buying protection (by paying the premium) is required to pay the fraction of coupon accrued from the last payment date up to the default date. This information would be specified in the agreement. Should the payment of the accrued coupon be necessary, this involves the calculation of an integral for each payment frequency. It can be shown (see O'Kane and Turnbull [65]) that this can be approximated and the premium leg can be written as

$$C \sum_i D_i \left\{ S_i + \frac{1_{PA}}{2} [S_{i-1} - S_i] \right\} dt_i \qquad (3.14)$$

where 1_{PA} is equal to 1 if we need to consider the accrued premium and 0 otherwise. The impact of considering or ignoring the accrued premium is small when valuing the present value of the CDS and, of course, is a function of the frequency of payments: the more frequent, the smaller.[13]

The recovery leg needs to assess the present value of the payment of $(1 - R)$ in case of default. Since default can happen at any time, we are going to approximate this (technically continuous) calculation with a discrete set of time steps by writing

$$(1 - R) \sum_n D_n [S_{n-1} - S_n] \qquad (3.15)$$

---

[13]This dependency is, however, not very important considering that the great majority of CDS contracts have quarterly premium payments.

where we have used a different suffix counter n and we assume, in order to better approximate a continuous integral, that $T_i - T_{i-1} \gg T_n - T_{n-1}$, that is, the summation frequency is higher in the recovery leg. Because we are approximating a continuous integral, we describe the possibility of defaulting at *any* time t by bracketing this time within a short interval $T_{n-1} < t < T_n$. In this case then, $S_{n-1} - S_n$ is the probability of defaulting in that interval *given* the survival up to T_{n-1}.

The only market information traded[14] in a CDS is the coupon premium C. Since at the beginning of the contract there should be no initial gain for either side, we must have

$$
C = \frac{(1 - R) \sum_n D_n [S_{n-1} - S_n]}{\sum_i D_i \{S_i + AT\} dt_i}
$$

$$
AT = \frac{1}{2} P_A [S_{i-1} - S_i] \tag{3.16}
$$

Our goal is the calibration of a hazard rate term structure. By using market information, a strip of CDS quotes for increasing maturities, we calculate the hazard rate for the equivalent maturity. We use a bootstrapping method similar to the one we have used in Section 2.5 to build a discount factors term structure, that is, we start by calculating the shortest maturity, then we move on to the next one, and so forth. Let us imagine that we have CDS quotes for one, two, and three years, respectively C_1, C_2, and C_3. Starting with the first maturity, by using Equation 3.13 we rewrite the above equation as

$$
C_1 = \frac{(1 - R) \sum_n D_n \left[e^{b_{0,1} T_{n-1}} - e^{b_{0,1} T_n} \right]}{\sum_i D_i \left\{ e^{b_{0,1} T_i} + AT_1 \right\} dt_i}
$$

$$
AT_1 = \frac{1}{2} P_A \left[e^{b_{0,1} T_{i-1}} - e^{b_{0,1} T_i} \right] \tag{3.17}
$$

where b_{01} is the hazard rate from the beginning of the contract up to 1 year, i has a quarterly frequency (per definition of CDS contract), that is, $T_{i=1} = 0.25$, $T_{i=2} = 0.5$, $T_{i=3} = 0.75, \ldots$, and we can decide to have m running at a monthly frequency, that is, $T_{m=1} = 0.08333$, $T_{m=2} = 0.16667$, $T_{m=3} = 0.25, \ldots$ Equation 3.17 can be solved using a solver that tries to guess values of $b_{0,1}$ until both sides of the equation are equal.

---

[14]The recovery R is also an input but it is not traded in a CDS, it is assumed. When it is traded it is done through recovery swaps, a different type of instrument.

Now that we have found $h_{0,1}$, we can use the information contained in the second piece of market information, that is, the rate C_2 for a CDS with maturity two years. We apply a solver algorithm to

$$C_2 = \frac{(1-R)\sum_n D_n \left[e^{\left(\sum_{k=0}^{k<T_{n-1}} h_{k,k+1}\right)T_{n-1}} - e^{\left(\sum_{k=0}^{k<T_n} h_{k,k+1}\right)T_n} \right]}{\sum_i D_i \left\{ e^{\left(\sum_{k=0}^{k<T_i} h_{k,k+1}\right)T_i} + AT_2 \right\} dt_i}$$

$$AT_2 = \frac{1}{2}\frac{p_A}{2} \left[e^{\left(\sum_{k=0}^{k<T_{i-1}} h_{k,k+1}\right)T_{i-1}} - e^{\left(\sum_{k=0}^{k<T_i} h_{k,k+1}\right)T_i} \right]$$

where we have used Equation 3.13, in order to find $h_{1,2}$. We repeat this process one final time by applying a solver to

$$C_3 = \frac{(1-R)\sum_n D_n \left[e^{\left(\sum_{k=0}^{k<T_{n-1}} h_{k,k+1}\right)T_{n-1}} - e^{\left(\sum_{k=0}^{k<T_n} h_{k,k+1}\right)T_n} \right]}{\sum_i D_i \left\{ e^{\left(\sum_{k=0}^{k<T_i} h_{k,k+1}\right)T_i} + AT_3 \right\} dt_i}$$

$$AT_3 = \frac{1}{2}\frac{p_A}{2} \left[e^{\left(\sum_{k=0}^{k<T_{i-1}} h_{k,k+1}\right)T_{i-1}} - e^{\left(\sum_{k=0}^{k<T_i} h_{k,k+1}\right)T_i} \right]$$

and we complete our simple term structure of hazard rates by finding $h_{2,3}$. (The only practical difference between the last two equations is the fact that the summation of the hazard rates is one step longer in the latter.) In the chapter About the Web Site we direct the reader to a web site where we offer a spreadsheet with an implementation of the process outlined above.

Could this process lead to negative hazard rates? In practice yes, particularly for heavily inverted CDS rate curves (in Section 4.2.3 we will see some examples of these in the case of emerging markets) but it should be taken as a numerical error. Absence of arbitrage (and in the case of credit, the absence of arbitrage that applies to short rate models is reinforced by common sense) dictates that we cannot have negative hazard rates since they would imply a probability of survival greater than one. With real, liquid, and up-to-date data, negative rates cannot occur.

If the data is stale, the bid-offer is wide, and the situation extreme (highly inverted curve and/or very large CDS rates), it can happen that hazard rates become negative. A typical example is CDS spreads for emerging market entities where one or two specific points are very liquid and the neighboring ones rarely traded. For example, Turkey's five-year point is very liquid, but the four-year and the six-year are certainly not as liquid. In the neighborhood of the five-year point, then we could encounter negative hazard rates.

Our approach should be to doubt the data for the illiquid points and assume that the true rate is a different one. In a real-life situation, if the hazard rate $h_{k,k+1}$ implied by CDS levels for maturities T_k and T_{k+1} is negative, two things can be done. We can overwrite the value for $CDS_{T_{k+1}}$ by shifting it a little upward until the implied hazard rate is positive. Otherwise, in our algorithm we can decide to floor the hazard rates at a small positive value (i.e., whenever the solution is negative we discard it and pick a small positive value, say, 0.00001). The result is broadly the same in both cases, but the advantage of the latter consists of being automatic; it has, however, the disadvantage of not communicating to what assumed-to-be-true new value of CDS rate the fictitious hazard rate corresponds. While tempting, hazard rates *should not* be floored at zero: if this were the case, that is, $h_{k,k+1} = 0$, we would be saying that $S_k \equiv S_{k+1}$, implying an impossibility of defaulting between T_k and T_{k+1}.

3.2.3 Different Quotations and Different Currencies

Let us consider the situation where we bought protection against the default of a certain borrower by entering into a CDS where we pay a premium C_1. Some time later, the credit of the same borrower deteriorates and we sell, for the same maturity and amount, protection receiving a higher coupon C_2. As far as our income is concerned we have a *risky annuity*

$$(C_2 - C_1) \sum_i S_i D_i dt_i \tag{3.18}$$

that is, an income that is heavily subjected to credit risk. During the financial crisis of 2007 to 2009 a new type of CDS quotation became common, one that would make any gain or loss immediate and eliminate a situation such as the one above.

In the new CDS contract, the premium paid by the protection buyer would be split into two parts, a coupon similar to the old one but taking only a small set of specific values (25, 100, 500, and 1,000 bps) and an up-front premium. Let us consider the situation above in the new framework. We buy protection against the default of a certain borrower by paying an up-front premium U_1 and a running coupon C_{100} of, say, 100 bps, so that the present value of the protection leg is

$$-U_1 - C_{100} \sum_i S_i D_i dt_i \tag{3.19}$$

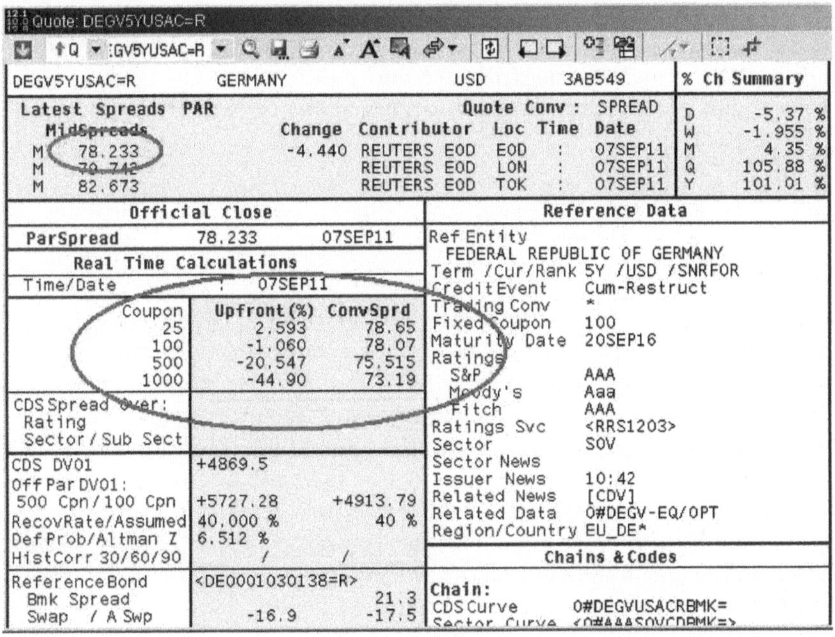

FIGURE 3.3 A quote screen for Germany CDS rate. *Source*: Thomson Reuters Eikon.

which is negative since we are paying for the protection. When the credit of the borrower deteriorates, we sell protection by receiving an up-front premium U_2 (with $U_2 > U_1$) and a running coupon *which remains* equal to 100 bps, that is, C_{100}, so that the present value of the protection leg is

$$U_2 + C_{100} \sum_i S_i D_i dt_i \qquad (3.20)$$

The difference between the two is $U_2 - U_1$, a gain that we realize immediately.

The new quotation is fairly recent and the trading community is still used to the old one. From Figure 3.3 we can see how the CDS is quoted in this transition period. In the top left corner we have circled the old quote. In the center of the page (also circled) we have the four quotes for the up-front we need to pay in case the running coupon is one of the four possible types (25, 100, 500, 1,000 bps). In the case of a borrower with as good a credit as Germany, we see that the up-front payment for the 100, 500, and 1,000 bps running coupon is negative. This might seem bizarre but it simply states that the present value of those coupons is already higher than the present value of the recovery leg and so, for the contract to be worth zero at inception, the up-front needs to be negative. We notice that next to the up-front there is the equivalent conventional spread, that is, that spread $\widetilde{C}_x$ for which the following is true

$$\widetilde{C}_x \sum_i S_i D_i dt_i = U_x + C_x \sum_i S_i D_i dt_i \qquad (3.21)$$

where $x = 25, 100, 500, 1,000$ and C_x is the running coupon paid in conjunction with the up-front U_x. We also note, surprisingly, that the conventional spreads are different from one another whereas we would expect them to be the same. The reason is that there are different levels of demand for the four types of up-front. For example, it would be strange to enter into a CDS contract on Germany agreeing to pay such a high running coupon as 1,000 bps and therefore the demand for that contract (and probably the 500 bps as well) is likely to be small. Not surprisingly the two equivalent spreads closest to the one in the top left corner are the ones corresponding to the 25 and 100 bps running coupons.

As far as the calibration of the hazard rates $h_{k,k+1}$ is concerned, the process is identical, except that now we need to apply our solver algorithm to

$$U + C \sum_i D_i \left\{ e^{h_{k,k+1} T_i} + \frac{1}{2} P A \left[e^{h_{k,k+1} T_{i-1}} - e^{h_{k,k+1} T_i} \right] \right\} dt_i \qquad (3.22)$$

$$= (1 - R) \sum_n D_n \left[e^{h_{k,k+1} T_{n-1}} - e^{h_{k,k+1} T_n} \right]$$

Those who have read the screen shown in Figure 3.3 carefully might have noticed that the quote displayed is for the CDS level in USD. What does the specification of the currency entail? This is a very complex field and we are simply going to describe what is available in the market.

There are four types of CDS traded in the market with varying levels of liquidity:

- CDS spread paid in USD to protect USD-denominated debt
- CDS spread paid in foreign currency to protect USD-denominated debt
- CDS spread paid in USD to protect foreign currency-denominated debt
- CDS spread paid in foreign currency to protect foreign currency-denominated debt

The first type is the one we have dealt with even though it was not explicitly stated. An entity issues debt in USD and we pay a premium in USD to buy protection against its default.

The fourth type tends to be the least common and this has to do with the willingness of investors to purchase debt in foreign currency. In general investors are wary of buying debt in local currency[15] since a government could *in principle* fend off default by printing money to pay off the debt: due to the subsequent inflation, investors would be holding something almost worthless. This is particularly true for small emerging markets (larger ones such as India can rely on local investors who are more willing to take the risk than foreign ones) and less so for large, developed countries (e.g., Japan, Canada, etc.).

As far as Euro zone members are concerned, the Euro should be considered, when it comes to debt, a foreign currency since individual members have no money-printing ability. As a consequence, the CDS spread in local currency to protect debt in local currency (e.g., spread in South African Rand to protect South African Rand-denominated debt) is usually very low. Since the government has the option to print money, the default on local debt is unlikely.

The second and third type are the most interesting ones and are sometimes referred to as *quanto CDS*. The third is becoming common in the context of sovereign European debt. The connection between FX and credit is very interesting. Ehlers and Schöbucher [35] look at it in great detail (their main focus is entities issuing debt not in their home currencies). The reason is that there is a strong correlation between credit and FX in case of default. When a country defaults (and one could argue the same for some very large and important corporates), the currency tends to depreciate very rapidly, that is, the value of X/USD, the number of X we receive for one U.S. Dollar, increases considerably. To model this can be very challenging in the sense that not only do we need a model where the correlation between FX and credit is not zero, but a diffusion model for FX (the standard approach) might not be enough and we need to turn to a jump-diffusion model. This is because we need to deal with a situation where the motion of the underlying is fairly

---

[15]The alternative use of local and foreign here is probably confusing, but we have already mentioned when discussing FX forwards that this is the way traders tend to think. Although USD is a currency foreign to many countries, it is so commonly used that it holds a special status. Currencies that are non-USD are referred to as foreign, and currencies that not only are non-USD but tend to be weaker currencies are referred to as local. A trading desk in say, South Africa, would have traders trading USD instruments and traders trading local instruments by which we intend South African Rand (ZAR) or other African currencies denominated instruments.

volatile on average but with sudden, rare and large jumps. While interesting to mention, these types of CDS would rarely be traded by a treasury desk or a development institution.

3.3   FAIR VALUE OF LOANS AND THE SPECIAL CASE OF DEVELOPMENT INSTITUTIONS

3.3.1   The Argument around the Fair Valuing of Loans

Among the many differences between a loan and a bond (we have mentioned in Section 3.1.1 how loans are over-the-counter instruments with a smaller number of variations than bonds, which can be exchange traded but come in different flavors), the one we are going to focus on is the fact that bonds are securitized instruments traded in the secondary market. The only secondary activity affecting loans, and only a small section of them, is loan syndication, which is a bespoke type of trading. This is very important when discussing the action of taking the fair value of financial instruments. Let us now remind ourselves of what we mean by fair value.

To fair value an instrument means to find a value that is fair. In order for something to be considered fair we must have this be the opinion of a collection of different parties. When it comes to financial instruments, the value that is fair is the value at which someone is willing to sell and someone else is willing to buy. In order to find a tradable value we need not only calculate the appropriate cash flows (for which the simple Equations 3.1 and 3.2 would suffice), we also need to find its present value, so that we know how much it is worth at the moment we pass it on/receive it to/from someone else. Not only this, we should also be able, since both loans and bonds carry credit risk, to assess the risk associated with the borrower, calculating in practice a risky present value. The fact that a fair value can be tradable means that the models and mechanisms used to obtain it fall within the risk-neutral framework.

There has been a general consensus as to whether derivatives should be fair valued since at least 1998 (see FAS 133 [39]). Few people would now argue against the soundness of the principle behind it. Whether loans should also be fair valued is a very different case, with sound arguments (and reasonable supporters) on both sides.

For the lender a loan is an asset. Let us consider the situation of an average bank extending a variable loan of, say, $1M to an individual or an institution. The bank would first consider the credit-worthiness of the borrower and, should it then decide to extend the loan, it would book the loan as an asset worth $1M. The risk against default would be taken into account with a *loan loss provision*, a sort of valuation adjustment on the loan value but something that is far from a calculation carried in a risk-neutral framework. The argument is, should this value be enough or should the loan be fair valued with a proper[16] calculation of the present value and an inclusion of the survival probability of the borrower?

One argument claims that if the loan is to be kept on the bank's book till maturity there is no real need of a fair value. After all, a way of defining fair value is as tradable value; if there is not going to be a secondary trade, what is the need for a fair value?

The opposite argument says that the goal is to assess correctly the value of the balance sheet of an institution. Let us imagine that the lending institution is bought by another one or it needs to be liquidated. Isn't it important to have a fair assessment of its assets? The fact that the drive toward fair value is driven by accounting concerns (note that the decision to fair value derivatives was agreed to by the Financial Accounting Standards Board) might mean that in the end the fair valuing of loans argument is going to prove decisive. At the time of writing, no final decision has been made yet.

With the view that one day the fair value of loans argument is going to be generally accepted, let us observe what fair valuing entails in practice. In Equation 3.1 we have given the definition of a loan by showing its general cash flow structure, but we did not show its present fair value. In order to do so we need to write it as

$$\sum_i S_i D_i \left[N_i \left(L_i + s \right) dt_i + \left(N_i - N_{i+1} \right) \right] + R \sum_j N_j D_j \left(S_{j-1} - S_j \right) \quad (3.23)$$

The first term in Equation 3.23 is very similar to Equation 3.1 except for the fact that we now include the discount factor D_i and the survival probability S_i, that is, the probability that the borrower has not defaulted before time T_i. The first term basically states that all loan interest payments and principal repayments are subject to the borrower being solvent.

The second term states what happens in the case of default: should the borrower default between times T_{j-1} and T_j, the lender receives the recovery rate of the loan (whatever that might mean) applied to the outstanding principal.

---

[16] A proper calculation of the present value would probably impact less than a correct measure of risk: in this example, which covers the case of the majority of loans, we have considered a variable rate loan. We have seen in Section 2.2.5.2 that, in general, a floating leg will price more or less at par, meaning that a riskless variable loan of $1M valued at $1M is not such a gross approximation.

It is when discussing default that we need to state that, in the case of loans, there are two common practices: one is to structure loans so that they are *accelerating* and the other so that they are *nonaccelerating*. The former means that in case of default the maturity at time T of the loan is brought forward and the recovery rate is to be applied to the entire outstanding principal. The loan shown in Equation 3.23 is an example of an accelerating one. In the case of a nonaccelerating loan it is assumed that although defaulted, the maturity of the loan remains unchanged: the fair value of nonaccelerating loans needs to take this into account and therefore apply the recover rate not to the entire principal but simply to its present value.

The fair value of a nonaccelerating loan could be written as

$$\sum_i S_i D_i [N_i (L_i + s) dt_i + (N_i - N_{i+1})] \tag{3.24}$$

$$+ R \sum_j \left[\sum_{n=j}^{T} D_n (N_n - N_{n+1}) \right] D_j (S_{j-1} - S_j)$$

where the content of the square bracket in the second term is indeed the fair value, at time of default, of the remaining principal payments. In the case of development organizations we shall return to the difference between accelerating and nonaccelerating loans when discussing the practice of converting loans through swaps.

For both types of loans we immediately see that fair valuing a loan changes its value dramatically (which is probably behind some of the resistance on the part of financial institutions to move toward the fair value of loans): a loan of $1M will not be worth its principal amount anymore. We have said that the effect of discounting will not impact as much as the effect of taking into account the credit risk of the borrower. We have seen in Section 3.2.1 that the survival probability S_t must be less than unity for any future time: this means that (see Section 3.2.2) the riskier the borrower, the smaller the survival probability and the smaller the fair value of the loan, or, to put it differently, the greater the difference between calculating and not calculating the fair value of the loan.

Let us, as promised earlier, focus briefly on the recovery value R. In the introduction to this chapter we mentioned how development institutions can see defaults in a different way from traditional financial institutions. This is because development banks often have *preferential creditor status*, meaning that, in case of default, they are the first to be repaid. Argentina, after the 2002 default, repaid in full the loans from the IMF and the World Bank, meaning that, for all intents and purposes, it did not default on those. If this seems unfair toward the other creditors, let us not forget that not only do development institutions offer terms of lending much more favorable than normal market participants, but they are also the only ones who, during a crisis, willingly and actively lend. All this has to be compensated somehow and the preferential creditor status is a way to do so.

Because of preferential creditor status, the value of R in Equations 3.23 and 3.24 for a development institution are necessarily higher than for the average market participants. It cannot be 1 because, although in the example of Argentina there was full repayment, we need to view R as an expected value and therefore the average of multiple scenarios. In practice it can be double the amount the average market player would use.

Let us stress an important point: for a development institution the value of R used to obtain the survival probabilities S_i through the methodology outlined in Section 3.2.2 is the same as for the average investment bank. When it comes, however, to valuing the recovery amount of a loan in case of default (the second term of Equations 3.23 and 3.24), then it takes a higher value. This is because everyone has to agree on the idea that default has taken place or is about to (and we know that, in the bootstrapping process, the recovery rate affects the value of S_i), however, once the default has taken place, an investment bank and a development bank will view the remains in a different fashion.

Fair valuing a loan is also crucial if we want to treat its prepayment and the option embedded in it, which we mentioned in Section 3.1.1. It is in this respect that we see the biggest difference between a normal financial institution and a development organization. We shall see how this works in practice in the next section.

3.3.2 Prepayment Option and the Case of Development Institutions

As we mentioned earlier, in the great majority of loans the borrower can choose to repay the principal before the maturity of the loan and doing so results in the presence of a financial option embedded in the loan. In order to model this option, we assume that the borrower acts according to sound financial reasons and we can identify two main drivers behind these reasons: credit and interest rates.

The basic question a borrower asks himself during the life of a loan is, if I were to repay my loan now, could I get something better elsewhere? If the loan is a fixed-rate loan, the rate was fixed at the moment of entering the contract and it matched the rate landscape at the time (it was basically that fixed rate that would make the loan be worth par). In case the landscape changes in the direction that results in overpaying on the part of the borrower, this might be tempting to prepay the existing loan and enter into a new one at a lower rate. If the rate of the loan is variable, the value of the interest rate option is very small since, with only a little time lag between rate resets, a resetting loan rate always reflects the current rate level, taking away the borrower's incentive to prepay. Let us always remember the fact (see Section 2.2.5.2) that a floating leg is always more or less worth par.

The other driver is the credit standing of the borrower. At the moment of entering the loan the lender would have set a spread s over LIBOR matching the creditworthiness of the borrower: the lower the latter the higher the former. If during the life of the loan the credit standing of the borrower improves, there is a chance that it might obtain a new loan at a spread lower than s.

If we want to describe the sensitivity of the option to credit and interest rates we could say that the option is a put on the prevailing interest rate (if the loan is a fixed-rate loan, the more interest rates decrease the more the option of switching loans is valuable) and a call on the credit risk of the borrower, the more this improves the more valuable the option. Of course if we describe the credit risk of the borrower, as we should after Sections 3.2.1 and 3.2.2, using CDS spreads and hazard rates, we could say that the option is a put on these, too: the more they decrease the more valuable the option.

How is this option priced in practice? Loans are fairly simple instruments and short rate models are usually sufficient to price the option embedded in them. Of course we will be dealing here with a model belonging always to the spread-based family of credit models: there are alternatives in terms of pricing the optionality with credit rating models (see for example Engelmann [36]), but they are outside the scope of a financial institution practicing investment banking in the traditional sense of the word. These institutions, which are the focus of our attention, tend to prefer, as we have highlighted in Section 3.1, risk-neutral models based on trading activity.[17]

Since, as we said, loans are fairly simple instruments, a further goal would be an analytic implementation (i.e., one not relying on numerical simulations). We offer an example in Appendix C where we will follow closely Schönbucher's [74] description of a PDE-based implementation.

Before discussing the behavior of the option with respect to its variables, let us first describe the special case of development institutions. Development institutions can be considered as some sort of credit cooperatives, a cooperative that, in the case of the larger development institutions, can reach a

---

[17]There is also, as an aside, the world of mortgage modeling that needs to rely heavily on empirical data (see for example Kau et al. [57]) and needs to value financial options that are not always exercised according to optimal reasoning (see for example Stanton [77] or Goncharov [43]).

very large membership. Members pool funds together that are then either lent internally or used to back a solid credit that can be used to borrow at favorable terms. This, combined with the fact that they are nonprofit organizations, has of course some advantages for its receiving members but also entails some restrictions on the decisions these can take with respect to a loan.

The first one has to do with fixed-rate loans. Let us first consider the normal situation found in the for-profit world. Let us imagine that we receive a loan at a fixed-rate C_1 and let us also assume, for simplicity, that the principal will be repaid at the end, that the fixed coupon is exactly like the prevailing swap rate S_1 at the time of entering the contract, and that we are discounting our cash flows simply using interest rate swaps.[18] This means that, in the case of a unit principal, we must have

$$\sum_i^T C_1 D_i(S_1)dt_i + D_T(S_1) \approx 1 \qquad (3.25)$$

where we have stressed the dependence of the discount factor on the swap rate. Let us imagine that the prevailing swap rate decreases considerably and now, at time T_2, is equal to $S_2 < S_1$. The loan now will be worth

$$\sum_i^T C_1 D_i(S_2)dt_i + D_T(S_2) > 1 \qquad (3.26)$$

(as we have seen in the previous chapter, a lower swap rate results in higher discount factors, so the above follows). The lender is now holding a more valuable asset since the present value of the loan is higher than the principal amount. We have assumed that the fixed rate on a loan follows closely the swap rate: this means that we could obtain a loan somewhere else at a rate C_2 whose present value would be approximately par. By switching loans it is easy to see that we would gain the present value of the difference between the two rates. Let us define it as P_1

$$P_1 = \sum_i^T (C_1 - C_2) D_i \qquad (3.27)$$

---

[18]This means that we are ignoring the curve construction techniques highlighted in Section 2.2.5.1. While this is not entirely correct as described in the previous chapter, for the situation, for example, of a USD loan for a USD-centered institution, it could be a fair approximation.

The situation in development institutions is different. Being nonprofit, the amount charged on loans is simply used to cover operating costs. These costs would increase considerably should borrowers switch from loan to loan too often. As a consequence, if a borrower chooses to prepay a fixed-rate loan it will be charged the exact amount P_1. This means that, irrespective of interest rate moves, a country borrowing from a development organization has no *interest rate driven* incentive to prepay a loan.

We have seen in the introduction, and we will analyze it in more detail later, that development institutions using the tools of investment banking toward development basically borrow using their good credit and pass on this good credit (plus a small spread to cover operating costs) to the borrowers. This results in the borrowers being able to obtain a loan at a level close to the one of a AAA-rated institution and certainly lower than the one they could obtain in the market.

Let us imagine that at time T_1 a development institution issues floating rate loans at $L_i + s_1$, that is, at LIBOR (we have shown the suffix to stress its floating aspect) plus a spread s_1. Let us imagine that at time T_2 the development bank manages to issue debt at an even lower level resulting in the ability to issue loans at $L_i + s_2$ with $s_2 < s_1$. A country might be tempted to prepay the loan with spread s_1 and enter into a loan with spread s_2: to prevent this the development institution would charge the borrower

$$P_2 = \sum_i^T \max(s_1 - s_2, 0)\, D_i \qquad (3.28)$$

This means that the borrower has no incentive driven by the credit standing of the development institution to prepay the loan. The combination of the two penalties P_1 and P_2 results in a prepayment option driven purely by the credit of the borrowing country and not, in any way, by the interest rate environment or other considerations. This means that from the discussion leading to Equation C.5 (in Appendix C) we need to ignore stochastic interest rates. If at first the presence of the above-mentioned penalties might seem a little harsh, let us remind the reader that development institutions provide loans to borrowers that are sometimes cheaper in the order of a few *percentages* with respect to what the same borrower could get, if at all, in the market. P_1 and P_2 are a small price to pay for this advantage.

The final point, originating from the special status of development organizations, is the fact that, being a credit cooperative, all loans, *at a specific time*, are issued at the same level irrespective of the credit standing of the borrower. All fixed-rate loans issued at a certain time will have the same fixed rate and all floating-rate loans issued at a certain time will have the same spread s over LIBOR. This has very important consequences, particularly when fair valuing loans. Although all loans are issued at the same level, we have seen in Equations 3.23 and 3.24 that the survival probability used to fair value a loan is driven by that borrower-specific credit standing (in practice, its CDS level).

The first consequence is that the lender is holding assets with very different values. A normal (for-profit) institution choosing to fair value its loans would issue loans at levels such that, roughly speaking, the combination of floating rate plus spread would balance the effect of discount factor plus survival probability. In practice, in the typical cash flow,

$$(L_i + cs) \, S_i \, D_i \qquad (3.29)$$

the discount factor D_i would be driven by the interest rate L_i (as we have seen in the previous chapter) and the spread cs charged to the borrower would match the survival probability S_i: the lower this one, the higher cs (in practice cs follows crudely, as we shall see later, the CDS level of the borrower). The combination of the two would make sure that a strip of cash flows such as the one in Equation 3.29 would be roughly equal to the principal amount of the loan. In the case of a development institution we have said that cs remains constant for all borrowers, meaning that to the institution, as an asset, the loan to a borrower with a poor credit standing will be worth less than the loan to a borrower with a better credit standing.

The second consequence appears when dealing with the prepayment option. We have said that valuing the prepayment option is akin to answering quantitatively the question asked by the borrower, is it more advantageous to me to remain with this loan or to switch to a different one? Fair valuing loans is a considerable advantage when dealing with this question because it enables us to value the loan in a way considered objective by the lender, the borrower, and a potential third party to whom the borrower might turn for an alternative loan.

3.4 NUMERICAL EXAMPLE: CALCULATING THE FAIR VALUE OF A LOAN

To illustrate the points mentioned in the previous section let us try to calculate the fair value of a set of four loans issued by a development institution to four borrowers, in this case China, Argentina, Uruguay, and Ukraine.

In Figure 3.4a we show the term structure of CDS rates used for each of the borrowers. We use these, as shown in Section 3.2.2, to find the hazard rates and survival probabilities of each borrower. We assumed that we have issued to each of the four borrowers on September 30, 2012, a 10-year loan with a principal of USD 100M linearly amortizing every six months and with interest payments of USD six-month LIBOR plus 30 bps.

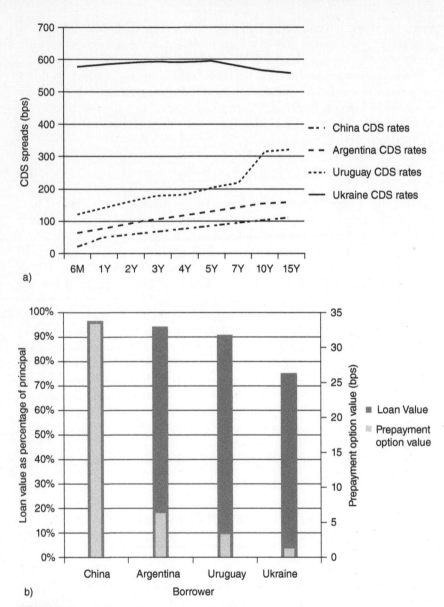

FIGURE 3.4   a) The term structures of CDS rates for the borrowers used in the example; b) the fair value of the loan as a percentage of the principal (primary axis) and the value, in basis points, of the prepayment option (secondary axis).

TABLE 3.1 The detailed output of the fair value of the loan to China.

Date	Principal amount (USD M)	USD discount factor	Survival probability	Interest amount	Principal repayment	Principal repayment in case of default
3/31/2013	100	0.9981	0.9864	333,624	4,922,833	233,878
9/30/2013	95	0.9954	0.9804	391,050	4,879,599	198,512
3/31/2014	90	0.9908	0.9739	535,299	4,824,587	203,161
9/30/2014	85	0.9847	0.9671	617,673	4,761,839	196,156
3/31/2015	80	0.9756	0.9592	812,351	4,679,175	213,757
9/30/2015	75	0.9647	0.9507	884,707	4,585,389	215,034
3/31/2016	70	0.9510	0.9407	989,924	4,473,151	229,360
9/30/2016	65	0.9357	0.9299	1,012,386	4,350,330	224,532
3/31/2017	60	0.9187	0.9200	1,011,958	4,226,389	184,876
9/30/2017	55	0.9003	0.9112	991,416	4,102,067	147,201
3/31/2018	50	0.8824	0.9025	866,369	3,981,816	129,997
9/30/2018	45	0.8638	0.8939	803,866	3,860,485	110,873
3/31/2019	40	0.8435	0.8846	760,387	3,731,093	101,774
9/30/2019	35	0.8227	0.8751	676,458	3,599,830	86,918
3/31/2020	30	0.8047	0.8656	497,733	3,482,845	71,536
9/30/2020	25	0.7866	0.8563	412,509	3,368,032	54,751
3/31/2021	20	0.7578	0.8470	338,312	3,251,605	40,110
9/30/2021	15	0.7488	0.8378	252,494	3,137,073	25,526
3/31/2022	10	0.7290	0.8274	172,847	3,016,060	14,210
9/30/2022	5	0.7093	0.8162	84,918	2,894,763	14,211

In Table 3.1 we show the results of the calculations in detail for one of the borrowers, China. In the first column we show the date on which the interest is paid and the principal amortizes; in the second column we show the principal on which, on that date, the interest is paid; in the third and fourth columns we show the USD discount factor and China's survival probability on that day; in the fifth and sixth we show the present value of the interest payment and the principal repayment contingent on China's survival; in the seventh column we show the present value of the payout in case of default.

Breaking down Equation 3.23 we can see that the interest payment at time T_j is given by

$$\left(L_{i,j} + s\right) N_j D_j S_j dt_j \equiv \left[\frac{1}{dt_j}\left(\frac{D_i}{D_j} - 1\right) + s\right] N_j D_j S_j dt_j$$

Using actual numbers for the interest payment due on March 31, 2014, we have

$$\left[2\left(\frac{0.9954}{0.9908} - 1\right) + 0.003\right] \cdot 90{,}000{,}000 \cdot 0.9908 \cdot 0.9739 \cdot 0.5 = 535{,}299 \tag{3.30}$$

as shown in Table 3.1. For the interest payment we have

$$(N_i - N_{i+1})D_i S_i$$

which, using actual numbers also for March 31, 2014, we have

$$5{,}000{,}000 \cdot 0.9908 \cdot 0.9739 = 4{,}824{,}587 \tag{3.31}$$

as shown in the table. The calculation of the payment in case of default is slightly more complicated. As seen in Equation 3.23 from the fact that the summation has a different index, for each payment date (if we want to visualize it as done in the table) we are supposed to integrate over the period to that date from the previous one and calculate the payout in case the borrower defaults on the amount outstanding in that time interval. In order to do that, we start at the end of the period and take two points, the last day T_N, and another point T_{N-1} a few days earlier (for example, two days, the shorter the time difference the more accurate the calculation); we calculate the probability of the borrower defaulting between T_{N-1} and T_N, conditional on survival up to T_{N-1} by taking $(S_{T_{N-1}} - S_{T_N})$; we multiply this by the outstanding principal amount in that interval; we multiply this by the assumed recovery rate; finally we discount this value.[19] We repeat the process now between T_{N-2} and T_{N-1} and so forth until we reach the beginning of the interval and then we sum all the values obtained. This is what is shown in the seventh column of Table 3.1.

Table 3.2 shows a summary of the same calculations done for the four loans. The value of the loan (without prepayment option) is also shown, as percentage of the loan principal, on the primary axis of Figure 3.4b. We immediately see what we meant by saying that the lender is holding assets of very different values. Not only is none of the loans worth par (the principal amount), but, for example, the loan to Ukraine is worth more than 10% less

---

[19]The choice of which discount factor to use is an open one. Since we are assuming the time between the two points tending to zero we could, for example, take the discount factor at a time $\widetilde{T_N} = \frac{1}{2}(T_N - T_{N-1})$.

TABLE 3.2 The summary of the fair values of the four loans.

	China	Argentina	Uruguay	Ukraine
Interest payment	12,446,282	12,229,563	11,656,080	8,788,762
Principal repayment	82,852,333	81,847,125	79,193,556	66,210,098
Total value without option	95,271,615	94,076,688	90,849,636	74,998,860
Prepayment option value	(333,332)	(63,174)	(32,773)	(11,630)

than the one to China (which implies, as we would expect, that the credit risk associated with China is a lot smaller than the one associated with Ukraine).

In Table 3.2 we present the value of the prepayment option, which is also shown on the secondary axis of Figure 3.4b. We have implemented the model mentioned in the previous section (and shown in Appendix C) by solving the PDE using an alternating direction explicit method. Essentially, the value of the option, like in any situation involving a prepayment or callable feature, is the difference between the value of the loan should the borrower prepay it and the value should the borrower hold it to maturity. Since it is the borrower who holds the option, the value is negative as we price the loan from the development bank's point of view.

Observing Figure 3.4b, we can immediately answer pictorially the question about the sensitivity of the option value to the credit standing of the borrower. If we assume that the par level (i.e., unity in our graph on the primary axis) is the level at which a borrower could get a loan in the market outside development institutions, how does this relate to the option value shown in basis points on the secondary axis? A borrower who *could* realistically obtain another loan somewhere else would attribute value to the option to do so; a borrower who cannot will consider the option as having almost no value at all. In the graph shown in Figure 3.4b, China's loan value is close to par, meaning that it is not inconceivable that its own credit standing might one day improve to the level of pushing the loan value above par (the trigger indicating that a loan in the for-profit market is an attractive alternative). Ukraine has almost no such hope. This is in line with the values of the four different options, which show that the optionality embedded in the loan to China is far more valuable than the one embedded in the loan to Ukraine. It is probably not a surprise to the reader the fact that, in general and in particular as we can see from our realistic example, the optionality embedded in loans extended by development organizations to developing countries is very small.

CHAPTER 4

Emerging Markets and Liquidity

We have reached a point in our narrative where we have introduced the role and activities of development banking, the fundamentals of discounting, and the fundamentals of credit. Before moving on to the topic of debt, we pause to discuss a topic that is important in a geographical and a conceptual way.

Emerging markets are not only important in being the geographical area where development banking plays its principal role, they are also a showcase of specific financial features that are not found elsewhere. We shall focus on these because each of them is, in a way, a manifestation of credit that is and remains our principal focus. We introduce the concept of liquidity, present the difference in trade maturities between developed and developing markets, discuss the explicit higher credit risk of emerging market entities; and finally, raise the specific topic of capital control.

We will conclude the chapter with an example of the involvement of development banks in emerging markets in terms of borrowing and lending, the latter with the help of a few realistic case studies.

4.1 THE DEFINITION OF EMERGING MARKETS

Paraphrasing St. Augustine, we could say: what then are emerging markets? If no one asks me, I know what they are. If I wish to explain it to him who asks, I do not know. The term was coined by Antoine Van Agtmael, an economist at the World Bank, in the 1980s, and particularly in financial as opposed to economic terms, it should describe countries that are developed enough so as to have at least a rudimentary financial market.

An emerging market is developed enough, but it is still a long distance away from a fully developed economy. This entails many differences, which we will describe in detail throughout this chapter.

Many indices of emerging markets are published by, among others, Dow Jones, Standard and Poor's, and MSCI, but they do not all agree on its members. Trading desks at investment banks might include countries that appear nowhere on more official lists. For example, South Korea is on a recent MSCI list, Taiwan is on the FTSE, MSCI, and Standard and Poor's lists, but Israel is not on any of those. However, on some trading desks Israel is considered an emerging market. They all have a similar GDP per capita. Portugal also has a similar GDP per capita but is not considered an emerging market (the fact that it has adopted the Euro complicates things as far as definitions are concerned but, as of 2011, Greece is considered by FTSE as an advanced emerging market).[1]

Before the beginning of the sovereign debt crisis in Europe we could have defined an emerging market, as opposed to a fully developed one, by answering the simple question: When things go bad do people look for safety in government debt? If the answer was yes, then the country was a developed one, otherwise it was an emerging market.[2] Events have caught up with this definition, making things more complicated: While we have seen Greece defined as an advanced emerging market (although it lacks the growth potential of proper emerging countries), it would be difficult to consider Italy or Spain (or even France, whose bond prices wobbled when fear took control of the markets) as emerging economies.

Emerging markets are particularly important for our discussion for two reasons, which we shall explore in detail in Section 4.3. They are important for any treasury operation because part of debt raising is finding new investors or offering new products to current investors: emerging markets are usually rich with cash that needs to be invested or are usually attractive, if risky, opportunities for investors in developed economies. They are important for development banking because, although possessing an embryonic financial market, this might not be sufficiently large for all the needs the country has. The government might still turn to a development institution, particularly to fund large projects.

Probably the best definition comes from observing one by one those characteristics of a financial market where the difference between an emerging market and a fully developed one are most striking. We shall treat them as issues in the sense that they might constitute a challenge to the practices we are used to.

---

[1]The case for Greece is a bit different, though. Even if we have not introduced the characteristics of emerging markets yet, it will not come as a surprise the fact that in general they are countries where investments are risky but potentially lucrative because of the vast reservoir of growth in the economy. To talk of Greece as possessing a vast reservoir of growth would be bringing denial to an unprecedented level.

[2]Since the question implies tradable debt, it excludes countries that have not even reached the minimum level of development needed to be considered as emerging.

4.2 THE MAIN ISSUES WITH EMERGING MARKETS

4.2.1 Liquidity

We define liquidity as the measure of the ease with which we can buy (and even more, sell) a financial instrument. The best measure of liquidity is the bid-offer spread, the difference between the price at which one is willing to buy and the price at which one is willing to sell.

The bid-offer spread is a proxy of the knowledge we possess of a particular market. If someone asked us the prices at which we would buy and sell a pint of milk we might not be able to exactly remember how much we paid last time we went shopping, but we would give two numbers fairly close to each other (and bracketing the average market value). If the same question was about a vintage sports car, we would not, except for the most fortunate among us, be able to show the same level of confidence, and the two prices would be much, much farther apart (and possibly not even bracketing the average market value). This is because knowledge is linked to the frequency with which an item is bought and sold, which in itself is a definition of liquidity.

Previously, we mentioned how even more important than the price at which we buy a financial instrument is the price at which we can sell it. Let us imagine that we would like to purchase a security and let us assume that we are told that there is going to be a certain amount of time in which we will not be able to find a buyer should we wish to sell it. What would be the relationship between the amount of time and the price we are willing to pay for the security? Financial common sense dictates that the longer the amount of time in which we would be unable to sell it, the lower the price we will be willing to pay for it. Similarly, let us assume that we want to sell a security but we are told that we won't be able to purchase the same or a similar one for a certain amount of time. Again, the longer the amount of time, the higher the price we are going to sell it for. Combining the two, the longer the uncertainty to find a buyer/seller, the lower/higher our bid-offer prices and hence the wider the bid-offer spread. The fact that the price at which we wish to sell is probably slightly more important is due to the fact that, in general, and this might be a gross generalization, the market is more risk averse in nature.[3]

Emerging markets are characterized by considerably lower levels of liquidity when compared to developed markets. This is due to general uncertainty and to a certain volatility of interest by which we mean that

---

[3]Shown, for example, by the fact that, at equal distance from current prices, equity put options are more valuable than equity call options.

EURAB6E5Y=		EUR 5Y IRS AB/6M EURIBOR
Pay	Receive	Contributor
1.9850	**2.0050**	ICM
1.9840 /	2.0040	ICM
1.9830 /	2.0030	ICM

CZKAM6PR5Y=		CZK 5Y IRS AM / 6M PRIBOR	L
Pay	Receive	Contributor	
1.6000	**1.6500**	CSOB	P
1.5900 /	1.6500	WALLICH&MATT	P
1.5900 /	1.6700	WALLICH&MATT	P

USDAM3L5Y=		USD 5Y IRS AM / 3M LIBOR
Pay	Receive	Contributor
1.1690	**1.1810**	BROKER
1.1690 /	1.1790	BROKER
1.1560 /	1.1860	ERSTE BANK

ILSAM3T5Y=		ILS 5Y IRS AM/3M TELBOR
Pay	Receive	Contributor
3.4300	**3.4900**	CITIBANK
3.4400 /	3.5000	CITIBANK
3.4500 /	3.5100	CITIBANK

a)   b)

FIGURE 4.1 A comparison between developed and emerging markets bid-offer spreads. a) Developed markets: USD and EUR five-year interest rate swap rates; b) advanced emerging markets: ILS (Israeli Shekel) and CZK (Czech Krone) five-year swap rate as of September 6, 2011. *Source*: Thomson Reuters Eikon.

the appetite for investment is particularly sensitive to news and information. On the back of current news there might be more or less appetite at unpredictable moments to an extent far larger than in the case of developed markets where appetite is driven perhaps by wider and less explicit considerations. Another important factor driving liquidity and lack thereof is the fact that the volume traded in emerging markets and its frequency are considerably smaller.

Figures 4.1 and 4.2 show a set of quotes for the five-year interest rate swap rates for a certain number of developed and emerging countries. The goal of the figure is to show the widening bid-offer spread. Figure 4.1a shows the quote for EUR and USD, the two most liquid currencies in the world: the bid-offer is less than 2 bps. Figure 4.1b shows two advanced emerging markets, Israel and the Czech Republic: the quote for the same maturity of the same instrument is now in the order of 5 bps. Figure 4.2a shows the same quote for two middle-ranking emerging markets, South Africa and Hungary: the bid-offer is now 10 bps. Finally Figure 4.2b shows the five-year swap rate for two emerging markets belonging to the least developed ones, Turkey and the Philippines: the bid-offer is now 30 bps and 55 bps respectively.

We have shown quotes for interest rate swaps because we wanted to show the difference in bid-offer spreads between developed and emerging market currencies: in developed markets, interest rate swaps are among the most common instruments. This, however, could be a bit misleading since a swap might not necessarily be the most common instrument in *all* markets. We said in Section 2.2.3 that in some emerging markets FX forwards are the

ZARQB3ZB5Y=	**ZAR 5Y**	**IRS QB / 90D BA**	
Pay	Receive	Contributor	
6.1800	**6.2800**	INVESTEC	
6.1900 /	6.2900	INVESTEC	
6.1500 /	6.2300	RMB	

TRYAM3T5Y=	**TRY 5Y**	**IRS AM/3M TRYIBOR**	
Pay	Receive	Contributor	I
7.7500	**8.0500**	CS	I
7.7000 /	7.8000	CS	I
7.7500 /	8.0500	CS	I

HUFAB6B5Y=	**HUF 5Y**	**IRS AB/6M BUBOR**	
Pay	Receive	Contributor	
5.8300	**5.9300**	ERSTE BANK	
5.8300 /	5.9300	ERSTE BANK	
5.8300 /	5.9300	ERSTE BANK	

PHPQB3P5Y=	**PHP 5Y**	**IRS QB / 3M PHIREF**	
Pay	Receive	Contributor	L
3.2500	**3.8000**	BROKER	G
3.2000 /	3.8500	STANCHART	S
3.2000 /	3.6750	STANCHART	S

a)   b)

FIGURE 4.2   A comparison between developed and emerging markets bid-offer spreads. a) Mid-development emerging markets: ZAR (South African Rand) and HUF (Hungarian Florin) five-year swap rates; b) low-development emerging markets: TRY (Turkish Lira) and PHP (Philippine Pesos) five-year swap rate as of September 6, 2011. *Source*: Thomson Reuters Eikon.

most liquid instrument type, more so than interest rate swaps. In the case of Turkey we see that the bid-offer is quite wide for swaps; it could be that for FX forwards it might not be so wide. To test this we are going to use the information shown in Figure 4.3a.

Let us remind ourselves of what we have discussed in the chapter about curve construction. If we want to obtain the discount factor at time T in TRY using FX forwards (see Equation 2.3), we need to use

$$D_T^{TRY} = \frac{FX_t}{FWD_T} D_T^{USD}$$

from which we can obtain the zero rate equivalent (which we have defined in Section 2.4.3 as a nontraded value useful for illustration purposes) by doing

$$\widehat{R_T^{TRY}} = \frac{1}{T}\left(\frac{1}{D_T^{TRY}} - 1\right)$$

in case of linear compounding or

$$R_T^{TRY} = \frac{1}{T\sqrt{D_T^{TRY}}} - 1$$

```
┌─ Quote: TRYF=                                                    _ □ × ─┐
│ ↓  ↑Q  ▼ TRYF=        ▼ Q ⊟ ⬛ A⁺ A⁻ ▦ ⬧▼  ⧉ ⬜⬛ ▣▦  ⤳▼  ⋮ ⌗      │
│          TRY Deps & Fwds                                                │
│        Bid     Ask    Srce Time   RIC              Bid     Ask    Srce Time
│        1.7609  1.7633 CISC 12:59                                        │
│        5.05    7.50        12:50   TRYON=          2.91    3.06        12:56
│        5.50    7.50        10:35   TRYTN=          3.02    3.12        12:53
│        5.50    7.50        10:35   TRY1W=          20.36   21.36       12:59
│        6.00    8.00        10:35   TRYSW=          20.36   21.36       12:59
│        6.15    6.65        12:56   TRY2W=          40.98   43.03  INGY 13:00
│        6.00    8.00        10:35   TRY3W=          60.85   63.32  INGY 13:00
│        6.15    8.15        10:35   TRY1M=          95.00   97.30       12:56
│        6.75    8.45        10:35   TRY2M=          176.50  182.60 INGY 13:00
│        7.00    8.55        10:35   TRY3M=          248.88  257.78 RTFX 12:51
│        7.25    8.70        10:35   TRY6M=          462.87  497.53 RBIS 12:59
│        7.70    8.85        10:35   TRY9M=          679.08  732.29 RBIS 12:59
│        7.95    9.45        10:35   TRY1Y=          904.24  975.81 RBIS 12:59
│        8.15    9.60        10:35   TRY2Y=          1897.00 1984.00 CSTL 11:49
│                                   TRY3Y=          2830.00 2949.00 CSTL 11:51
│                                                                        │
│ ◄                                                                   ►  │
└────────────────────────────────────────────────────────────────────────┘
```

a)

```
┌─ Quote: ABAF03                                                   _ □ × ─┐
│ ↓  ↑Q  ▼ ABAF03       ▼ Q ⊟ ⬛ A⁺ A⁻ ▦ ⬧▼  ⧉ ⬜⬛ ▣▦  ⤳▼  ⋮ ⌗      │
│ 15:06 07SEP11   ABSA BANK LIMITED AFRICA CONTRIBUTION ZA01291    ABAF03 │
│                                                                        │
│                 ABSA AFRICA FWDS AND LT FX                             │
│                                                                        │
│         NGN NDFS        USDNGN (LVL)      USDMZN (LVL)LTFX AFRICA - LVLS│
│ 1M 156.78 157.67   ON  -3.1     9.6      0.4   1.0  KES        TZS      │
│ 2M 157.70 158.85   TN  -3.1     9.6      0.4   1.0  2Y 2322 2602 2Y 255  367
│ 3M 158.53 160.10   1W   8.6    36.9      2.7   6.8  3Y 3327 4019 3Y 428  595
│ 6M 161.05 164.16   1M  56.7   149.9      12.1  31.1 5Y 5820 6927 5Y 808  119
│ 9M 164.00 168.21   2M 160.2   268.1      15.8  40.8                     │
│ 1Y 166.61 172.15   3M 240.8   400.7      34.5  88.5 ZMK        UGX      │
│    FIX OFF NIFEX01  6M 485.8   795.2      74.9 182.5 2Y 1112 1604 2Y  796 1075
│                     9M 791.7  1208.0     116.0 278.6 3Y 1675 2406 3Y  104 1459
│                     1Y1050.1  1599.4     159.4 375.0 5Y 4983 6152 5Y  180 2602
│                                                                        │
│          USDGHS          USDNAD          USDAOA    GHS                  │
│ ON    3    5           9    12         4    5     2Y 2948  4466         │
│ TN    3    5           9    12         4    5     3Y 4579  7736         │
│ 1W   24   33          63    84        25   37     5Y 1058 15639         │
│ 1M  120  147         286   379       120  178                          │
│ 2M  239  290         543   722       222  331     BWP         NGN LVL   │
│ 3M  367  444         787  1054       312  476     2Y -203 -134 2Y 2105 3352
│ 6M  685  952        1459  2081       637  963     3Y -307 -187 3Y 3315 6996
│ 9M 1052 1456        2166  3108      1017 1509     5Y -458 -308 5Y 4870 10744
│ 1Y 1361 1897        2864  4116      1430 2083                          │
└────────────────────────────────────────────────────────────────────────┘
```

b)

FIGURE 4.3 FX forward rates for a) Turkish Lira (TRY); b) a selection of African currencies as of September 7, 2011. *Source*: Thomson Reuters Eikon.

in case of continuous compounding. We show both types of compounding since a zero rate is not an officially traded quantity with specified characteristics: both could be valid. The same calculation applies, of course, to bid and offer prices.

From Figure 4.3 we see that the bid-spot FX rate is 1.7618 Turkish Liras for one U.S. Dollar and the offer FX rate is 1.7644. We are going to calculate the zero rate equivalent for a maturity of three years (the farthest available). The bid pips are 2,837 and the offer pips are 2,956. Assuming the USD discount factor (which we know is a big assumption, but since our goal is to find a relative measure, i.e., the bid-offer spread, the impact of this assumption is limited), we obtain the discount relative to the bid quote, $D_T^{TRY,bid} = 0.819455$ and the one relative to the offer quote, $D_T^{TRY,offer} = 0.814888$. Since it is difficult to compare discount factors and get a feel for a market spread, we convert them into zero rates.

The bid and offer zero rates[4] linearly compounded are

$$\widehat{R_T^{TRY,bid}} = 7.3352\% \quad \widehat{R_T^{TRY,offer}} = 7.5653\%$$

and

$$R_T^{TRY,bid} = 6.8546\% \quad R_T^{TRY,offer} = 7.0558\%$$

if continuously compounded. If they seem different from the rates quoted in Figure 4.2b let us not forget that they must be different; those are swap rates (the coupon in Equation 2.4), these are zero rates (the r in Equation 2.2).

If we now calculate the bid-offer spread we see that it is 20 bps in the case of the continuously compounded rate and 23 bps in the case of the linearly compounded rate. This is roughly two-thirds of the bid-offer on the swap rate,[5] that is, it shows a far greater liquidity. Nevertheless, the bid-offer is far from the levels found in a developed market. As an emerging market develops, as different market participants enter into it, as the principal amount of trades increases, the bid-offer tightens.

---

[4]To be more correct, the calculation is slightly more complicated and can be seen in Appendix A; however, for a feel of the magnitudes involved, these numbers are sufficiently precise.

[5]The three-year quote is not shown in Fig. 4.2b, but its bid-offer was also 30 bps.

4.2.2 Maturity

The second characteristic that greatly differs between developed and emerging markets is the maturity of traded instruments.

From what we might know already and from what we have hitherto said, emerging markets are associated with a feeling of uncertainty and risk. The fact that someone might be unwilling to enter into too long a contract in an uncertain environment results in the maturities of financial instruments being considerably shorter in emerging markets.

In developed markets such as USD or EUR we can have swaps going up to maturities as long as 40 or even 50 years. This is very different from a situation such as the one in Figure 4.3b, which shows quotes for FX forwards for a collection of African currencies. These currencies belong to countries that are even less developed than the one appearing in Figure 4.2b: only FX forwards are traded and we can see that the bid-offer is extremely wide. For example, if we try to imply a one-year zero rate for Ghanian Cedi (GHS), we obtain a bid-offer larger than 300 bps; for three year it is greater than 500 bps! The argument on the width of the bid-offer is not only to continue the discussion on liquidity started in the previous section, it is to show that at such wide bid-offers, the actual bulk of trades will be conducted at much shorter maturities.[6]

The attentive reader might argue that we have seen that in emerging markets, FX forwards are the most common instruments traded, we have seen that FX forwards are essentially fully collateralized, so where is the risk involved? Why can't we trade longer maturities? This is an interesting point that begs for some further explanation. We shall enter into greater detail in the following chapters but we can now ask the question, why do people enter into financial transactions of the type shown here as examples?

A commonly held view (and a view that the great recession has done nothing but strengthen) is that all financial transactions of derivative instruments are carried out as a form of betting and/or speculation. While certainly this is true of some of them, this view ignores or forgets that derivatives are meant to constitute an insurance against the sensitivity to some market parameter of a primary investment or economic activity.

While it is true that many market participants use FX forwards to speculate on the vagaries of an exchange rate, it is also true that FX forwards are used for the purpose they were intended: to convert future cashflows in foreign currencies at an exchange rate agreed today, something that retrospectively might result in a loss but that eliminates uncertainty

---

[6]The type of quotes shown in Figure 4.3b are what brokers call indicative levels: they are not actual trades. This means that we cannot know at which maturity the majority of trades take place: a fair guess would be in the less than one year region.

from the primary activity (the one whose cash flows we are hedging). This means that the FX forwards shown in Figure 4.3b are most probably used as a hedging tool for some other activity, which can be a private investment in some concrete economic activity returning a profit in local currency or to hedge the cash flows of a bond in local currency.

Let us imagine we purchase a bond in Ghanian Cedi (GHS) maturing at time T. As a U.S. investor, the present value will be given by

$$FX_t N^{GHS} \sum_i^T D_i^{GHS} C dt_i$$

where FX_t is the FX rate today, N^{GHS} is the principal in Cedi, C is the coupon, and D_i^{GHS} are the Cedi discount factors. The present value will be very sensitive to the forward FX rates since these are the main drivers of the foreign discount factors. An alternative would be, for each cash flow, to enter into an FX forward so that each cash flow is a USD amount, in practice

$$N^{GHS} \sum_i^T D_i^{USD} FWD_i C dt_i$$

By doing so we have eliminated any sensitivity to the Cedi market and we only have USD interest rate risk. This means that (it might be an obvious statement but it is perhaps worth making anyway), like in all forms of hedging, we might end up worse off than if we hadn't done anything: the only certain thing is that we have eliminated a form of uncertainty. Because of the risk involved in either activity (economic investment or bond buying), neither is likely to be entered for too long a period. As a consequence, the financial market will match fairly closely those maturities.

The above should be seen also in the context of what we discussed in the chapter about curve construction. It is important when making decisions about pricing (curve construction should be considered pricing) to observe what actually takes place in the market and what is the biggest picture we can consider at once. We could have simply looked at the GHS bond and discounted it on the GHS curve. By asking ourselves what is the actual activity taking place (the hedging of the bond), we see that it can be priced in a completely different way by discounting it on the USD curve.[7]

---

[7]In some cases, we shall discuss nondeliverability. In Section 4.2.4, we have no choice and we have to convert all cash flows in USD as the country does not allow foreign investors to deal in local currency.

4.2.3 Credit

From what we have mentioned in the previous section about emerging markets being characterized by uncertainty and risk, it is only natural that we touch upon the issue of credit risk.

In Section 3.2 we have shown how the credit risk of a borrower can be hedged through credit default swaps. As a consequence, at first glance, the CDS rates are the best indicators of the riskiness of a certain borrower. Let us add immediately that they are perfect indicators in a *risk-neutral framework* in the sense that through them we can imply risk-neutral survival probabilities. In other frameworks, other indicators are preferred (e.g., credit ratings published by rating agencies).

In emerging markets, CDS levels are considerably higher than in developed countries, and in Table 4.1 we show the one-year and five-year CDS rates for a selection of emerging markets. For comparison we also show the CDS rates for two developed countries (the United States and Germany) and two corporates (Ford Motor Company and Sony Corporation). To offer a common comparison tool, these are CDS rates for contracts offering protection against borrowing in USD, not in local currency. We mentioned in Section 3.2.3 that CDS levels for non-USD denominated debt would be different.

TABLE 4.1 Credit spread of selected emerging markets sovereign shown against a few developed markets' sovereign and corporate for comparison, as of March 4, 2013.

Entity	One-year CDS spread (USD)	Five-year CDS spread (USD)
United States of America, Government of	20.01	37.68
Germany, Federal Republic of	9.46	38.81
Israel, State of	40.84	127.16
South Africa, Republic of	61.35	172.72
Czech Republic, Government of the	15.00	59.05
Turkey, Republic of	56.93	136.98
Philippines, Republic of	19.17	98.99
Kazakhstan, Republic of	41.45	156.61
Ukraine, Republic of	381.94	565.73
Argentina, Republic of	7,027.76	3,208.80
Ford Motor Company	29.41	168.24
Sony Corporation	51.47	216.24

The data shown in Table 4.1 is very interesting because it shows that not all emerging markets are equally risky (and it gives an idea of why it is so difficult to lump them together), but the same data should come with a caveat. From CDS rates we can imply survival probabilities, in other words default probabilities,[8] but CDS rates are driven by many considerations that go beyond pure credit. There could be liquidity issues—the less frequently a CDS is traded, the more false could be the credit information embedded in it; there could be speculation involved in the trading of that CDS. Let us not forget that a CDS is a derivative with a link to an underlying (the credit of a borrower) but, as we discussed in Section 3.1.1, sometimes this link becomes broken and the two values (the derivative's value and the underlying's value[9]) move in very different directions. The amount of debt involved (which could or could not match the principal of the CDS contracts) can have a distorting effect through leverage.

As an example of the above, let us look at the most striking piece of data from the table: Argentina's one-year CDS level at $7,027.76$ bps. One can show (see Appendix B) that the probability of default (expressed as one minus the survival probability) can be approximated, particularly for a short maturity T, by

$$1 - S_T \approx \frac{CDS_T}{1 - R}$$

where CDS_T is the rate for a CDS with maturity T and R is the assumed recovery rate. Using a recovery of 24%, for Argentina this implies a probability of default greater than 80% within a year. This means that we are considering Argentina 170 times more likely than Kazakhstan to default within a year. While for some this might seem reasonable (some argue that Argentina has never fully left the 2002 default behind and is drifting more and more toward uncertainty), these numbers are difficult to grasp. Similarly hard to believe is that the one-year CDS spread for the Philippines and the Czech Republic is lower than the U.S. Treasury. This difficulty also originates from the fact that above we have presented a risk-neutral probability of default (we shall introduce risk neutrality in Section 7.2.1), which should not be confused with an actuarial probability of default. Rating agencies publish

---

[8]Since, of course, if there is a probability S_T that a borrower is solvent, there is a probability $1 - S_T$ that it has defaulted.
[9]Which, in the case of credit, unfortunately is not visible unlike, say, equities where one can easily see quoted stock and option prices. It is true that one could consider the bond as the underlying, but a bond still gives an *implied* view of credit as opposed to a share price, which is the underlying itself.

probabilities of default based on historical data (and therefore not implied from CDS levels), which are considerably lower.

Despite the caveats and the surprises that CDS levels can lead to, they are very useful indicators, and it is helpful to compare emerging market levels to the levels of developed countries to comprehend the different levels of magnitude of the risk involved.

Another interesting aspect of the above data is the fact that Argentina presents a so-called inverted curve, that is, the short end (represented by the one-year point) of the CDS rate's term structure is higher than the medium-long end (represented by the five-year point). This is counterintuitive since we would expect to pay more for longer-dated protection. This happens in dire situations (and almost always in emerging markets), the market thinking being roughly "if country X survives the immediate difficult situation, there is a greater chance that it might survive in the longer term as well."

Figure 4.4 shows how for Ukraine and Kazakhstan the shape of the curve is usually normal (i.e., one-year point lower than the five-year point) except during the peak of the 2007 to 2009 financial crisis when the points switched positions.

Figure 4.4 is also useful to show what kinds of magnitudes the CDS rates of emerging markets can reach during a crisis.

4.2.4 Capital Control

The final issue we are going to discuss, capital control, is one that is peculiar to emerging markets and is not a matter of degree (shorter versus longer maturity, small versus large bid-offer spread, etc.), but only of being present there.

A government has the ultimate tool to control FX rate in its own currency: by being able to print money in that currency it can always offer a two-way price in the currency market. This two-way price is rather a bottomless one way since this tool works very well in one direction, devaluation. In the other direction, the government's tools do not differ from those of any other big market players (i.e., it needs to have large foreign reserves to buy back its own and make it appreciate).

In the case of small countries, whose currencies' total amount is significantly less than the one of larger developed ones, there is sometimes the fear that a powerful external player might be able to manipulate the currency in the same way that the government would. For small countries the fear is usually of devaluation; for large, export-driven countries like China, the fear can be the opposite, that is, of their currency appreciating too much.

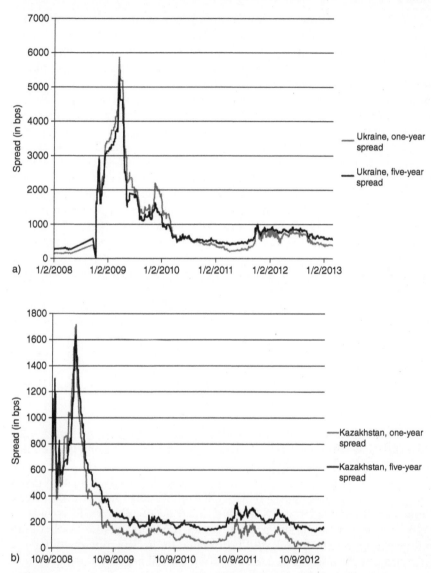

FIGURE 4.4 An example of curve inversion for a) Ukraine; b) Kazakhstan.

The answer to these concerns is capital control. To exercise capital control means to forbid the trading of a certain currency outside the currency's home country. This entails the creation of an *on-shore* market (in the currency's home market and open only to locals) and an *off-shore* market open to foreigners. It also entails, as a consequence, the creation of *nondeliverable instruments*, instruments dictating that, where they prescribe a payment in the protected currency, the actual settlement should occur in another currency (usually USD).

The most common types of instruments are nondeliverable FX forwards where the MTM of the trade, that is, the difference between the realized FX rate and the expected one at the beginning of the trade, is settled in the foreign currency only. Since we have seen in Section 2.2.3 that, through the interest rate parity, FX forwards are closely linked to discount factors, this mechanism has a profound impact on the interest rate market and creates a mirror on-shore, off-shore market for interest rates as well. Some of the more developed protected markets also have nondeliverable cross currency swaps, where the cash flows of the leg in local currency is settled in the foreign one (usually USD).

Figure 4.5 shows quotes for nondeliverable FX forwards premia for Chinese Renmibi (CNY). Let us consider the one-year points, whose mid value in pips is −500 (negative). By using

$$D_{1Y}^{CNY} = \frac{FX_t}{FWD_{1Y}} D_{1Y}^{USD}$$

to obtain the one-year value for the discount factor in CNY, we find a value of 1.00102 resulting in a zero rate $R_{1Y}^{CNY} \approx -10$ *bps*. Not only is the value puzzling for being negative but it is also in clear contrast to the value found in Figure 4.6, which shows the fixings for the SHIBOR, the Chinese LIBOR equivalent (Shanghai Interbank Offer Rate). We have said at great length how the rates implied from FX forwards are conceptually very different from LIBOR, but they should still be in the same order of magnitude, as they both in the end represent some cost of borrowing. In this situation the difference is enormous considering we are comparing a small negative rate with one— we are focusing on the one-year SHIBOR rate—that is fixed at more than 5%. The reason for this difference lies in capital control. SHIBOR rates are the rates at which *Chinese* banks lend to each other: it is a market closed to foreigners. The zero rate we have implied from the nondeliverable forwards is one that is open to foreigners.

Let us state immediately (and this should alleviate the concern caused by the sight of negative rates) that the implied negative rate is purely fictitious

0#CNYF= USD/CNY FORWARD ENHANCED GUIDE

CNY= 6.3833 / 43

Term	Bid	Offer	Source	Time	Start	Maturity	Outright	DayCount
CNYON=	-2.00	-1.00	MUSH	05:56	08SEP11	09SEP11	6.383700/5000	1
CNYTN=	-5.00	-3.00	MUSH	05:56	09SEP11	13SEP11	6.383600/4800	4
CNYSN=	-2.00	-0.50	ICHO	04:16	13SEP11	14SEP11	6.383100/4250	1
CNYSW=	-10.00	-3.00	MUSH	05:56	13SEP11	20SEP11	6.382300/4000	7
CNY2W=	-11.30	-6.30	BPSH	04:40	13SEP11	27SEP11	6.382170/3670	14
CNY3W=	-9.00	-4.00	CTSH	04:10	13SEP11	11OCT11	6.382400/3900	28
CNY1M=	-10.00	-1.00	MUSH	05:56	13SEP11	13OCT11	6.382300/4200	30
CNY2M=	-23.00	23.00	MUSH	05:56	13SEP11	14NOV11	6.381000/6600	62
CNY3M=	-50.00	0	MUSH	05:56	13SEP11	13DEC11	6.378300/4300	91
CNY4M=	-79.18	-52.58	CTSH	04:10	13SEP11	13JAN12	6.375382/9042	122
CNY5M=	-118.35	-95.16	CTSH	04:10	13SEP11	13FEB12	6.371465/4784	153
CNY6M=	-165.00	-135.00	MUSH	05:56	13SEP11	13MAR12	6.366800/0800	182
CNY7M=	-210.60	-190.60	ICHO	04:10	13SEP11	13APR12	6.362240/5240	213
CNY8M=	-266.20	-246.20	ICHO	04:10	13SEP11	14MAY12	6.356680/9680	244
CNY9M=	-330.00	-290.00	MUSH	05:56	13SEP11	13JUN12	6.350300/5300	274
CNY10M=	-385.22	-360.33	ICHO	04:10	13SEP11	13JUL12	6.344778/8267	304
CNY11M=	-452.61	-422.66	ICHO	04:10	13SEP11	13AUG12	6.338039/2034	335
CNY1Y=	-530.00	-470.00	MUSH	05:56	13SEP11	13SEP12	6.330300/7300	366
CNY2Y=	-1600.0	-900.00	CTSI	04:10	13SEP11	13SEP13	6.223300/4300	731
CNY3Y=	-2850.0	-1550.0	CTSI	04:10	13SEP11	15SEP14	6.098300/9300	1098
CNY4Y=	-4500.0	-2500.0	CTSI	04:10	13SEP11	14SEP15	5.933300/4300	1462

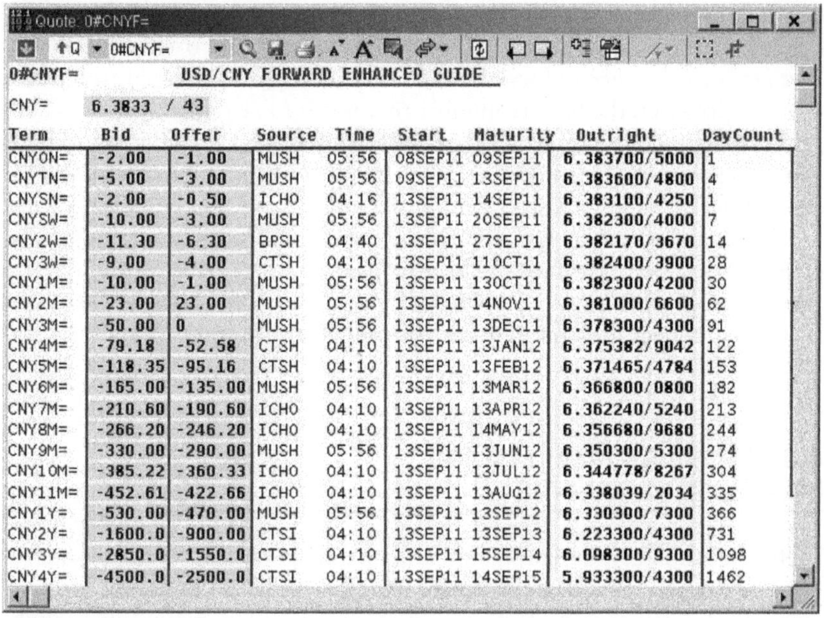

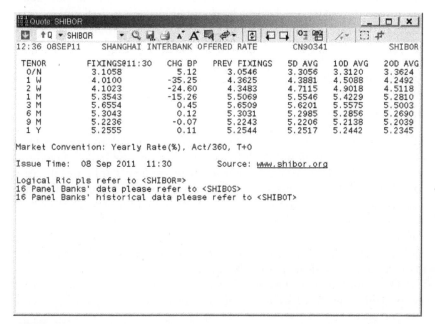

FIGURE 4.5 FX forwards premia for Chinese renmibi (CNY). *Source*: Thomson Reuters Eikon.

12:36 08SEP11 SHANGHAI INTERBANK OFFERED RATE CN90341 SHIBOR

TENOR	FIXINGS@11:30	CHG BP	PREV FIXINGS	5D AVG	10D AVG	20D AVG
O/N	3.1058	5.12	3.0546	3.3056	3.3120	3.3624
1 W	4.0100	-35.25	4.3625	4.3881	4.5088	4.2492
2 W	4.1023	-24.60	4.3483	4.7115	4.9018	4.5118
1 M	5.3543	-15.26	5.5069	5.5546	5.4229	5.2810
3 M	5.6554	0.45	5.6509	5.6201	5.5575	5.5003
6 M	5.3043	0.12	5.3031	5.2985	5.2856	5.2690
9 M	5.2236	-0.07	5.2243	5.2206	5.2138	5.2039
1 Y	5.2555	0.11	5.2544	5.2517	5.2442	5.2345

Market Convention: Yearly Rate(%), Act/360, T+0

Issue Time: 08 Sep 2011 11:30 Source: www.shibor.org

Logical Ric pls refer to <SHIBOR=>
16 Panel Banks' data please refer to <SHIBOS>
16 Panel Banks' historical data please refer to <SHIBOT>

FIGURE 4.6 SHIBOR fixings as of September 8, 2011. *Source*: Thomson Reuters Eikon.

and it is used either for illustration purposes (as we have done here) or for operational ones. (In some trading systems one needs to visualize the rate *that leads to the correct* forwards, in other words, and paraphrasing the famous expression, the bizarre number that needs to be plugged in, in order to give the right value.) As we have stated many times, FX traders trading forwards are simply concerned about cash flows in different currencies and they are indifferent to and uninterested in the interest rate implied from them.

With capital control, probably the most peculiar of emerging markets characteristics, we conclude the brief exposition of the issues one might meet when dealing with less developed markets. We shall now observe how these issues can impact in particular the borrowing and lending of a development institution.

4.3 EMERGING MARKETS AND DEVELOPMENT BANKING

In the eyes of many, development banking and emerging markets, which are often referred to as developing markets, are closely linked. This is certainly true and, for our specific purposes, in more ways than commonly thought.

As we have said before (and will explore in greater detail later), development institutions lend to underdeveloped or developing countries roughly in two ways: by using funds given by donors (this term is used with a certain freedom) or by using funds raised in the capital markets, that is, by using the tools of investment banking. As we shall see in the following sections, in the former situation they are in contact with emerging countries only through lending, in the latter also through borrowing.

4.3.1 Borrowing

We can observe in Figure 4.2 the outstanding principal amounts of bonds issued by the International Bank for Reconstruction and Development (part of the World Bank Group), the European Investment Bank, and the Asian Development Bank in emerging market currencies. The range of currencies is extremely varied. We shall see later how a treasury business works, but the first question one would probably ask is, why would a development institution issue debt in an emerging market currency? The reasons are twofold, the first applying to any treasury operation and the second being relevant only in the case of development banking.

One could say that the goal of a treasury desk is to borrow at the cheapest possible rate. In order to do so they must issue bonds that attract the

TABLE 4.2 Principal outstanding of bonds issued in emerging market currencies by selected development institutions as of September 13, 2011 (in millions of local currency).

Currency name	World Bank/ I.B.R.D.	European Investment Bank	Asian Development Bank
Bulgarian Lev (BGN)	–	230	–
Brazilian Real (BRL)	6,205	4,307	2,447
Botswana Pula (BWP)	266	–	–
Chilean Peso (CLP)	275,000	–	–
Chinese Renmibi (CNY)	500	–	3,200
Colombian Peso (COP)	581,360	–	–
Ghanian Cedi (GHS)	194	44	–
Hungarian Florin (HUF)	6,150	13,750	–
Indonesian Rupee (IDR)	–	6,855,272	–
Indian Rupee (INR)	4,000	1,000	5,000
Kazakhstan Tenge (KZT)	–	–	1,200
Mexican Pesos (MXN)	15,720	1,055	669
Malaysian Ringit (MYR)	607	–	500
Nigerian Naira (NGN)	21,210	–	–
Philippine Peso (PHP)	–	5,000	–
Polish Zloty (PLN)	858	2,700	–
Romanian Leu (RON)	280	450	–
Russian Ruble (RUB)	31,765	30,010	–
Saudi Arabian Riyal (SAR)	1,000	–	–
Thai Bhat (THB)	1,250	–	6,500
Turkish Lira (TRY)	2,227	7,975	3,167
Uruguayan Peso (UYU)	1,982	–	–
South African Rand (ZAR)	56,397	25,019	30,018
Zambian Kwacha (ZMK)	335,500	240,000	–

highest level of interest in order to sell the bond at the highest price (the details on how this takes place are left vague on purpose and are left for future chapters).

Bonds in emerging markets' currencies issued by development banks are particularly attractive to investors for several reasons. They offer diversification by being only as risky as the issuing institution they offer exposure to a currency and its rates that would be otherwise much riskier; it is an attractive way to invest funds gained within a certain country (e.g., a manufacturer needing to invest profits in local currency). These reasons could be the same as those of any financial institution looking for investors.

One usually considers the commitment to development as being purely expressed through favorable lending terms; however, this is an incomplete picture. If a developed financial market is believed to be important for the overall development of a country, then issuing good quality debt in that currency is a fundamental step. Let us imagine that a country with currency X has practically a nonexistent financial market except for deposits which are short dated, illiquid, and accessible mainly to locals (although we are not assuming that the currency is controlled).

Let us imagine that a development bank issues a two-year bond in currency X: the bond pays a semiannual fixed coupon in X. An investor buying this bond will receive four fixed amounts of X and might want to hedge this exposure; another market participant agrees to enter into an agreement with the investor to exchange these amounts into USD at an agreed price, in practice creating an X/USD FX forwards market. The market participant is now in possession of X, which he might want to invest. He can do this either in the economy itself (which, under the point of view of development, is a positive consequence) or by investing in proper government bonds, which, by now, due to the presence of new investors, might have started being issued.

When confidence and liquidity grows, interest rate swaps and floating-rate bonds would eventually follow. The initial issue of debt in currency X by an institution with good credit can therefore create a virtuous circle to the benefit of the development of a financial market.

4.3.2 Lending

The main link between development institutions and emerging markets, of course, takes place through lending. Being that loans are private financial instruments (as opposed to bonds, which are publicly traded), it is difficult or impossible to access the proprietary information needed to create a table similar to the one for bonds shown in Figure 4.2. It would not necessarily be more varied (as we have mentioned before, the majority of loans are in USD), but it would probably cover nearly as many currencies.

In Section 4.4 we shall look at some sample projects that should mimic the type of project a development institution carries out in a typical emerging market. In particular, we shall see how a loan instrument is structured around a project. In the rest of this section we shall look at some peculiar, technical issues that characterize development lending.

In Section 3.3.1 we have seen how to fair value a loan in the presence of credit risk. We shall repeat now a fairly important concept that we have introduced when dealing with the prepayment option of a loan. When it comes to loans extended by development institutions to sovereign borrowers (of which the great majority are developing countries), there is a fairly important detail concerning the assumption of the recovery rate. Although the probability of default is calibrated using the same assumptions used by the market (this is important in order to use CDS spreads[10]), when the fair value of the loan is calculated, a different, higher recovery rate is used.

Development institutions, we have already mentioned, can be seen as credit cooperatives: its members contribute funds (some more than others, of course) and then the institutions lend these funds back. This cooperative approach combined with the fact that development institutions are lenders of last resort makes default of payment to a development institution very unlikely. This entails an assumption of a recovery that is much larger than the, say, 25% assumed by the market.

When it comes to development lending, a fairly common instrument is the *guarantee*. A guarantee is not a loan but a promise made by a development institution that a loan, or part of it, taken on by a sovereign entity will continue to meet its obligations even in the case of default of the sovereign entity. From its description it seems conceptually similar to a CDS written by the development institution to sell protection to the sovereign entity. Conceptually, it is similar, but the main differences consist of the fact that a guarantee is not a swap (hence it is not regulated by ISDA); it deals with an underlying, which is usually amortizing (as opposed to a CDS which protects a non-amortizing instrument such as a bond); and most of the time there are issues of nonacceleration, which we have mentioned in Section 3.3.1.

These types of differences are central to the way development institutions hedge loans, and are useful to describe the risk involved in mixing different types of instruments. As an example, let us consider

---

[10]One could be led to think that the obvious solution would be to use Equation 3.17 with the spread as quoted by the CDS contract and a different recovery rate. Although we have said that the recovery rate is not a traded quantity, it is still closely linked to *that particular* CDS rate. To be more specific: should one go to a market maker asking for a quote on a CDS with a specifically stated recovery rate, the quote received would differ from the standard one, which in turn would lead to a different implied survival probability.

the case in which we have issued a nonaccelerating, floating-rate loan of the type

$$
\sum_i S_i D_i \left[N_i \left(L_i + s \right) dt_i + \left(N_i - N_{i+1} \right) \right]
$$

$$
+ R \sum_j \left[\sum_{n=j}^T D_n \left(N_n - N_{n+1} \right) \right] D_j \left(S_{j-1} - S_j \right)
\tag{4.1}
$$

Now let us consider the case where we have issued a nonaccelerating, fixed-rate loan

$$
\sum_i S_i D_i \left[N_i C dt_i + \left(N_i - N_{i+1} \right) \right]
$$

$$
+ R \sum_j \left[\sum_{n=j}^T D_n \left(N_n - N_{n+1} \right) \right] D_j \left(S_{j-1} - S_j \right)
\tag{4.2}
$$

with a coupon C and at the same time a swap (which we have written on one side of the equal to stress that we *receive* floating) such that the following is true

$$
\sum_i \left(L_i + s \right) D_i dt_i - \sum_i C D_i dt_i = 0
\tag{4.3}
$$

If we enter into the swap with the borrower, assume that the swap amortizes in the same way as the loan and we do not ask for collateral postings from the counterpart, we could be tempted to think that the floating-rate loan or the combination of a fixed-rate loan plus a swap, such as the one shown above, are identical. In both situations we end up receiving LIBOR plus spread. This is tempting but incorrect because it does not take into account the fact that the typical development loan does not accelerate, whereas a derivative regulated by an ISDA agreement does.

To illustrate this, let us rewrite the swap more precisely taking into account the amortizing principal and also the credit risk of our counterpart (because in this particular type of swap no collateral is exchanged irrespective of the credit rating of either party). To simplify the notation we make the assumption, far from implausible, that, given we are an institution with an excellent rating and the borrower is a developing country, our credit risk is negligible compared to our counterpart and therefore we are going to ignore first-to-default considerations and the equation will only feature S_i, the survival probability of the borrower.[11] Doing so we have

$$\sum_i S_i D_i \left[N_i \left(L_i + s \right) dt_i + \left(N_i - N_{i+1} \right) \right]$$

$$- \sum_i S_i D_i \left[N_i C dt_i + \left(N_i - N_{i+1} \right) \right] \tag{4.4}$$

$$+ R \sum_j MTM_j^+ D_j \left(S_{j-1} - S_j \right)$$

where in the recovery term, MTM_j^+ means the mark-to-market of the swap only when it is positive (since we are seeing the issue from our perspective). From this we can see that, in case of default, the recovery of the swap is on the value of the MTM at time T_j; in the case of the loan the recovery is on the *present value* of the principal at time T_j. We can ask ourselves the question, is the floating-rate loan given by Equation 4.1 equivalent to the combination of the fixed-rate loan given by Equation 4.2 and the swap given by Equation 4.4? The answer is no: although the second term in Equation 4.4 cancels with the first in Equation 4.2, Equation 4.4 is still different from Equation 4.1 because of the recovery amount.

The substitution of a combination of accelerating and nonaccelerating instruments instead of a nonaccelerating one, although in terms of cash flow makes sense, it creates a discrepancy in case of default, which is easy to see when we calculate the fair value of both situations.

---

[11]The way we are going to rewrite it is not necessarily more precise, it is only a way that is more suited to our argument. The discrepancy between the way we usually write swaps and loans as in Equations 4.2 and 4.3 is given by the fact that, in general, swaps are collateralized and therefore, as opposed to loans, do not need to feature survival probabilities in the cash flows. In our example, we assume that our swap is not collateralized and consider the counterparty risk through an explicit survival probability factor and not in other ways (such as, for example, through a CVA). Another way would have been, of course, not to fair value the loan in this example, but then we would have had two external terms, a CVA-like number for the swap and a loan loss provision for the loan, which would have rendered things even less clear. We have preferred to write the swap as given in Equation 4.4, which, although slightly odd, is a least consistent with our argument.

4.4   CASE STUDIES OF DEVELOPMENT PROJECTS

We shall now take a closer look at the type of action a development institution can take in order to offer help to a developing country. These are sample projects, and while realistic, they are in no way identical to actual ones.

The goals of these examples is to show how developing projects are structured and also to show, once the deal is structured, how the risks are shared among the different participants. Often in these projects, the introduction of financial risks in the local market is accompanied by thorough technical help on the part of the development institution so that, by dealing with the risks, the local capital market grows in sophistication.

4.4.1   Rural Development in X

ABC Development Bank and the government of X agreed that a hurdle that needed to be overcome in order for X to grow was the development of its vast rural areas. In this context three points were essential: an encouragement toward private enterprise; a development of market economy, in particular, the banking sector; and easier access to funds for the rural poor.

The project was structured as a wholesale banking operation, meaning that the initial lending was done not to the individuals but to participating financial institutions. This had several advantages including an automatic development of the country's banking system through the competition between the participating financial institutions; a more specific tailoring to the ultimate project through a more personal connection between the participating financial institution and the final borrower; and, in this type of operation, the decrease of the initial lender's credit risk through diversification. This type of operation decreases, through diversification, the credit risk of the initial lender.

The initial lender, the tip of the pyramid in the wholesale operation, was going to be the central bank of X. ABC would offer the initial loan to X and technical assistance to the central bank of X in order to learn how to supervise a wholesale banking operation, to the participating financial institution to teach how to appraise projects and the fundamentals of accounting and financial control, and to the rural poor to increase financial literacy.

The loan was structured as shown in Figure 4.7. ABC would lend to the central bank of X, the central bank of X would lend to the participating financial institutions, which in turn would lend to each individual project. For every 100 units of currency finally used for the project

- Fifteen were put up by the ultimate borrower, the undertaker of the rural project.
- Ten were put up by the participating financial institution.

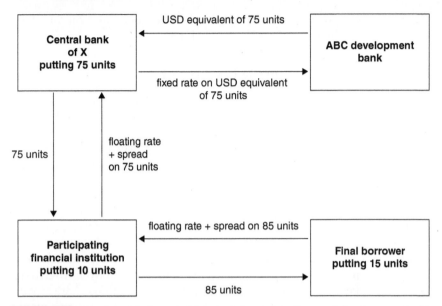

FIGURE 4.7 A schematic representation of the project for rural development in X explaining the provenance of the final 100 units of funds dedicated to an individual project.

- Seventy-five were put up by the central bank of X, which was disbursing the funds obtained by ABC.

Taking account of each actual exposure, the risks were such that

- The participating financial institution would bear the *credit risk* of the final borrower on 85 units of principal.
- The central bank of X would bear the *credit risk* of the participating financial institution on 75 units of principal.
- The central bank would bear the *currency risk* linked to the exchange rate between the currency X of the loans disbursed to the participating financial institutions and the USD loan it received from ABC.
- ABC would bear the *credit risk* of X (in the form of its central bank) on 75 units of principal.

As seen in Figure 4.7, the loan from ABC was a fixed-rate loan and the loans from the central bank to the participating financial institutions and subsequently to the final borrowers were variable-rate loans where the rate was fixed quarterly using the deposit rate as a benchmark on top of which a spread was included to cover the costs of operations.

4.4.2 Development of Textile Exports in Y

ABC Development Bank, after a thorough study of Y's economy, had highlighted an important opportunity for growth in the development of the important textile business toward export. The textile sector already constituted an important part of Y's local economy but, with a loan from ABC, investment could be made to contribute even more toward growth by benefiting from global trade.

The goals were specifically two: the growth of the textile exporting industry and, through influx of hard currency in the country, the development of the currently rudimentary capital market into a more developed kind. The loan from ABC would be accompanied by technical aid. The local participants would be the Industrial and Commercial Bank of Y (a state-backed financial institution, in charge of lending the funds received from ABC to the textile manufacturers) and participating financial institutions charged with initiating transactions between local and hard currency. Consultants would work with the textile manufacturer to offer advice on anything from project management to foreign marketing, and others would work with the participating financial institutions in order to advise on key concepts of public-side banking such as compliance, control, collateral, and risk management, and so on.

The project was structured as shown in Figure 4.8 with the following key transactions:

- ABC would issue a loan in USD to the Industrial and Commercial Bank of Y at LIBOR plus spread.
- For a portion of the total size of the loan, the Industrial and Commercial Bank of Y would enter into a USD versus Y currency cross currency swap with a participating financial institution in which there would be initial and final exchange of principals, and the ICB would pay a fixed rate in Y currency and the participating financial institution would pay LIBOR plus spread on the USD principal.
- The Industrial and Commercial Bank of Y would lend the Y currency principal obtained from the participating financial institution at a fixed rate to a textile manufacturer.
- The textile manufacturer would invest the funds into the exporting business and receive income in USD.
- The textile manufacturer would enter into an FX derivative with a participating financial institution in order to hedge the FX exposure

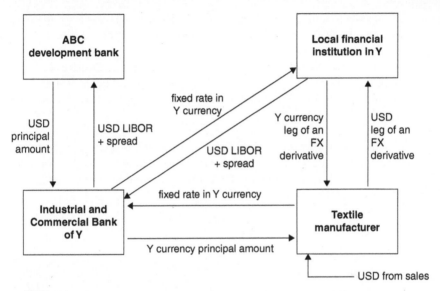

FIGURE 4.8 A representation of the relationship between the different parties involved in the textile export development project.

resulting from the difference in currency between its income and its liability to the Industrial and Commercial Bank.

The structure described above ensures that ABC's loan is repaid in USD with the hard currency income earned from the export business. The route through which the income returns to ABC is such that it injects liquidity and development in the local capital market. Some of the risks faced by each party are:

- ABC is exposed to the *credit risk* of the Industrial and Commercial Bank of Y.
- The Industrial and Commercial Bank of Y mitigates[12] some of the *FX risk* through the cross currency swap but is exposed to *USD LIBOR risk*.
- The Industrial and Commercial Bank of Y is also exposed to the *credit risk* of the manufacturers.

---

[12]The risk is only mitigated and not completely canceled since the swap is fixed for floating.

- The textile manufacturers hedge their *FX risk* through the FX derivative with the participating financial institution but are exposed, through the loan, to *local interest rate risk*.
- For the participating financial institutions, the FX derivative with the manufacturers and the cross currency swap with the Industrial and Commercial Bank of Y partly offset their *FX risk* but they are still exposed to *USD LIBOR risk*.

This particular project, with its focus on local and foreign currencies and local and foreign interest rates, is important in showing how a development project, if successfully carried out, can bring considerable financial expertise to a developing economy.

CHAPTER 5

Bond Pricing

We have built all the tools needed to approach the topic that is at the center of any discussion of credit and the activity of a treasury: debt. We have seen how to generate and discount future cash flows, we have seen how a choice of discounting is highly sensitive to the credit environment, and we have explicitly discussed credit. It is now time to use this knowledge to observe and price debt instruments.

In order to build a self-contained narrative we shall begin with an introduction to the basic concepts surrounding a bond. We shall then move on to the very important issue of trying to isolate the credit component of a bond in a more or less explicit way; we shall present the concepts of benchmarks, asset swaps (introduced here and revisited in the following chapters); and an analysis of the relationship between bonds and credit default swaps. We shall conclude with a section on how to price distressed and/or highly illiquid bonds and one where this final topic is presented through a numerical example.

5.1   WHAT IS A BOND?

We have defined a bond as a way for an entity to raise capital without relinquishing control. Bonds are among the oldest financial instruments and among the first types of securitization,[1] a way of turning the scattered revenues of a government or a corporation into a well-defined and tradable instrument. An entity forecasts a fairly regular set of revenues (from sales for a company or from taxes and investments for a government) but needs an immediate and large cash amount: on the back of its revenues it will issue a bond in which it promises to return the amount at maturity and to

---

[1]The interested reader is directed toward Niall Ferguson's *The House of Rothschild* for a riveting narration of what bond trading was in truly illiquid markets.

pay interest at regular dates. The regularity of the entity's revenues should ensure the regular payment of coupons.

An investor will decide to buy a certain amount of this bond (effectively lending money to the entity) and the price for this bond will be driven by the investor's trust in the entity's abilities to meet its obligations. The price at a time t of a bond B with unit principal is defined as

$$B_t = \sum_i^T C_i D_i dt_i + D_T \tag{5.1}$$

where we remind ourselves that C_i are fixed or variable coupons, D_i are the discount factors, and $dt_i = t_i - t_{i-1}$ are the day count fractions.

Let us state first what might puzzle the mathematically minded reader who appreciates the form given by the above equation: a bond price is just a number. The prices of bonds are driven by people reacting to different stimuli but who almost never think of those prices as given by the neat sum of cash flows described above. This is not saying that traders trade in an imprecise fashion, it simply means that, through instinct and experience, the bond price is enough to mean everything to them. A musical comparison would be with those musicians (rare but who apparently can count Louis Armstrong in their midst) who cannot read music and yet are fully at ease with scales and (basic) musical theory. Of course, siding with the mathematically minded among us, we need to admit that this can only take the practitioner up to a point: the same way one cannot write the *Art of the Fugue* without reading music, one cannot go much beyond bond trading by simply thinking in terms of bond prices.

Derivatives are priced through models that require calibration. To calibrate means to take an observed (i.e., traded) quantity and use it to arrive at another, often more than one, hidden variable in the model: these model variables are implied from market data. The trader only sees the market data and it is enough for him, the quant sees the model variables as well.

Let us consider, for example, the CDS definition given by Equation 3.17: a quant, particularly one fairly new at his job, is often baffled by the ease with which traders think of CDS spreads, their movement, sensitivities to their movement, and so on. This is because, for the quant, what counts is the left-hand side of Equation 3.17, with its integrals, survival probabilities, and optimization. The trader's only concern is the fact that if he sees the value of C go up, the credit standing of the entity in question is deteriorating; if it goes down it is the opposite.

The same applies to bond prices: the quant sees a long list of coupons, forward rates (if it is a variable coupon bond), and discount factors; the trader sees the price. We shall see that this is not entirely true when dealing with a bond's yield, but the main point of this aside is a warning to the young mathematically minded practitioner not to freeze in front of a perceived great complexity. A final analogy will be with language. When learning a foreign language written in a different alphabet, at first we are forced to read words by going through each letter. We are amazed at the speed with which native speakers read, thinking that they must read the letters at great speed. We forget that with practice no one reads a word by scanning the letters, we read words by reaching stored images in our brain of the word itself. Although a bond is made of coupons and discount factors, the seasoned practitioner does not scan and price each of those, he simply concentrates on the overall image, the price.

The relationship between the different elements of Equation 5.1 is, however, very much real and crucial to understand for those of us who are interested in the meaning of the deeper factors that drive an entity's debt. These factors are often implicit and therefore need to be implied from the full definition of a bond. In order to do so let us introduce a few important concepts about bonds. These concepts are presented at an introductory level to render this chapter self-sufficient and to present them in the same formalism and with the same spirit of the remaining part of the book. For a more thorough and extensive discussion of bond fundamentals, the reader is directed toward Fabozzi [38] or Smith [76].

5.2 A FEW FUNDAMENTAL CONCEPTS OF THE BOND WORLD

5.2.1 Par

The price of a bond is expressed as 100 times the percentage of its principal value. The principal value is the amount the investors will receive at maturity: this means that 100 is taken to be the full amount. When the price B_t of a bond is equal to 100 we say that the bond is worth *par*. We have already encountered the concept of par when dealing with swaps and we have already mentioned how, only mathematically though, a bond is similar to the leg of a swap.

Bonds tend to be issued at par, that is, an investor pays the amount that he is expecting to receive at maturity. We already see how this means that at the issue date one of the variables of Equation 5.1 is fixed: $B_0 = 100$.

If the price is given and the discount factors D_i are known, then would all issuers in one currency issue bonds of similar maturity with the same coupon simply chosen so as to lead to 100 when discounted? Of course not.

Within the Euro zone, for example, we know very well that the coupon on a German bond will be much smaller than the coupon on a, say, Spanish bond. This is because we have not considered yet the element of credit.

A further issue with the price of a bond is the concept of *accrued interest*. Accrued interest is the amount accrued by the coupon between the last coupon date and now. We call the price given by Equation 5.1 *clean price* and the price given by the clean price plus the accrued interest is called the *dirty price*. On coupon dates the two prices will be equal, otherwise the dirty price is, of course, always higher: this is to compensate the seller of a bond for the missed coupon payments. If one investor sells on March 1 a bond that pays every first day of December and June, the investor who buys the bond, on the following June 1, will receive the full coupon although he will only have held the bond for half of the accrual period: to compensate the seller he pays the dirty price.

5.2.2 Yield

In the previous section we said that the price of a bond at issue date is always 100: this is not entirely true, however. Since it is very close to par let us continue to consider it as a fix point. What makes bond pricing very interesting is that in a very simple way it allows the user to experience what implying a value means; moreover, since the variables entering the calculation are all roughly equally important, there is a true sense of choice in what we consider a given and what we want to imply.

Let us be more specific by using an example from a different financial field. In the case of an equity option, even assuming that price and volatility are equivalent in importance (which is not the case since a trader will always think in terms of volatility but a quant in terms of price), there are many other variables which enter into a fairly complex equation (Black and Scholes formula) in order to obtain either price or volatility. Interest rates (in the equity world) are always inputs; one would never think of using Black and Scholes' formula to imply them. On the contrary, Equation 5.1 is of a simplicity that anyone with a grasp of arithmetic can appreciate. In addition, we shall see how all its inputs are more or less equally important.

If at issue the bond price is, if not fixed, very close to a fixed value, if the coupon is fixed (we are considering for the moment the case of a fixed rate bond) then something else has to give way for the calculation to be correct. Indeed this is the case and our attention needs to focus on the discount factors.

We have assumed that D_i in Equation 5.1 are the same as the discount factors we have seen up to this point, values implied from interest rate instruments such as deposit, FRAs, swaps, and even overnight rates. This is no longer the case since those instruments implied two specific types of risk. If the trade was collateralized, the implied risk rate was the overnight risk, otherwise, being those types of trades between market participants, it implied a level of risk of type LIBOR.

A bond is not collateralized (it would defeat the purpose of raising cash) and the issuance of a bond is not limited to financial institutions. This means that the level of risk is specific to the institution issuing the bond and this means that D_i is no longer the same as the discount factors we have seen up to this point.

Let us then rewrite Equation 5.1 in the following way

$$B_t = \sum_i^T C_i \, D_i \, \widetilde{D}_i \, dt_i + D_T \widetilde{D}_T \tag{5.2}$$

where $\widetilde{D}_i$ is a new variable. This notation is very different from the one found in the literature: it has its drawbacks and we shall soon converge to the more usual way of discounting bond cash flows. The wish here is to put discounting as far as bonds are concerned in the same mathematical form as discounting in the context of swaps, and discounting and survival probabilities in the context of CDSs. If this notation seems awkward now, when discussing the comparison between the debt and income of a financial institution, hopefully the reader will see how it has significant conceptual advantages.

We can consider $\widetilde{D}_i$ in Equation 5.2 as a correction applied to the discount factor we are familiar with. This correction reflects the credit standing of the issuer.

Let us consider the case of two issuers, A and B, who on the same day issue a bond with maturity in five years' time. Let us consider a situation here similar to the one we have mentioned about Germany and another Euro country: A is the best issuer in one currency and B is one that has a considerably worse credit standing than A.

At issue date, A issues at 100.115 a five-year bond paying a 1.25% annual fixed coupon and B issues at 100.087 a bond with identical maturity and a 3.00% annual coupon. Table 5.1 shows the details of each bond. The first column displays the discount factor D_i obtained through market instruments as discussed in Chapter 2, the third and fifth columns show the cash flows, that is, the coupon each year and the principal payment at maturity, and the second and fourth columns show the correction $\widetilde{D}_i$ for A and B respectively. The correction for issuer A is equal to one: this means that the average rate (let us say the five-year swap rate as a proxy) used to build the

TABLE 5.1 Cash flows of two similar bonds issued by two issuers with different credit standings.

D_i	$\widetilde{D_i}$ for A	Cash flows for A	$\widetilde{D_i}$ for B	Cash flows for B
0.99560	1	1.25	0.98275	3.00
0.98974	1	1.25	0.96585	3.00
0.98069	1	1.25	0.94924	3.00
0.96430	1	1.25	0.93291	3.00
0.94027	1	100.25	0.91683	103.00
	$B_0^A =$	100.115	$B_0^B =$	100.087

discount factors must be very close to 1.25%, the coupon value.[2] The issue price of bond A, B_0^A, is equal to 100.115 to make it realistic: had we insisted on exactly 100, the correction would have been slightly different from 1. The price at issue of bond B, B_0^B, is also close to par but the corrections to the discount factors are very much different from 1.

We have implied the values of the corrections to the discount factors used in B's case by keeping both the issue price and the coupon fixed. The issue price is usually reached through an auction-type sale. There is an announcement of an imminent debt issuance on the part of an entity; the bond has a certain coupon and investors subscribe to the sale. The interest (or lack thereof) drives the issue price. This means that in real life things happen in a slightly different order. The corrections to the discount factors are driven by a market feeling for the entity's credit. The entity itself then sets, *before the auction*, the coupon so that, taking into account the market's feeling, the price is going to be roughly par.

Because the coupon usually takes values no more granular than a quarter of a percentage and because at the auction itself, market feeling can change, the price of the bond cannot be exactly par at issuance. This does not change the fact that an investor at maturity receives the par value. When the price is greater than par, the bond is said to be sold at a *premium*; when it is lower, it is sold at a *discount*. From this little exercise we hope we have shown what was considered interesting as far as bond pricing was concerned: we have played with three elements, the bond price, the coupon, and the corrections and we have shown how, at different moments, some can be kept fixed and some others can be implied.

---

[2]If we pay the same rate we use to discount, we must be at par or, to see it in the same light as this exercise, if we are at par, the rate we use to discount must be the rate we are paying.

It is probably time to stop calling $\widetilde{D}_i$ a correction and move toward a notation more in line with the literature. In Section 2.2.1 and elsewhere where we discussed zero rates, we have shown the relationship between a discount factor and a simple rate. Using a similar approach, let us write

$$D_i \widetilde{D}_i = \frac{1}{(1 + Y)^{T_i - t}} \tag{5.3}$$

substituting into Equation 5.2 we obtain

$$B_t = \sum_i^T \frac{C_i}{(1 + Y)^{T_i - t}} dt_i + \frac{1}{(1 + Y)^{T - t}} \tag{5.4}$$

where we have introduced Y, the *yield* of the bond, or to be more precise the *yield to maturity* of the bond since the calculation assumes that we intend to hold the bond up to maturity. (When pricing bonds, details are very important but some are beyond the scope of this book. The accounting for time, which we have simply expressed as $T_i - t$, presents many nuances based on conventions, day count, holiday calendars, etc. The interested reader is directed toward Smith [76] for an in-depth treatment.)

It is important to note that the yield is one single number. Someone, admittedly misled by our previous formalism, might have been inclined to draw a parallel with discount factors or survival probabilities and write something along the lines of

$$D_i \widetilde{D}_i = \frac{1}{(1 + R_i)^{T_i - t}} \frac{1}{\left(1 + \widetilde{R}_i\right)^{T_i - t}} \tag{5.5}$$

or even

$$D_i \widetilde{D}_i = \frac{1}{(1 + Y_i)^{T_i - t}} \tag{5.6}$$

(note the suffix as opposed to Equation 5.3). This would have been radically different from the concept of yield, which draws its strength exactly from the fact that it is one single number (in nature it is similar to the concept of internal rate of return). Why is this important?

We have stressed at length how, once we set ourselves the target of par value, the higher the coupon the larger the credit-driven correction needs to be and vice versa. Conversely, fixing the coupon price, different levels of corrections will lead to different bond prices. To think in terms of $\widetilde{D}_i$, however, is not easy.

In its simplicity a bond yield allows us a very quick calculation (or at least a feel for the magnitude): knowing either only the bond price but not the coupon or only the coupon but not the bond price, the yield lets us estimate the other very quickly. For example, if a bond trades below par and the yield is y, then we know that the coupon c must be such that $c < y$. Conversely, if we know that a bond pays a coupon C and I know that the yield is such that $C > Y$, we also know that the bond trades above par.

Let us stress the importance of the concept of yield by looking at the word itself. A bond can be roughly considered to be made of two parts, the principal and the coupon. The principal is the amount of money the investor lends to the borrower and is the main component of the deal, the coupon payments can be seen as the compensation the investor requires for delaying the consumption of the principal.[3]

We have seen that the borrower sets the coupon by making sure that, once the bond is discounted and taking into account the market's perception of the borrower's own credit risk, the price is more or less par. This means that the coupon is the element taking care of the borrower's credit. Bonds, however, can be very long dated instruments and between the time the coupon is set and a subsequent time, the credit standing of the borrower might change, making the coupon value irrelevant as a credit signal. Moreover, irrespective of the price paid for the bond, at maturity the investor receives the full principal amount, the unit of measure being the principal amount. Here is where the yield plays a crucial role in telling how much the investment is really yielding. If an investor pays 95 for a bond with a 5% (of 100, of course) annual coupon, then the investment *yields* more than simply 5%.

For the most liquid bonds the yield plays such an important role that it can be traded alongside the bond price (not separately, of course, as the trader chooses to quote one or the other).

5.2.3 Duration

We have not mentioned up to now in any context the concept of sensitivity, that is, the impact of the price of a financial instrument due to a small movement in one of the variables leading to its value. This, of course, is very

---

[3]This might seem a very roundabout, economics-driven way of defining coupon payments. It is meant to be general and linkable to the time value of money; other interpretations can be thought of.

important in finance as it constitutes the foundation of replication, hedging, and risk-neutral pricing. In the interest rate world the most important of these sensitivities is the *PV01* (short for Present Value of 1 basis point), the sensitivity of the instrument to a shift of 1 bps in one of the underlying rates. The fact that we have said "one of" illustrates how a PV01 calculation is not as simple as it is in other asset classes. In equity, the idea of shifting the underlying stock by a fixed amount is fairly clear. When we ask to shift an interest rate by 1 bps, what do we mean exactly?

In Chapter 2 we said how constructing a curve means to calibrate to market data one or more index curves and one discount curve. Each of these curves will have a corresponding PV01.

Let us consider the case shown in Equation 2.13 of a curve built using interest rate, currency basis, and tenor basis swaps. The outcomes of the process are three functions: a discount function D_t and two index functions $f(L_{3M})$ and $f(L_{6M})$ linked to the three- and six-month rates respectively. We then have three PV01s since we have a sensitivity to the market instruments that drive the discounting and a sensitivity to the market instruments that drive each of the index curves. How do we calculate these sensitivities in practice?

Let us imagine that we are calculating the present value V_t of an instrument paying every six months the difference between the five-year and the one-year swap rates

$$V_t = \sum_i D_i \left(S_i^{5Y} - S_i^{1Y} \right) dt_i$$

and we need to estimate its sensitivity to the three curves we have built in our curve construction process.

A small but crucial point is that in a proper PV01 calculation we do *not directly shift* the functions D_t, $f(L_{3M})$, and $f(L_{6M})$. Instead, once we have V_t, we shock the instruments leading to each of them,[4] solve Equation 2.13 each time we do that, recalculate the price of the instrument, take the difference with the original V_t, and obtain three different PV01s. Why is it important each time to go through a calibration process and why can't we simply shock the function we have calculated?

---

[4]Note that in this example, when we shock the instruments we shock them all: if the curve is constructed with, say, deposits, FRAs, and interest rate swaps, we shock all three types of instruments. There is another type of PV01, sometimes called *bucket PV01* or *key rate PV01* where we only want to know the sensitivity to one instrument with a certain maturity and therefore we shock only, for example, the one-year interest rate swap.

First, let us appreciate the fact that the two processes are not equivalent. If, for example, we shift C by 1 bps in Equation 2.13, this will not necessarily translate to a 1-bps shift in $f(L_{6M})$ (the amount will be probably close but not exactly 1 bps). Second, let us think of a PV01 as a hedging tool. If we shift the actual market instrument once we know the sensitivity, this will tell us how much of that market instrument we need to buy or sell to hedge V. While seemingly more complex, the route each time of recalibrating the curve allows us to plug the result directly into our hedging strategy.

Bond pricing has been presented up to now as deliberately simpler than other types of valuation. We have shown in particular a continuous effort to combine interest rate and credit elements in single parameters. The calculation of sensitivity is no different. While we can and often do calculate a bond PV01, we have seen that the main driver of a bond price (at least in the short term) is the market perception of the credit standing of the borrower.

The same way we have introduced the yield as a number able to capture the information of coupon and price (or coupon and credit) simultaneously, we are going to introduce the concept of *duration* as a measure of sensitivity to a shift in yield. If we wanted an analogy, we could say that the duration is to the PV01 what the yield is to the coupon.

The first type of duration we are going to introduce is *modified duration*. Although probably less frequently used, modified duration is closer in spirit to what we would expect sensitivity to look like. Modified duration gives us the sensitivity to a change in yield as a percentage of the bond price, that is,

$$MD = -\frac{1}{V}\frac{\partial B_t}{\partial Y} \tag{5.7}$$

where the minus sign is so that we obtain a positive value. To someone used to Greeks, PV01 and the idea of a sensitivity being a derivative, modified duration is an intuitive concept.

The most frequently used duration, however, is the *Macaulay duration* which is defined as the time-weighted average of the cash flows, that is,

$$McD = -\frac{1}{B_t}\left[\sum_i^T (T_i - t)\frac{C_i}{(1+Y)^{T_i-t}} + (T-t)\frac{1}{(1+Y)^{T_i-t}}\right] \tag{5.8}$$

When we decide to approximate the discrete compounding of the yield with a continuous compounding (using the notation introduced at the beginning of Section 5.1) by doing

$$D_i \widetilde{D}_i = \frac{1}{(1+Y)^{T_i}} \Rightarrow e^{-YT_i}$$

then Macaulay and modified durations are identical. When we do not, which is the majority of situations, the relationship between the two (proof can be found in Appendix D) is

$$MD\,(1 + Y) = McD \qquad (5.9)$$

While similar, the two are profoundly different in terms of quotation. Modified duration, as we said, is a percentage whereas the Macaulay duration is expressed in *years*. The fact that a sensitivity such as duration (from here onward we are going to drop "Macaulay" and treat Macaulay duration as the default, specifying when we mean modified duration) is expressed in years might seem very odd, particularly to the more mathematically minded users. A sensitivity being a derivative, the argument would be, should be in the units of the numerator by the units of the variable we shift or, as in the case of PV01 where we accept a standard shift, in the unit of the numerator.[5]

While none of these will probably dislodge completely the feeling in some readers' minds that duration does not look like a real sensitivity, there are many reasons for it. Some of these reasons are due to ease of calculation, some are born out of practice, and others have a real financial character. First we need to stress that the concept of duration was introduced in the 1930s as a computationally easy tool to assess a bond's risk. Nowadays, particularly for a simple instrument such as a bond, shocking curves, coupons, and maturities are trivial exercises: in the days before spreadsheets it was a lot more labor intensive.

A more financially minded (and less mathematical) way of seeing duration is the idea of the time taken for a bond to cover its cost, where by cost here we mean a measure that includes the cost of risk. If we have a zero coupon bond, that is, a bond that pays only the principal at the end, we recover our cost only at maturity. Needless to say, this entails not only a large credit risk but also a great sensitivity to interest rate moves. If we have coupons paid between now and maturity, in a way we bring forward that date on which we will have recovered our cost/risk. The duration in years is the time between now and that date brought forward. For zero coupon bonds, duration is equal to maturity for coupon bearing bonds—the higher

---

[5]In practice in a PV01 calculation, if we are observing the sensitivity of instrument f to rate r we do

$$PV01 = \frac{df}{dr}\Delta r$$

where Δr is the standard amount of 1 bps. The units of PV01 are therefore the units of f, that is, money.

the coupon the shorter the duration is and it is always less than the time to maturity.

A final way of thinking about duration is to say that the yield sensitivity of a coupon bearing bond is equal to that of a zero coupon bond with maturity equal to the duration of the coupon bearing bond. This in turn is helpful since the sensitivity of a zero coupon bond is quite easy to grasp being roughly linear with time. The importance of duration, at least as far as terminology is concerned, matters to us since many times swaps set in place to hedge interest rate sensitivity are referred to as duration swaps.

5.3 EXPRESSING CREDIT EXPLICITLY WHEN PRICING A BOND

In Sections 5.2.1 and 5.2.2 we spoke at great length of the role played by the credit standing of the borrower when it comes to pricing a bond. In particular, we have seen how the concept of yield plays a fundamental role by simply and directly combining information about the coupon of a bond and the worth (hence the implicit credit risk) of the investment.

There are, however, situations in which we do not want to use such an immediate tool and we wish to isolate the credit element of bond price. We shall introduce some of the most useful ones.

5.3.1 Benchmarks and z-Spreads

In Equations 5.5 and 5.6 we have shown how *not* to calculate a bond yield. Those equations nonetheless are examples of other attempts to separate the interest rate component from the credit component in the discount factor applied to bond cash flows.

We have repeated many times, beginning in Chapter 2, that when we deal with a set of payments that includes a final principal, and if we discount with the same rate we use for coupon payments, the value of the leg is more or less par. This means that if we have a par leg paying a higher coupon rate than the one used for discounting or if we have a leg paying a similar coupon but which prices to less than par, there must be some further parameter involved in discounting. An intuitive way of visualizing this extra element is to think of a spread we add on to the normal discount rate (by normal we mean the one implied from interest rate instruments).

We would then write the bond value as

$$B_t = \sum_i \frac{C_i}{(1 + R_i + b)^{T_i - t}} dt_i + \frac{1}{(1 + R_i + b)^{T_i - t}} \tag{5.10}$$

where R_i is some interest rate and b is some spread we add to it. For the avoidance of doubt, in the absence of b, we would imply from R_i the usual discount factors D_i. In the way the discounting is written in Equation 5.10, we have separated an interest rate component from a credit component. The credit component should be technically defined as a non-interest-rate component in the sense that it might include factors (such as liquidity for example, see Schwarz [75]) that are beyond credit; however, since credit risk is the main driver of b we can safely call it a credit component. One could even claim that nowadays to suggest the existence of a pure interest rate component (with its risk-free connotation) does not make much sense since, one of the main arguments of this book, credit is everywhere. To be more precise then, we could call R_i the component that *could*[6] be implied from interest rate instruments and b the other, mainly credit-driven, component. Being a rather awkward set of definitions, we will remain with the former being the interest rate and the latter the credit component.

Once we have separated the two components we can decide what rate we use as reference point, that is, what the rate R_i is that we want to measure the credit risk of our bond relative to. The choice of reference points is usually driven by the habits of the trader using it. Some options are shown highlighted in Figure 5.1 where we look at the quote for a French government bond paying a 3.75% coupon and expiring on January 12, 2012.

The most important reference point is the *benchmark*, that is, a benchmark bond to which the bond we are considering is compared to. This is usually the most liquid and least risky bond in a certain currency. For example, in the case of the French government bond shown in Figure 5.1, the benchmark bond is the German three-month government bond.

The benchmark spread of x bps states that the bond we are considering yields x bps more (hence is riskier) than the benchmark. The number is usually always positive since, as we said, the benchmark tends to be the least risky bond available in that currency. In the example shown in Figure 5.1, the French government bond yields 30.9 bps more than the three-month German government bond. All the bonds issued by Euro area countries are measured against German treasuries (government bonds are often referred to as treasuries). In late 2011 the spread varied from a few tens of basis

---

[6]The italics are due to the fact that, as we shall see throughout the rest of the chapter, to imply variables from one traded quantity, the bond price, is not very easy, which means that not everything can be precisely implied at the same time. Being people usually more interested in credit, the interest rate component is generally assumed rather than implied and used as a springboard toward implying the credit one.

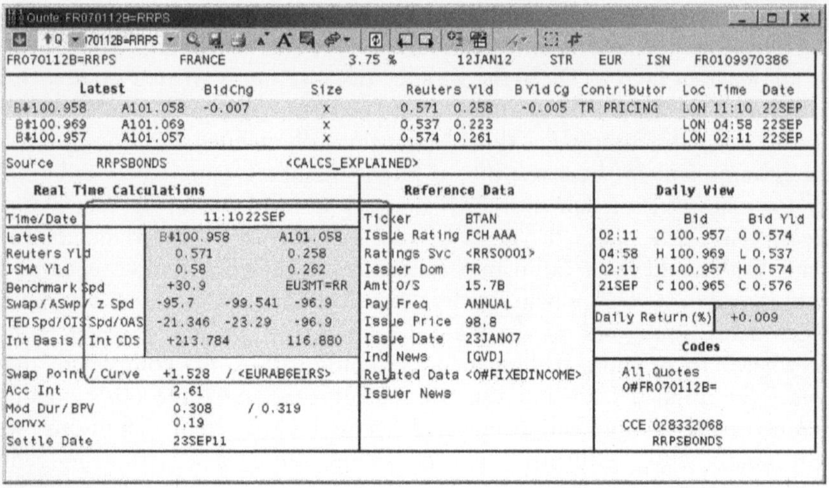

FIGURE 5.1 A sample quote for a French government bond with the different benchmarks highlighted. *Source*: Thomson Reuters Eikon.

points, as in the case of France, to a few thousand basis points, as in the case of Portugal and Greece.

If we want to apply the benchmark spread information we take the yield Y of the benchmark and we set $R_i = Y$ (note the suffix: we set *all* R_i equal to the yield) in Equation 5.10 and then set b in the same equation equal to the benchmark spread. In light of what we have just said about interest rate and credit components, it might seem a little odd to set R_i equal to Y. Didn't we just say that a yield also contains credit information and R_i shouldn't? The question is certainly valid but we are making the assumption that the benchmark is so devoid of credit risk that its yield is almost solely driven by interest rate moves.

The next reference point of note is the spread given in comparison to a *reference swap rate*. In this case we take a swap rate—in Figure 5.1 the value shown is 1.528% and we are told, not surprisingly, that it is the local EUR interest rate swap rate—and we add the swap spread, which we are also told is −95.7 bps. This combined value is then used as a yield in our calculations.

In the case of a government bond of a country with a good credit standing such as France, we are not surprised to see that the spread is negative. Let us remind ourselves that a swap rate is a LIBOR-driven value, that is, it carries a risk of borrowing of the same order of magnitude of an investment bank. One would assume a financially sound government to have a lower level of risk. Let us do a little check to see if all these numbers make sense.

All spreads are relative measures, however, we also have an absolute quote, the reference swap rate. If we take the reference swap rate and add the (negative) swap spread we are left with 0.571%; if from this value we subtract the benchmark spread of 30.9 bps we have 26.2 bps. What should this value represent? It should give us the yield of the German treasury, which, with an actual value of 25 bps (not shown in the figure), is close to the implied value we have just calculated.

The benchmark spread and the spread relative to the swap rate are very important because they give each a sense of relative measure compared to two very different worlds: the almost riskless world of treasuries and the risky world of interdealers borrowing.

The next spread and probably one of the most commonly used is the *z-spread*. This spread is the value that one would add to the zero rate of the corresponding maturity. This means that in Equation 5.10 R_i is the zero rate corresponding to the cash flow at time T_i and b is the z-spread.[7]

We have mentioned before in Section 2.4.3 that a zero rate is not a traded instrument and as a consequence, although it has the same structure as a cash deposit, it is not an official quantity as to whose value all market participants agree. However, because of its simplicity it is also a quantity everyone can easily grasp conceptually. If a bank A wants to borrow a certain amount of money, what is the simplest rate it can be charged? A rate fixed today payable every year, that is, the zero rate. Once we grasp this very simple concept and imagine the situation of a second borrower, a nonfinancial institution B, it is easy to see the extra cost B will be charged as a spread over the zero rate.

We have been surprisingly specific as to the nature of the business of A and B. Why? Although the zero rate is not a traded quantity, it is assumed that it is a quantity calculated after having built a curve according to the methodologies shown in Chapter 2. Since those methodologies involved the use of a great deal of LIBOR-driven market instruments, it is assumed that a zero rate would carry the intrinsic risk level of a financial institution. It is then understandable that a government such as France would have a negative z-spread since we would expect it to have a safer credit standing than the average institution relying on LIBOR levels of borrowing.

As one can see from Figure 5.1 there are other spreads shown in a standard bond quote. Some go beyond our scope and some, such as the relationship between bonds and CDS, will be treated later. The last of the most

---

[7] As a reminder, we have defined the relation between the zero rate R_i and the discount factor D_i as

$$D_i = \frac{1}{(1 + R_i)^{T_i}}$$

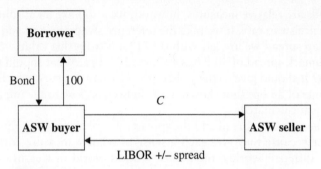

FIGURE 5.2   A schematic representation of a (par) asset swap at inception.

common reference spreads is the asset swap spread, and since it is central to our discourse on funding, we shall discuss it in a specially dedicated section.

5.3.2   Asset Swaps

In Figure 5.1 between the spread to a reference swap rate and the z-spread we see the *asset swap spread* quoted. In order to appreciate its importance we need to show the basics of an asset swap structure.

As represented in Figure 5.2 an asset swap consists of a structure where an investor (the asset swap buyer) holding a bond transfers the bond's coupon onto another party (the asset swap seller), who in returns pays the investor LIBOR plus or minus a spread, the asset swap spread.

One could consider an asset swap as a way, on the bond holder's part, to achieve two things: to monetize the bond's credit risk and to do this relative to a standard benchmark such as a LIBOR. The ownership of the bond remains with the bond holder (the asset swap buyer); in case of default the bond holder will bear the brunt of it settling for the recovery rate of the bond. In case of default the swap does not terminate automatically, meaning the bond holder is still liable for the swap coupon payments unless the swap is exited (which usually is done at terms that are suboptimal for the asset swap buyer in these situations[8]). The asset swap spread is meant to offer the bond holder a way to hedge the credit risk of the bond. How is the asset swap spread calculated in practice?

---

[8]This is true in general; however, as we shall see later, Treasuries use asset swaps in the opposite direction, that is, they issue a bond and then they swap the liability. In these situations there is a clear linkage between bond and swap, and usually when the bond terminates so does the swap (but not vice versa).

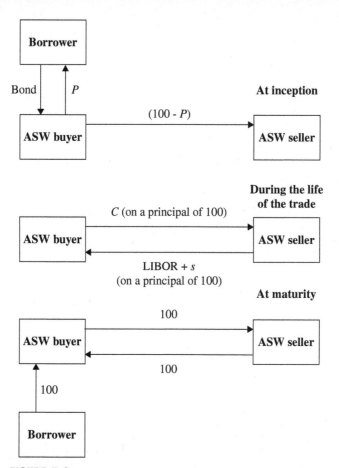

FIGURE 5.3 A detailed representation of a par asset swap, where P is the bond price.

Before proceeding let us elaborate on our simple picture given by Figure 5.2 where we specify that it shows a par asset swap at inception. This means that the swap was entered into at the same time the bond was issued and both instruments were worth par. While, we shall see in great detail later, a treasury entering into an asset swap structure will always do so at inception and usually at par, let us for the moment maintain a general tone and assume that we are dealing with the situation of an investor who purchases a (fixed rate, for simplicity) bond not at inception and wishes to swap it for a stream of floating payments. The investor has two options, either to enter a *par asset swap* as shown in Figure 5.3 or a *market* or *proceeds asset swap* as shown in Figure 5.4.

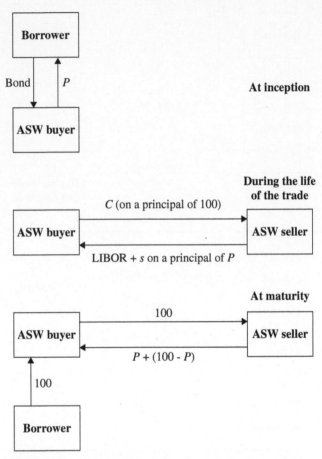

FIGURE 5.4 A detailed representation of a market (or proceeds) asset swap, where P is the bond price.

In Figure 5.3 we have assumed that the bond the investor is swapping is worth less than par. In this situation, one of a par asset swap, the investor needs to pay the asset swap seller up-front the difference between par value and the current bond price. This is because otherwise the investor would begin the swap with a free mark-to-market gain. One could think of this in terms of a fictitious principal exchange: if we were to exchange par principals, the seller would offer the full principal and the buyer would need to do that as well, hence the difference between the bond price and par. During the life of the swap the buyer turns over the coupons C (on a full principal) to the seller and the seller pays a spread over LIBOR to the buyer. At maturity each would pay the full final cash flow and the buyer would also receive the principal from the bond issuer. Now that we have seen the picture in full, how do we calculate the asset swap spread? The situation when the bond is currently worth P, seen from the point of view of the investor, can be expressed mathematically as

$$-(1 - P) + \sum_i (L_i + s_A) D_i dt_i - \sum_j C_j D_j dt_j$$
$$= -P + \sum_j C_j D_j \widetilde{D}_j dt_j + D_T \widetilde{D}_T \tag{5.11}$$

In the above on the right-hand side we have the purchase of the bond at a price P and an income stream of coupons discounted on a curve adjusted for the credit risk of the issuer. On the left-hand side we have the up-front payment and, for the investor, an income stream of LIBOR payments plus a spread s_A and a cost stream of coupons all discounted on a LIBOR-driven (or OIS-driven as shown in Chapter 2) curve. The asset swap spread s_A is calculated such that at inception the above structure is fair. In the above we have assumed only one currency for the sake of simplicity and we have assumed that the frequency of the bond is the same as the floating leg payments. We now see how useful it is to use the terminology introduced in Section 5.2.2 in which we use a credit correction $\widetilde{D}_j$ to the discount factor. This means that on the right-hand side of Equation 5.11 we do not need to concern ourselves for the moment with how we discount the bond, how we get to the correct yield, and so on. What is crucial is that the same fixed coupon C_j is discounted in two different ways on two sides of Equation 5.11.

In Figure 5.4 we describe the situation of a market (or proceeds) asset swap. The investor (or asset swap buyer) has bought a bond at a price P, which is less than the full par value, and instead of entering into a swap with principal 1 he enters into a swap with principal P. During the life of the swap the investor pays the coupons from the bond and receives a set of floating payments on a P principal. However, the coupons and, crucially, the final payment, since they need to match the bond, refer to a full principal which means that the asset swap buyer will pay 1 at maturity to the asset swap seller who will need to increase the natural final payment of the swap, which would have been P, by an amount $(1 - P)$. Mathematically we can express this, again from the point of view of the investor, as

$$P \sum_i (L_i + s_{MA}) D_i dt_i + P D_T + (1 - P)D_T - \sum_j C_j D_j dt_j - D_T$$
$$= -P + \sum_j C_j D_j \widetilde{D}_j dt_j + D_T \widetilde{D}_T \tag{5.12}$$

The asset swap spread s_{MA} is again the spread that renders the whole structure above fair at inception. For other types of asset swaps and an interesting discussion on the sensitivities of asset swaps, one should see O'Kane [66]. In Equation 5.11 we have highlighted the initial up-front payment that corrects for the fact that the bond price is not par. Previously, in Equation 5.12 we have highlighted the last additional payment, and in order to do so we have included the last principal exchange cash flows in the swap on the left-hand side. As odd as it might seem, this is to show that, whereas in the par asset swap the principal is the same on both swap legs (the principal exchanges are nonexistent since it is a single currency swap), in the market asset swap it isn't and this is because the coupon leg of the swap always has to mirror the bond. Perhaps it is useful to stress it again to avoid confusion. There isn't a real principal exchange at the end, only the additional payment on the asset swap seller side. We have written it in this form in Equation 5.12 for didactic purposes only.

Of the spreads that can be used to characterize the credit risk of a bond, benchmarks, swap spreads, and z-spreads are useful indicators to compare different issuers, even across different types of maturities. They are, however, not useful calculation tools and certainly they are not trading tools. No trader would trade a bond using the reference spreads to swap rates, benchmark bonds, or z-spreads (we shall see later, however, how they can be useful to arrive to tradable values for illiquid bonds).

Asset swap spreads, on the other hand, are not useful credit indicators because they are driven by the bond price, which in itself is driven by many factors, credit or noncredit related. The spread can be useful to compare two issuers only if we compare two bonds trading roughly at the same price and with similar issue and maturity dates. (For this precise purpose, on the other hand, an asset swap is an extremely useful tool and probably the only one rigorous enough.) However, asset swap spreads are real calculation tools and are tradable values, that is, it is a number a trader would quote. They are particularly important for our discussion because, as we shall see later, asset swap structures constitute the essence of funding and treasury operations. The funding level of an institution is in essence the asset swap at inception of a recently issued bond.

We shall conclude our analysis of bond credit with a look at the relationship between bonds and credit default swaps.

5.3.3   Constructing a CDS-Implied Credit Framework for Bond Pricing

After discussing the credit element of a bond price, the reader might be tempted to wonder, given that credit default swaps were created to offer protection against bond defaults, can we leverage the information given by a CDS rate in order to price a bond? In principle this would be possible, but there are a few important caveats to consider.

Let us first take an intuitive step: we are going to obtain the price B_t of a bond by multiplying each cash flow by the survival probability of the issuer in a way similar to the one we used to fair value loans in Section 3.3.1. In this framework a bond with principal N will have a price B_t given by

$$B_t = N \sum_i C_i e^{-r_i T_i} S_i dt_i + N e^{-r_T T} S_T \tag{5.13}$$

where we have simplified the discounting by setting $D_i = e^{-r_i T_i}$ with r_i some continuously compounded rate (very similar in nature to a zero rate). We have seen in Section 4.2.3 (and prove in Appendix B) that one could approximate the probability of default by dividing the CDS rate by one minus recovery, that is,

$$1 - S_i \approx \frac{CDS_i}{1 - R}$$

In turn, by using a simple binomial expansion one can show that, at least for short maturities,

$$S_i = e^{-h_i T_i} \approx 1 - h_i T_i$$

Combining the above two equations we obtain

$$h_i \approx \frac{CDS_i}{1 - R} \tag{5.14}$$

(Note that we have written h_i instead of $h_i T_i$: this is because, in our approximation, we assume it to be an annualized rate like the CDS rate on the other side of the equation.)

Writing the survival probability explicitly in Equation 5.13 and using as hazard rate the value found in Equation 5.14, we obtain for B_t

$$\begin{aligned} B_t &= N \sum_i C_i e^{-r_i T_i} e^{-\frac{CDS_i}{1-R} T_i} dt_i + N e^{-r_T T} e^{-\frac{CDS_i}{1-R} T} \\ &= N \sum_i C_i e^{-\left(r_i + \frac{CDS_i}{1-R}\right) T_i} dt_i + N e^{-\left(r_T + \frac{CDS_i}{1-R}\right) T} \end{aligned} \tag{5.15}$$

We also know, using Equation 5.10 with a rate continuously compounded, that the price of a bond can be expressed by adding a z-spread z to an interest rate component and therefore write B_t as

$$B_t = N \sum_i C_i e^{-(r_i+z)T_i} dt_i + N e^{-(r_T+z)T} \qquad (5.16)$$

From Equation 5.15 and 5.16 we see that a CDS rate is (roughly because of some approximations) equivalent to a z-spread in the special case of a zero recovery bond. The situation of a zero recovery bond, however, is an idealized one and in practice (as shown in great detail by Berd et al. [12] and Pedersen [68]) things are more interesting.

From the above we see that the shortcut taken by some of simply treating the CDS rate as a z-spread and using it to build a correction to the discount factor is fundamentally flawed. To divide the CDS rate by one minus recovery (essentially using Equation 5.15) is an improvement. A more sophisticated approach would be to calibrate a set of survival probabilities S_i to CDS rates as shown in Section 3.2.2 and write the bond price B_t taking into account recovery, that is,

$$B_t = N \sum_i C_i D_i S_i dt_i + N D_T S_T + N(1-R) \sum_j \left(S_j - S_{j-1}\right) D_j \qquad (5.17)$$

where we have returned to writing discount factors as D_i, the more general form.[9] Equation 5.17 states that we have a stream of cash flows including a final payment that are all contingent on the survival of the issuer plus a payment of one minus recovery in case of default.

The approach given by Equation 5.17 is more sophisticated, but sometimes it can misrepresent reality. However, at this point we need to state our objective clearly. To calibrate or to imply (as we will discuss further in Section 5.4.1) model variables means using a model to reprice a market variable: it is crucial that one is observable and the other is not.

Although the above statement is correct in all situations, if we assume that whenever something is not observable we are using a model to find it, let us rephrase things slightly differently. In finance we often use one piece

---

[9]Some readers might be slightly annoyed by this continuous change in the discount factor formalism. As an apology we can only say that we find the general form D_i intellectually pure, based on the fact that everyone agrees on what the concept of present value is (but not on how to get there). We abandon it only when it is really necessary and try to revert to it as soon as possible.

of market information to find another piece of information/variable. Almost by definition, if we are trying to find the latter, this is unknown. There are some situations, however, where this is not the case and we are facing what at first appears to be an inconsistency.

When dealing with bonds and CDSs we might be in one of three situations: we have bond prices, easily available but not CDS rates, we have CDS rates easily available but not bond prices, or both are easily available.

In the first situation, Equation 5.17 will be a calibration tool rather than a bond pricing tool. Since we do not have CDS rates easily available we cannot arrive at Equation 5.17 with an already calibrated set of survival probabilities obtained as shown in Section 3.2.2. Instead we would use it to obtain S_i. Of course in order to build a term structure of survival probabilities we would need an equation such as Equation 5.17 for several different maturities.

In the second situation (an absence of bond prices), we would use Equation 5.17 as a pricing tool and we would be satisfied with the value of B_t. Note that in this statement we are using an "absence of evidence is evidence of absence" approach: if we cannot show that the bond price obtained through the use of Equation 5.17 is wrong, then it must be correct. In this we are using a principle similar to the one that can be applied to the currency basis swap introduced in Section 2.3: if it is not traded we can assume it to be zero.

The mentioning of the currency basis (in the context of the calibration of S_i to existing CDS quotes) is not casual. We could find ourselves in the third situation, one where we use Equation 5.17 and it does not lead to to the traded price B_t. The discrepancy between the two is explained by the *bond-CDS basis*. We have mentioned before that in finance a basis is a way of quantifying and trading what appears to be an inconsistency. In this case the inconsistency is the fact that the survival probabilities implied from CDS rates do not describe the credit risk associated with a bond. We said in Section 3.1.1 that a CDS is a way of turning a risky bond into a riskless one. If we purchase a risky bond we have a large risky return: if we choose to use some of that return to purchase protection in the form of a CDS then we expect to have the same (lower) return as a riskless bond (e.g., a treasury bond). This is valid in theory but in practice we can find ourselves with a higher or lower return according to the sign of the bond-CDS basis. In this situation we need to write Equation 5.17 as

$$B_t = N \sum_i C_i D_i \overline{S_i} dt_i + N D_T \overline{S_T} + N(1-R) \sum_j \left(\overline{S_j} - \overline{S_{j-1}} \right) D_j \qquad (5.18)$$

where the new survival probability $\overline{S_i}$ is obtained (a variation of Equation 3.16) calibrating to

$$
\begin{aligned}
(C + CDS_{basis}) \sum_i D_i & \left\{ \overline{S_i} + \frac{1}{2}_{PA} \left[\overline{S_{i-1}} - \overline{S_i} \right] \right\} dt_i \\
& = (1 - R) \sum_n D_n \left[\overline{S_{n-1}} - \overline{S_n} \right]
\end{aligned}
\tag{5.19}
$$

where, for simplicity, we have assumed the old quotation with only a running coupon C and where CDS_{basis} can be either positive or negative.

Although the idea of calculating a bond-CDS basis (in itself a double calibration, of the basis and of the survival probabilities) might seem pointless when we have both CDS rates and bond prices, there are situations in which it could be useful. First, there could be a situation where the presence of both bond prices and CDS rates happens only for certain maturities: the basis found for those maturities can then be applied with some extrapolation to those maturities where we only have, say, CDS rates. In the same spirit, which we shall apply in Section 5.4.3, a basis found for a certain issuer can contain useful information that we might use to price similar bonds issued by other entities.

5.4 ILLIQUID BONDS

In Section 5.2.2 we argued, when trying to separate the interest rate from the credit component in the discounting of a bond, that other factors next to credit contribute to the correction to the usual discount factors: one of these was liquidity. Liquidity has a great impact on the pricing of bonds (see Schwarz [75] or Acharya and Pedersen [1]), impact that presents itself, in a more or less explicit way, in the form of a spread over a risk-free rate.

An investor choosing between two bonds would apply the same reasoning valid for any asset. Between two assets the preference would go toward the one offering an easy secondary market, that is, the possibility to exchange the asset for cash in an easy and fast manner. The more difficult one must compensate with a more attractive price and/or a higher coupon.

There are many concatenated issues around this. There is a link (see Brunnermeier and Pedersen [22]) between the funding liquidity of an institution and market liquidity in general (traders are unable to fund their positions) that translates into liquidity premia on assets in general. Another interesting point is made by Adrian and Shin [2] on the connection between leverage and liquidity. This in particular will be important shortly, appearing in the form of market presence, when discussing the pricing of bonds in emerging market currencies. A common feature throughout the literature is to stress an inverse relationship between liquidity and volatility.

In this section we will try to give a few examples of situations where we might need to price bonds with very low liquidity.

5.4.1 Pricing at Recovery

In Section 3.1.2, when introducing the concept of credit default swap, we mentioned the recovery rate of a bond. In the past the protection buyer would exchange the bond itself for the par value and the protection seller would be left with whatever was left of the bond, the recovery rate.

The recovery rate is not a clear concept and, as we have said before, it is not a value that, at least in the context of CDSs, is traded in itself: it is always assumed. When an entity is rather safe from default, a CDS is quoted, sometimes using the rule of thumb that a sovereign offers a recovery rate of 25% and a corporate a recovery rate of 40%. This is because, in case of corporate defaults, there is usually a well-structured process in place where investors can hope to seize a decent amount of assets. This process, because of their rarity and because by definition it would be a transnational one, is not in place for sovereign defaults.

This simple rule of thumb is valid when we are estimating the recovery rate of an entity that is still in good credit standing. As the entity's credit deteriorates however, the concept of recovery, becoming more real in the mind of investors, starts becoming more precise.

Let us place ourselves in the position of a protection seller. The more the default of the entity we are asked to provide protection on seems certain, the more we are going to charge an amount very similar to the one we are eventually going to offer, that is, the difference between par and the recovery rate. The more we are edging closer to default, the more the credit default swap price and the bond price itself will make the recovery rate value almost explicit. This of course is because the element we are usually solving for, default probability, becomes almost an input and frees the role of unknown variable. In this situation a bond is said to trade at recovery, meaning that its price is close to its (assumed) recovery rate.

In Figure 5.5 we are showing quotes of corporate bonds trading at recovery (respectively AIFUL Corporation, Clear Channel Communications Inc., Energy Future Holdings Corporation, and The PMI Group Inc.) and in Figure 5.6 we are showing quotes for Greece government bonds, also trading at recovery.

The first thing we notice is, of course, how low the prices of these bonds are. Values of this order of magnitude are usually easier to find in the corporate bond world than in the sovereign one: Greece is, hopefully, an exception.

| JP011231063=RRPS | | AIFUL | | 3.5 % | | 05JUN15 | STR | JPY | ISN | XS0112310635 |

Latest		BidChg	Size	Reuters Yld		B Yld Cg	Contributor	Loc Time	Date
B↓39.503	A39.803	+0.033	x	33.236	32.971	-0.007	TR PRICING	LON 05:35	03OCT
B↑39.524	A39.824		x	33.217	32.952			LON 05:15	03OCT
B↓39.501	A39.801		x	33.238	32.973			LON 02:55	03OCT

| 184502AX0=RRPS | | CLEAR CHA COMM | | 5.500 % | | 15DEC16 | STR | USD | ISN | US184502AX06 |

Latest		BidChg	Size	Reuters Yld		B Yld Cg	Contributor	Loc Time	Date
B↓38.0000	IA40.0000	+2.0000	x	29.570	28.1469	-1.511	TR PRICING	NYC 10:48	03OCT
B↓36.0000	IA38.0000		x	31.093	29.5702			07:21	03OCT
B36.0000	A38.0000		x	31.093	29.5702			21:21	02OCT

| 873168AN8= | | ENERGY FUTURE HD | | 6.500 % | | 15NOV24 | STR | USD | ISN | US873168AN84 |

Latest		BidChg	Size	Reuters Yld		B Yld Cg	Contributor	Loc Time	Date
B↓36.0000	IA37.0000	-2.0000	x	20.981	20.4849	+0.973	TR PRICING	NYC 11:42	03OCT
B↓38.0000	IA39.0000		x	20.009	19.5549			07:21	03OCT
B38.0000	A39.0000		x	20.009	19.5549			21:20	02OCT

| 69344MAK7=RRPS | | PMI GROUP | | 4.500 % | | 15APR20 | CNV | USD | ISN | US69344MAK71 |

Latest		Contributor	Loc Time	Date	Equity	Edge(%)	Prem(%)	ImplVol(%)	Delta(%)
B↓30.7733	IA31.7733	TR PRICING	NYC 07:28	03OCT	0.2	-74.32	26.1000		82.048
B30.7733	A31.7733		21:00	02OCT					
B30.7733	A31.7733		16:04	30SEP					

FIGURE 5.5   A collection of corporate bonds pricing near recovery. *Source*: Thomson Reuters Eikon.

At this point we need to state that the concept of trading or pricing at recovery does not necessarily fall within the discussion of illiquidity: the bid-offer spreads shown for the quotes in Figures 5.5 and 5.6 are quite tight despite the dire financial situation of the respective issuers. However, it is not unusual, particularly in the situation of emerging markets, for the two phenomena to appear simultaneously, that is, a drying up of the market combined with a worsening credit situation.

| GR035733302=RRPS | | GREECE | | 1.66 % | | 11APR16 | FRN | EUR | ISN | XS0357333029 |

Latest		Bid Chg	Size	Reuters Yld		B Yld Cg	Contributor	Loc Time	Date
B↑39.538	A41.538	-0.248	x	24.904	23.594	+0.188	TR PRICING	LON 10:55	03OCT
B↓38.895	A40.895			25.341	24.007		TR PRICING	LON 06:03	03OCT
B↑39.810	A41.810			24.714	23.414		TR PRICING	LON 02:21	03OCT

| GR19071910G=RRPS | | GREECE | | 6 % | | 19JUL19 | STR | EUR | ISN | GR0124031650 |

Latest		BidChg	Size	Reuters Yld		B Yld Cg	Contributor	Loc Time	Date
B↓40.163	A42.163	+2.121	x	23.314	22.246	-1.214	TR PRICING	LON 11:28	03OCT
B↑40.185	A42.185		x	23.302	22.234		REUTERS_EVAL	LON 11:08	03OCT
B↑40.169	A42.169		x	23.311	22.243		REUTERS_EVAL	LON 10:55	03OCT

| GR20071810G=RRPS | | GREECE | | 4.6 % | | 20JUL18 | STR | EUR | ISN | GR0124030645 |

Latest		BidChg	Size	Reuters Yld		B Yld Cg	Contributor	Loc Time	Date
B↑40.067	A42.067	+0.342	x	22.707	21.614	-0.188	TR PRICING	LON 11:28	03OCT
B↑40.095	A42.095		x	22.691	21.600		REUTERS_EVAL	LON 11:08	03OCT
B↑40.069	A42.069		x	22.705	21.613		REUTERS_EVAL	LON 10:55	03OCT

| GR2008145YG=RRPS | | GREECE | | 5.5 % | | 20AUG14 | STR | EUR | ISN | GR0114022479 |

Latest		BidChg	Size	Reuters Yld		B Yld Cg	Contributor	Loc Time	Date
B↓40.256	A42.256	+0.012	x	47.738	45.073	+0.023	TR PRICING	LON 10:55	03OCT
B↑40.315	A42.315		x	47.657	44.997		REUTERS_EVAL	LON 10:08	03OCT
B↑40.328	A42.328		x	47.639	44.981		REUTERS_EVAL	LON 09:28	03OCT

FIGURE 5.6   A collection of four Greek government bonds pricing near recovery. *Source*: Thomson Reuters Eikon.

Official Close			Reference Data	
ParSpread 6442.570 29SEP11			Ref Entity	
Real Time Calculations			HELLENIC REPUBLIC	
Time/Date : 30SEP11			Term /Cur/Rank 3Y /USD /SNRFOR	
			Credit Event Cum-Restruct	
Coupon	Upfront(%)	ConvSprd	Trading Conv "	
25	59.437	10345.31	Fixed Coupon 500	
100	58.743	9255.79	Maturity Date 20DEC14	
500	55.042	7733.442	Ratings	
1000	50.42	7207.51	S&P CC	
CDS Spread Over:			Moody's Ca	
Rating			Fitch CCC	
Sector / Sub Sect			Ratings Svc <RRS1230>	
			Sector SOV	

Official Close			Reference Data	
ParSpread 4720.240 30SEP11			Ref Entity	
Real Time Calculations			THE PMI GROUP, INC.	
Time/Date : 03OCT11			Term /Cur/Rank 10Y/USD /SNRFOR	
			Credit Event Ex-Restruct	
Coupon	Upfront(%)	ConvSprd	Trading Conv "	
25			Fixed Coupon 500	
100	70.317	0	Maturity Date 20DEC21	
500	64.230	0	Ratings	
1000			S&P CC	
CDS Spread Over:			Moody's	
Rating			Fitch CCC	
Sector / Sub Sect			Ratings Svc N/A	
			Sector OFN	

FIGURE 5.7   CDS quotes of entities trading at recovery. *Source*: Thomson Reuters Eikon.

It is useful to combine the information given by Figures 5.5 and 5.6 to the one shown by Figure 5.7 where we show the three-year CDS quote for the Hellenic Republic of Greece and the 10-year CDS quote for The PMI Group Inc. In a deteriorating credit situation we appreciate the importance of the new CDS quotation we discussed in Section 3.2.3 where the protection buyer pays a standard coupon plus an up-front fee. As the default of the entity on which protection is traded becomes more and more certain, the protection seller needs to make sure that the funds needed to offer protection are there to compensate the buyer.

From Figure 5.5 we see that the mid price for the PMI Group bond expiring on April 15, 2020, and paying a coupon of 4.5% is 31.2733. From Figure 5.7 we see that the 10-year CDS on PMI Group trades with a quarterly coupon with an annual rate of 500 bps and an up-front payment of 64.230%. This means that as a protection buyer we are asked to pay upfront 65.48% (the up-front payment plus a quarter of the coupon). In the case of a very likely default within a short period of time (let us imagine a probability of 95%) we are in the situation where a CDS simplifies to

$$65.48\% = (1 - R)\,95\%$$

from which it follows that the recovery is 31.07%, which is close to the bond price.

The same could be said for the Greek bond. Let us consider one of the bonds shown in Figure 5.6, for example, the bond paying a 5.5% coupon and expiring on August 20, 2014: the mid price is 41.256. From Figure 5.7 we see that the Hellenic Republic three-year CDS quoted up-front consists of an annual coupon paid quarterly of 500 bps and an up-front payment of 55.042%. This means that in order to buy protection against the default of Greece we need to pay up-front 56.292%. Again, assuming a very likely default in the near future (let as assume a 95% probability of default) the CDS reduces to

$$56.292\% = (1 - R)\,95\%$$

from which it follows that the recovery is 40.75%, close to the bond value.

We need to stress again that the phenomenon of trading at recovery is linked first and foremost to distressed debt rather than illiquid debt per se. However the concept of pricing at recovery is an important tool that can be used to price illiquid debt of which, almost by definition, there is little market information.

To calibrate a model, as we have shown in Section 3.2.2, means to imply model variables from market variables and often is not unlike trying to cover something with a very small blanket. Usually there is a one-to-one relationship between the number of model variables and the number of market variables:[10] when this one-to-one relationship is missing we make do with some sort of bootstrapping. In the case of CDSs, not only do we need to resort to bootstrapping, but we also need to assume the value of the recovery rate.[11]

To summarize: we use the market variable, the CDS rate, we assume the recovery rate and we imply the model variable, the hazard rate, or survival probability. This process exists in what we could call the investment grade world, that is, the realm of good debt. When we move toward highly illiquid and/or distressed debt, things simplify considerably. Instead of assuming the recovery rate, we assume the survival probability. There could be two situations we might be dealing with: the situation of an illiquid bond issued by an entity whose CDS rates is more available than the bond price and the situation where neither the bond price nor the CDS rates are available.

In the first situation we apply the principle we have applied in the examples above (with the difference, of course, that in the examples above we had

---

[10]In equity, for every implied volatility that we try to solve, there is one option price.
[11]There have been some recent attempts, namely by Vrugt [81], to build a parametric model that solves simultaneously for implied survival probabilities and recovery rates.

all the needed market information and we were simply proving the validity of the argument): we assume an almost certainty of default, we use the CDS (up-front) quote and we obtain the recovery rate that, because of the near certain default, must be close to the bond price.

In the case where even the CDS rates are not easily found, a trader would take an even cruder approach: he would estimate the recovery rate (assessing the realistic chances of an investor to recover some of the issuer's assets) and would use that value as bond price. This practice was often used to price emerging markets bonds during the peak of the 2007 to 2009 financial crisis.

5.4.2 Case Study: The Default of Greece

In Section 5.4.1 we used the debt of Greece as an example on how to price bonds to recovery. Next to what we have said, which stands true, as an added feature we can use the default itself of the government of Greece as an important tool in the understanding of credit events. At the end of a drawn-out process and with little surprise on the part of the markets, Greece agreed to restructure its debt on March 19, 2012.

In the case of events so recent and so charged with different meanings and interests to different parties, it is difficult to point the reader to formal literature other than the major financial newspapers and specialist sites such as Vox or Breakingviews. A few key issues render the situation of Greece particularly difficult:

- Defaults by developed sovereign entities are extremely rare and there is a general wish for them to remain so. This has resulted in an unwillingness on the part of the public and the politicians to accept the fact that a default was unavoidable, and in the default itself, taking place well after the market had taken it for granted. The lateness of the default brought with it all the problems of a self-fulfilling prophecy: contagion of other European countries' debt, capital flight from Greece, and so on.
- Greece is part of the Euro zone: the membership resulted in a series of considerations and discussions that probably would not have taken place had Greece been unattached. (There are, of course, those arguing that Greece's membership in the Euro zone is precisely the reason for its default.) The general effort was directed toward finding voluntary arrangements that would minimally disrupt the complicated links between sovereign debtors and corporate creditors.
- The majority of Greece's debt is in Euros, which, as we have mentioned before, can be considered at the same time a domestic currency, but also as a foreign currency since the Greek government has no monetary control over it.

Instead of focusing on the economics of the issue, which not only are controversial but also subject to change resulting in statements easily obsolete, let us discuss a few numbers and figures in order to illustrate what we have discussed about distressed and illiquid debt.

In Figure 5.8a we show a plot of the price of the bond in EUR paying a coupon of 6.14% and expiring on April 14, 2028, together with the (EUR) up-front premium needed to purchase five-year protection against the default of Greece. In Figure 5.8b we show the plot of the price of the bond in USD paying a coupon of 4.625% and expiring on June 25, 2013, together with the (USD) up-front premium needed to purchase five-year protection against its default.

Let us remind ourselves that Greece has defaulted on its EUR, not USD, denominated debt.[12] We see that near the default, the price of the USD bond is (relatively speaking considering the abysmal levels) considerably higher than the EUR bond. Both plots are striking in their being X-shaped from the summer of 2010 when the sovereign debt crisis roughly began: the price of the bonds starts veering off the par value and the price of the up-front protection increases accordingly.

In the previous section we introduced a rough relationship between protection premium, recovery, and probability of default, namely

$$\text{Protection premium} = \frac{\text{Probabilty of default}}{1 - \text{Recovery}} \qquad (5.20)$$

This means that in a situation nearing default, since the probability of default is essentially 100% and the recovery is very close to the bond price, the sum of protection premium and bond price should be close to 100% of the bond's face value. We plot this in Figures 5.8a and 5.8b and we find our view broadly confirmed. There are, however, some details that are interesting to focus on. First of all is the difference between the EUR and USD scenarios. Since the probability of default cannot be more than 100% we would expect the sum of bond price and protection to be *below* 100: this is because the protection premium must also involve the scenarios where the underlying *does not* default. An event cannot be more than certain, to be certain is the most probable it can be, therefore protection must be progressively cheaper as we move away from certitude and therefore the sum of bond price and protection should have, according to this very simple reasoning, 100 as an upper bound.

---

[12]This is also because the size of the EUR debt dwarfs by roughly two hundred times the size of its USD-denominated debt

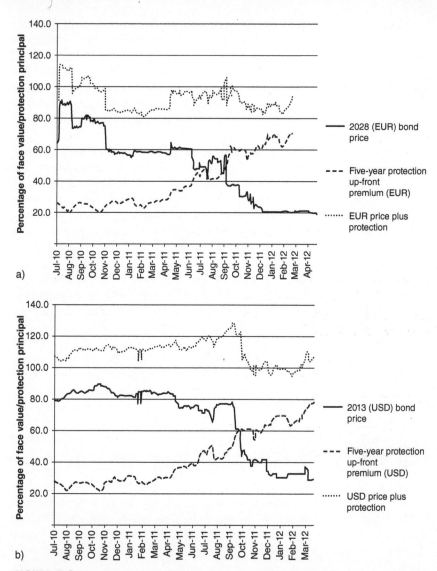

FIGURE 5.8 A plot in time of the market price of the Greek government bond, the up-front premium to buy five-year protection against the default of Greece, and the sum of the two for a) the 2028, 6.14% bond (EUR) and b) the 2013, 4.625% bond (USD).

Of course this is very simple reasoning indeed since it does not take into account the estimate of the recovery level, liquidity, or the effect of interest rates (and the coupon value) on the bond price (we have assumed that in a situation like this one credit trumps any other consideration). We notice that in the case of EUR the sum tends to be below 100, whereas in the case of USD the sum tends to be above. This could be because the price for protection is very similar in the two currencies whereas the bond price in USD is considerably higher.

Protection is determined with respect to a pool of reference obligations, that is, debt instruments whose default triggers the protection payment. The USD bond we are considering is essentially the only USD bond issued by Greece: this means that the five-year protection premium, being of a tenor much longer than the maturity of the bond, is an approximation. Moreover, the protection premium is linked to the reference obligations but is also very much driven to market feeling: once accounted for FX basis and the like, it only makes sense that the cost of protection in USD would follow closely the cost of protection in EUR. This irrespective of the fact that repaying its USD debt is a drop in the ocean of obligations facing the Greek government.

Relating to what we have just mentioned about the fact that 100 should be an upper bound for the sum of bond price and protection, let us observe another characteristic of the shape of each curve. Judging from Figure 5.8a, by the end of December 2011 the market seemed to have settled on the price at which Greece would eventually default (21.5% of face value). Figure 5.8b shows that, similarly, the USD bond price reaches a more or less stable price at the same time. Despite the fact that these values remained stable for more than three months before the actual (EUR) default, the protection premia are not as stable. For more than a year before the actual default of Greece the market believed that it was unavoidable, yet, more than once, the European governments managed to rescue the situation and postpone its solution for a brief period. This means that the default possibility, while present, was not seen in the immediate future (in this context immediate really means immediate). This means that, since we said that the further away from certitude, even for a small period, the cheaper protection must become, protection level would be lower than it should be judging by bond prices.[13]

In Figures 5.9a and 5.9b we show the plot of a two-year strategy beginning in the summer of 2010 and ending at the time of default. We imagine

---

[13]This option-like argument based simply on the time value of protection is compounded by legal arguments centering around the possibility that a non-CDS-triggering default could take place.

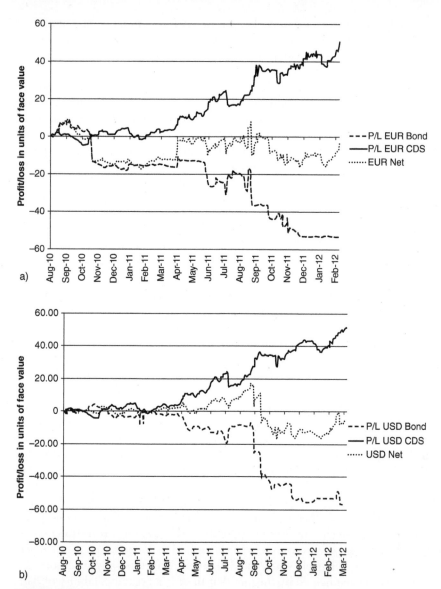

FIGURE 5.9 The cumulative profit and loss resulting from holding bond and protection from August 16, 2010, up to the default of Greece for a) EUR-denominated debt and b) USD-denominated debt.

that in the summer of 2010 we bought our two bonds and at the same time we purchased the corresponding protection against their defaults. In the two plots we show the P/L (profit or loss) deriving from holding bond and CDS, that is, hedging the bond with its corresponding CDS.

The P/L associated with the possession of a bond is fairly easy to understand: if the price of the bond increases we could make a profit by selling it at a higher price than the one we bought it at. Should the price decrease the opposite would be true. What does P/L mean in the case of protection? It means roughly the same thing: if we bought protection at a certain price, should the cost of protection increase, we make a profit because we are holding something that has become more valuable than when we bought it. In order to realize the profit (i.e., monetize it) we could sell protection at the new (higher price) and, a process made even more transparent by the new CDS quotation convention, we would gain the difference between the upfront premia. It might not seem obvious and tangible, but as far as judging the worth of our strategy is concerned, we mark a profit or loss even if we do not physically realize it.

A perfect hedge in which the price of the bond and its corresponding protection move in perfect sync would result in a net P/L, which is a fairly constant line near the zero level.[14] Of course this is not possible since there are considerations such as liquidity, the assumption of recovery rate, and the effect of interest rate that affect the two prices in different ways. Having said that, we would still expect the line to be roughly constant and end (this is the interesting aspect of doing this exercise on the obligation of a borrower who has defaulted) at zero. Both plots confirm the final part, as in both situations the final net P/L is close to zero. Otherwise the two plots illustrate in a different way what we have already mentioned. The cost of protection at the beginning differs little between the two currencies, however, the EUR bond drops in price more quickly and sooner than the USD bond. The strategy therefore during the first half shows a net loss in the case of the EUR and a profit in the case of USD. Later both turn negative and reach the final, zero, net value from below, that is, confirming the fact that the bond prices reached a stationary value sooner than the corresponding protection premia.

The example of Greece has been very useful to understand the movement of bond and CDS levels when the dynamic is driven mainly by credit. The exercise has been helped by the fact that there is a great availability of data.

---

[14]How constant and how near zero would depend on some secondary factors such as the size of the running coupon in the CDS (indicating the relative weight of the up-front premium in the cost of protection), the time to maturity, the distressed level of the debt (the more distressed the more credit plays the dominant role), and so on.

We shall now concentrate on situations where the credit situation not only might be dire but also where the data is scarce.

5.4.3 Building Proxies

What happens when we need to price a truly illiquid bond, a bond on whose issuing entity little information is known in terms of other bond prices, CDS rates, reference spreads, and so on? Here the same principles apply that hold true for any illiquid asset: we try to find a valuation through proxies.

Illiquid assets tend to be worth considerably less than liquid ones in the sense that an investor, if offered the option between two similar products, will choose the one that offers him the possibility of an easy subsequent sale. This is the reason why during a liquidity crisis there is a general tendency to write off assets, that is, to assume a loss. Let us stress here that this might not necessarily reflect the health of the issuer: we have seen that the price of a bond contains a correction driven by credit to the plain discounting of the cash flows. We have also said, however, that a bond price is just a number and many factors can drive it, liquidity being one of them.

A bond price can decrease because of a deteriorating credit standing but it also can decrease because nobody wants to buy it at that time. This implies then a deterioration of credit standing, which might not apply in the first place.[15]

It was rumored that traders at Credit Suisse were paid a bonus in 2008 in illiquid assets. If true, this was a clever move on many fronts. Having written the assets off the bank was giving away something that nominally was worth very little. On a public relations front, traders were made to stand behind their trades (crudely speaking, to put their money where their mouth was). As for the traders, if the problem was really a matter of liquidity, there was a large gain to be made. Imagine that a trader is expecting \$1M as a bonus but the bank gives him instead \$500,000 in the form of a bond trading at 25 (as a percentage of par). If the problem was only one of liquidity and the issuer honors its obligations then the trader at maturity will receive \$2M plus the coupon payments throughout the life of the bond. The question here however is, how do we arrive at the value of 25?

---

[15]Unfortunately for the issuer the two tend to feed off each other: If nobody wants to buy an issuer's bond it means that funding will be difficult, the financing of essential activities will be difficult, and this in turn will affect its credit standing. This is why there is an intense argument as to whether the financial crisis of 2007 to 2009 was principally a liquidity or a credit credit crisis: the two are often indistinguishable.

In Section 5.4.1 we explored the concept of trading at recovery, something that, while valid for truly illiquid bonds, holds true in particular for distressed debt. We shall now consider the concept of proxy, which is probably less sophisticated in terms of finance and mathematics but more complex under an economical point of view.

As the name suggests, to build a proxy is to find market data that could apply to our illiquid assets because of similarities between the issuers. We shall explore here some of the possible proxies.

5.4.3.1 The Case of Missing Maturities   The first case is one where out of a set of bonds issued by a certain entity, only a few are so illiquid as not to have any market information associated to them. In this case we apply a simple interpolation between the price of neighboring bonds (neighboring both in case of maturities and coupon size) and price the illiquid ones.

5.4.3.2 The Case of Quasi Government Entities   A phenomenon present in emerging markets (but not limited to them) is the one of state-owned or state-backed enterprise. This is an entity that competes on a local or global stage but has a strong link to a particular government. When this entity issues debt it is not exactly identical to government debt, but an investor can be assured that the government would intervene in case of trouble. If we had to price an illiquid bond issued by a quasi government entity we would take a reference spread of the respective government (say a z-spread or survival probabilities calibrated on CDS rates), add a further spread because of liquidity and the fact that, all considered, the entity must be at least a little riskier than the government, and price the bond.

5.4.3.3 Similar Countries   When trying to price an illiquid sovereign bond a sensible starting point is to look at similar countries. Similarity can be considered in many forms. The first option is to look at neighboring countries.

Let us say that we need to price a bond[16] issued by the Kingdom of Cambodia. We could use the credit information of Vietnam. This, however, would be a bit simplistic since Vietnam is far larger and wealthier than Cambodia and participates more actively in the wider financial system.

---

[16]We discuss bonds in this section, but the same principles could be applied without modification to the fair value of loans as seen in Section 3.3.1.

We could then consider a proxy basket and, Cambodia belonging to ASEAN (the Association of South East Asian Nations[17]), we could take an average of the credit information (in the form, as usual, of z-spreads, benchmarks, or CDS rates) of the liquid members, add some spread, and price Cambodian debt. In this case a lot would depend on the spread we are adding since the liquid members have a considerably higher credit standing due to their wealth.

Another option would be to forgo regional similarity and focus on using proxies based on alternative economic indicators such as credit ratings, similar GDP, similar level of debt, or similar type of economy. Sometimes similarity can group countries very far from each other. One could argue that as members of the BRIC countries,[18] Russia and Brazil have more in common with each other than with some of their neighbors. This is not necessarily useful for our exercise since BRIC countries have fairly liquid debt (however, not all of them have USD-denominated debt).

5.4.3.4 Similar Companies
The priority in which we use the criteria mentioned in the previous section is of course very subjective; in the most desperate situations often one needs to use what is available. This is even more true when trying to price corporate debt.

If we are trying to price a bond issued by an entity lacking any sort of government backing, one could apply some of the principles discussed above or alternatively some of the following ones.

We could consider another company in the same country similar in terms of activity, level of debt, or credit rating.

We could consider a foreign company in the same industry, claiming that the credit health of our issuer is linked to the global health of the industry.

We could use a foreign company in a similar industry with the same weight within its respective country.[19]

We could also claim that if industry X plays a role in country A similar to the one played by industry Y in country B, we should use the liquid information of a member of X to price the illiquid debt of a member of Y. This can easily be seen in terms of different commodities (although one could argue that they are not different industries): If we agree, say, that rice is to

---

[17]The other members are Brunei, Burma, Indonesia, Laos, Malaysia, Philippines, Thailand, Singapore, and Vietnam.

[18]The term BRIC was coined by Goldman Sachs to group together Brazil, Russia, India, and China. In the press there have been modifications in the form of an extra I and/or S to include Indonesia and South Africa.

[19]The author remembers a former colleague's heroic but futile effort to sell Yasar Holdings as a sort of Turkish Parmalat.

Vietnam what cocoa is to Côte d'Ivoir, then we could use the credit information of a Vietnamese rice producer (assuming we have it) to price a debt issued by an Ivorian cocoa producer. The information can be used either in absolute terms or relative to their respective country, that is, by thinking that the spread of the rice producer with respect to Vietnam credit must be the same as the spread of the cocoa producer over the one of Côte d'Ivoir (assuming that we have it). These two approaches mean that we need to weigh whether the credit of each producer is driven more by the agricultural commodities market or by their own national markets.

The question, like all the questions one needs to answer when choosing a proxy, is far from trivial. To conclude, the exercise of choosing a proxy is very useful and can be applied to any illiquid market information beyond the specific one of bond prices we have mentioned.

5.5 NUMERICAL EXAMPLE: ESTIMATING THE COUPON OF AN EMERGING MARKET DEBT INSTRUMENT

Let us apply the combined knowledge we have obtained from the previous two chapters in a numerical exercise in which we imagine we are helping a developing world entity to issue a bond.

Let us imagine we are working closely with Electricity of Vietnam to issue a fixed-rate two-year bond and we need to decide what the coupon of the bond is going to be either in local currency, Vietnamese Dong (VND), or in USD.

Vietnam is a developing country with a rudimentary financial market. It is dynamic and with a growth rate averaging around 7% over the past decade. Electricity of Vietnam is a public utility company backed by the government of Vietnam. In establishing what the coupon should be in a two-year fixed-rate bond, we should, as we have seen throughout this chapter, take into account considerations of credit and the general interest rate landscape of the denominating currency. These two considerations need to be combined so that, irrespective of the currency in which we issue the bond (USD or VND), given the chosen coupon, at inception the bond price is equal to par.

We have chosen the example of a fixed-rate bond because this is what happens in practice at the developing stage of a debt market. Investors want to purchase debt that is easy to hedge with the instruments available in the market. In order to hedge a floating-rate bond one needs floating-rate instruments, which are not easily available in developing markets. Although interest rate swaps are traded in Vietnam, they are not very liquid and/or the

TABLE 5.2   Data, on interest rate instruments as of March 1, 2012, relevant in the assessment of the coupon of a two-year Electricity of Vietnam bond.

Instrument type	Currency	Maturity	Rate
VNIBOR	VND	1Y	13.50 %
VNIBOR	USD (loc.)	1Y	4.10 %
VNIBOR	USD (fgn.)	1Y	2.36 %
Swap rate	VND	2Y	13.00 %
Prime rate	VND	1M	9.00 %
Swap rate	INR	2Y	5.85 %
JIBOR	IDR	1Y	4.87 %
JIBOR	USD	1Y	1.49 %
Swap rate	IDR	2Y	6.05 %

sizes of contracts would put a serious cap on the principal of the bond we are trying to issue.[20] As we have mentioned many times before, the first instruments to appear in the market are FX forwards, which are ideal instruments to hedge fixed-rate bonds. As the coupon is fixed, we are only concerned about the combination of interest rate and credit, which will result in that discount factor leading to an initial par level.

Vietnam, like many other emerging economies as outlined in Section 4.2.4, exercises capital control: VND cannot be exchanged freely and, as a consequence, the dealing of USD within the country is also controlled. From Table 5.2 we see that there is one interbank rate, VNIBOR, fixing in VND and representing the rate at which banks lend VND to each other. We also see that there is another VNIBOR rate fixing in USD and representing the rate at which banks lend, *within* Vietnam, USD to each other.

It is not surprising that the first rate is higher than the second (even allowing for the further detail that the VNIBOR rate in USD depends also on the local versus foreign nature of the bank that does the lending). We offer the additional example of Indonesia where we also see a different fixing in the interbank rate (JIBOR) depending on whether the fixing is in USD

---

[20]Since investors need to hedge the bond, we cannot issue a bond with a principal that exceeds the principal of the hedging instruments. For example, if the average interest rate swap is traded with a size of 100M it would be risky to issue a bond with a principal much greater than, say, 50M. We want the hedging instrument's size to be not only larger than the size of the instrument that needs hedging but much larger in order to avoid any market distortion.

or in Indonesian Rupees (IDR). Again, the USD fixing is lower. For Vietnam in Table 5.2 we have also shown the prime rate, which is the rate, set by the government, at which commercial banks can lend on a monthly basis. Intuitively we would expect it, being shorter maturity, being set by the government and applying only to commercial banks, to be lower than the interbank rate. We see that this is indeed the case.

In Section 5.4.3 we have shown how, when trying to price an illiquid or an unusual debt instrument, we proceed with a strategy of looking for proxies. Since in the case of Electricity of Vietnam we do not have a measure of the credit standing of the issuer (the only information we have on its credit is a USD loan expiring in three years issued at 290 bps over LIBOR) we need to look at similar entities and see what we can achieve by imitation. The process consists of modifying little by little what we mean by similar until we have built a set of proxies we are confident with.

In this particular example we decide to focus on three criteria of similarity: geographical proximity, type of industry, and role of the company within the economy and/or its relation to the government. Using these criteria we decide to focus on India, Indonesia, and Thailand for similar geographical location and type of country (i.e., fast growing and relatively wealthy by developing world standards). Within these countries we then focus on Electricity Generating Authority of Thailand (Thai EGA in Table 5.3) and Perusahaan Listrik Negara of Indonesia (PLN in Table 5.3) as two examples of electricity companies. Finally we add Indian Oil Corporation (Indian Oil in Table 5.3) as an example of a government-owned power company. The bonds were chosen such that those that needed to be compared pairwise were issued close to each other in time and therefore in a similar credit environment.

In Section 5.3.1 we have shown how one of the most common benchmarks for a bond is the debt of the most creditworthy government issuing in that currency. As the Vietnamese government is the only issuer of debt in VND, in estimating the coupon of our (VND) bond we shall try to work toward establishing a benchmark value between the Electricity of Vietnam bond we are issuing and a similar government bond. When it will be the moment of estimating the value of the coupon of our USD bond, the benchmark will be against a U.S. government treasury bond. Benchmarks against government bonds are given in the form of yields. Since our problem is not to price a bond but is the easier one of estimating the coupon of a bond about to be issued, we can use the yield as a coupon. We know that at inception the yield is equal to the coupon. In the spirit of showing the additive nature of yields as quoted, we show as an example the yield of the 10-year U.S. Treasury note: at 1.98% is indeed 254 bps (plus or minus a few basis points) lower than the yield of 4.55% of the November 2021 PLN bond.

TABLE 5.3 Data, on debt instruments as of March 1, 2012, relevant in the assessment of the coupon of a two-year Electricity of Vietnam bond.

Instrument type	Currency	Maturity	Entity	Price/yield/ spread	Benchmark if spread
Loan	USD	27-Oct-2015	Electricity of Vietnam	290 bps	USD LIBOR
Bond	VND	20-Feb-14	Vietnam	10.98%	
Bond	USD	29-Jan-20	Vietnam	5.39%	
Bond	USD	29-Jan-20	Vietnam	395 bps	US7YT
CDS	USD	20-Mar-19	Vietnam	361 bps	
Loan	USD	22-Mar-16	Indian Oil	120 bps	USD LIBOR
Bond	USD	2-Aug-21	Indian Oil	5.28%	
Bond	USD	2-Aug-21	Indian Oil	327 bps	US10YT
Bond	INR	21-Dec-16	Indian Oil	9.32%	
Bond	INR	21-Dec-16	Indian Oil	79 bps	IN1YT
Bond	INR	12-Dec-41	India	8.61%	
Bond	USD	17-Jan-42	Indonesia	4.82%	
Bond	USD	17-Jan-42	Indonesia	169 bps	US30YT
Bond	IDR	15-Jul-21	Indonesia	5.73%	
CDS	USD	20-Mar-22	Indonesia	213 bps	
Bond	USD	22-Nov-21	PLN	4.55%	
Bond	USD	22-Nov-21	PLN	254 bps	US10YT
Bond	IDR	8-Jul-22	PLN	7.77%	
Bond	IDR	8-Jul-22	PLN	224 bps	ID10YT
Bond	THB	27-Aug-14	Thai EGA	3.50%	
Bond	THB	27-Aug-14	Thai EGA	41 bps	TH2YT
CDS	USD	20-Mar-14	Thailand	77 bps	
Bond	USD	2-Aug-21	USA	1.98%	

In Table 5.3 we show a set of bonds belonging to the set of proxies we have chosen. When relevant we have shown the same bond twice, once with its value in the form of yield and once in the form of spread with respect to some benchmark. We have one bond in USD and one in VND issued by the government of Vietnam; we have one bond in USD and one in Indian Rupees (INR) issued by Indian Oil; we have one bond issued in INR by the government of India; we have one bond in USD and one in IDR issued by the government of Indonesia; we have one bond in USD and one in IDR issued by PLN; finally, we have one bond in Thai Baht (THB) issued by EGA.

In the table we have also included some CDS levels to test and display what we have learned in the previous chapters. For example, we see that the January 2020 Vietnamese bond yields 395 bps over the relevant U.S.

Treasury note. Since U.S. government bonds are as close as one can get to a risk-free instrument, one can (very) roughly consider them as a purely interest rate instrument. We have said many times that a CDS rate is not something one can apply as it is, as tempting as it might be, onto an interest rate to add a credit element. However we have seen in Equation 5.14 that we can manipulate a CDS rate so that we can do something in that direction. Let us take Vietnam's CDS rate shown in the table and scale it, taking into consideration the recovery rate

$$\frac{361}{1-R} \xrightarrow[\text{recovery}]{\text{with 15\%}} 424$$

This number, with the not unreasonable assumption of 15% recovery, is quite close[21] to the spread of 395 bps yielded by the Vietnam bond over the U.S. Treasury note. The excitement about seeing two numbers making sense of each other needs to be dampened by applying the same test to Indonesia. We see that the January 2042 bond yields 169 bps over the 30-year U.S. Treasury note. By taking the CDS spread shown in Table 5.3 (the required 30 years CDS rate is equal to the 10 years shown) we can calculate

$$\frac{213}{1-R} \xrightarrow[\text{recovery}]{\text{with 20\%}} 266$$

which is almost 100 bps higher than the spread between the government bond's yield and the U.S. Treasury note. The fact that we are treating very long dated and illiquid instruments means that in this context 100 bps is not a very large difference; however, it also shows that these calculations should only be used to support a general view and not to demand high precision. We have used 20% recovery simply on the basis that one would think that a country with a higher credit rating than Vietnam would have a higher recovery rate. Using the same recovery rate of 15% would lead to a value of 250 bps, which is close to the spread over the U.S. Treasury.

In trying to assess what should be the relation (spread) between the bond we are about to issue and the Vietnamese government bond, let us begin with the local currency bond. From the table we see that the spread between the

---

[21]When comparing instruments that are not quite the same and particularly in the realm of emerging markets, the definition of close becomes considerably generous. The author remembers that when pricing illiquid EM bonds, after having considered all inputs, spreads of up to 250 bps were added in the name of liquidity. It was more like saying, we are walking blind, in the dark, in a room with a potentially low ceiling, let us put a large pillow in front of our face in case we bump into something.

Indian Oil INR bond and the one-year Indian Government bond is 79 bps; the spread between the EGA bond and the two-year Thai government bond is 41 bps; the spread between the PLN IDR bond and the 10-year Indonesian government bond is 224 bps. The average between these three values is 115 bps and this would be the first guess for a spread over the Vietnamese government bond. We could set the coupon at 12.15% by rounding up the sum of 10.98% (the government bond's yield) and 115 bps.

There are few considerations that could make this value higher or lower.

On one side Vietnam offers a riskier environment, judging from the CDS levels, than Indonesia and Thailand (there are no CDS levels for India) and therefore our value should be higher than the arithmetic average. The immediate counterargument, however, is that we are discussing *relative* values, that is, we are not concerned by how risky the government of Vietnam or Electricity of Vietnam are, but by how Electricity of Vietnam is *riskier* than the government.

On the other side the spread for the PLN bond over the Indonesian government bond is for 10 years, a maturity far greater than the one we are considering and one where we would assume that spreads increase. According to this argument our value should be lower than the arithmetic average. Since both these arguments are valid at first order[22] we could then accept the value of 115 bps.

We could round up the value of the coupon, in the name of uncertainty, to, say, 12.50% but we need to be aware, in case we are tempted to increase it even more, that we are soon reaching an important upper bound.

In Table 5.2 we show the value of the one-year VNIBOR rate to be equal to 13.50% and the value of the two-year swap rate to be equal to 13.00%. We know little about the liquidity of these numbers and their market depth (meaning how large the size of the average trade is), however, intuitively we would expect that a government-owned company would be able to raise capital at a lower cost than a financial institution.

We now focus on estimating the coupon of the USD bond Electricity of Vietnam is wishing to issue. A first approach would be to consider the spreads over U.S. Treasury notes of the two other companies for which we have data. PLN's bond trades at 254 bps over the U.S. 10-year note and Indian Oil's bond trades at 327 bps over the same note: the average is 290 bps. We could then argue, although admittedly we have information only for Indonesia's CDS levels, that we should scale this number by the

---

[22]A more thorough analysis would involve a more serious assessment of liquidity and the legal relationship between each of these companies and their respective governments.

ratio in CDS levels between the countries from which we have worked out the spread and the country in which we are trying to apply our calculation. We are basically trying to answer the question: this spread is valid for a credit regime given by one certain CDS level, how would this spread change in a different CDS environment?

We are switching again to a relative view. PLN and Indian Oil are to Indonesia and India what Electricity of Vietnam is to Vietnam: if the spread between the two companies and the USD note is of a certain value in a country with a certain CDS level, wouldn't the spread between Electricity of Vietnam and the U.S. note be increased by the fact that that company is in a country with a larger CDS rate? Indonesia's CDS level is 213 bps and Vietnam's is 361. Therefore, the spread we are looking for could be calculated in the following way

$$\frac{254 + 327}{2} \frac{361}{213} \approx 491$$

The coupon of our bond should be then given by the U.S. Treasury note's yield plus 491 bps.

A second approach could be to take the number we have obtained in the previous calculation, when we were estimating the coupon of the VND bond, as the spread between Electricity of Vietnam and the Vietnamese government bond (115 bps) and add it on top of the spread between the government of Vietnam's bond and the relevant U.S. Treasury note, which, as shown in Table 5.3, is 395 bps. This operation would lead to a spread of 510 bps, meaning that the coupon of our bond should be given by the U.S. Treasury note's yield plus 510 bps. We note that the numbers obtained with these two methods are not far from each other (which is a good sign).

With these calculations we have shown how traders and bond issuers try to make sense of very scattered and illiquid information. We have produced numbers that at first seem reasonable. This was far from a scientific process: the same numbers could be argued and proved meaningless from several points of view. The main role played by the data provided is to offer a view of the situation and a feel for the credit environment, the rest is open to debate. We could finish this section with two statements often heard among physicists. The first is to never run a simulation unless one already knows the result. The second, which could be applied to the type of data we deal with, is that statistics to a scientist is like a lamppost to a drunk, it is more of a support than a source of illumination.

CHAPTER 6

Treasury Revisited

T he main focus of our discussion, credit and debt, is seen through the activity of a treasury, its role, and the way certain risks are managed. We have seen how a financial institution and in particular a development institution work; we have seen how discounting plays a crucial role in assessing the value of any financial instruments; more importantly we have seen how the concept of credit and in turn the concept of funding cost is closely linked to it. On the issue of credit we have seen how this is treated under a modeling point of view and what it entails when applied to the lending side of a financial institution (with a focus on development). We have seen how financial instruments behave differently in less developed markets and what this entails in terms of borrowing and lending. We have seen how bonds are priced and, crucially, the role played in this by credit.

The above are some of the most important tools needed to understand the role and activities carried out by a treasury desk and in particular to understand the role played by funding when it comes to treating financial instruments. In this chapter we shall try to show how the goal of a treasury desk is to raise funds by issuing debt in the most attractive way to investors. How to get to this price, where and how to issue it, and the impact of the price on the credit standing (or vice versa) of the issuers are all points that will leverage the knowledge we have acquired in the previous chapters. We shall conclude this chapter with a discussion on borrowing and investment benchmarks with a special focus on these in the domain of development banking.

6.1 FUNDING AS AN ASSET SWAP STRUCTURE

6.1.1 Asset Swaps Revisited

In Section 5.3.2 we defined what an asset swap is. At first Figures 5.2 and 1.3 do not seem identical, but if we focus on what in essence an asset swap means, we shall see how they are.

Probably the most general and essential definition of an asset swap one could give is the one where we define it as a way of capturing the credit risk of a bond through a fixed spread over a LIBOR. This can be written (we generalize Equation 5.11) as

$$\sum_i (L_i + s_A) D_i dt_i - \sum_j F_j D_j dt_j \rightleftharpoons 1 - \sum_j F_j D_j \widetilde{D}_j dt_j - D_T \widetilde{D}_T \quad (6.1)$$

where, in our preferred fashion, we have kept the discount factor expressed in a general form D_i and where $\widetilde{D}_i$ is a correction to the discount factor driven by the credit standing of the bond issuer. In Equation 6.1 F_j is the coupon of the bond where, in order to generalize, we assume that it can be anything from a fixed rate to a floating rate to a complex structure. As usual L_i is the LIBOR and s_A is the asset swap spread. The symbol $\rightleftharpoons$ means that each side of the equation is as seen by each counterparty. The right-hand side is the side of the bond issuer, which sees (positive) 1 as the money received from the investors (bond buyers) and the bond payment to the investors as negative, that is, a liability. The left-hand side is the side doing the swap, which sees the LIBOR payment made by the bond issuer as positive and the coupon leg payments as negative. (Had we used a simple equal sign, Equation 6.1 would not have satisfied the simple rules of algebra. In Equation 5.11 we did use an equal sign, but the signs in front of the terms are different: the rules of algebra were satisfied and, at the time, we did not need to be too precise about the directions of the trade.)

With the asset swap framework in mind, a treasury desk would gauge the market appetite for a certain type of bond (e.g., fixed rate or with a more complicated payoff) after which it would issue the bond and, as a consequence of the market response, the bond acquires a price. At this stage, the right-hand side of Equation 6.1, that is,

$$1 - \sum_j F_j D_j \widetilde{D}_j dt_j - D_T \widetilde{D}_T$$

becomes known (with the bond price driving the value of $\widetilde{D}_j$). Not only the right-hand side is known but also the term

$$\sum_j F_j D_j dt_j$$

on the left-hand side is now known. This means that the only remaining element needed for a fair price is the asset swap spread s_A. After the trading desk (or any unit acting as the other party in the asset swap) and the treasury desk agree on this, the swap part of the asset swap structure is completed.

In practice the operation does not really follow this order; the issuing and the swapping happens simultaneously. More important the bond and the swap are often legally linked. For example, if something were to happen to the bond in terms of interruption, such as recall or prepayment, the swap would often reflect the consequences. This is slightly different from a normal asset swap situation where the bond holder *after having purchased the bond* swaps it in order to monetize the bond's risk. This helps to explain the difference between Figure 5.2 and Figure 1.3; however, if we look at an asset swap spread as an easily tradable proxy for a bond's credit, the two situations immediately become very similar.

The bond shown in Equation 6.1 matures at time T, which of course means that the swap also matures at time T. From this we say that the asset swap spread s_A represents the *cost of funding* or *funding level* up to year T and we shall rewrite it as s_A^T. Similarly if the treasury desk issues a swap with maturity $S > T$, the asset swap spread s_A^S will represent the cost of funding up to year S. It would be unlikely for the two costs of funding to be identical. If we repeat the same process (which is of course what happens in practice) of issuing bonds with different maturities we build a *term structure of funding levels*. For the better issuers in the past this term structure would be almost flat, that is, asset swap spreads were very similar at different maturities. After the financial crisis of 2007 to 2009, however, the overall reconsideration of credit (which we have seen affecting discounting in Chapter 2) has not left any corner undisturbed, and now almost all term structures of funding costs present some (usually upward) movement.

In Table 6.1 we show the asset swap levels of selected bonds issued by the Republic of Italy as a display of a term structure of funding costs. Next to it we show the approximate CDS rate, quoted in USD (see Section 3.2.3), corresponding to the maturity of the bond: this is only for illustration purposes since we know, after discussing it in Sections 5.3.2 and 5.3.3, that asset

TABLE 6.1 Example of USD funding level term structure for the Republic of Italy as of October 17, 2011.

Maturity	s_A	Approx. CDS rate (USD)
10/05/2012	385.40	390.27
09/16/2013	353.86	423.66
09/20/2016	395.93	446.67
09/27/2023	451.91	429.00 (interp.)

swap spreads and CDS rates, while often close in value, are quite different in principle.

To be more precise we would need to say that the funding levels shown in Table 6.1 are USD funding levels: why is the specification important? A borrowing entity, corporate or sovereign, can decide to issue a bond either in its local market (even multinationals have a principal or local market) or in a foreign one. The decision for an institution to issue debt abroad is driven by the notion that there will be interest in purchasing its own debt in that specific country and in that country's currency.[1] The question however is, how much interest?

Will a bond issued by, say, Coca Cola, an American company, be considered more valuable in the United States, Coca Cola's local market, issued in USD or in Japan issued in JPY? This is a very important question that, once answered (through subscribed debt issuances) by the market over multiple occasions, enables an issuer to build term structures of funding levels in different currencies. These funding levels, one in USD and one in JPY, will almost certainly be different.

Remaining with Coca Cola's example, let us try to answer the question on the view of the credit of the company as held by American versus Japanese investors. Probably a Japanese investor would think that, should a default of Coca Cola occur, an American investor would have easier access to the spoils of the firm, so to speak.[2] In this case, a Coca Cola bond in Japan would be worth less than a similar Coca Cola bond in the United States. We should know by now, after reading Chapter 5, that to be worth less means a higher yield, which in turn could mean a higher coupon paid by the bond (in order to attract Japanese investors). Using Equation 6.1 we can easily see that the higher the coupon F_j, the higher the asset swap spread s_A must be. This means that the asset swap level, that is, the cost of funding, for Coca Cola in Japan would be greater. Unless something changes in our simple reasoning (which could happen since our reasoning was very simple indeed and ignored many possible market scenarios), Coca Cola has little interest in issuing debt in Japan. Since the same principle we have used for Japan would apply to any non-American market, it should concentrate in issuing debt only in the United States.

---

[1] We assume that a bond issued in a certain country will be denominated in the currency of that country. While this is not always the case it is the most common situation.

[2] Which is not necessarily true but market sentiment, particularly when it comes to credit, can be fairly irrational or at least overcautious.

TABLE 6.2 Example of EUR funding level term structure for the Republic of Italy as of October 17, 2011. Indicative levels are shown for the currency basis swap as spread to be paid over EURIBOR versus USD LIBOR flat.

Maturity	s_A	Approx. CDS rate (EUR)	Currency basis spread (bps)
15/10/2012	207.96	344.94	−65
1/11/2013	273.45	387.49	−55
20/09/2016	323.26	402.78	−37
27/09/2023	304.05	387.00 (interp.)	−18.45 (interp.)

Not many institutions issue debt in multiple currencies, that is, in foreign markets: it is interesting to see what happens to the few that do. Table 6.2 shows bonds issued by the Republic of Italy in EUR: the maturities and issue dates of the bonds have been chosen so as to be as similar as possible to those of the bonds shown in Table 6.1. The values are considerably different. Let us express each situation as an asset swap. The Republic of Italy could issue a EUR-denominated bond and enter into an asset swap

$$
N^{EUR} \left\{ \sum_i \left(L_i^{EUR} + s_A^{EUR} \right) D_i^{EUR} dt_i - \sum_j F_j D_j^{EUR} dt_j \right\}
$$
$$
\rightleftharpoons N^{EUR} \left\{ 1 - \sum_j F_j D_j^{EUR} \widetilde{D_j^{EUR}} dt_j - D_T^{EUR} \widetilde{D_T^{EUR}} \right\}
$$
(6.2)

where N^{EUR} is the principal in EUR, D_i^{EUR} are the EUR discount factors, and L_i^{EUR} is the EURIBOR floating rate. Alternatively it could issue a USD-denominated bond and enter into an asset swap

$$
N^{USD} \left\{ \sum_i \left(L_i^{USD} + s_A^{USD} \right) D_i^{USD} dt_i - \sum_j F_j D_j^{USD} dt_j \right\}
$$
$$
\rightleftharpoons N^{USD} \left\{ 1 - \sum_j F_j D_j^{USD} \widetilde{D_j^{USD}} dt_j - D_T^{USD} \widetilde{D_T^{USD}} \right\}
$$
(6.3)

where, similarly, $N^\$$ is the bond's principal in USD, $D_i^\$$ are the USD discount factors, and $L_i^\$$ is the USD LIBOR. These two bonds would have two different asset swap spreads s_A^{EUR} and $s_A^\$$ indicating two different costs of funding, one in each currency. From Table 6.2 it would appear that the government of Italy could issue bonds in EUR at a cheaper (i.e., more advantageous) level than if it did the same in USD. This is true, but the extra column in Table 6.2 explains part of the difference. The government of Italy could either issue a bond in USD and pay $L_i^\$ + s_A^\$$ or issue a bond in EUR and pay $L_i^{EUR} + s_A^{EUR}$. Isn't there something we have encountered before that enables us to compare floating rates from different currencies? In Section 2.2.5.2 we have seen that a EUR versus USD cross currency basis swap would be structured as

$$N^{EUR}\left\{-1 + \sum_i \left(L_i^{EUR} + b_C\right) D_i^{EUR} dt_i + D_T^{EUR}\right\}$$

$$= N^{USD}\left\{-1 + \sum_i L_i^{USD} D_i^{USD} dt_i + D_T^{USD}\right\}$$

where b_C is the cross currency basis. From Table 6.2 we see, for example, that the cross currency basis quote with tenor similar to the first bond is (negative) -65 bps: this means that, in the floating rate exchange, the EURIBOR level is higher than the USD-LIBOR level by 65 bps. This also means that, because the rate itself is higher, an asset swap spread/funding level quoted in EUR must be intuitively lower.[3] As a consequence, in order to compare two funding cost levels in a meaningful way, one should at least add the currency basis. This means that we need to compare

$$L_i^{EUR} + s_A^{EUR} + b_C$$

with

$$L_i^{USD} + s_A^{USD}$$

in order to compare $s_A^\$$ with s_A^{EUR}. The basis b_C can be either added to the floating rate or subtracted from the asset swap spread. This, confusingly since it is negative, means that if we want to compare the asset swap spread given in EUR in Table 6.2 to the one given in USD in Table 6.1 we need to subtract the -65 bps from the 207.96 bps of the asset swap spread leading to a total of 272.96 bps. This value is still very much lower than the 385.40 bps we see quoted for a USD bond with similar maturity, leading us to conclude

---

[3]Should this seem hard to grasp one can think that floating rate plus asset swap spread must be *very roughly* equal to the coupon value: if the floating rate is lower, the asset swap spread must be higher and conversely if the floating rate is higher, the asset swap spread must be lower.

that for Italy it is cheaper to issue debt in EUR than in USD. The fact that a quick glance at Italy's outstanding debt shows that EUR debt principal is roughly 100 times larger than USD debt principal would confirm this.

The relationship between funding levels and cross currency basis cannot be stressed enough. In the example above we have used cross currency levels to manipulate asset swap spreads, but the real relationship starts at the other end. In Section 2.3 we said how the cross currency basis is the level that represents the ease with which investment banks borrow in a certain currency, this meaning that it represents the view that a certain country's market has of the credit standing of the *average* foreign bank. This means that cross currency basis swaps exist exactly, because when a bank tries to issue a bond outside its native market, the cost of funding is different. Bond prices, or more generally borrowing instruments, drive the basis. To conduct an exercise similar to the one we have done for Italy on several investment banks would be more difficult since banks issue a greater number of smaller denominated bonds with varying liquidity and varying complexity of payoff (we shall describe in Section 6.2 why this is an issue). Such a study however would lead to interesting results when compared to the traded cross currency basis levels.

6.1.2   The Impact of Discounting on Asset Swap Levels

In Chapter 2 we discussed at great length the role of discounting. In Section 2.4.3 in particular we tried to gauge the impact of discounting on the value of a swap. We have concluded that a par swap (which we have also called at the money) is affected less than an out-of-the-money swap by a change in discount curve. We could ask the same question in relation to the asset swap spreads.

If an entity is issuing a bond and the bond price will result in a corresponding funding level/asset swap spread, wouldn't the choice of discounting for the swap part of the structure (i.e., the left-hand side of Equation 6.1) have an impact on the asset swap spread itself?

Let us imagine that, following the lead of the major financial institutions and clearinghouses in which all swaps are discounted with overnight index swaps, Equation 6.1 would be rewritten as

$$
\begin{aligned}
\sum_i (L_i + \overline{s_A})\, D_i^{OIS} dt_i - \sum_j F_j D_j^{OIS} dt_j \\
\rightleftharpoons 1 - \sum_j F_j D_j^{LIB} \widetilde{D}_j dt_j - D_T^{LIB} \widetilde{D}_T
\end{aligned}
\tag{6.4}
$$

where D_i^{OIS} indicates a discount factor driven by the overnight index swap and D_i^{LIB} indicates a discount factor driven by the LIBOR (we have left the correction $\widetilde{D}_i$ untouched since it is a credit-driven correction). The spread $\overline{s_A}$ is the new asset swap spread, which could be different from s_A. From Equation 6.4 we notice something that is important, perhaps obvious, but often forgotten when the reasons behind a choice of discounting is forgotten: the move toward OIS discounting only affects swaps and leaves bonds unchanged. OIS discounting is a discounting that takes into account the posting of collateral, in the case of bonds there is of course no such thing. To be precise we should not be writing D_j^{LIB} either because, as we discussed at great length when dealing with bond cash flow discounting, it does not make much sense to try to put too precise a label on the interest rate component of a bond discount factor. If we need to break the unity of such a discount factor it is better to be vague and say that there is some interest rate element and some credit element contributing to it. In the above we wrote D_j^{LIB} simply to stress that it is definitively not an OIS-driven discount.

In Equation 6.4, D_i^{LIB} is identical to D_i in Equation 6.1; we have only written it differently to stress its origin. This means that the right-hand side of the two equations is the same, which is comforting since it corresponds to a traded price, that is, the bond's price. However, the left-hand sides of the two equations, although overall they need to equal each other (by being equal to the right-hand sides), they are not the same in essence because of the different choice of discounting. In each we have only one free parameter, the asset swap spread, and the structural difference between the two might mean that the two asset swap spreads, s_A and $\overline{s_A}$, might be different.

We have already mentioned the interesting discussion on asset swap sensitivities found in O'Kane [66]. Here it is slightly different because we are not wondering what the effect of interest moves is on the swap level, rather we are decoupling the index and discount curve and, holding the former constant, we ask ourselves what the impact is on the asset swap spread of a change in the latter. It turns out the impact of discounting on the asset swap spread is not very significant. If we assume that the asset swap we enter into is at the money (which is not always the case in a normal asset swap but it is often the case in the asset swap made against a bond in the type of transaction carried out by a treasury desk) then the impact of discounting is limited as it is for all at-the-money swaps.

By estimating the sensitivity to a change in discount factor in the left-hand side of 6.4, we show this in detail in Appendix E.

6.2 FUNDING LEVEL TARGETS

6.2.1 The Objective of Ever-Smaller Funding Levels

The goal of any treasury desk is to borrow money for the institution in the cheapest possible way, this way lowering the funding cost as much as possible. We have seen that this consists of swapping a bond for the lowest possible asset swap spread. How is this achieved?

An asset swap spread reflects the credit risk of a bond and is proportional to the yield of the bond itself: the more attractive the bond appears to investors, the lower the yield will be. The goal of a treasury desk, the treasury division within an institution, or the debt management agency for a sovereign entity is to find a way of making its debt appear as attractive as possible to investors.

A simple approach, as is the case with many products, is through novelty. By issuing debt in a novel form, an institution not only can issue something scarce and hence valuable, but also something that, being difficult to price in comparison with similar instruments, can gain from some sort of bid-offer premium. In Section 4.2.1 we discussed the bid-offer spread size in relation to liquidity—the wider the spread, the less liquid the instrument. When it comes to selling an instrument, the seller can price it at a higher value than the true value more easily than in the case of a more liquid asset. Using the same terms of comparison, there is a greater gain from selling vintage sports cars than pints of milk. A bond, which is unlike any other bond, will fetch a high price at auction.

We have seen in a previous example, where we used Coca Cola, that a corporate entity usually finds it difficult to issue a bond abroad where its credit standing might seem less appealing to foreign investors than to local ones. While this intuitive reasoning holds in a large number of situations, it is not a general rule. There might be situations where issuing a foreign bond might be to the institution's advantage. If the institution has a particularly good credit standing in general, it might choose to issue a bond in a country where there is a lack of similar institutions of similar standing. The rarity of the bond might make it advantageous to issue in that particular country and foreign currency where the funding level might be even lower than in the institution's own market.

Another possible advantage might come from a choice of maturity. Figure 6.1 shows the debt profile of the USD equivalent outstanding principal value for a few selected borrowing entities: two sovereign, Belgium and Mexico; one supranational, the IBRD; three financials, Société Générale, Morgan Stanley, and Deutsche Bank; and one manufacturer, Boeing.

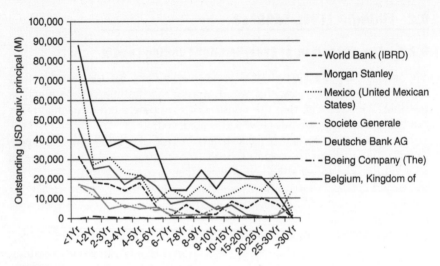

FIGURE 6.1 The debt profile in time as of October 19, 2011, for a few selected entities.

The first thing we notice, as an aside, is that nonsovereign debt pales in size when compared to sovereign debt. This is true even if it is matched against the one of two countries such as Mexico and Belgium, which are far from being the largest borrowers (to include large borrowers would have meant rendering the graph illegible). This, of course, is partially due to the fact that corporations and financials can raise money through shares; however, in the face of a debt crisis, sovereigns are more exposed.

Leaving the comparison between sovereign and corporates aside, however, what we notice is that the majority of debt crowds the short end of the maturity spectrum, tapering fairly quickly. If an investor wishes to purchase long-dated debt there are not many options and an institution, particularly one in good standing, could try to raise capital at a relatively cheap level by tapping the long-dated market. Immediately we need to state that funding cost, apart from some peculiar exceptions, tends to rise with maturity. This is why we said relatively cheap level: we mean relative to this general upward trend. The attentive reader might have noticed a spike in Société Générale's debt profile for maturities greater than 30 years: this is due to several perpetual bonds,[4] that is, bonds that have no maturity.

---

[4]Perpetuals are a very old type of bond (also called rents or consols) that pay a usually low coupon in perpetuity: a little present value calculation will show that this is not as outlandish as it might seem.

Liquidity would be another factor in a bond price, which could play in favor of the issuer. To issue in an illiquid or exotic currency (particularly if combined with a long maturity) is the equivalent of selling a vintage sports car: the bond could fetch a price well above its true value resulting in a lower cost of funding for the issuing entity. When discussing emerging markets, we mentioned in Section 4.3.1 the role played by development institutions when issuing debt in developing markets' currencies. This brings liquidity and development to the local financial markets but also, through the appetite for good debt in that currency, results in an attractive funding level for the issuing entity.

Complexity is probably the most common element played by issuing entities in order to lower their funding costs. Up to now we have described the coupon on a bond either as fixed or, vaguely, as some function. The nature and complexity of this function plays an important role in the appetite generated by a certain issue. In the same way as a long-dated or an illiquid bond can earn a considerable markup (or markdown in the funding spread), a complex structure in the coupon can render a bond attractive. (Another way of seeing it is by saying that it makes the bond more difficult to value in comparison with other bonds and therefore there is some bid-offer premium.)

We have hitherto defined as C_j a fixed coupon paid at time T_j and as F_j a coupon variable with the value linked either to a floating rate or to a function. This function can be literally anything. The bond coupon might take the form of an equity linked basket option

$$F_j = \max\left[0, \frac{1}{N}\sum_i^N S_i\left(T_j\right) - K\right]$$

where we pay at each coupon the average positive performance of a basket of N stocks with respect to a strike K. Such a bond would be very valuable when the correlation between the stocks is high, resulting in the investor taking a long position with respect to equity correlation. It could be a five-year versus two-year constant maturity swap (CMS) spread range accrual of the form

$$F_j = C\frac{\sum_{i=T_{j-1}}^{T_j} \mathbf{1}_{S_i^{5Y} > S_i^{2Y}}}{N}$$

where the coupon consists of a fraction of a fixed value C determined by the number of days, out of a total N in a certain period, in which the five-year swap rate S_i^{5Y} at time T_i is greater than the two-year swap rate S_i^{2Y} at time T_i. This bond is very valuable in the presence of a steep swap curve, one in which swap rate values grow as the swap maturity grows. It could be a targeted redemption note (TARN) of the form

$$
F_j = \begin{cases} X_j & \text{if } \sum_{i=0}^{j} X_i \leq K \\ 100 & \text{if } \sum_{i=0}^{j} X_i > K \text{ after which the bond terminates} \end{cases}
$$

where X_j is some variable (a stock price, an FX rate, an interest rate, etc.) and K is a target: the bond pays a coupon X_j until the sum of the past coupon payments exceeds a set target K, at which point the principal value of the bond is returned to the investor and the bond terminates.

The above are just examples out of the vast and ever-growing family of exotic structures, the goal of which is to tempt the investor, by offering him exposure to a specific quantity (volatility, correlation, swap curve dynamics, etc.), to pay a higher price for the bond in which the structure is embedded. We are now going to discuss what the impact is of complexity in the value of the funding level/asset swap spread.

6.2.2 Different Funding Levels for Different Types of Debt

It is tempting to think that, by issuing bonds with more and more complex structures embedded into them or bonds denominated in highly illiquid currencies, the result is an attractive low funding cost. This is partly true but the issue is more complex.

Let us imagine an institution issues a simple bond with fixed-coupon C in a liquid currency and using

$$
\sum_i (L_i + s_V) D_i dt_i - \sum_j C D_j dt_j \rightleftharpoons 1 - \sum_j C D_j \widetilde{D}_j dt_j - D_T \widetilde{D}_T
$$

we obtain a funding level s_V (where V stands for vanilla). Let us assume that the product is so liquid that the bid-offer on s_V is almost negligible. Now let us imagine that the same institution issues a complex structure

$$
\sum_i (L_i + s_E) D_i dt_i - \sum_j F_j (X_j, Y_j) D_j dt_j
$$
$$
\rightleftharpoons 1 - \sum_j F_j (X_j, Y_j) D_j \widetilde{D}_j dt_j - D_T \widetilde{D}_T
$$

where the value of the coupon is based on two variables X and Y. We also know that the structure is long dated and the volatility levels σ_X and σ_Y are not very liquid. We know that the structure is sensitive to the skew of these volatilities, that is, $\partial_K \sigma_X$ and $\partial_K \sigma_Y$ (where K is the strike). Being a multi-asset structure, it will be sensitive to the correlation $\rho_{X,Y}$ between the two variables. This bond results in a funding cost s_E (where E stands for exotic) with, as we have discussed earlier, $s_E \ll s_V$, that is, the funding cost obtained from the exotic structure is considerably smaller than the one derived from a vanilla one. We conclude that funding is cheaper through exotic bonds.

The lower funding cost seems attractive until we ask ourselves two questions. The first is, are we sure of the value of the bond leading to s_E? The second is, what will be the cost of hedging the risk involved in that structure?

To assess the value of an illiquid structure is not an easy task, particularly as the number of variables grows. The most common approach is to value it using mid values (i.e., the average between bid and offer) and then put aside some reserve in case to value it at mid was wrong.

The true value of the entire structure (from which one will be roughly able to imply the correct value of its variables) will only be known if the structure will be retraded, which might not even happen. This future possible value is sometimes known as exit price since it signals the cost of exiting the trade.

To summarize, the bond is valued at a certain price, however, the real value of the trade as far as profit for the institution is concerned is adjusted (downward, i.e., conservatively) to take into account the fact that some of the variables used in the calculation were a bit doubtful. Should the trade be exited before maturity, the reserve will be used to cover potential losses originating from thinking that the bond was worth more than market value. Should the trade reach maturity (or is exited at a more favorable price than expected) the reserve will be then, and only then, considered as realized profit.[5]

This approach is applicable to trades in general; when it comes to trades that are treasury issued bonds, we should change the word profit and use instead liquidity or funds, which can be passed on to the rest of the institution.

---

[5]In practice the part of the reserve that is not meant to cover hedging costs but that is only meant to constitute a buffer in case of wrong valuation will not be treated as a lump sum: as the trade seasons, a proportion of the reserve will be considered as realized profit. On a, say, 20-year trade the risk of misvalue after 15 years is, of course, lower than after one.

This last point is crucial in linking the uncertainty in the bond price with the respective uncertainty in the funding cost. A reserve in the bond value must, when swapped, result in a different funding spread. Does this make sense? Is this correct? After all, the spread in an asset swap is a contractual quantity, it is a number agreed between the two parties and a fixed value to be added on top of the floating rate each time this sets. This is indeed the case and there is no such thing as a reserve spread; however, in light of model or market data uncertainty, a more critical view of the funding spread is needed for two reasons mainly. Should we exit the swap, the same way as the reserve on the bond price should reflect the more realistic market value of the bond, an add-on on the asset swap spread should reflect the cost of unwinding the asset swap. The second reason is that, as we shall see in Section 6.4, the funding level, in the form of a benchmark, is an extremely important quantity against which many things, including the institution's profitability, are measured. A more conservative internal value for the funding spread, which could be in the form of an add-on onto the asset swap spread, would help toward more realistic measurements.

There are a few ways to assess the impact of the illiquidity on the funding spread. The easiest to implement is to calculate the sensitivity of the funding spread to a change in the input variable and then multiply this sensitivity by what we think is the potential uncertainty in the value (which could be the bid-offer spread). In practice we want to find the spread s'_E

$$s'_E = \frac{\partial s_E}{\partial \sigma_X} \left(\sigma_X^{BID} - \sigma_X^{OFFER} \right) + \frac{\partial s_E}{\partial \sigma_Y} \left(\sigma_Y^{BID} - \sigma_Y^{OFFER} \right)$$

where we have assumed, for simplicity, that the sensitivities are not correlated to each other (i.e., there are no cross derivatives). Each sensitivity is obtained by calculating a numerical derivative. We subtract the value of the funding cost corresponding to the official bond value (the one calculated with a mid level of volatility) from the value of the funding cost corresponding to the bond calculated with a volatility $\sigma + \Delta\sigma$ and then divide this by $\Delta\sigma$. We do this for σ_X and σ_Y.

Another approach would be, of course, to avoid calculating the sensitivity first and simply calculate the value of the bond twice, once with the bid, once with the offer values and take the difference between the resulting funding spreads. This is faster, but calculating the sensitivity first enables the user to use it for alternative scenarios. Let us imagine we want to calculate the impact not only of the current bid-offer but also of historical bid-offers, or the impact of the average volatility variance for the past year or over some other horizon. If we have the sensitivity we do not need to keep valuing the bond, we simply multiply it by the desired volatility move.

A very similar approach applies to correlation. With the exception of the most liquid foreign exchange rates where one can calculate implied volatilities from traded option values, correlation is always a historical value. Similarly to volatility we could calculate a spread s_E''

$$s_E'' = \frac{\partial s_E}{\partial \rho_{X,Y}} \, Var \, [\rho_{X,Y}]$$

given by the sensitivity of F_j to the correlation between its variables multiplied by some measure of the variance in the correlation itself. This is important because the historical correlation we might use to price the trade, even assuming that there is such a thing as a historical value agreed upon by all, might not be the one leading to a tradable price in case of exit. A reserve for correlation would be put aside in the same way as for volatility.

The two examples above are linked to uncertainty about market inputs. Earlier, however, we mentioned that next to the question about the real value of our asset, we were also wondering what the cost of hedging the risks associated to the trade were, or in general if there should be reserves held against modeling choices.

In our example we said that the value of the coupon F_j is sensitive to the volatility skew of both variables X and Y. At this point we need to answer, are we able to model this skew, meaning, do we have a framework modeling $d\sigma_X$ and $d\sigma_Y$ as stochastic variables? We have not specified what X and Y are: in case they are equity prices or FX rates almost all market participants would have a model with their volatilities stochastic. Should they be rates, the same would probably be true; however, in case of more exotic variables, let us imagine that if X and Y are (forward) CDS rates, then we cannot assume that everyone has the ability to model their volatility skew.

Assuming that the transaction takes place despite this modeling deficiency, then we should account for the shortcoming. The typical way is to try to see what happens to the trade if we try to mimic the effect of skew by moving underlying and volatility together[6] and reprice the trade.

The outcome would be reflected in a corresponding funding level spread impact, which we shall call s_E'''. Should we be able to model (and therefore hedge) this feature, this would also have an impact in terms of hedging costs

---

[6] We remind the reader that the essence of a stochastic volatility model is one that not only models the volatility as a stochastic process but one that has a *non-zero correlation* between the volatility and the underlying itself. This is to take into consideration the cases where the underlying moves across the strike and the volatility changes accordingly.

on the bond value and therefore on the funding spread. For simplicity, we shall let s_E''' incorporate both effects (and for even greater simplicity, let us have it encapsulate other, maybe unusual, hedging costs, the point being that they all will have *some* impact).

We now have three correction spreads s_E', s_E'', and s_E''' and we ask ourselves whether this is still true

$$s_E + s_E' + s_E'' + s_E''' \overset{?}{\ll} s_V \qquad (6.5)$$

that is, whether it is still *very* much cheaper to fund ourselves with an exotic structure than with a vanilla one. The answer is probably no.

The point raised by Equation 6.5 is an important one and there are certainly many reasons beyond the purely mathematical ones driving the choice of structure and hence the funding level.

With the exceptions of governments (in particular those with an extremely good credit standing, let us think of Germany, Japan, the United States, etc.) that can limit themselves to issue plain vanilla bonds with the knowledge that investors will always buy them, all institutions need, for purely marketing purposes, to look for novelty and complexity in their debt management. This means that an exotic bond is not necessarily always issued with the goal of lowering the funding cost. Sometimes the simple goal is to attract investors. This is not unlike other industries: car manufacturers of middle-ranking brands often build one flashy model, not necessarily for profit but to attract attention to the rest of their plain vanilla fleet.[7]

A related point, which is not arguable, however, is whether an institution should have two correction factors $\widetilde{D_i}$, one for exotic structures and one for plain vanilla structures, applied to the discount factor D_i to price its bonds. To be more specific: if we need to calculate $F_i D_i \widetilde{D_i}$, that is, the present value of a cash flow of an institution's bond, do we need to know whether F_i is an exotic coupon or a plain vanilla coupon so as to use two different $\widetilde{D_i}$, one corresponding to s_E and the other to s_V? The answer is no: the credit of a bond is just one and there should be just one type of discounting. Although one might not be able to show that the two sides of Equation 6.5 are identical, the credit standing of an institution is unique irrespective of the type of structure.

---

[7]This is known as the *halo effect* and its usefulness is often argued over as it is in the financial instruments industry.

6.3 THE FUNDAMENTAL DIFFERENCES BETWEEN INVESTMENT BANKING AND DEVELOPMENT BANKING

In Section 3.3.2 we saw how the difference in spirit and practice between a for-profit and a not-for-profit institution leads to a fundamental difference in the pricing of the prepayment option in a loan. There are other differences that are closely reflected in the way trades are structured and/or priced.

The goal of a development institution is lending and it needs to ensure that the highest and safest amount of money is available for this purpose. In order to achieve this goal a development institution in general does not manage the risk of the bonds it issues, that is, it does not hedge them dynamically. Although we shall discuss this in more detail in Section 7.2.2, we can easily see how this not only would entail considerable risks and losses that would damage the capital intended for lending, it would also direct some of that capital toward building infrastructures and resources capable of the hedging activity. Development institutions tend to avoid this at the source and instead swap the bond with an external market participant, usually an investment bank.

If we look at Figure 6.2 we see that this structure is similar to the asset swap structure involving a general treasury desk (see Figure 1.3), the difference being that in an investment bank the swap would be between the

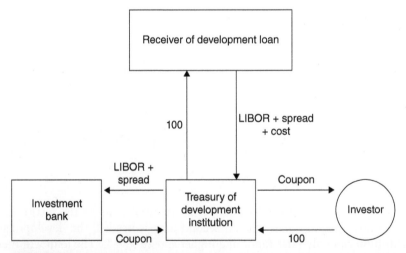

FIGURE 6.2 A graphic representation of the lending and borrowing carried out by a development institution.

treasury desk and another desk, whereas in the case of a development bank the asset swap would be with an external party.

The fact that development institutions enter into these types of structures ("swap out the bond" in the jargon), means that they do not face the usual financial risks inherent in the bond since these risks offset each other between the bond and the coupon leg of the asset swap. This also means that the importance of pricing an instrument correctly, as far as a development institution is concerned, is mainly due to counterparty risk and funding risk. (We shall see this in more detail in the next chapter and it is why we focused on discounting in Chapter 2.)

The previous point, although true of most development institutions, could also apply to medium-sized institutions not wanting to invest in a hedging infrastructure. In Figure 6.2 we notice, however, the role of the borrower in the structure of a development institution, in particular we see how and at which point the borrower is charged a cost. As a not-for-profit institution, this cost would be the only cost charged to the borrower. A development bank, after taking into account the cost of borrowing, will charge, in addition to this cost of borrowing, only the costs of maintaining the institution operational. This is in contrast to a normal investment bank, which seeks to maximize profits by borrowing as cheaply as possible and, simplifying the situation, lend the borrowed funds at the highest possible rate.

Let us imagine a development bank issuing a bond and swapping it out with

$$\sum_i (L_i + s_A) D_i dt_i - \sum_j F_j D_j dt_j \rightleftharpoons 1 - \sum_j F_j D_j \widetilde{D}_j dt_j - D_T \widetilde{D}_T$$

resulting in a cost of funding s_A. Let us imagine that the nominal value of the bond obtained from the investor is lent to a borrower through a loan (see Equation 3.23)

$$\sum_i S_i D_i [N_i (L_i + s_A + s_C) dt_i + (N_i - N_{i+1})] + R \sum_j N_j D_j (S_{j-1} - S_j)$$

$$(6.6)$$

where s_C is deemed enough to cover the running costs of the institution. Let us now imagine that, when a second loan is needed, the development institution can only raise funds at a higher spread $s_A + \epsilon$. The loan will then be issued with a spread over LIBOR of $s_A + \epsilon + s_C$. Conversely if the second loan could have been funded with a cheaper bond with spread $s_A - \delta$, the spread over LIBOR would have been $s_A - \delta + s_C$. (We need to remind the reader, however, as explained in Section 3.3.2, that the receiver of the first loan has no incentive to repay the first and switch the cheaper one since they would be charged the difference.)

The loan shown in Equation 6.6 is a fixed-spread loan, a loan with a variable coupon driven by the LIBOR level but where the spread, representing the funding cost of the lending institution, is fixed at the beginning of the loan. There is another type of loan, even more typical of development institutions, which is a loan where the cost of borrowing is passed through to the borrower with a variable rate. This loan could be written as

$$
\sum_i S_i D_i \left[N_i \left(L_i + s_A^i + s_C \right) dt_i + (N_i - N_{i+1}) \right] + R \sum_j N_j D_j \left(S_{j-1} - S_j \right)
$$

(6.7)

where s_A^i is now a variable changing with the same frequency as the LIBOR (although this is not a strict requirement). We shall see this with greater detail in the next chapter, but the value of this variable spread is roughly obtained by averaging the cost *at that moment in time* of all debt funding variable spread loans. In this type of loan it is even more evident the lack of profit for the development bank since the rate paid by the borrower rises and falls with the credit of the bank.

The above, combined with the special posting of collateral and the peculiar characteristics driving prepayment optionality we have seen in Section 3.3.2, are the main differences between a for-profit and a not-for-profit financial institution. In the next chapter we shall see, while discussing the risk management issue linked to combined borrowing and lending operations, how these have some profound and technical consequences.

6.4 BENCHMARKS FOR BORROWING AND INVESTING

We have seen the fundamental role of a treasury desk: borrowing for the institution in the most advantageous way. We have seen how a series of debt issuances can be combined to build a term structure of funding levels. This term structure, which we know is asset swap driven, is usually seen through a benchmark. Also, as we mentioned in Section 1.4, an important part of banking activity is investment, which is also measured against a benchmark. The relationship between the two is important.

We mentioned in Section 5.3.1 the concept of benchmark. In the context in which we presented it—the relative price of a bond—it represented an issuance against which other bonds could be compared. We mentioned that often, but not always, it is the better rated and most liquid bond within a certain group of debt instruments sharing the same currency.

The concept of benchmark as instrument of comparison can be applied to many other situations. Fund managers, for example, choose a benchmark so that the performance of their fund is never absolute but always relative. A fund manager dealing with equity underlyings might choose a stock index having several individual shares in common with his own fund so that the fund is considered to outperform or underperform the benchmark. The skilled manager will choose to populate the fund with the best performing stocks out of the index so that the fund always outperforms the index. A mathematically minded view of this is that the fund manager is trying to approximate a complex function with its tangent plus something, that something being hopefully positive. The idea of the tangent has percolated in the common terminology of alphas and betas where alpha is the slope of the straight line, the tangent, and the elusive beta is the outperformance.

In finance nothing is absolute, every variable and every performance can be seen in another context (the easiest example would be another currency) and therefore to be able to measure something in as solid a relative way as possible is very important. This is particularly important as far as borrowing and investing is concerned.

6.4.1 Borrowing

A financial institution of any kind borrows through a large number of debt instruments and each time, as we have seen, the search is for the cheapest possible funding cost. What is the best possible way of monitoring whether our borrowing capabilities are improving or worsening? It is through deciding on a benchmark.

The outcome of an asset swap is in fact a benchmark and one of the most rigorous possible.[8] An issuer, by swapping each debt instrument into a simple flow of interest rate plus spread, expresses the value of its debt pool relative to that floating rate, in practice the issuer's benchmark. From the expression "institution ABC borrows for five years at X plus Y" we gather that ABC's benchmark is the rate X. Here we need to specify that not all benchmarks are the result of an asset swap: retail banks that have access to deposits or commercial banks with access to some central bank lending facility will have the deposit rate and the overnight rate as benchmarks. Our

---

[8] Let us remind ourselves of what we said in Section 5.3.1: although other measures, such as z-spreads or spreads over a swap rate are useful indicators, only the asset swap spread constitutes a rigorous and unambiguous value.

focus, however, will be on benchmarks, which are the result of an asset swap. This means that we are trying to attach a relative value to debt issuance.

In Section 6.1 we showed the example of an entity issuing debt in different currencies and in Section 6.2 we discussed some of the reasons entities might choose to do so. How does this affect the construction of a benchmark? The question should be, does the issuer want to have exposure to any foreign currency Y at all or it does it only wish to have exposure to its own currency X? Should the issuer wish to be exposed to Y, the currency of the bond, then it will enter into an asset swap

$$
N^Y \sum_i \left(L_i^Y + s_A^Y \right) D_i^Y dt_i \; - \; N^Y \sum_j F_j D_j^Y dt_j
$$

$$
\rightleftharpoons N^Y \left\{ 1 - \sum_j F_j D_j \widetilde{D}_j^Y dt_j - D_T^Y \right\} \widetilde{D}_T^Y
\tag{6.8}
$$

The above means that although its native currency is X, the issuer chooses to borrow against a foreign benchmark, in this case the Y-LIBOR L_i^Y (calling it LIBOR and losing some of the general tone helps to picture a practical situation). The exposure to L^Y will need to be managed.

Should the issuer choose not to be exposed to L^Y, it has two options. The first and most obvious one is to issue a bond directly in X resulting in the following asset swap

$$
N^X \sum_i \left(L_i^X + s_A^X \right) D_i^X dt_i \; - \; N^X \sum_j F_j D_j^X dt_j
$$

$$
\rightleftharpoons N^X \left\{ 1 - \sum_j F_j D_j \widetilde{D}_j^X dt_j - D_T^X \right\} \widetilde{D}_T^X
\tag{6.9}
$$

with asset swap spread s_A^X. Alternatively it can issue a swap in Y and swap the bond through a cross currency asset swap of the type

$$
N^X \left\{ -1 + \sum_i \left(L_i^X + s_A^{\widetilde{X}} \right) D_i^X dt_i + D_T^X \right\}
$$

$$
- N^Y \left\{ -1 + \sum_j F_j D_j^Y dt_j + D_T^Y \right\}
\tag{6.10}
$$

$$
\rightleftharpoons N^Y \left\{ 1 - \sum_j F_j D_j \widetilde{D}_j^Y dt_j - D_T^Y \right\} \widetilde{D}_T^Y
$$

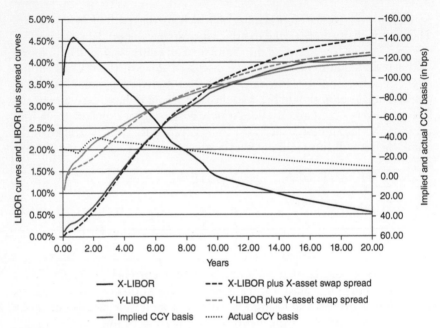

FIGURE 6.3 A plot, on the primary axis, of the LIBOR and funding curves in currencies X and Y and an inverted plot, on the secondary axis, of the currency basis between X and Y and the implied currency basis.

In the previous situation, although the bond was issued in Y, the credit standing of the borrower is measured, through the asset swap spread $s_A^{\widehat{X}}$, against the X-LIBOR L_i^X. In Equation 6.10 we note the two -1 in the swap; they indicate the principal exchange in the swap, and the fact that the asset swap spread $s_A^{\widehat{X}}$ has the index $\widehat{X}$ to denote that it is different from the two previous equations.

Figure 6.3 tries to draw a picture of the preceding situation for an institution of good credit standing that uses X as its operating currency. In the plot we show some realistic curves for LIBOR in currency X and Y and the funding curves in each currency for the institution. These funding curves are basically $L_t^X + s_{A,t}^X$ and $L_t^Y + s_{A,t}^Y$.

In Section 6.1, using as an example the debt of the Republic of Italy, we touched upon the relation between asset swap spreads in different currencies and the cross currency basis between the same two currencies. Asset swap spreads and currency basis are after all constants added to the same rate; it would only be normal to be curious about the differences between the two funding curves on one side and the currency basis on the other. To put it differently, from a currency basis swap we are told that we can substitute one rate plus basis whenever we see the other one. What happens when we do that in the context of an asset swap? On the secondary axis of Figure 6.3 we have two plots, the difference between the two funding curves, continuous line, and the actual cross currency basis between currencies X and Y, dashed line, that is, that number b_c such that

$$N^Y \left\{ -1 + \sum_i \left(L_i^Y + b_C \right) D_i^Y dt_i + D_T^Y \right\} = N^X \left\{ -1 + \sum_i L_i^X D_i^X dt_i + D_T^X \right\}$$

holds true. Before interpreting the plot, let us recap that there are three possible situations for our institution issuing in X or Y. It can issue a bond in X and swap it against X-LIBOR (as described by Equation 6.9 and leading to $L_t^X + s_A^X$); it can issue a bond in Y and swap it against Y-LIBOR (as described by Equation 6.8 and leading to $L_t^Y + s_A^Y$); finally, it can issue in Y and swap it against X-LIBOR (as described by Equation 6.10 and leading to $L_t^X + s_A^{\hat{X}}$).

The difference between the second and third situation is that in the second the institution takes exposure to Y-LIBOR and its funding spread s_A^Y is truly measured against a foreign benchmark. In the third situation, although the institution is issuing a bond in Y, we cannot say that its funding level $s_A^{\hat{X}}$ is measured against a foreign benchmark. We would expect the second situation to be independent of the currency basis levels whereas the third to be closely linked and one could almost say implied. To express this formally

$$s_A^Y + b_c \neq s_A^X$$
$$s_A^{\hat{X}} + b_c = s_A^X \tag{6.11}$$

In Figure 6.3 we have plotted, for currency Y, the funding curve corresponding to the second situation, a full exposure and benchmarking to Y-LIBOR. This means that if we take the difference between that curve and the funding curve in X we are asking ourselves the question

$$L_i^X + s_A^X - \left(L_i^Y + s_A^Y \right) \overset{?}{=} 0$$
$$L_i^Y + b_C + s_A^X - \left(L_i^Y + s_A^Y \right) \overset{?}{=} 0 \tag{6.12}$$
$$s_A^Y - s_A^X \overset{?}{=} b_C$$

with the answer being no, as we see from the plot in Figure 6.3 where the actual currency basis is plotted.

The same exercise with the third situation would have been equivalent
to asking ourselves

$$L_i^X + s_A^X - \left(L_i^Y + s_A^{\widehat{X}}\right) \overset{?}{=} 0$$

$$L_i^Y + b_C + s_A^X - \left(L_i^Y + s_A^{\widehat{X}}\right) \overset{?}{=} 0 \qquad (6.13)$$

$$b_C + s_A^X - s_A^X - b_C \overset{?}{=} 0$$

with the tautological answer being yes since, as we stated in Equation 6.11,
we know that $s_A^{\widehat{X}}$ is derived from the currency basis itself.

The plot in Figure 6.3 is interesting for another reason, which is connected to what we mentioned in Section 5.3.3 about the relation between
CDS spreads and other relative measures of a bond's credit.

We mentioned how each form of risk is different, although, in rough
qualitative terms, they all indicate the same thing: a large spread added to
any rate indicates a worse credit standing than a smaller one.

We explained why, for many reasons some of which were the inclusion
of the recovery value, one cannot simply take the CDS spread and add it
unto a zero or LIBOR the same way one can add a z-spread or an asset
swap spread.

Figure 6.3 shows the example of a fortunate institution, which in the
short term can borrow at sub-LIBOR, meaning that the spread over LIBOR
is negative: one could never find a CDS spread value smaller than zero. Of
course the immediate counterargument to this reasoning is that one should
not see a CDS spread as potentially a spread over LIBOR but over a risk-
free/overnight-like rate, which of course would be lower. Over the same rate
an asset swap spread, although it would be technically meaningless but let us
for a moment take a rough qualitative view, would also be positive. However,
since a CDS is not meant to be seen as a spread on anything, the counterargument is as open to interpretation as the initial argument. Perhaps the
interesting point out of this is that the LIBOR is a rate high enough in value
so as to serve as a benchmark to negative spreads, something that, in the
previous example, we had not seen yet.

Why is it important that the difference between the X funding curve
and the Y funding curve is smaller (note the inverted secondary axis) than
the actual cross currency basis? Anyone who can borrow at X-LIBOR can,
by virtue of the definition of a cross currency basis swap[9] borrow in currency

---

[9]We remind ourselves of the fact that, the same way the X-LIBOR is the average rate
at which financial institutions lend to each other, Y-LIBOR plus currency basis is the
rate at which foreign, with respect to Y, banks borrow in the Y currency market.

Y at Y-LIBOR plus (minus in this case, as the basis is negative) the currency basis. We have seen that our institution can borrow in currency X in the short term at less than X-LIBOR; there would be no point in issuing debt in currency Y if it could not get something a lot better (that is, cheaper) than what it would get anyway by trading a simple cross currency basis swap.

6.4.2 Investing

We started the present section by mentioning that one of the most common uses of the term benchmark was in relation to fund management and investment. It is only natural to finish it by mentioning in what way investment activity can be related to a chosen benchmark.

Although it is not absolutely necessary, it is helpful to have a similar benchmark for borrowing and investments within the same financial institution. The institution knows at which level, with respect to the chosen benchmark, it borrows and therefore, using a similar benchmark for investments, knows whether its investments are returning a profit or a loss. An institution using, for example, the LIBOR as a borrowing benchmark would also measure the return of its investments with respect to LIBOR.[10] Of course an institution could have more than one benchmark, for example, a Treasury benchmark or a constant duration LIBOR benchmark for the main bulk of its long-term, relatively less liquid, investments and an overnight type benchmark for a smaller, more liquid, portfolio of investments.

The investment activity of a traditional financial institution would cover the entire visible (and probably also the invisible to the commoner's eye) spectrum of financial activities. To cover those would be beyond the scope of this book. The investment activities of a development institution are, on the other hand, more vanilla and resemble those of a conservative fund. Let us not forget, as we have mentioned in Section 1.4, that in a development institution the fundamental goals of its investment division are upkeeping its equity and, most important, providing an emergency liquidity buffer. Because of the latter requirement its investments tend to be very liquid and, for the most part, short-dated instruments. The type of investments would fall roughly in four categories: deposits, bonds, asset-backed securities (ABS), and liquid instruments such as Equities and FX.

A deposit as an investment consists of, as one would imagine, placing a certain amount of money with a (usually foreign, we shall discuss why

---

[10]We have omitted, for simplicity, the fact that we would specify further which type of LIBOR we would use as benchmark, the three-month LIBOR, the six-month LIBOR, and so on.

toward the end of this section) bank. The time horizon for this type of investment is usually short, less than a year.

We discussed bonds at length, and we understand what an investment in a bond, that is, its purchase, would entail. We are lending money to the issuer and receive a coupon in return. Although our discussion took us away from it when we introduced asset swaps, we showed that they can, of course, be used not only when we are the issuers but also when we are the investors. We shall discuss this in more detail in Section 7.3.1, but when we, as a development institution,[11] invest in a bond (and the same applies to a deposit) we immediately enter into an asset swap so that our income is not the coupon itself of the bond but the spread over some floating rate we earn from the asset swap counterpart. The spread we earn over the floating rate, which hopefully for illustration purposes would be similar to our benchmark, would be the visible monetization of the credit risk of the issuer. Later in this section, after discussion on the role of FX in investment strategies, we shall return to this idea.

According to the type or according to the conceptual depth at which they are analyzed, Asset Backed Securities can be either fairly simple or very complicated. The fundamental idea is straightforward: the investor receives a set of coupons paid with the cash flows from a set of receivables. At first this does not seem different from a normal bond. A government issuing a bond will pay the bond's coupon with the government's income, for example its tax receivables. A manufacturer will honor its obligation using, say, its revenues from sales. The difference however is that an issuer of a normal bond does not have to specify what will be used to repay its debt,[12] whereas the issuer of an asset-backed security will. For example an issuer would take receivables from, say, credit cards, student loans, mortgages, and so on, and on the back of them pay a coupon to an investor.

The link between the disparate set of receivables and the ABS is the pinnacle of securitization. This repackaging, using the rather ugly term often seen in the popular press, brings out a first credit issue. The issuer of a normal bond has a certain flexibility in repaying its debt: even if, for the sake of argument, an entire region of a country were to stop paying income tax, that country's government would still have other income to repay its immediate

---

[11]We stress this, not because it is important that we are a development institution, but because it is important for our discussion that we do not attempt to hedge the bond ourselves and choose to asset swap it with a third party. The same could apply to the investment unit of a corporate institution.

[12]The French government will never state, for example, that the coupons of the August 16, 2016, fixed-coupon bond will be paid with the taxes from the citizens of Lille.

debt. On the other hand, if a few loans linked to a certain ABS default, even if the ABS issuer has other income, the coupons of the ABS itself are affected and the ABS investor would suffer. In order to take this into account, an ABS is usually segmented into tranches, which can be seen as safety buffers: should only a few loans default, not all investors will be affected in the same way, some actually will not be affected at all.

Let us give an example of an ABS built on the back of the receivables from a pool of 10 loans. The issuer decides to create three tranches. Tranche C will pay a coupon of 10% if *at most* two loans default: should three or more loans default, coupon payments cease. Tranche B will pay a coupon of 5% if *at most* four loans default: should five or more loans default, coupon payments cease. Finally, tranche A will pay a coupon of 2% if *at most* six loans will default: should seven or more loans default, coupon payments will cease. It is easy to see that the tranches are ordered by increasing riskiness from A to C, which is also why an investor in the C tranche receives a far higher coupon than an investor in the A tranche.

For our purposes the credit risk of an ABS can be monetized in the same way as the credit risk of a bond or a deposit through a swap. We shall see in Section 7.3.1 that there are a few ways to hedge an ABS and each would lead to a different return over a floating benchmark.

Finally, a conceptually simple form of investment is to buy shares. In Section 7.3.1 we will see how even an equity investment can be turned, using an equity return swap, into a spread over a floating rate and thus as a return over a benchmark. Shares can also be held on their own without swapping them, but of course this strategy is riskier. In general, for a prudent investor an equity position is not necessarily interesting: if hedged through a swap it looses its risk but it also leads to a modest return; if held on its own it can, of course, lead to a great profit but at a great risk.

Before returning to discussing investment returns with respect to a certain benchmark, let us point out some interesting aspects of investing in different currencies, a topic we have touched in the previous section when discussing the relationship between the funding curves in different currencies.

Let us first discuss the basics of investing in different currencies. Let us leave aside for a moment all that we have said about issuing debt, let us just imagine that we already have the funds we want to invest and therefore ignore the cost of borrowing. Why would we invest in a different currency? The first naive look at interest rates would tempt us to say, let us choose a currency in which the nominal interest rate is very high or at least higher than the one in our own currency and simply change our funds into that currency and let the interest rate increase our capital. A closer look would show that this is not as attractive as it sounds. Our strategy, to summarize, would be to exchange our funds N_X from our currency X into currency Y, let interest rate R_Y (which is higher than our own interest rate, that is, $R_Y > R_X$) increase our capital in Y, and then exchange it back into X to realize the profit. Formally this amounts to

$$N_X \frac{1}{F X_{X/Y}^0} (1 + R_Y)^T F X_{X/Y}^T \qquad (6.14)$$

where $F_{X/Y}^T$ is the forward FX rate at time T. This, we think at first, is a more attractive investment than simply investing at our own interest rate, a strategy that would yield $N_X (1 + R_X)^T$. However, we know from the definition of forward FX rate that the equation above could be written as

$$N_X \frac{1}{F X_{X/Y}^0} (1 + R_Y)^T F X_{X/Y}^0 \frac{(1 + R_X)^T}{(1 + R_Y)^T} = N_X (1 + R_X)^T \qquad (6.15)$$

meaning that there is no difference between our strategy and doing nothing at all. The reasoning is that all financial variables are part of an arbitrage-free world: the FX forward rates are there, one could say, exactly for this purpose, to compensate the temptation to exploit an interest rate differential.

It turns out, however, that our naive reasoning was not so naive and that practice shows that it can yield a profit. This is part of the phenomenon known as the forward premium puzzle first shown by Bilson [13]. Before we have decided to leave aside the need for borrowing. We can easily see, however, that the strategy mentioned above works also when it comes to borrowing. We could be tempted to think that we could borrow in the X currency where the interest rate R_X is low, exchange the principal into currency Y where the interest rate R_Y is higher, and then at time T after having realized a profit in X, exchange the needed amount in Y so that we can repay the initial debt.

The fact that the above has worked in practice (going against our arbitrage-free reasoning) is due again to the forward premium puzzle and is at the origin of the so-called carry trades. Carry trading is a vast topic (see, for example, Candelaria et al. [25] or Plantin and Shin [71]) but it can be summarized in the forward puzzle given by the fact that the FX spot will *consistently* not follow the expected forward and therefore, by changing our principal at time T not at the forward level but at a rate *close to the spot* level, we make a profit. To explain this let us rewrite Equation 6.14 stressing the profit as the difference between our final and initial situation (our initial situation being our possession of N_X).

The theoretical profit $P_{\text{Theoretical}}$ would be

$$
\begin{aligned}
P_{\text{Theoretical}} &= N_X \frac{1}{F X^0_{X/Y}} (1 + R_Y)^T F X^T_{X/Y} - N_X \\
&= N_X \frac{1}{F X^0_{X/Y}} (1 + R_Y)^T F X^0_{X/Y} \frac{(1 + R_X)^T}{(1 + R_Y)^T} - N_X \\
&= N_X (1 + R_X)^T - N_X \\
&= N_X R_X
\end{aligned}
$$

which, of course, is identical to the one we would have obtained by not going through the strategy and simply investing in our local interest rate. The other strategy consists of taking advantage of the fact that we know, actually we feel, that the spot FX rate at time T will be very similar to the spot FX today and therefore our actual profit P_{Actual} will be

$$
\begin{aligned}
P_{\text{Actual}} &= N_X \frac{1}{F X^0_{X/Y}} (1 + R_Y)^T F X^0_{X/Y} - N_X \\
&= N_X (1 + R_Y)^T - N_X \\
&= N_X R_Y
\end{aligned}
$$

which, by virtue of the difference in the interest rates, is higher than $N_X R_X$. Needless to say, the strategy is rather risky since, once we accept that the actual FX rate is disjoint from the expected forward value, it becomes difficult, pun not intended, to know what to expect.

Why this phenomenon exists is a fascinating topic that tends to leave the realm of finance toward the one of economics (see for example Burnside et al. [24], Backus and Smith [6], or Bansal and Dahlquist [9]). In essence one could say that, using an almost scientific terminology, the financial system in these situations is not isolated or autonomous anymore and thus the presence of external macroeconomic variables leads to the failure of common arbitrage assumptions. Remaining with the scientific simile, this situation is similar to those physical experiments (actual or numerical) where one realizes that energy is not conserved and to understand the problem one has to consider external variables. In the situation of the forward premium puzzle, these variables might be of macroeconomic nature not easily quantifiable with capital markets parameters.

Why this digression discussing carry trades and foreign currency investments? We have mentioned how the investment tools of a development institution are limited (because of risk aversion) when compared to those of a traditional investment bank. A large part of these tools consists of fairly vanilla cross currency transactions aiming at converting costs, spreads, and basis from one currency to another in search for a profit. Previously we have described the concept of carry trade to depict the context in which these transactions take place. In order to continue we need to state that what we have shown in Equations 6.14 and 6.15 is actually not quite true or at least is a bit more subtle. To the reader who has followed our discussion from curve construction in the beginning to the considerations of credit in the chapter on bond pricing, the choice of a rate R_Y must have seemed a little too generic. This feeling would be justified and therefore let us try to be more specific.

Let us remind ourselves of a very important point we raised in Section 2.4.2. When trading an FX forward, an FX trader will think of nothing but an exchange of two principals in different currencies, and only his perception of their future relative value will drive the price. However, we also know that the rate one implies from an FX forward (a less risky instrument) is a rate that is less risky, hence lower, than the LIBOR in the same currency. This consideration should help qualify our statement in Equation 6.15 and, in particular, our use of R_X and R_Y.

The summary of our situation is the following: We have an amount N_X and we could either lend it to a financial institution in the country with currency X and earn L_X (X-LIBOR) or exchange it at the spot $F_{X/Y}^0$, lend it to a financial institution in the country with currency Y, earn L_Y (Y-LIBOR), and then exchange back into X at $F_{X/Y}^T$. We assume, although it is not essential in this version of the example (we shall understand this later), that $L_Y > L_X$.

Let us assume that, since we said that the rate implied by an FX forward is lower than LIBOR, we can write the FX forward used in Equation 6.14 as

$$FX_{X/Y}^T = FX_{X/Y}^0 \frac{(1 + L_X - c_X)^T}{(1 + L_Y - c_Y)^T} \approx FX_{X/Y}^0 \frac{(1 + L_X)^T (1 - c_X)^T}{(1 + L_Y)^T (1 - c_Y)^T} \quad (6.16)$$

where the approximation is to render subsequent calculations easier. The two unspecified amounts c_X and c_Y denote the fact that the rates implied by an FX forward are lower than LIBOR. If we insert the above consideration in Equation 6.15 we have

$$N_X \frac{1}{FX_{X/Y}^0} (1 + L_Y)^T FX_{X/Y}^0 \frac{(1 + L_X)^T (1 - c_X)^T}{(1 + L_Y)^T (1 - c_Y)^T} = N_X (1 + L_X)^T \frac{(1 - c_X)^T}{(1 - c_Y)^T}$$

$$(6.17)$$

If we have that[13] $c_X < c_Y$, the preceding leads to a better strategy than simply investing in currency X where we would earn L_X.

How can this happen? The extra earning we obtain is because we are assuming the higher credit risk of the institution in the country with currency Y. Let us stress again that the values c_X and c_Y are purely for illustration purposes; they are a way of constructing for the reader an interest rate that is lower than LIBOR. Nothing in the definition of FX forward and in the way they are traded indicates the formal existence of such rate. Having said that, the values c_X and c_Y bear some similarities to cross currency basis. We have mentioned that a cross currency basis can be thought of as a correction to the interest rate parity (the FX interest rate relationship we are using in these equations). The nature of this correction, we need to stress again, can only be gathered when comparing rates *implied* from these instruments and not in any formal rates.

To illustrate the issue of credit encapsulated in c_X and c_Y, let us consider another example, one where we do not use FX forwards that might confuse us a little but instead we use cross currency basis swaps. Let us then take the further step of choosing two specific currencies USD and EUR instead of X and Y. This is so that we become (as many institutions are) USD-centered and we adopt the currency against which the majority of currency basis are quoted.

We have mentioned at the beginning of this section the investment in deposits and bonds and the fact that often these are foreign. Let us imagine that we have an amount N_{USD}, which we could invest in our own country and earn L_{USD}. Let us imagine an alternative scenario in which we undertake two transactions: one EUR-USD cross currency floating for floating swap and the purchase of a bond of an average EUR-centered financial institution.

We know from the definition of cross currency basis swap (Equation 2.8) that we have an initial and a final exchange of principals, which means that we exchange, with our swap counterpart, N_{USD} for N_{EUR} (its EUR equivalent) at the beginning of the swap and we exchange *the same amounts* at the end of the swap. This means that we have N_{EUR} with which we can purchase a floating-rate bond of an average EUR-centered financial institution paying L_{EUR} flat. The maturity of the bond and the swap are the same and the payment frequency of the EUR leg of the swap is the same as the one of the bond.[14] The final repayment of N_{EUR} in the bond will be used for the final exchange in the swap. The standard cross currency basis swap, the

---

[13]The choice of currencies in this strategy would be such that this would be true.
[14]This transaction, while similar in principle, is not an asset swap. First, the two transactions are not formally linked other than in our strategy. Second, here we are

one where we exchange USD-LIBOR flat for EUR-LIBOR plus (a negative) basis, is quoted in the market as having a basis $-b_C$.

The overall transaction therefore is such that, by simply looking at the cash flows and not the initial and final exchange/purchase (which we have already described in words), from the bond, we earn

$$N_{EUR} \sum_j L_{EUR}^j$$

and in the swap we pay and receive the following

$$-N_{EUR} \sum_j L_{EUR}^j + N_{USD} \sum_i \left(L_{USD}^i + \widehat{b_C} \right)$$

Combining the two we see that we earn $\widehat{b_C}$ over USD-LIBOR. (If, from the definition of EUR-USD cross currency basis swap, EUR-LIBOR minus something is equal to USD-LIBOR flat, EUR-LIBOR flat must be equal to something[15] greater than USD-LIBOR.)

This strategy can exploit an investment across currencies to earn a profit above one's benchmark. An institution that has an investment benchmark of USD-LIBOR can earn a basis on top of its benchmark by monetizing the higher credit risk of EUR-centered institution. We can observe this return not only in terms of the benchmark but also in terms of the funding cost we have seen in Section 6.4.1: If an institution borrows at a level lower than LIBOR and earns a return at a level higher than LIBOR, of course, this is not a bad outcome.

A clarification is needed, though, when this involves a development bank. While it is the goal of a traditional investment bank (not to mention a hedge fund) to fund financial investment through borrowing, the same is usually not in the mandate of a development bank. Borrowing should be used for the sole purpose of funding lending[16] toward development goals: only

---

simply trying to match the values of the cash flow values of the two transactions rather than the values of the instruments themselves.

[15]This, which is obvious once we look at the equation, will not be exactly equal to b_C. If we take the basis from one side of the equation to the other in Equation 2.8 we see that we must have

$$\widehat{b_C} = b_C \frac{\sum_j D_j^{EUR}}{\sum_i D_i^{USD}} \qquad (6.18)$$

[16]Lending in the context of development banking would not be considered a financial investment; in the context of traditional banking it might.

funds obtained otherwise should be used toward financial investment. This means that measuring investment returns against the funding level, although interesting (one should be worried if the former were consistently lower than the latter), is not really meaningful as the two activities are clearly separated. This is why the benchmark, while similar, is not necessarily the same. The same can usually be said of a government that would not borrow to fund financial investments. Sovereign wealth funds invest money that has been obtained through extra income and not through borrowing.

6.4.3 Case Study: A Note on the LIBOR Scandal

It is probably appropriate to end this section, where the LIBOR has been mentioned so many times, with a topical note on the LIBOR scandal taking place at the time of writing. We introduced the LIBOR in Section 2.2.4 where we briefly stated that it is an interest rate set in London every day for a range of currencies. Every morning a number of financial institutions are asked at what rate they could borrow a reasonable amount of money if they needed to. The four highest and lowest rates are eliminated and the remaining ones are averaged: the resulting rate is the LIBOR published by the British Bankers Association (BBA).

Although we have not mentioned hedging yet, we have discussed activities resulting in the two possible positions an institution can take with respect to a rate, that is, long and short. A long position with respect to an interest rate benefits from an increasing rate and suffers from a decreasing one. A short position has an opposite behavior. It is not difficult to see how debt linked to a floating rate such as LIBOR is inherently a short position with respect to it[17] and a loan or an investment is inherently a long position.

The financial institutions involved in setting the LIBOR might have been balanced in terms of direction in their overall positions, however, some of the individuals at a more granular level had a strong incentive for the rate to take certain values. Because of this, some of them allegedly tried and sometimes succeeded in manipulating the LIBOR. Since, as we said, the four extreme values on each side are eliminated, in order for the manipulation to be effective quite a few players need to be involved. The reasons for the manipulations or foul play were essentially two: either an individual had a

---

[17]Although we shall discuss this later by introducing the concept of cost and income in the context of reset risk, let us state here that we are simply discussing the sensitivity to the value of the actual rate: *we are not considering discounting*. Basically we are asking the question, if tomorrow we fix the rate of the next coupon on a bond or a loan, what is the effect of the LIBOR on its value?

derivative position linked to LIBOR that would benefit from a specific (higher or lower) fixing or the institution would benefit from submitting a (lower) figure to be averaged in order to show the market its (relatively good) credit standing. The former would be effective only if enough players participated in the manipulation, while the latter, which was essentially only a form of signaling, could always be effective. The ambiguity lied in the fact that these figures were not results of actual trades but only answers to a hypothetical question. Further research would be needed to ascertain whether the manipulators were clever enough not to do so on days in which the bank would issue actual debt, since a blatant discrepancy between the rate submitted and the coupon paid on the bond would have given the game away.

What was the impact of these manipulations on the wider financial world and what would they look like in the context of the benchmarks we have been discussing? Trillions of dollars (the LIBOR in USD is the most important of the rates published by the BBA) worth of contracts are linked to the LIBOR. These range from bonds to swaps, from corporate loans to home mortgages. Each of these positions is one-sided in the sense that if the rate is manipulated, that is, is different from a true value (if such thing even makes sense), then there is an actual gain or loss. If I have a mortgage linked to the six-month LIBOR and the next rate fixes at 3.12% instead of the true 3.15%, then I make an implicit gain of 3 bps of principal. (The mortgage lender makes an identical loss.) Should one know exactly on which dates the rates have been manipulated and by how much, it is not impossible to assess the global gain or loss caused by the manipulation. The exercise would be nonetheless far from trivial.

When discussing benchmarks as we have done in the past few sections, the situation is, however, a little different. It is going to be only in Chapter 7 that we are going to study in detail the relationship between income and cost, but we have already seen how essentially the business of a simple financial institution is to borrow at a certain rate and lend at another. The same way as borrowing and investing, as we have shown in the previous sections, are linked to a benchmark, so is lending. It makes sense to have the same benchmark for both activities or at least benchmarks that are easily relatable. Let us imagine for simplicity that both lending and borrowing is linked to the LIBOR, which we call L. Then our income will be given by

$$\text{Income} = L + l$$

where l is a positive lending spread and our debt is given by

$$\text{Debt} = L + b$$

where b is a positive borrowing spread. Crucially we have $l > b$. This means that our net income is

$$\text{Net} = l - b$$

It is easy to see how in the case of a simple borrowing and lending activity such as the one illustrated above, where both activities are benchmarked to the same LIBOR L, our net income is unaffected by the actual value of the LIBOR. This means that as far as our discussion is concerned the effect of manipulations on the LIBOR is nonexistent.

Of course, the above example is a particularly oversimplified scenario: even assuming that both lending and borrowing activities are linked to the same benchmark, the rate L will not be necessarily the same since it is unlikely that it will fix exactly on the same day. We shall discuss this in great detail in Section 7.4.4, as it is the essence of the problem of reset risk. Here we can say that if indeed the rate L appearing in the two equations above is not the same because they are in fact two different LIBOR set on two different days, then the manipulation could have an effect on our activity. Let us imagine that one of the two rates L has been manipulated away from its true value by an amount ϵ (which can be either positive or negative).[18] We assume only one has been affected since manipulations did not happen every day. This means that our net income now is $l - b + \epsilon$ and we are not anymore indifferent to the effect of the manipulation.

---

[18]The tendency was for the manipulations to lower the LIBOR, however, we shall assume that they could act in either direction.

CHAPTER 7

Risk and Asset Liability Management

Throughout this book we have switched more or less freely in our discussion between traditional investment banks and development institutions. In a development institution (or a small financial institution) the financial activities carried out by the treasury amount to the near totality of all the financial activity of the institution since the remaining ones are fairly basic. In a traditional investment bank the treasury desk is just one of many. As far as risk is concerned we need to introduce the subject with a qualifier as to which type of institution we will be mainly focusing on. Throughout this book we have been focusing on debt (bonds) and loans, and it is the relation between the two that we will be focusing on now: the managing of this relation and the risk involved is defined as asset liability management, as we have mentioned in Section 1.4.

We will begin by discussing leverage and in particular how much of the lending activity is funded by debt; we shall then digress a little with an introduction to hedging and risk neutrality in order to explain what it means when bonds are hedged dynamically or statically. An important section, the core of asset liability management, on the types of funding risks follows; it will be supported by two numerical sections in which we explain these concepts through examples.

A traditional financial institution would face and manage risks (currency, credit, etc.) that in their complexity are beyond our scope. Although throughout the chapter asset liability management is going to be our main focus, in Section 7.3 we will show some examples of simple management tools for credit and other simple market variables.

7.1 THE ISSUE OF LEVERAGE

In Section 3.1.2 we touched upon the issue of leverage and the potential havoc it can create in a market. The same way as a lever enables us to lift a great weight with little effort, financial leverage enables us, to put it crudely, to make a lot out of a little. The functioning of a lever, however, abides by the rules of classical mechanics and calculus. The functioning of financial leverage resides instead in the realm of stochastic calculus, meaning that, in order to work we need to accept the possibility of losing a lot out of a little. To be precise, what makes financial leverage dangerous is that, since we cannot physically lose more than everything we have, the loss gets propagated toward someone else.

The simplest example of leverage is the type of mortgage that used to be popular before the financial crisis of 2007 to 2009. Let us imagine that we have $5,000, we borrow $95,000 to purchase a house worth $100,000, and agree with the bank to pay $5,000 a year to service the debt. At the end of one year the price of the house rises to $125,000, we sell it and, once interest payments are taken into account, we make a profit of $15,000, 300% of our initial capital. The extraordinary profit is explained by the fact that we took exposure to 20 times our initial capital. The danger we were mentioning before is the contagious nature of this structure: had the house price dropped below $95,000 (and entered the famous negative equity zone gripping the news headlines), the loss would be on the bank's side.

The type of approach shown above in the domestic sphere is key to the functioning of hedge funds in the financial markets sphere. A central strategy to hedge fund trading is taking a spread position and betting that a difference between two variables is going to take a certain direction. Since the difference is usually small, profit is made only if the overall position is very large. Profit is also made if the position is held until the outcome of the bet becomes known: should the position be exited beforehand, there is a great danger of a liquidity ripple effect. This is basically what happened during the crisis originated by the default of Long Term Capital Management, and the link to liquidity is explored by Jorion [56] and by Adrian and Shin [2].

We are looking closely at the core of any bank's activity, the relationship between its borrowing and lending operations. Liquidity risk is strongly linked to this core and to the funds that sustain lending. Funding liquidity risk is defined (see Drehmann and Nikolau [31]) as the inability to settle obligations with immediacy: this inability can lead to default.

We shall observe in Section 7.4 the dynamics of the flow going from the income generated by the lending to the cost represented by the borrowing. If this careful balancing exercise is interrupted, the institution faces liquidity risk.[1] Leverage exacerbates all this. Since income must be *overall* greater than the costs necessary to serve our debt, when the debt principal becomes similar in size to, or even greater than, the income principal (lending income for financial institutions or revenues for sovereign or corporate entities) there is a great risk. Particularly considering the fact that often the cost is fixed and the income is variable (the simplest picture is a country paying a fixed coupon on a bond using revenues coming from a variable tax collection), should the expected income not be enough to meet the immediate obligations, unless there are some assets (basically cash) that can be used to do so, there is a possibility of default.

These considerations are at the center of the discussions about capital requirements for financial institutions, the most recent expression of which are the Basel II agreement [8] and the forthcoming Basel III agreement. Capital requirements are a way of ensuring that financial institutions have those assets mentioned above such that they can immediately and safely meet obligations in case income is less than anticipated. These are not unlike one of the Euro convergence criteria, which was a debt-to-GDP ratio of less than 60%. The capital requirement can be seen as a number of units of principal needed as capital against every 100 units of principal lent. If one institution lends 100, the same institution needs to have X units in cash (or an equivalent liquid asset), which is similar to say that it cannot have a debt with principal greater than $100 - X$ units.

Since to keep cash is not very profitable, financial institutions in general have historically tried to push for the lowest possible capital requirements. After the 2007 to 2009 financial crisis this position is harder to defend since, should there be large write-offs, the government needs to intervene, and it is only fair that banks, through their own cash, cover a larger portion of these write-offs. Development institutions, not surprisingly, maintain an equity pool that far exceeds any past, or potentially agreed in the future, capital requirements. In Section 1.6.1 we discussed how there are broadly two types of development institutions, those that lend money already held and those that borrow first in order to subsequently lend. The former would essentially meet a 100% capital requirement (although in their situation it probably does not even make sense to talk about capital requirements), the latter, with varying degrees between institutions, would still meet a number that is several multiples the one of the average investment bank.

---

[1]This, of course, is at the core of the Euro sovereign crisis of 2010 to 2011. Central to it was the question, is a country insolvent, that is, will it *never* be able to meet its liabilities, or does it have liquidity issues, that is, it cannot generate revenues in time to meet its next liabilities?

We shall return to the issue of leverage in Section 7.4.1 to see how it can distort the pillars of risk neutrality. In Section 7.2.1 we shall look at leverage when dealing with funding gap risk, that is, the breaking in the balance between the amount one borrows versus the amount one lends.

7.2   HEDGING

7.2.1   Risk Neutrality and the Meaning of Hedging

In the previous chapter we showed how central to a borrowing activity (particularly in the context of development banking) is the simultaneous trading of a bond and a swap where one leg of the swap mimics the bond. We have seen that the remaining leg of the swap is a vanilla leg (floating rate plus asset swap spread), which means that as far as the complex structure in the bond and the swap is concerned we have two opposite positions, short in the bond and long in the swap. Because of this we are protected against the risks originating from the complexity of the structure. This is a form of hedging in which we replicate, by copying it exactly in the swap leg, the bond's structure. The fact that we hedge our position is actually very important when it comes to assessing its value, and to understand this better we are going to give a brief overview of the concept of replication using as an example, for their simplicity, equity options.

In finance an assumption that applies to the near totality of situations is that when we assess the value of a financial instrument we do so within a risk-neutral framework. Risk neutrality, as the name implies, means that, when assessing the value of a financial instrument, we are indifferent to risk.

Although it is not always obvious to say whether risk neutrality is at the source of hedging or vice versa, one can say that there are some fundamental concepts that support both. Crucial is the absence of arbitrage. We have already mentioned this in Section 2.2.4, but the absence of arbitrage means the impossibility of making a riskless profit. This in turn hinges on the assumption that information travels freely in the marketplace (everyone has the same level of knowledge) and on the assumption that everyone has the same tools, including speed, with which to act upon this information. Knowledge and tools mean that, should there be the possibility of making a riskless profit, everyone would know about it and acting on it would immediately erase this possibility.[2]

---

[2]Of course some players try to build powerful means (often nonhuman) that enable them to act faster than everybody else and hence exploit the possibility to make a riskless profit: the presence of these players, however, is not strong enough to change the assumption of risk neutrality.

Absence of arbitrage is a requirement, replication is what makes risk neutrality what it is and one cannot discuss replication without mentioning hedging. Hedging can be described as taking opposite positions in two similar financial instruments or assets: this definition is left vague on purpose and much depends on the meaning of similar.

In its simplest form hedging is a form of protection, a known curtailing of one's profit for the sake of protecting oneself against potential losses. Cases of it have been known to take place in ancient times. As hedging became more sophisticated, also thanks to advances in the divulgation of financial information, Black and Scholes [14] built a theory out of it, a theory based on replication. After Black and Scholes' rigorous construction, hedging became even more precise and frequent.

The biggest difference between classical physics and finance is that in the latter the action of the user has a direct impact on the variables *and* the model itself. To put it bluntly, a financial model is only valid if people use it. This means that the activity of hedging gave birth to a theory that prompted even more precise hedging, which in turn gave further backing to the theory itself. Let us be more specific.

Central to Black and Scholes' theory is that if we sell an option with value V that depends on an underlying S, by building a portfolio

$$\Pi = \frac{\partial V}{\partial S} S - V = \Delta S - V \tag{7.1}$$

in which next to the selling of V we purchase an amount of S as dictated by the quantity Δ, we are indifferent to risk and this enables us to find the risk-neutral price of V. Since these are the foundations of finance, volumes have been written on it (to this day one of the clearest descriptions is the one given by Baxter and Rennie [10]). It is probably useful, however, to remind the reader that the act of replication exemplified by Equation 7.1 has a profound impact on the probabilities governing what, after all, are events driven by stochastic variables (to this end in Appendix F we remind briefly how replication leads to probability values). These probabilities are risk-neutral probabilities as opposed to real-world probabilities, which govern nonfinancial events.

Making a very general and approximate statement, the value V of an instrument offering a payout C in case some events X take place, can be written as

$$V = P(X)\, C \tag{7.2}$$

where $P(X)$ is the probability that the event takes place. The loss of a suitcase is a stochastic event as much as the behavior of a Ford Motor share.

The probability of the former event, however, which is behind the premium charged by an insurance company, is very much different in nature from the one driving the latter and as a consequence the value of an option written on the share.

An insurance premium is driven by probabilities belonging to the real-world measure, an option price is assessed using probabilities from the risk-neutral measure.

While we can buy and sell shares in Ford Motor according to the Δ in Equation 7.1, we cannot do the same with suitcases: this fact gives rise[3] to two different types of probabilities. This means that the value of an instrument, such as an option, offering protection against an event, although it can roughly be calculated with Equation 7.2, will be driven by very different $P(X)$ depending on whether we can purchase the underlying or not.

The assumption of risk neutrality is so general that it often is applied to situations that, under closer scrutiny, should instead be exempted. Let us observe a few examples.

Let us imagine that bank ABC trades a vanilla option written on Ford Motor stock with bank XYZ. Both will use Black and Scholes and they will more or less agree on the value of the option. Let us imagine that ABC also sells to retail clients (the Italian old ladies or the Mrs. Watanabe of retail banking lore) a structured product with an embedded option that is identical in structure to the one just traded with XYZ. A structured product with this embedded option can be thought of as a bond, such as the one discussed in Section 6.2.1, with F_j a vanilla equity option on Ford Motor.

The value of the option by itself within the bond (i.e., the value of F_j) will be priced and sold in an identical way to the one traded with XYZ, and the retail client will accept the price. Is this correct? Both ABC and XYZ are able to trade the underlying whereas, no matter how much financial prowess one attributes to Mrs. Watanabe, the retail client cannot. Since we have said that it is the act of replication that drives the probabilities, which in turn drive the option price, the investment bank and the retail client should envisage two different prices so the answer to the question is no. This in practice does not matter since the retail client is ready to purchase the structured product anyway and to view essentially this investment equal to the purchase of a lottery ticket.[4]

---

[3]As mentioned previously, much has been written already about the theory behind this, but the reader is directed, as a reminder, toward a rigorous mathematical backing given, for example, by Baxter and Rennie [10] or by Etheridge [37].
[4]The probabilities of a winning lottery are drawn from a real-world probability distribution.

A similar concern surrounds options written on underlyings difficult to purchase: should they be priced within a risk-neutral framework? This is very important in the context of the use of historical versus actively traded (and therefore implied) data.

Let us imagine that we need to price an option, exotic or vanilla, on the Nikkei index. The most important input, the volatility of the index, is readily available since options on the Nikkei are actively traded and the Nikkei futures used to hedge them are also actively traded. In this case we would be more than justified in pricing the option within a risk-neutral framework.

Let us imagine now that we are going to price an option not on the Nikkei but on some proprietary index. A proprietary index is an index, that is, a variable tracking the performance of some assets, published usually by investment banks at their own discretion whose value is obtained through a proprietary algorithm. Neither futures nor options are traded on it, the only available data would be past fixings of the index. Using past fixings we can of course calculate historical volatility and pretend we can simply plug this into, say, Black and Scholes formula. Would it be correct though?

The essence of risk neutrality is that when trading an option we can at the same time purchase the underlying. In this case we cannot, so we should not, technically, be pricing this option the same way we would price the option on the Nikkei. In practice, however, many market participants would do it anyway. The danger is that, should something dramatic happen to the components of the index (let us imagine that they are stocks) affecting in turn the index and the option written on it, we would not be able to hedge ourselves since futures on the index are not traded and the composition of the index itself, which could enable us to trade on the stocks directly, is not openly known being the index composition proprietary.

A counterargument has been made by Derman and Taleb [30] and by Taleb [78]. To the extent that pure dynamic replication within the requirements of Black and Scholes is most of the time an illusion,[5] by making a virtue out of a necessity and following market practice, one *should* price options written on non-easily tradable underlyings in the same way one would price them when written on liquid ones. The fact that, as we have said before, in finance only the model that is actually used is considered valid, which gives some support to this view.

---

[5]The argument goes roughly along these lines: the assumptions of Black and Scholes are so strict theoretically that in practice, particularly as far as the idea of continuous and costless hedging is concerned, they can never be satisfied and therefore the use, sometimes, of historical data and/or nontradable data is not as serious as one would think.

The final issue we are going to consider has to do with leverage as we anticipated in the previous section. In Section 3.1.2 we introduced how the danger of derivatives consists of breaking the nexus between option and underlying. We specifically described the situation where one would trade the protection offered by a CDS without ever holding the bond the CDS was supposed to render riskless.

When we trade an underlying there are physical limits attached to it: for bonds it is the total outstanding principal of debt, for shares it is the market capitalization of the company. If a company has a market capitalization of $1M, it is impossible to purchase more than that amount (assuming all of it is traded). However, is it possible to write on the same underlying an option with a principal of $5M? Certainly. When we use Black and Scholes to price it and we are told, from Equation 7.1, that we need to buy, say, $2.5M of Δ, what are we going to do?

This is another side effect of leverage, the one of making the fundamental assumptions of financial modeling dangerously inapplicable. However, this is not as bizarre as it might seem. Although an extremely large principal would make a trader think twice about trading a particular option, a large but reasonable principal would not push a trader to actually make sure that there is enough stock to buy in order to hedge.[6]

We have outlined in Equation 7.1 (and in Appendix F) the basic principles of replication. We are now going from simple replication to full hedging.

7.2.2   Static and Dynamic Hedging

In Equation 7.1, we see how the action of buying or selling a certain amount of underlying in conjunction with an option written on it makes us indifferent—neutral—to the risk posed by movements in the underlying. However, an option is almost never simply a first-order function of the underlying only and full-scale hedging consists of protecting ourselves from other risks.

The ability to trade a certain security is crucial to the pricing of a derivative on that security. This is because we have said that the pricing of a derivative in the risk-neutral valuation hinges on the concept of replication, the ability to express a derivative with a similar object. In a certain sense this is similar to the action of synthesizing. A concept that is very useful to have in

---

[6]Of course the issue is not necessarily with the amount of stock available at inception: we need to remember that the more in the money an option goes, the greater the Δ becomes and therefore the greater the need for the underlying becomes.

mind is that of sound: the complexity of sound can be reproduced syntheti-
cally with a Fourier series, a sum of terms more or less long that will never
be like the original sound but that could resemble it remarkably well.

The pricing of a derivative in the risk-neutral framework is quite similar
in principle and all this is at the heart of hedging. As we have said, hedging
means taking two similar and opposite positions with respect to a certain
financial instrument. To be more precise we need to outline how the trading
of a derivative happens in practice.

A very useful statement would be to say that the essence of derivative
trading is that one sells the function and buys the Taylor series.[7] This is the
real core of the matter; all else, if one understands this, falls easily into place.

Imagine that we priced a derivative $f(S)$ expiring in one year on an
underlying S and we sold it. Imagine that we could express $f(S)$ so that its
value when we move the value of the underlying by an amount dS is given
by

$$f(S + dS, t) = a_1(S, t)dS + a_2(S, t)dS^2 + O(dS^3) \qquad (7.4)$$

This means that after selling the option we would buy $a_1(S, t)S$ and
$a_2(S, t)S^2$, ignoring the higher-order term, hold them for one year, and then
sell them. (Note that these are functions of time so when we say "hold them"
we actually mean that we hold them as they vary in time by buying and
selling portions of them as their value increases or decreases.) The dynamic
represented by the right-hand side would mimic the dynamic of the function
itself.

In a purely theoretical world, without transaction costs and infinite liquidity, if higher-order terms are negligible this strategy would lead to neither
loss nor gain. However, in real life the trader would sell $f(S, t)$ at a price
higher than the fair price (to take into account the fact that there will be

---

[7]We remind the reader that a Taylor series, like all series expansions, is a way of
expressing a function through a power series, a sum of terms in increasing powers of
the function's variable whose coefficients are calculated in a certain way. This certain
way is what differentiates a type of series from another. In the case of a Taylor series
we say that around a point $x = b$

$$f(x) = \sum_n a_n \frac{(x - b)^n}{n!}$$

with

$$a_n = \frac{df}{dx^n}\bigg|_{x=b} \qquad (7.3)$$

some costs involved with the purchase of the hedging instruments $a_1(S, t)$ and $a_2(S, t)$) and probably he would take a certain personal view of the market and not buy all the needed hedges or buy part of them. This would lead to a profit with a clear contained risk.

This is truly all there is to know about hedging, however, as they say, the devil is in the detail. How do we calculate the coefficients of the series? Does the series converge? How do we know how many terms to neglect? And most important: how many variables do the coefficients depend on?

Each term on the right-hand side of Equation 7.4 represents a certain risk (we could see the first, $a_1(S, t)$ as being the same as Δ in Equation 7.1) and, because they are all functions of time, to hedge as outlined above is a dynamic process. How dynamic this process really is depends on many factors and on the discrepancy between the theoretical assumptions behind Black and Scholes (continuous and costless transactions, etc.) and the reality of trading.[8]

---

[8]It is probably interesting to mention at this stage a topic that has been widely discussed in the financial press: the multibillion-dollar losses made by a trader (the "Whale") at the London office of JP Morgan. The issue has been discussed at length both with detail and with passion, although not always at the same time. We shall only concentrate on those aspects that can be used as an example of the point we were making about replication, risk neutrality, and hedging.

Of all the different types of hedging we can do, only equity (and to a certain extent FX) Delta hedging can be done surgically, so to speak, by buying the actual underlying. All other forms of hedging need to be done indirectly. What does this mean exactly? If we have a position that is sensitive to the movement of a stock price, we can buy a delta amount of that stock and we become risk neutral. If we hold a position that is sensitive to the volatility of a stock, to the value of an interest rate, or to the credit of an issuer, then we cannot buy volatility as it is, interest rate as it is, or credit as it is. All three need to be bought implicitly through simpler instruments with an exposure of their own to the same variables. By making sure that the exposure has an opposite sign we ensure risk neutrality. However, hedging through derivatives, as opposed to hedging by buying a stock, leaves some loose ends in the sense that the hedging instruments themselves will have exposures that will need hedging. For example, although it is not large, a CDS has some exposure to interest rates. If we use a CDS to hedge credit exposure from our initial position then we open ourselves to interest rate risks through the use of the CDS itself as a hedging instrument.

We hedge in order *not* to have open (essentially risk-partial) positions; if the hedging instruments we use keep us open on other fronts, what is the point? In the example of the CDS above we said that the interest rate exposure was small. It is not difficult to imagine situations, particularly those involving synthetic credit as it was in the JPM case, where, by hedging, we open ourselves to more than a little interest

Despite the apparent digression on replication, our focus is always the treasury business and the issue of debt. In this context hedging plays a much reduced role. Portrayed in Equation 7.4 is dynamic hedging; an alternative would be a static version of it.

Static hedging is not a definite term, but it is understood as a way of reducing the frequency of purchase or sale of the underlying. Dynamic hedging can be very difficult and potentially costly; some market player might wish to avoid it and enter into some transaction that offers protection without the need for continuous correction. Of course, as is the case with everything in finance, anything that offers peace of mind comes with a price: a form of static hedging is in general more expensive than a dynamic one. It is, however, cheaper than a dynamic one gone wrong.

In our context we could view an asset swap as a form of static hedge. Let us imagine that we have issued a bond with a coupon depending on the same option $f(S, t)$ of Equation 7.4 (which we are going to write as $f(S_j)$ to use the time indication of the coupon payment). We could write once again the asset swap structure

$$\sum_j (L_j + s_A) D_j dt_j - \sum_j f(S_j) D_j dt_j \rightleftharpoons 1 - \sum_j f(S_j) D_j \widetilde{D}_j dt_j - D_T \widetilde{D}_T$$

$$(7.5)$$

Before entering into the asset swap we were exposed to a certain number of risks intrinsic to f: through the asset swap we have passed these risks on to our counterpart (for us, the bond and the coupon leg of the swap cancel each other) and we are left with a sensitivity (risk exposure) only to the LIBOR. To be more precise we are left with a sensitivity to the LIBOR and our own credit standing since the extent to which the bond and the coupon leg cancel each other depends on the way we discount our bond (in essence the impact of the correction $\widetilde{D}_j$). This is linked to what is sometimes referred to as the liability paradox (see Fries [40] and also Gregory [44]), the fact that,

---

rate exposure. The issue is very important because it shows that when regulators try, with the so-called Volcker rule, to ban proprietary trading (which we defined in Section 1.5.2), the task is not an easy one as one cannot be absolutely sure where the line between trading to hedge and proprietary trading can be drawn. One would have naively thought that a trade carried out for hedging leaves the trader risk neutral whereas a trade carried out for proprietary trading leaves the trader risk partial: as we have tried to explain in this note, the distinction is not so easy to make. The trade carried out by JP Morgan was supposed to be a hedge, and yet, we don't know if it intentionally left the bank with an open position eventually resulting in the enormous loss.

through the calculation of present value, a company's liability decreases as the company's credit deteriorates. We shall return to this, but at the moment we are ignoring this sensitivity.

We can say that we have decided to exchange a series of (since we have many coupons) hedging transactions for a series of payments of LIBOR plus spread, which, combining Equations 7.4 and 7.5, could be written as

$$\sum_j a_1(S_j)dS_j + a_2(S_j)dS_j^2 + O(dS_j^3) = \sum_j (L_j + s_A)\, dt_j$$

Because of the complexity of curve construction, as discussed in Chapter 2, the sensitivity of the LIBOR leg in the asset swap is not only to the LIBOR itself (which would constitute, as opposed to the a_n terms in Equation 7.4, a unitary derivative, or Delta 1) but technically to other parameters. Having said that, the one to the LIBOR represents by far the largest single sensitivity left for the bond issuer after an asset swap.

To summarize: we have issued a bond that could have had a series of sensitivities (let us recollect Section 6.2.2 where we mentioned sensitivities to FX, volatility, volatility skew, etc.), each one of which can be represented by a term in a series like the one shown in Equation 7.4; by entering into an asset swap of the form given by Equation 7.5 we have passed on to our swap counterpart this series of risks; having opposite sign, the bond and coupon leg of the swap have also opposite sensitivity to each of the risks appearing in the Taylor series; after the asset swap we are left with a LIBOR leg that has a trivial sensitivity to interest rate. Should we be seeking absolute peace of mind we could enter into a swap

$$\sum_j (L_j + s_A)\, D_j dt_j = \sum_j FIX D_j dt_j \tag{7.6}$$

where *FIX* is some fixed rate and the direction of the left-hand side of Equation 7.6 is opposite to the left-hand side of Equation 7.5, that is, after the asset swap we are left *paying* LIBOR plus spread and in Equation 7.6 we *receive* LIBOR plus spread. With this last transaction we have eliminated all source of uncertainty.[9]

---

[9]Of course, we have eliminated sources of uncertainty only as far as our actual cost is concerned, that is, we know exactly how much we pay to service our debt. As far as the fair value of our debt is concerned we are, of course, still open to interest rate risk through discounting.

If we look at a treasury desk alone we see how, once all the transactions related to a bond issuance are carried out, it is left with a simple sensitivity to interest rates and all the difficult hedging is outsourced, so to speak. If we differentiate between the treasury of an investment bank and the treasury of a development institution, we notice that in the former the risk is away from the desk but still within the same firm, in the latter the risk is passed on to a completely different entity.

A question worth asking, and we shall do so in the next section, is whether correct pricing still matters in a situation where, after an asset swap, what we are always left with is simply a LIBOR leg.

7.2.3 Valuation in the Absence of Dynamic Hedging

If we hold the point of view of a treasury desk, particularly one of a development or small financial institution that swaps the bond straight away with another counterpart, why do we care about correctly pricing an instrument? After all, the bond and the coupon leg of the asset swap cancel each other, so technically *any* value would do. The argument would seem even stronger for institutions with good credit ratings for which the discount factors of the bond and the coupon leg of the swap are fairly close (there is a small correction $\widetilde{D}_i$).

At first the above theory seems sensible, however, there are a few cases and reasons why it is not. The first and most important has to do with the exit price of a trade. We have already mentioned this in Section 6.2.2 when we discussed the valuation of exotic structures.

For transactions that, like the majority of swaps and the totality of exotic swaps, are not quoted officially on an exchange but rely on internal valuations, the exit price is the last agreed price before the transaction is interrupted, usually, voluntarily.

A swap is made of a series of payments that each side owes the other. At payment date the amount is a known quantity and each side settles with the other. However, as we mentioned in Section 2.4.1, there needs to be an agreement on the net present value of both legs (the present value of one minus the present value of the other, which we called mark to market [MTM]) for collateral issues. The party who sees a negative MTM needs to post collateral in quantity equal (or at least proportional) to the MTM. This means that the suggestion in the opening paragraph that *any* value would do for the coupon leg of the asset swap does not hold. Unless we have a value that is reasonably in line with our counterpart there will be collateral disputes.

Collateral issues would be a strong enough reason for the importance of a correct valuation, however, at closer inspection, there might be reasons for grayness. Because of netting agreements (collateral is managed not at trade level but at portfolio level) one side might wish to accept a mistake on the other if it allows it to pay less collateral. Since the real payment on settlement date is not in dispute, the issue is only of collateral. There might be even more business-driven reasons, such as a client's line of credit.

Each institution, in order to disperse credit risk, sets itself limits on how much business it does with a specific counterpart and this limit is in terms of MTM. An investment bank eager to do business with the treasury of another institution might be willing to accept a lower MTM (from its own point of view) if this means it will remain within the limits of the treasury.

Let us imagine that investment bank ABC and treasury XYZ have two swaps between them, a plain vanilla with fixed coupon C, easy to value, and an exotic one. From ABC's point of view the vanilla one has MTM MTM_V

$$\sum_i L_i D_i dt_i - \sum_j C D_j dt_j = MTM_V > 0$$

large and positive. The exotic swap linked to some function $f(L_m)$ has MTM MTM_E

$$\sum_n L_n D_n dt_n - \sum_m f(L_m) D_m dt_m = MTM_E < 0$$

which is large and negative. We have, however,

$$|MTM_V| - |MTM_E| = \epsilon > 0$$

that is, the difference in mark-to-market results in an overall positive collateral position for ABC and the treasury XZY would need to post collateral of an amount ϵ.

Let us imagine that XYZ makes an error in valuing the exotic swaps resulting in an even greater MTM (i.e., more negative for ABC) $\widetilde{MTM_E}$ such that

$$|MTM_V| - \left|\widetilde{MTM_E}\right| = \tilde{\epsilon} < \epsilon$$

Although this on paper would technically mean ABC owes more to XYZ, ABC might let it pass because, overall (after netting the two swaps), it reduces the collateral it receives from XYZ to $\tilde{\epsilon}$. This is a bit risky, but otherwise XYZ (treasuries usually have stricter limits than banks) might go somewhere else for business if net MTM had gone above the accepted limit for counterparty ABC. In general ABC sees this type of error as an involuntary way on XYZ's part to free the credit line and therefore allow ABC to do more business. ABC knows that on settlement date all will be solved by the fact that the payment becomes a certainty.[10]

If collateral management offers reasons going beyond the strictly mathematical/financial ones for accepting a misprice of a transaction, exit prices constitute a different matter. As the name suggests, an exit price is the last agreement between two counterparts: whereas a collateral dispute will be cleared, in part, by the actual settlement, there is nothing beyond the exit price, so it is in both parties' interest to value it correctly. We could envisage the need to calculate an exit price in two main situations: the bond terminates and we, as issuers of the debt, need to interrupt the asset swap accordingly or we need to transfer the asset swap to another counterpart.

In the following discussion let us lighten the notation a little. Let us define by B_t the value at time t of a bond with nominal value N paying a coupon linked to some function f_j (which can be a fixed or floating coupon), that is,

$$B_t = N \sum_j f_j D_j \widetilde{D}_j dt_j - N D_T \widetilde{D}_T$$

and let us define the mark to market of an asset swap as $MTM_t \left(s_A^{t_1}, N \right)$, that is, the value at time t of a swap with principal N that pays LIBOR plus a fixed spread $s_A^{t_1}$ fixed at a time t_1 in exchange for the coupons of the bond, as

$$MTM_t \left(s_A^{t_1}, N \right) = N \sum_j \left(L_j + s_A^{t_1} \right) D_j dt_j - N \sum_j f_J D_j dt_j$$

Using the above the bond plus asset swap structure at inception (we choose inception to be time t_1) will be given by

$$MTM_{t_1} \left(s_A^{t_1}, N \right) \rightleftharpoons N - B_{t_1} \qquad (7.7)$$

Assuming the bond was issued at par, both sides of the above at time t_1 are equal to zero. Let us imagine now the situation in which the bond is terminated. The reasons for which a bond terminates can be multiple, however, the most common ones are either a trigger event such as the one shown for a TARN structure in Section 6.2.1 or the issuer deciding to call the bond, or a buyback, that is, an institution repurchasing its own debt. Let

---

[10]Providing a little shock to XYZ for whom the difference between the reality and what it *thought it was owed* becomes apparent.

us consider the second situation as an example and consider thus the case in which the issuer at time $t_2 > t_1$ returns the nominal value to the investor.

Assuming the issuer follows financial logic, the bond is called when it is worth more than par by an amount δ, that is, $B_{t_2} > B_{t_1} > N + \delta$. From our perspective, *immediately before* we call the bond

$$N - B_{t_2} = -\delta < 0 \qquad (7.8)$$

at the same time the liability we have on the bond is compensated by our gain on the swap since, always from our own perspective,

$$MTM_{t_2}\left(s_A^{t_1}, N\right) = \delta > 0 \qquad (7.9)$$

The above is not entirely true. We mentioned in Section 7.2.2 that a change in the issuer's own credit rating has an effect on the relation between the bond and the swap price: one could imagine a strange scenario in which all market inputs are frozen except for a progressive deterioration/improvement of the the credit rating of the issuer, in which case the bond would decrease/increase in value without being matched by a respective move in the asset swap mark to market. In this scenario we could not have the same variable δ in both Equations 7.8 and 7.9. We are going to ignore this scenario and imagine instead a situation in which the credit rating of the issuer, our credit rating, is fairly constant and good, meaning that the present value of the coupon payments are the main drivers of bond and swap prices.

As far as the value of our assets is concerned, everything is fine only if we agree on the value of δ with our swap counterpart. Otherwise, should the δ on the swap side be smaller than the one we see on the bond side, we would be registering a loss.

If the example of early termination might seem a bit hard to grasp, after all, one might say the loss is simply between what *we thought we had*, and as far as the transaction itself is concerned there is no real loss. Let us not forget that in the modern economy the records of a company, in the form of financial statements, are crucial instruments and the belief a company has of the value of its own assets[11] is a fundamental pillar of the economy because it is central to the way others see the health of the institution.

An example even more clear, however, is the case where we need to change, for some reason, swap counterpart. Let us imagine ourselves again at a point where Equation 7.8 is true. In order to change counterpart we

---

[11] Of course, we are discussing the value of assets that need some form of valuation, not assets, such as cash or shares, that have an objective value.

have two options: either we enter into the same swap we had with the first counterpart, that is, a swap with mark to market

$$MTM_{t_2}\left(s_A^{t_1}, N\right)$$

or we enter into a market asset swap (see Section 5.3.2) where the swap has principal equal to the value of the bond and a new asset swap spread $s_A^{t_2}$ such that the swap prices at par, that is, with

$$MTM_{t_2}\left(s_A^{t_2}, B_{t_2}\right)$$

equal to zero. Let us consider the first case, which is probably easier and more common: we thus maintain constant the characteristics of the function f_j appearing in the bond and coupon leg of the swap and we maintain constant the asset swap spread $s_A^{t_1}$. In the simplest scenario we terminate the swap with the first counterparty, receive δ (the value of the MTM of the swap, which is positive for us) and give it to the second counterpart to cover the fact they start the swap at a disadvantage, that is, with a negative MTM from their point of view.

This simple scenario relies on the assumption that the second counterpart also sees the value of the MTM of the swap as being equal to δ and this situation is an argument in favor of the importance of valuing an instrument correctly even when carrying out static hedging. It is unlikely that all three parties—us, the first counterpart, A, and second counterpart, B—will agree on the value of δ. There could even be a situation in which B sees the MTM value as larger than δ, meaning that the lump sum we receive from A (assuming that at least the two of us have agreed) will not be enough to give to B and, assuming we proceed with B, the extra amount will be a realized loss. This loss, as opposed to the disagreements we were mentioning in the context of collateral, is real.

Another way of changing counterpart is through the process known as *novation*. This process is usually more common since the payment of a lump sum, as in the example above, while possible, rarely happens due to the likelihood of a disagreement in the value of the MTM. A novation is a legal process in which one of the parties in an agreement is exchanged for another. In our swap, we were facing A and now we are facing B. Should we all agree on the value of δ, the process then becomes a purely legal one. In most cases, however, B will want to be paid the difference between what they see and what we see as the value of δ.

From the examples above one obtains the impression that when exiting a trade there is always a loss for the debt issuer, after all, why can't it be the opposite, and why can't we receive something from B? There are many reasons for it, let us try to name a few.

A debt issuer, particularly one that is swapping the trade with an external institution, prizes static hedging exactly because it is static, a transaction that takes all hedging worries away until the maturity of the debt. If it *needs* (as opposed to wants as in the case of a buyback) to exit a trade, it is usually because something serious has happened, possibly a grave deterioration or even default of the swap counterpart. Because these types of events are never isolated, there is a great chance that the market itself is in turmoil with liquidity and optimism in short supply. In this environment the second counterpart will need an incentive to take on the trade.

A further reason, closely linked to the first though, is that a treasury desk swapping a bond might not be aware of the hedging costs incurred by a swap counterpart, and these hedging costs tend to increase in the type of environment when a change of counterpart is carried out.

All these considerations should be enough to realize that static hedging is not an alternative to a proper valuation of a financial instrument. These considerations are the reasons for which we have discussed treasury business and risk management only after having introduced topics such as curve construction, credit, and emerging markets' liquidity, which at first might have seemed unrelated. Discussing these topics was a way of showing how theoretical and practical elements can add complexity to the valuation of financial derivatives.

7.3 MANAGING RISK RELATED TO FINANCIAL OBSERVABLES

As we have shown, development institutions tend to practice static hedging, meaning that a trade is hedged as a block at inception and with a virtually perfect off-setting position. This is different from dynamic (continuous) hedging practiced by traditional financial institutions where specific elements of a trade are hedged separately at numerous points throughout the life of the trade. Nonetheless, within the static hedging framework, it is useful to paint a picture of how an institution manages the risk associated with a few key parameters linked to financial variables. We shall begin with what relates to interest rate and FX risk (the two can be viewed together) and then a brief description of the (explicit) management of credit risk.

Since we focus mainly on the hedging itself, that is, the interaction between the asset and the swap, we shall treat together situations originating from the lending, borrowing, or investing activity of the institution. Between

TABLE 7.1 The hedging of a fixed-coupon bond issued to borrow capital.

Instrument type	Pay/Receive	Leg structure
Fixed/Structured Bond	Pay	$-\sum_i^T CD_i \widetilde{D}_i dt_i - D_T \widetilde{D}_T$
Fixed/Structured Swap Leg	Receive	$\sum_i^T CD_i dt_i - D_T$
Floating Swap Leg	Pay	$-\sum_j^T (L_j + s) D_j dt_j + D_T$
Result	Pay	$-\sum_j^T (L_j + s) D_j dt_j + D_T + \Phi$

these different situations, the difference in the sign and in the discounting used will be crucial.

7.3.1 Interest Rate and FX Risk

The underlying theme of this book is that credit is ever present in the value of basically any (and particularly fixed income) financial instrument. The presence of credit can be, however, more or less explicit. In this section we shall focus mainly on interest rate and FX when they dominate a certain instrument value or its corresponding hedge. We shall focus on the hedge of bonds, loans, and, insofar as the corresponding hedge is swap driven, instruments such as equity positions and credit-linked investments such as asset-backed securities.

7.3.1.1 Hedging a Fixed or Structured Bond   Let us begin with the situation in which the institution has raised debt through a fixed-coupon bond.

In Table 7.1 we show the bond as a negative stream of cash flows where we pay a fixed rate C. We have mentioned several times before (beginning with our introduction of cross currency basis swaps in Section 2.2.5.2) that the present value of a floating leg is always near par. Conversely, the present value of a fixed leg can, throughout the life of the trade, differ greatly from par. To hedge this sensitivity we enter into a swap where we receive the same fixed value paid in the swap and we pay a floating rate plus a spread where the spread is such that both transactions (bond and swap) are financially equivalent. The outcome is shown in the bottom line where, after summing the individual legs, we pay the resulting stream of floating rates plus spread. The resulting leg has a present value that will always be nearer par (depending on the value of the spread) than a fixed-rate one.

Note that in the resulting trade there is the quantity Φ: this represents the fair value of the difference between the discounting used on the swap (which is market driven, either by LIBOR or OIS rates) and the discounting on the bond, which is driven by the credit standing of the issuer. Although the cost and income (see Section 7.4.2) are perfectly offsetting, the same does not apply to their present value. One could define the difference as

$$\Phi = \sum_{i}^{T} \left(1 - \widetilde{D}_i\right)$$

(Some readers might have felt puzzled, if not worse, by the way we have expressed the discount factor of a bond as decomposed in a normal discount factor D_t and a credit correction $\widetilde{D}_t$. We hope that the ease with which we can express the discrepancy between the value of the bond and the corresponding swap leg in the equation above will go some way toward allaying their feeling.)

The same principle applies to the hedging of structured bonds as we introduced them in Sections 6.2.1 and 6.2.2. In Table 7.1 we view C as a structured coupon. At the moment the coupon sets, meaning it is determined with certainty for settlement purposes, its value would perfectly match between bond and swap. Before that, however, its present value would differ when calculated in the context of the bond or the swap, resulting in a net difference of Φ.

7.3.1.2 The Unhedgeable Nature of the Discount Spread Φ Before proceeding with other examples of hedging, it is probably necessary to focus a little longer on the term Φ introduced above. It is a very important variable and some say it represents the core issue of any funding business.

Let us repeat what Φ represents: it represents the discrepancy between the way we discount the same identical cash flow in a bond on one side or in the corresponding coupon leg of the asset swap on the other. Let us imagine we live in a LIBOR discounting world: should we be able to issue bonds at zero spread versus LIBOR, then Φ would be an almost vanishing quantity.[12] Let us imagine we live in an OIS discounting world: if we were able to issue bonds at zero spread with respect to the overnight rate, then Φ would be an almost vanishing quantity. We know, however, that this is seldom, or never, the case and thus when we value our asset (the swap) and liability (the bond) there will be a difference in the two MTMs, and this difference will have a variance driven by our own credit standing. What can we do about it?

---

[12]The reluctance to say that Φ would be exactly zero originates from what we have seen throughout the previous chapters and in particular the one on bond pricing. Because of the limited tools, in the form of market prices, at our disposal when implying variables, the relation between credit spreads, rates, and discounting is not an absolutely exact or uniquely defined one at granular level.

Not very much is the simple answer and the reason is broadly twofold. The usual way one would hedge any credit element would be through credit default swaps, however, in this situation an institution would need to buy CDSs *against its own default*. The first problem would be that this would create a form of liability paradox similar to the one we mentioned in Section 7.2.2: the protection we hold would gain in value the more our credit worsens. One might wonder, why can an individual purchase, say, unemployment insurance and an institution cannot buy CDSs against its own default? This question or problem is another way of illustrating the difference between the real and risk-neutral world we were mentioning earlier. The financial instruments in the risk-neutral world are tradable and they have, or should have, a unique value at which every market participant is willing to trade. If an individual is close to losing his job, he will be glad for the purchase of unemployment insurance and this insurance will gain in value *to him only*: he will not be able to pass the insurance on to someone else. In the case of an institution purchasing CDSs against its own default, the same is not true: the value of the protection we are holding gains in value for *every market participant*. Theoretically, as the credit standing worsens, the institution could monetize this gain by *selling* protection in a mirror trade to the one executed earlier to *buy* protection. It is not difficult to see how this can easily turn uncomfortable.

Let us, however, for the sake of argument, imagine that the problem just mentioned is not a great one and that we can in principle purchase protection against our own default. How would we know how much to purchase? For an interest rate derivative we know the PV01 (see Section 5.2.3) and we know therefore how much of certain interest-rate hedging instruments to buy. For a credit derivative we generally use a CDS model to price it and therefore the credit PV01 (or CV01) will tell us how much of a set of CDSs to buy. Even a bond, which does not have an explicit or unique pricing model, can be hedged with CDSs since that is the original definition itself of a CDS, an instrument to hedge a bond. However, what can we do to hedge Φ? Let us remind ourselves that Φ is driven by a credit correction to the pure interest rate discount factor, but let us also remind ourselves of the fact that

$$D_T \widetilde{D}_T \neq D_T S_T$$

where S_T represents the survival probability, in this case our own, calibrated to the quoted CDS rates. If the two sides of the equation above were equal, then we could use CDSs. We know, however, from Section 5.3.3, that there is such a thing as a bond-CDS basis, which means that as the equation above is true, the two sides are not equal. For them to be equal we would need to calibrate a credit curve using our own bond prices. However, when we discussed in Section 5.3.3 the idea of building a credit framework to price bonds, it was principally to value them only and also to do so when we might be missing some market information (either the bond price or the CDS rate). Here we are discussing a hedging issue (as opposed to valuation only) and in a situation where potentially we have both bond prices and CDS rates. This means that even if we were to calculate the bond-CDS basis and obtain a survival probability $\overline{S_T}$ (using the formalism of Equation 5.18) so that

$$D_T \widetilde{D_T} = D_T \overline{S_T}$$

it would not be very useful because our supposed hedging instrument would be the sort of shifted CDS introduced in Equation 5.19 and not a real market instrument.

In this brief aside we have tried to show why the discrepancy between the fair value of our own debt and the fair value of the corresponding asset swap introduces a very challenging unhedgeable factor. This challenge is in essence due to the fact that an institution is reluctant to purchase protection against its own default and also the fact that, even if it did, it would not lead to a clean hedge.

One could however raise a point that would throw all this aside and question the premises on which our discourse is based. Why do we need to fair value our own debt in a way that takes into account our own credit risk? When valuing our own debt, why do we need $\widetilde{D_T}$ in the first place? It is a legitimate question. Of course, the fact that throughout this book we *have* used the credit correction $\widetilde{D_T}$ means that we believe that it is correct, if only because it allows us to value our own debt in the way other market participants value it. Since, of course, other market participants do take into account our credit when valuing our debt, we believe that the fundamental assumption of risk-neutral valuation, that is, the unique nature of the price of any tradable security, trumps all other considerations and we need to price our own debt the way everybody else does. The other side of the argument, a side that has many intelligent followers, is that the paradoxes and intractability introduced in this section are enough to take a different approach and ignore our own credit risk.

This argument, which, like the one on the fair value of loans (see Section 3.3.1) or the one on funding adjusted discounting (see Section 2.4.4), does not have a clear solution, yet another example of how in recent years everything that deals with credit or funding has come to the forefront of any financial discussion and intellectual challenges.

7.3.1.3 Hedging a Fixed-Rate Loan Let us continue with our discussion on the different types of basic static hedges one might encounter. Another

TABLE 7.2 The hedging of a fixed-rate loan.

Instrument type	Pay/Receive	Leg structure
Fixed Loan	Receive	$\sum_i^T D_i \left(C N_i dt_i + N_i - N_{i+1} \right)$
Fixed Swap Leg	Pay	$-\sum_i^T D_i \left(C N_i dt_i + N_i - N_{i+1} \right)$
Floating Swap Leg	Receive	$\sum_i^T D_i \left[(L_i + s) N_i dt_i + N_i - N_{i+1} \right]$
Result	Receive	$\sum_i^T D_i \left[(L_i + s) N_i dt_i + N_i - N_{i+1} \right]$

exposure one would want to hedge, for the same reason outlined in the case of the bond, is the one to a fixed-rate loan.

In Table 7.2 we present the situation where the institution has extended a fixed-rate loan and therefore receives a stream of fixed cash flows made of a coupon and a principal repayment. Note how in the first line of the table we have written the expression for the loan in a way different from the previous ones in the sense that we have omitted any reference to the survival probability of the borrower. This is because in this section we want to highlight the dealing with interest rates and FX-related risk: we assume that the credit risk of the borrower is dealt with elsewhere (we shall discuss it in Section 7.3.2) and here we only concern ourselves with the interest rate sensitivity due to a fixed or a floating rate.

At this point one could ask: why didn't we do the same when dealing with the hedging of the fixed coupon bond? Why didn't we leave the discount factor correction $\widetilde{D}_t$ aside and only treat the interest rate component?

A bond, as opposed to a loan, is a securitized instrument: this means that the price of the bond is a market price that cannot be easily broken. At most, as we have done before, we can imply certain things. A loan is not a securitized instrument and the discussion around the fair value of loans (see Section 3.3.1) shows that there is not a single official way of valuing these instruments.

To hedge the exposure to the fixed rate of the loan, the institution would enter into an amortizing swap where it would pay the same fixed rate of the loan and receive a stream of floating rates plus spread where the spread would be chosen so that the two transactions (loan and swap) are financially equivalent. The sum of these three legs results in a net stream of floating cash flows.

As we have said before (see Section 4.3.2), when hedging a loan with a swap, not only are there considerations such as the one we have just illustrated above about the fair value of the loan, but there are others more important about what happens to the combined hedge (swap and loan) in

TABLE 7.3 The hedging of a bond in a foreign currency issued to borrow capital.

Instrument type	Pay/Receive	Leg structure
Foreign Currency Bond	Pay	$-N^Y \sum_i^T F_i D_i^Y \widetilde{D_i^Y} dt_i - D_T^Y \widetilde{D_T^Y}$
Foreign Currency Swap Leg	Receive	$N^Y \sum_i^T F_i D_i^Y dt_i - D_T^Y$
Domestic Currency Swap Leg	Pay	$-N^X \sum_j^T \left(L_j^X + s \right) D_j^X dt_j + D_T^X$
Result	Pay	$-N^X \sum_j^T \left(L_j^X + s \right) D_j^X dt_j + D_T^X + \Phi_Y$

case of the default of the borrower or the swap counterparty. Loans are, we have repeated many times, nonsecuritized instruments, meaning that many of the features of the agreement are set between lender and borrower on an almost ad hoc basis.[13] Swaps on the other hand, although there are specific deviations such as the waiver on collateral payment for some institutions, have much more standardized features, in particular those dealing with the situation of default. The presence of these different features, such as if the loan is accelerating or nonaccelerating,[14] would have an impact on the solidity of the hedge.

7.3.1.4   Hedging a Foreign Currency Bond or Loan   Let us now consider the case of a bond issued in a foreign currency Y different from our domestic currency X. This actually applies not just to foreign and domestic currencies in a strict sense, but we could define more loosely Y as a currency the institution *does not* want to have exposure to and X as a currency the institution *does* want to have an exposure to. An institution will always have one and only one reporting currency (the currency in which its financial statement is published) and therefore all exposure to all currencies will always be measured against its reporting currency. However, this does not mean that the institution will not have exposure to currencies other than its reporting currency.

Let us illustrate how the conversion works and then we shall offer some examples of the types of currencies that might be involved in the conversion.

In Table 7.3 we show the situation where we have issued a bond in currency Y with a coupon F_i which can be anything from a fixed coupon, a

---

[13]Although each lender certainly has a standard set of loan types, it is not technically impossible that each loan would have different important features.

[14]We remind the reader that an accelerating loan is one where at the moment of the default of the borrower, the lender calculates the recovery value on the outstanding principal; in a nonaccelerating loan, the recovery is calculated on the present value of the outstanding amount.

simple floating-rate coupon, or a structured coupon. The bond's true nature is not relevant here; what matters is only the fact that the currency of the bond is not one to which we care to have exposure. All the symbols have the usual meanings, in particular D_t^Y is the discount factor in currency Y and $\widetilde{D}_t^Y$ is the correction to the market discount factor due to the cost of borrowing in currency Y.

After issuing the foreign currency bond we would enter into a cross currency swap where we would receive a stream of cash flows equal to those of the bond and pay a set of cash flows in currency X, constituted by the X currency floating rate plus a spread. The spread, as usual, is such that the two transactions (bond and swap) are financially equivalent.

The outcome of this strategy, as shown in the last line of Table 7.3, is that we pay a stream of floating cash flows in currency X. Note that, similar to the situation shown in Section 7.3.1.1, when calculating the present value of the bond and the Y currency leg of the swap, the two do not perfectly offset. This is due to the fact that we discount the two sets of cash flows with two different curves: with a discount curve driven by LIBOR or OIS rates in the case of the swap and by our own cost of funding in currency Y[15] in the case of the bond. We have defined this difference with the quantity Φ_Y, which is given by

$$\Phi_Y = \sum_i \left(1 - \widetilde{D}_i^Y\right) \tag{7.10}$$

At the beginning of the section we explained how for every institution there is only one reporting currency, but there could be multiple currencies to which the institution wishes to gain exposure. An institution, particularly a development institution as seen in Section 4.3.1, would issue in a great variety of currencies: the choices behind issuing in these currencies go from specific development reasons to a search for an attractive funding level. After the issuance we have seen the institution enter into a cross currency asset swap (a static hedge).

Let us imagine that the reporting currency of the institution is USD: this means that many cross currency asset swaps would be into USD. However the institution might choose to have additional active exposure to, say, EUR, JPY, and GBP. This means that not only some debt will be issued directly in EUR, JPY, and GBP but also that debt issued in, say, Indonesian Rupees (IDR) could be swapped into either USD, the main reporting currency, or EUR, JPY, and GBP.

---

[15] See Section 6.4.1, where we discussed funding in different currencies.

Let us mention here the special case of nondeliverable currencies. We mentioned in Section 4.2.4 that some (developing) countries exercise capital control on their currencies, meaning that their currencies cannot be freely transferred outside of the country. This control of capital results in the creation of nondeliverable bonds and nondeliverable swaps, instruments where, every time there is a cash flow in the controlled currency Z, in order for a foreigner to take possession of it, it needs to be converted into (usually) USD. These types of bonds are issued only to foreigners and the currency in which the cash flow will be delivered is stated in the bond's terms.

An investor purchasing this type of instrument applies a strategy similar to the one mentioned in Section 6.4.2, where the divergence between FX forward and FX spot is exploited. The coupon in the bond will be high because there is an expected (and therefore reflected in the FX forwards) depreciation in the nondeliverable currency; however, this depreciation might not actually materialize at the moment of exchanging the cash flow in USD.

The net result is that the investor is purchasing a USD floating-rate note with a coupon that could be higher than if the note had been in USD to start with.

If parties A and B enter into a nondeliverable swap contract where A pays USD cash flows to B and B pays Z-denominated cash flows to A, in practice both parties will receive USD. One can generalize and say that the near totality of capital-controlled trades involve fixed cash flows and therefore in order to hedge a bond issued in a nondeliverable currency one should not consider the situation shown in Table 7.3, but rather the one shown in Table 7.4.

In order to vary our examples and also because it is easier to appreciate the difference between deliverable and nondeliverable currencies, we have

TABLE 7.4 The hedging of a bond in a nondeliverable currency Z purchased as an investment.

Instrument type	Pay/Receive	Leg structure
Bond (denominated in Z but deliverable in USD)	Receive	$\sum_i^T CN^Z F X_i D_i^\$ \widetilde{D_i^\$} dt_i$ $+ N^Z F X_i D_T^\$ \widetilde{D_i^\$}$
Floating Swap Leg (in USD)	Pay	$- \sum_i^T CN^Z F X_i D_i^\$ dt_i$ $- N^Z F X_i D_T^\$$
Floating Swap Leg (in USD)	Receive	$\sum_j^T \left(L_j^\$ + s \right) D_j^\$ dt_j + D_T^\$$
Result	Receive	$\sum_j^T \left(L_j^\$ + s \right) D_j^\$ dt_j + D_T^\$ - \Phi_\$$

TABLE 7.5 The hedging of a fixed- or floating-rate loan in a foreign currency.

Instrument type	Pay/Receive	Leg structure
Loan in currency Y	Receive	$\sum_i^T D_i^Y \left(F_i N_i^Y dt_i + N_i^Y - N_{i+1}^Y \right)$
Swap Leg in currency Y	Pay	$-\sum_i^T D_i^Y \left(F_i N_i^Y dt_i + N_i^Y - N_{i+1}^Y \right)$
Swap Leg in currency X	Receive	$\sum_i^T D_i^X \left[\left(L_i^X + s \right) N_i^X dt_i + N_i^X - N_{i+1}^X \right]$
Result	Receive	$\sum_i^T D_i^X \left[\left(L_i^X + s \right) N_i^X dt_i + N_i^X - N_{i+1}^X \right]$

considered the situation where instead of selling, that is, issuing, a bond, we purchase one. This could be the situation encountered by the investment arm of the institution.

After purchasing the (fixed-rate) bond denominated in the nondeliverable currency Z, we know immediately that at every coupon date we shall receive an amount $CN^Z F X_i$ of USD, where C is the coupon, N^Z is the principal amount in currency Z, and $F X_i$ is the spot FX rate at time T_i between Z and USD. We are therefore in the position in which we receive a set of varying coupons in USD. We can then enter into a purely USD swap in which we pay the set of cash flows we receive from the bond and receive a set of floating rates linked to a USD floating rate plus spread. As usual, the spread is such that the previous transactions are financially equivalent. Although we have said that the swap is purely USD, this is true only in practice. The actual definition of the swap is as nondeliverable, that is, one where we pay flows in currency Z: the fact that Z is a nondeliverable currency results in us making USD payments in practice.

The outcome is a stream of floating USD-denominated cash flows. In this case the amount $\Phi_\$$ refers to the discounting discrepancy between the effectively USD value of the bond and the corresponding leg in the swap.

For completeness we shall mention the situation in which we want to hedge the exposure to a currency Y in which we have extended a loan. As shown in Table 7.5 we are receiving a set of coupons F_i (which can be either fix or floating) on a principal N^Y and repayments of the same principal. We would enter into an amortizing cross currency swap in which we pay the same coupons and receive a set payment made of a coupon indexed to a floating rate L_j^X plus spread on a principal N^X and repayments of the same principal. The outcome is an exposure to a floating rate in X.

Typically an institution would set itself currency diversification targets: set percentages of the assets, debt, and equity need to be denominated in those currencies to which the institution wishes to have exposures. If, after operations such as the ones shown in these sections, the actual net (hopefully

TABLE 7.6 The hedging of an investment in an ABS with an asset swap.

Instrument type	Pay/Receive	Leg structure
Fixed/Floating ABS	Receive	$\sum_i^T C_i D_i \widetilde{D}_i dt_i - D_T \widetilde{D}_T$
Fixed/Floating Swap Leg	Pay	$-\sum_i^T C D_i dt_i - D_T$
Floating Swap Leg	Receive	$\sum_j^T (L_j + s_{ASW}) D_j dt_j + D_T$
Result	Receive	$\sum_j^T (L_j + s_{ASW}) D_j dt_j + D_T - \Phi$

positive) income does not fall within these percentages, this will be corrected with spot FX transactions.

7.3.1.5 Hedging a Credit-Linked Instrument Such as an Asset-Backed Security
We have seen in Section 6.4.2 that some instruments an institution can invest in are asset-backed securities, instruments that pay a coupon linked to the receivables from a specific pool of assets. These instruments can be hedged with an asset swap, however, as they can be fairly risky, the type of hedge that isolates market and credit risk is either a total return swap or a repurchase agreement, which are similar, although the latter tends to be more present in mature and liquid markets.

Hedging an asset-backed security with an asset swap does not differ greatly from hedging a fixed or floating vanilla bond.

In Table 7.6 we show the situation in which we have purchased an ABS paying a coupon C_i, which can be either fixed (in which case C_i will be the same for all i) or floating. The value of this instrument is obtained by discounting with a cumulative discount factor $D_t \widetilde{D}_t$. It is worth reminding that the credit correction $\widetilde{D}_t$ will, of course, be different for each of the examples in this section. (In this example it is the credit correction due to the credit of the ABS issuer.) After purchasing the instrument, we enter into a swap in which we pay the coupon received from the bond and receive in return a floating rate plus a spread s_{ASW}. The net outcome is that now we are receiving floating rate plus s_{ASW}. As usual, Φ denotes the difference resulting from the different discounting of the bond and the swap.

As we have said, asset-backed securities can be considerably risky and therefore can dramatically decrease in value or can default.[16] We know that in an asset swap after the initial setting of the spread s_{ASW}, the link between the security and the swap is not a tight one. Although the value of

---

[16]This, of course, applies to all securities, but in the case of ABS there is a stronger argument to be made.

TABLE 7.7 The hedging of an investment in an ABS with a total return swap.

Instrument type	Pay/Receive	Leg structure
Fixed/Floating ABS	Receive	$\sum_i^T C_i D_i \widetilde{D}_i dt_i - D_T \widetilde{D}_T$
Fixed/Floating TRS Leg	Pay	$-\sum_i^T \left[C + \left(B_{t_i} - B_{t_{i-1}} \right) \right] D_i dt_i - D_T$
Floating TRS Leg	Receive	$\sum_j^T \left[L_j + s_{TRS} + \right] D_j dt_j + D_T$
Result	Receive	$\sum_j^T \left[L_j + s_{TRS} + \right] D_j dt_j + D_T$

the coupon leg in the swap and the value of the bond will change in a similar (but of course *opposite*) fashion, this will be only if the change is linked to the coupon value or the pure interest rate element of the discount factor. If the change in the bond value is driven by the credit standing of the issuer, that is, it is driven by the discounting correction $\widetilde{D}_t$, then the bond and the coupon leg of the swap will be out of sync and, should the change be such that the bond loses value, the bond holder faces an overall loss. From the bond holder perspective, in this case the institution investing the bond, the income received from the bond is worth less than the liability represented by the coupon leg of the swap.

A type of static hedging that solves the issue presented above is one where the institution purchasing the bond enters into a total return swap. The situation is shown in Table 7.7.

The payout of the bond is, of course, similar between the situation presented in Tables 7.6 and 7.7. In a total return swap (TRS), the bond holder passes on to the swap counterpart not only the fixed coupon but also any appreciation *or depreciation* of the bond: of course to pass an appreciation is to pay something and to pass a depreciation is to receive something.

In Table 7.7 we have expressed the bond value at time t_i as B_{t_i} and the appreciation/depreciation between two coupon dates t_{i-1} and t_i as $B_{t_i} - B_{t_{i-1}}$. In the table the pay leg of the swap is seen from the point of view of the bond holder so, should the bond appreciate (i.e., $B_{t_i} > B_{t_{i-1}}$), the positive amount of the difference, with the negative sign in front, results in a payment on the bond holder part. Should the bond depreciate (i.e., $B_{t_i} < B_{t_{i-1}}$), the negative amount given by the difference, with the negative sign in front of the leg, results in a payment *from the counterpart to the bond holder* in addition to what the swap counterpart is already paying in the form of a floating rate plus spread. This does not apply to the final cash flow because, by definition, if the bond issuer has not defaulted, the bond is worth par.

We see why the transaction is called total return swap, because what is transferred between the two parties is not just the coupon of the security but the total mark-to-market (MTM) gain or loss as well. Should the bond

TABLE 7.8   The hedging of an equity investment with an equity return swap.

Instrument type	Pay/Receive	Leg structure
Equity investment	Receive	$\sum_i^T [S_i - S_{i-1}] D_i dt_i$
Floating Equity Swap Leg	Pay	$-\sum_i^T [S_i - S_{i-1}] D_i dt_i$
Floating Equity Swap Leg	Receive	$\sum_j^T (L_j + s) D_j dt_j$
Result	Receive	$\sum_j^T (L_j + s) D_j dt_j$

issuer default during the life of the swap and the bond price drop to some recovery value, the swap counterpart will pay the bond holder the difference between that value and par.

We are now able to comment on the relative returns of the two types of static hedges. As the TRS offers considerable protection to the bond holder, it is not difficult to see why the return in terms of spread over the floating rate is lower than in the case of a simple asset swap and we have therefore $s_{TRS} < s_{ASW}$. It is for the institution to decide whether it is worth taking the risk of hedging an ABS with an asset swap. A traditional financial institution, where the goal is the maximization of profit, would probably opt for an asset swap hedging; a development bank, whose goal is simply to gain a positive return over the benchmark (we can assume that L_j represents the benchmark), would probably opt for the TRS hedging.

Let us note as well that in Table 7.7 we do not have Φ anymore: this is because the difference between the bond price and the corresponding swap leg driven by the change in the credit, and therefore the discounting, of the bond is now included in the passing of the appreciation/depreciation of the bond between the bond holder and the swap counterpart.

7.3.1.6   Hedging an Equity Position   We have mentioned in Section 6.4.2 that a possible investment is to purchase equity in the form of shares. Equity return swaps (or simply equity swap) can be used to hedge this type of investment and to transform the return in a spread over a floating rate.

In Table 7.8 we show the example in which the institution has invested in S, a certain amount of shares. The return on this investment is measured at each time t_i and defined as the share value at that time minus the share value at the previous time, that is, $S_i - S_{i-1}$. This return is passed on to the swap counterpart, which in turn pays a floating rate plus a spread s. Note that, as we have mentioned in the previous section referring to the bond price, the return in the share price $S_i - S_{i-1}$ can be positive or negative. Thus the pay leg of the swap (from the bond holder's point of view) can result in a payment (if $S_i > S_{i-1}$) or in receiving a payment instead from the swap counterpart

TABLE 7.9 Taking a view on interest rates by locking a fixed rate.

Instrument type	Pay/Receive	Leg structure
Net income (floating)	Receive	$\sum_j^T (L_j + s) \, D_j dt_j$
Floating Swap Leg	Pay	$-\sum_j^T (L_j + s) \, D_j dt_j$
Fixed Swap Leg	Receive	$\sum_i^T C D_i dt_i$
Result	Receive	$\sum_i^T C D_i dt_i$

(if $S_i < S_{i-1}$). As mentioned before, the payment in the latter is in addition to what the swap counterpart is already paying in the form of floating rate plus s.

7.3.1.7 Locking an Interest Rate Position

All the strategies shown in the previous sections, the conversion of a fixed or structured coupon bond, the conversion of a fixed-rate loan, the conversion of a foreign currency bond, or the conversion of an investment in equity or credit-linked securities, means that we are net receivers[17] of floating cash flows in a set of currencies.

Let us imagine that the institution decides to take a view on interest rates in currency X where it believes that either these are about to decrease throughout the entire rate's term structure or that the swap curve is inverted, that is, the very long-term rates are lower than the short-term ones.

Let us imagine, as shown in Table 7.9, that we are in the unlikely but not completely inconceivable position in which all our net receivables can be bundled in a set of floating cash flows indexed to a floating rate L_j plus a spread s. We would enter into a swap where we pay exactly the same cash flows and receive a fixed coupon C. The value of the coupon would be such that the two transactions are financially equivalent at the time where we enter into this structure: should the interest rates decrease as expected we will be making a profit. Note that in the above table we have omitted the final cash flow: as opposed to the representation of the other structures in the previous sections, the first line is rather fictitious in the sense that it should bundle all our (hypothetically never ending) net receivables. Since it is not an actual transaction, there is no real value in adding a final principal repayment.

---

[17]Our net, hopefully positive, position is the result of summing our lending, borrowing, and investing activities.

7.3.2 Credit Risk

Throughout this book credit has been, more or less explicitly, our main focus. Although we have said at the beginning of this chapter that it was going to be mainly about asset liability management, it is only natural to mention very briefly the issue of credit risk management.

If our goal has been achieved, the reader will realize that there is no such thing as an absolute risk-free frame of reference or safe haven. Credit considerations permeate all financial variables either directly and explicitly mentioned such as in the case of CDS contracts, or directly but implicitly mentioned such as in the case of interest rates or indirectly because we know that all financial activity needs to be funded and funding means credit.

Dealing with credit risk is a very complicated matter and the financial crisis of 2007 to 2009 showed how there is no limit to the power of invention (with a neutral connotation in the term) when it comes to translating and diluting the idea of debt and ultimately of credit. To deal with full credit risk management is beyond the scope of this chapter and this book. Once more we shall look at the far simpler situation of a development institution to touch very briefly on a few important concepts.

What type of credit risk does a development institution or a small financial institution that deals in a borrowing and a simple lending activity face? It faces credit risk on two sides, of course: on one side it faces the credit risk of its borrowers and on the other side it faces the credit risk of its asset swap counterparts.

Before offering a few more details, let us first concentrate in a general way on the magnitude of credit risk and how its size can affect the institution. Why is too much credit risk bad? The question seems obvious but if we look at it closely it is more subtle than it appears.

Risk indicates an exposure/sensitivity to a financial variable or phenomenon. If properly calculated it shows the impact of an adverse movement on our position. What separates credit from other risks is that, although it depends on our view and model, credit can lead, through the phenomenon of default, to a scenario that is either/or. This, however, is not what we want to concentrate on here, rather we need to answer the question, why is too much risk bad? An institution cares not only about what the measuring of risk can communicate about a *potential* scenario, but also about the presence of risk itself. It is a difference of order.

If we are long variable A, we are concerned about what happens if A decreases and this is a first order concern about the potential behavior of A: the concern becomes effective, so to speak, when A truly goes down. However, a second order concern is that we are exposed in the first place and this concern has an impact even before knowing what variable A does.

The presence of credit risk, more than other types of risk, affects an institution's credit itself and this can be seen in a few different ways. There is the shareholder view in which credit risk affects the return on investment. The terminology is borrowed from a for-profit perspective but it does easily apply to a development institution as well. Our own exposure to credit risk is known to the outside world and therefore, casting a shadow on our solvency, it will affect the spread we offer bond holders when we issue debt. If it becomes onerous for us to issue debt, our net income, that is, the income we obtain from our lending/investment activity once we factor in the cost of borrowing, will suffer.

This problem affects more traditional financial institutions: development banks, where the net spread between loans and debt (we shall study this in detail in the next sections) is *roughly* constant, are less concerned about diminishing returns in the face of rising costs of funding. However, since the cost is passed on to borrowers and insofar as the borrowers' financial well-being is a cause for concern for the institution, this issue affects development institutions as well.

The other view is one that a credit agency might take. We already mentioned in Section 7.1 the concept of capital requirement and leverage. Without entering into details as the calculations are fairly complicated, the way these figures are obtained is by taking into account the credit risk involved in the assets (financial instruments) held by an institution. The outcome is a view of the institution that will affect its rating and as a consequence its borrowing ability. Both views at the end lead to a view on the borrowing ability of the institution. What one can consider the difference between the two is the motive, so to speak, and therefore a sometimes different threshold of acceptance of risk.

We have seen the role played by credit risk itself and different points of view from which to observe it. Let us now return to the management of credit risk and to the two principal sources, borrowers and counterparts, we were mentioning above.

The credit risk linked to a bank's borrowers is fairly easy to understand particularly in the fair value framework we showed in Section 3.3. We have valued each loan with each cash flow discounted by a risky discount factor that was the exact product of the normal discount factor D_t implied from interest rate instruments and the survival probability S_t of the borrower. The survival probability was implied in a way that would price CDS contracts correctly. In order to manage the credit risk associated with the loan we only need to know its sensitivity to it and hedge using credit default swaps. Leaving aside the complicated issue of the second order credit effect given by the fact that CDSs are contracts themselves with a counterparty risk of their own, let us observe what hedging through CDS entails for our sample bank of choice, the development institution.

A development institution is, as we said many times, a credit cooperative. Its loans are, usually,[18] purely sovereign loans to members of the cooperative. The purchase of a CDS, as natural and as sensible a choice it might
be, is a clear statement of confidence, or lack thereof, in a member country.
Although it is not an impossible step to take, the significance of it would
need to be considered. A further consideration would be the potential conflict between the profit and loss resulting from the CDS trading and the loan
issuance itself.

Let us imagine a small borrowing country whose five-year CDS trades at
600 bps that has a loan from development institution ABC. The market has
a fairly negative outlook on its finances. ABC sells protection with a principal N_1 on the country. Shortly after, ABC issues a large loan of principal
N_2 to the country, which boosts considerably the liquidity of its funds and
quickly lowers its five-year CDS rate to 500 bps. ABC now buys protection
on the country (of a principal $N_1 + N_2$). Not only did it buy protection on
the country but it also made 100 bps on N_1 of profit (either as a running
spread or as an up-front according to convention) by selling protection at
600 bps and buying it back at 500 bps.

Wouldn't one say that ABC had almost certain knowledge that its loan
would lower the CDS spread? Of course, ABC could limit itself to deal only
in covered protection, that is, only purchase the sell protection linked to a
specific outstanding loan principal, but the issue is certainly a complicated
one that needs careful consideration to avoid conflict of interest.

The credit risk linked to a loan issuance is fairly clear because it is unilat-
eral: the only concerned party is the one issuing the loan. More complicated
is the situation when it is bilateral, when both parties are concerned by the
other's credit risk. The typical situation is the one of a swap. The subject is
vast (see, for example, Brigo and Capponi [18] or Gregory [44]) and here we
are only going to offer a brief and practical summary simply to show what
is beyond asset liability management in terms of fundamental risks.

In Section 7.2.3 we discussed the concept of mark to market (MTM)
and its relation to collateral. The MTM of a swap is the net present values
of the two legs and it is such that when seen from counterpart A it has
exactly the opposite value from the one seen by counterpart B. We have seen
that (leaving aside the netting of multiple trades) when A sees the MTM as
positive, B has to post an amount of collateral equal to the MTM to A.

If all counterparts paid collateral and the payment would be instantaneous, collateral posting would take care of all risk associated with the

---

[18]Not all development institutions lend only to sovereign entities, but the credit cooperative view applies practically to all.

counterpart's credit. We have seen, however, that some institutions do not pay collateral either because of special arrangements due to their high credit ratings (which nonetheless does not mean they are exempt from the probability of default) or because they do not want to part with precious cash. Also, it is easy to see that collateral posting cannot be instantaneous either because of logistics or because sometimes collateral disputes take time to be solved and during their time part of the MTM may be uncovered by the collateral.

The solution to this is a credit value adjustment (CVA), which is a bilateral agreement to adjust the riskless value of the trade by a certain amount. The crucial point to this is that it is bilateral, which means that it is symmetric (each side does not consider itself riskless) and its value is equal in size and opposite in sign.

Let us define with MTM_t^A the mark to market as seen at time t by A, and with MTM_t^B the mark to market as seen at time t by B with

$$|MTM_t^A| \equiv |MTM_t^B|$$
$$MTM_t^A = -MTM_t^B$$

Using a view similar to Brigo et al. [21], we need to focus on two things when calculating a CVA: when the defaults of the parties happen (if before the end of the contract at time T) and whether the mark to market is positive or negative at the time of the default of the other party. Let us define as τ_A the time when A is going to default and τ_B the time when B is going to default. Then, if we take the point of view of party A we have the adjustment given by

$$\mathbf{E}_t \left[(1 - R_A) \, \mathbf{1}_{\tau_A \leq \tau_B \leq T \bigcup \tau_A \leq T \leq \tau_B} D_{\tau_A} \left(MTM_{\tau_A}^A \right)^+ \right] - \qquad (7.11)$$
$$\mathbf{E}_t \left[(1 - R_B) \, \mathbf{1}_{\tau_B \leq \tau_A \leq T \bigcup \tau_B \leq T \leq \tau_A} D_{\tau_B} \left(MTM_{\tau_B}^B \right)^+ \right]$$

where all the symbols have the usual meaning (R_A and R_B are the recovery rates of A and B, and D_{τ_A} and D_{τ_B} are the discount factors at the time of A's and B's default respectively) and where $\tau_X \leq \tau_Y \leq T \bigcup \tau_X \leq T \leq \tau_Y$ indicates the situation where either they both default before the end of the contract but X defaults first or only X defaults before the end of the contract. To express Equation 7.11 in words we could say, to simplify an otherwise confusing grid of ifs, that in case of default the defaulting party will receive the whole of the MTM if it sees it as positive and will only return a fraction of it if it sees it as negative.

Once we understand the different combinations of times of default and signs of the MTM, Equation 7.11 is fairly simple and intuitive. The only difficult part is given by the fact that, for example, in the case of the default of A, we do not have MTM_t^A but instead $MTM_{\tau_A}^A$. Computationally this makes an enormous difference because it means that we need to simulate the mark to market[19] of the trade *correlated* to the future credit risk of each counterpart. Depending on the type of trades, this could involve literally hours and hours of computations. Once a value is obtained the adjustment will be made on to the value, which is supposed to be default free. There are simplified assumptions that could be made to this full-scale calculation and this is usually the road taken by institutions that do not have sufficient computational power.

The advantage of a calculation based on something like Equation 7.11 is that it is absolutely symmetric: each term is identical once we change A for B. The value will be seen by each as equal in size and opposite in sign. A calculation where each party considered itself as riskless would not be symmetric. The disadvantage, although one should not necessarily describe it as such, more as a puzzle, is that it leads to situations where an institution's revenues (which include credit value adjustments) increase when the institution's credit deteriorates. This is similar in nature to the liability paradox we have mentioned already (see Fries [40] and also Gregory [44]) in which an institution's balance sheet seems to improve in the face of the worsening of its own credit standing.

As we have said at the beginning of this chapter, we have focused on the risk linked to the management of the relationship between debt and income and this was simply a partying note on some of the issues linked to credit risk. The subject is vast and, particularly in the context of for-profit banking, it would need a dedicated discussion, all the more important as the financial world has realized since the financial crisis of 2007 to 2009 that no corner is left untouched by credit, so the managing of its risk is of the essence.

7.4 FUNDING RISK

7.4.1 Funding Gap Risk

In Section 7.1 we have mentioned the concept of capital requirements: these were debt-to-loan ratios imposed by an external body. Even without an intervention from outside, an institution usually tries to maintain a balance between the amount it raises in debt and the amount it issues in loans. To understand why this is important, let us build a concrete example. In this example we are going to look at the balance between bonds and loans. We

---

[19]When we say mark to market we mean, of course, as we have introduced at the beginning of the section, the portion of mark to market that is not covered, for reasons of delay or dispute, by the collateral posted.

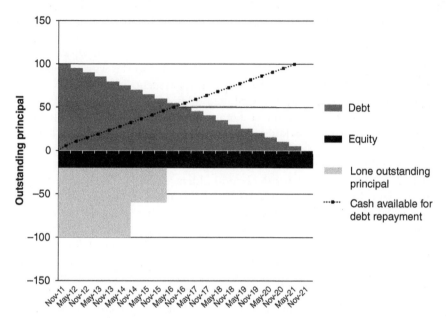

FIGURE 7.1 A representation of the debt-to-loan balance of a possible portfolio.

are using bonds and loans because it is the simplest possible way of picturing the management of debt and income. This will allow us to make specific points that are nonetheless applicable to the more general mechanism of a financial institution in which debt is issued in order to generate income.

Let us imagine that today is November 3, 2011, and we have disbursed a 10-year loan with 100 units of principal. Let us also imagine that we have issued two five-year bonds, each with a principal of 40, one and two years ago respectively (on October 27, 2009, and on November 10, 2010). Let us also assume that we had 20 units of equity.

Figure 7.1 offers a graphic representation of our situation in terms of principal profile, a plot in time of the outstanding principal of debt and loans. The first thing we need to state is that, as we gather from the plot and as we have mentioned in Section 3.1.1, loans are amortizing instruments and bonds are not. This is true in the near totality of situations (there are some exceptions in the form of bullet loans where the principal is repaid at the end, but they are not the norm). Describing the situation as depicted from the figure, we had 20 of equity, we raised 80 in debt from the two bonds, and we lent 100 over a 10-year period with repayments of principal in semiannual amounts of five.

Before entering into the merit of the dynamic balance between debt and loans, we can comment on the leverage of the situation to continue what we discussed at the beginning of the chapter. At the moment we are simply discussing principals and not interests payments, so the way to repay the bonds' principals is through the principal repayments in the loan. We have used 20 units of equity and a combined 80 units of debt to fund 100 units of loan: overall we are balanced. Let us assume that very early in the life of the loan the borrower defaults on the entirety of the loan. In this situation the amount of equity we have used to fund the loan (the rough equivalent of the capital requirement) is crucial: the equity amount is a loss for us but the debt is potentially a loss for the bond holders, should we be unable to raise other debt. In our case, should we be unable to raise another 80 units, the loss of 80 would be transferred to someone else. There is a push toward high capital requirements exactly to avoid contagion since the lower the amount of equity used to fund the loan, the more the loss from one defaulting loan will propagate throughout the financial world.

Leverage aside, looking at Figure 7.1 we can see that, although overall we are balanced, since debt maturities and loan repayments take place at different times throughout the lives of the different instruments, we are far from balanced. In three years' time, for example, we will need to pay the bond holders of the first bond, the one expiring on October 27, 2014. If we look at the plot of the cash that has been repaid by the borrower and is available to pay the bond holder, on that date we will only have 30 units, not enough.

In order to repay our bond holders we need to issue additional debt on that date; hence, on October 27, 2014, we are going to issue our first rebalancing bond, a four-year bond with a principal of 20 units. With the cash thus raised, plus the one we have received from the borrower, we can return the face value of the bond to the investors. On November 10, 2015, we will be facing the same problem when we need to return the face value of 40 units to the investors of the second original bond. We can issue another, a second, rebalancing four-year bond on that date with a principal of 20 units. With this amount, what we have from the first rebalancing bond and what we are receiving from the borrower we can return the 40 units from the bond holders. The loan proceeds are enough to repay the first rebalancing bond, however, we need to issue a third and final rebalancing bond on November 10, 2019, with a principal of 5 in order to repay the second. A summary of all the instruments in our portfolio is given in Table 7.10.

This seemingly complicated process is shown in Figure 7.2 where we plot the principal profile of the initial situation plus the additional rebalancing debt. In this new plot the proceeds from the loan are reduced each time we use them to repay the bond holders.

TABLE 7.10 A summary of the debt and loan portfolio in our example.

Instrument type	Issue date	Maturity date	Principal
Loan	November 3, 2011	November 3, 2021	100
Bond 1	October 27, 2009	October 27, 2014	40
Bond 2	December 10, 2010	December 10, 2015	40
Bond 3	October 27, 2014	October 27, 2018	20
Bond 4	December 10, 2015	December 10, 2019	20
Bond 5	December 10, 2019	December 10, 2021	5

To rebalance a debt/loan portfolio (or, in general, a debt/revenue one) is crucial and it is a particularly common mechanism carried out by sovereign treasuries. During a sovereign debt crisis sometimes we experience quiet moments: these are the moments in between principal repayments (at the moment we are excluding coupon payments).

The reader might wonder why there is a need to enter into such a complicated mechanism, why bonds and loans can't have the same maturity and the same profile, wouldn't it simplify things considerably? It would simplify things, but it is not done for many reasons, two of which we are going to

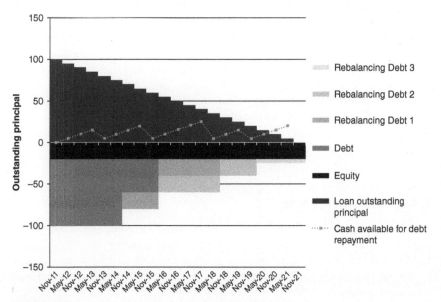

FIGURE 7.2 A representation of the debt-to-loan balance of a possible portfolio after additional debt has been issued to rebalance.

present. Under a legal point of view a loan is a different instrument from, say, a derivative: crucially, no collateral is paid. No collateral is paid on bonds either, but bonds are securitized instruments for which there is a, sometimes active, secondary market.

It would be a generalization to say that loans are usually extended to entities that would have difficulties raising funds in the bond market, but not a gross one. Should a loan have a profile similar to a bond, that is, with the largest payment at maturity, the risk for the lender would, of course, be much greater and the terms for the borrower would certainly be harsher. It therefore suits both parties for loans to have an amortizing profile.

The second reason, which shall be discussed in the next section, can be understood by considering what we have up to now ignored: coupon payments. In the rebalancing exercise we have carried out, we were only rebalancing principal; we have ignored the fact that both bonds and loans carry interest payments.

The bonds *pay* a coupon, which we service not directly but through an asset swap structure, meaning that we have a funding cost usually linked to a LIBOR. From the loan we *receive* a coupon, which we assume, for simplicity, to be also linked to a LIBOR. In all cases, for the sake of the profitability of the institution, our income from the loans must be greater than the cost we incur through servicing the debt. In addition to this we should try to maximize this positive difference between the rate we receive and the rate we pay. In case we are an investment bank, this is in order to increase our profits; in case we are a development bank charging only costs, in order to issue loans with the lowest possible rate.

We have already seen that funding costs, not surprisingly, tend to increase with the maturity of the debt. Therefore one of the best ways to maximize the spread between income and costs is to issue short-dated debt to fund long-dated loans. This is possibly the single most important reason for the mismatch in maturity between loans and bonds and we are going to discuss this in greater detail in the next section.

7.4.2 Refinancing Risk

The act of issuing new debt to repay a previous one while the accompanying loan is not matured yet is called, with a term familiar to any mortgage holder, *refinancing*. In the previous section we have stated how the practice of issuing short-dated debt to fund long-dated loans is carried out in order to maximize profit. In order to observe this in detail, let us first establish a formalism that should help us to simplify the expressions we have been using up to now.

We are going to define by L_t the value at time t of a loan of the form we saw in Section 3.3.1, that is,

$$L_t = \sum_i S_i D_i \left[N_i \left(L_i + s_L^{T_0} \right) dt_i + (N_i - N_{i+1}) \right] + R \sum_j N_j D_j \left(S_{j-1} - S_j \right)$$

where $s_L^{T_0}$ is the spread paid by the loan over the floating rate and set at time T_0, the start date of the loan.

With the operator $I^{+/-}[\ ]$ we are going to define the interest rate income generated by an instrument, the plus or minus sign indicating whether it is an income (plus) or a negative income (minus), that is, a cost. By income we mean the profit or cost the instrument is going to generate in the future: the actual profit at the moment it will become realized, not its present value. For example, for the loan above, the total income will be

$$I^+[L] = \sum_i \left(L_i + s_L^{T_0} \right) dt_i \tag{7.12}$$

By adding an index i, with $I^+{}_i$ we mean the income in one single period, for the loan above this would reduce to $(L_i + s_L^{T_0}) dt_i$. We stress that since by income we mean realized profit, we discard any notion of discount and/or default risk.

By B_t we are going to define the value of a bond of the type

$$B_t = \sum_i f_i D_i \widetilde{D}_i dt_i - D_T \widetilde{D}_T$$

however, since we have swapped the bond in an asset swap structure leading to a funding spread $s_A^{T_0}$, not only we are indifferent to the nature of the coupon f_i but we can say that

$$I^-[B] = \sum_i \left(L_i + s_A^{T_0} \right) dt_i \tag{7.13}$$

where the income operator now has a negative sign since, when applied to a bond, becomes a cost. In the case of a bond, the cost for a single period is then $(L_i + s_A^{T_0}) dt_i$. Let us stress the role of the time stamp as it is very important and key to understanding the challenges of refinancing risk. T_0 is the time at which we disburse the loan amount and we issue the *first* bond: the spreads $s_L^{T_0}$ will be constant for the *entire life of the loan* and the spread $s_A^{T_0}$ will be constant for the entire life *only of the first* bond.

The profit P we are going to make from our operation is thus going to be given by

$$P = \sum_i \left(s_L^{T_0} - s_A^{T_0} \right) dt_i \qquad (7.14)$$

where we have assumed (in Section 7.4.4 we are going to see what happens when this assumption does not hold) that the loan frequency and payment dates coincide with those of the bond, meaning that L_i is literally the same in Equations 7.12 and 7.13. If this is the case, when summing income and cost, the two L_i cancel each other.

In the previous section we stated that the situation, which at first might seem logistically simpler—having the maturity of the bond coincide with the maturity of the loan—would yield little profit because it could very well be that $s_L^{T_0}$ would be of a size comparable to $s_A^{T_0}$. If we assume that (with T being the maturity of the bond)

$$s_A \downarrow \text{ as } T \downarrow$$

that is, the funding spread decreases for short-dated bonds (a reasonable assumption based on reasonable credit considerations), then, keeping the maturity of the loan constant,

$$P \uparrow \text{ as } T \downarrow$$

The above means that in order to maximize our profit we should issue the most short-dated debt possible. This is true in principle but it needs to be balanced with the fact that the more we rebalance our debt/loan pool by refinancing (what we have shown in Figure 7.2), the more we are exposing ourselves to *refinancing risk*.

Refinancing risk can be defined as the risk that, having to issue new debt at the expiry of the old one (while the loan is still in part outstanding), we do so at a funding level higher than expected and therefore we are unable to make the same profit as expected from Equation 7.14.

To understand this better let us introduce the quantity

$$\mathbf{E}_{T_i} \left[s_A^{T_j} \right]$$

as the expected value of the funding level at time T_j as seen at time T_i. If T_i is now, the above expression would tell us at what level we would expect to issue a debt starting at time $T_j > T_i$. We have said that funding levels tend to increase with the maturity of a bond *starting today*. This means that, like any rate term structure, even the funding levels of bonds starting in the future tend to increase with time, hence we expect

$$s_A^{T_0} < \mathbf{E}_{T_0}\left[s_A^{T_1}\right] < \mathbf{E}_{T_0}\left[s_A^{T_2}\right] < \mathbf{E}_{T_0}\left[s_A^{T_3}\right] < \ldots < \mathbf{E}_{T_0}\left[s_A^{T_N}\right]$$

(where we stress the importance of the time notation).

This adds some complexity to Equation 7.14, which appears slightly simplistic in the present form. Since we expect to issue further debt during the life of the loan, we should not compare one loan spread with one funding level, rather we should be comparing one loan spread with *all* the funding levels of all the bonds issued to fund the loan. If we issue N bonds to fund one loan, the cumulative profits then would be

$$
\begin{aligned}
P = & \left[\sum_{i=T_0}^{T_1}\left(s_L^{T_0} - s_A^{T_0}\right)dt_i\right] + \left[\sum_{i=T_1}^{T_2}\left(s_L^{T_0} - s_A^{T_1}\right)dt_i\right] \qquad (7.15)\\
& + \left[\sum_{i=T_2}^{T_3}\left(s_L^{T_0} - s_A^{T_2}\right)dt_i\right] \\
& + \left[\sum_{i=T_3}^{T_4}\left(s_L^{T_0} - s_A^{T_3}\right)dt_i\right] + \ldots + \left[\sum_{i=T_N}^{T_{N+1}}\left(s_L^{T_0} - s_A^{T_N}\right)dt_i\right]
\end{aligned}
$$

(if the summation signs above seem strange, let us not forget that the index i tracks the LIBOR L_i, which, since we have assumed for the moment it is the same for loans and bond, has disappeared).

In the above we want P to be positive, of course (and either of a certain amount if we are a development institution or as large as possible if we are an investment bank), but that does not mean that in each of the terms above we require $s_A^{T_n} < s_L^{T_0} \; \forall \; n$. If one wished, one could see the above as a swap where the loan spread plays the role of the fixed rate we receive and the expectation of the future funding levels the role of the floating rate we pay. The valuation of a swap is based on the fact that, although toward the beginning the fixed rate will be higher than the floating rate and toward the end the fixed rate will be lower, the present value of the sum leads to a fair value. Similarly the combination of all the terms in 7.15, where in some the funding level will be lower and in some higher than the loan spread, should lead to $P > 0$. Let us remind ourselves that the only parameter over which we have full control is the loan spread $s_L^{T_0}$: we set it accordingly to what we need or want to obtain in terms of P.

There are three possible scenarios we could be facing now and we shall present them in increasing order of complexity.

7.4.2.1 The Case of Constant Funding Level
In a calm credit environment, one the world is not going to see for a long time after the financial crisis of 2007 to 2009, funding costs, particularly for borrowers in good standing, are roughly constant and tend to have very low variance and they tend to come true. This means not only that

$$s_A^{T_0} \approx \mathbf{E}_{T_0}\left[s_A^{T_1}\right] \approx \mathbf{E}_{T_0}\left[s_A^{T_2}\right] \approx \mathbf{E}_{T_0}\left[s_A^{T_3}\right] \approx \ldots \approx \mathbf{E}_{T_0}\left[s_A^{T_N}\right]$$

but also that

$$s_A^{T_n} \approx \mathbf{E}_{T_{n-1}}\left[s_A^{T_n}\right]$$

meaning that when at time T_n the asset swap spread corresponding to a bond issued at that moment became certain, it was approximatively equal to the value we were expecting earlier at time T_{n-1}. This environment offers no particular challenges or risks.

7.4.2.2 The Case of Funding Level Lower Than Expected
There are many situations in finance where one hears the expression "the spot does not follow the forward." This is particularly frequent in the FX world[20] but it can be applied here as well. The expression means that when something actually takes place it does so in a way that differs consistently from its previously expected value. The expression is also usually intended in a favorable sense. In our context it would mean that

$$s_A^{T_n} < \mathbf{E}_{T_{n-1}}\left[s_A^{T_n}\right]$$

The above means that when the time comes to issue a new bond, the actual asset swap spread is lower than what we had expected previously. If this is the case, the value set for $s_L^{T_0}$ was too conservative: it was set for a certain series of funding levels and these turned out to be lower than expected. The profit we are going to make is higher than initially foreseen.

---

[20]The consistency with which the spot USD/JPY rate did not follow the forward was at the origin of the famous "Yen carry trades," which we mentioned in Section 6.4.2.

7.4.2.3 The Case of Funding Level Higher Than Expected

It is not difficult to imagine the opposite of the previous scenario and envisage the situation where

$$s_A^{T_n} > \mathbf{E}_{T_{n-1}}\left[s_A^{T_n}\right] \tag{7.16}$$

that is, when the time comes to issue the refinancing debt, the asset swap level is higher than we had anticipated.

This is the simplest expression of the danger of refinancing risk. We set a spread for the loan, which should lead to a profit based on the assumption of a certain funding level term structure; however, the actual funding levels turn out to be much higher leading to a smaller than expected (or negative) P.

This situation is particularly treacherous and is easily compounded by external factors such as leverage, liquidity, and contagion. During the Euro sovereign crisis of 2010 to 2012 an important issue was the difference between insolvent countries like Greece, where[21] $s_L^{T_0}$ in any scenario was never going to be enough to lead to a positive P, and countries essentially solvent like Spain and Italy, where the positive value of P was jeopardized simply by the fact that in a credit and liquidity crisis $s_A^{T_n}$ follows Equation 7.16 to a dramatic level. Banks [7] offers a thorough analysis of the relationship (with examples from important financial crisis) between the problems of liquidity occurring during a credit crisis and funding.

7.4.3 Numerical Example: Estimating Refinancing Risk

Using our fictitious portfolio of one loan and five bonds shown in Table 7.10 we shall describe in numerical detail the issue of refinancing risk.

Let us assume that our funding spread, or cost, in the short term is 20 bps below the six-month LIBOR and after that it evolves as shown in Figure 7.3, meaning that in the long term our funding cost, as implied by our current debt stock, is considerably higher than LIBOR. Let us assume that to cover our institution's costs we need an income of 50 bps. Based on the short-term funding of LIBOR minus 20 bps we price our loan so that the borrower needs to pay an interest of LIBOR plus 30 bps. Assuming for simplicity that all bonds are, like the loan, referenced to the same LIBOR six-month rate,

---

[21]The spread $s_L^{T_0}$ has been defined here as a loan spread, in a qualitative argument it can be extended to mean income in general.

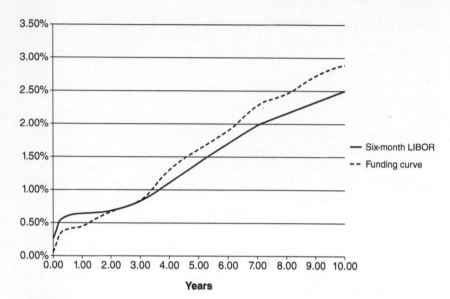

FIGURE 7.3 The six-month LIBOR curve and the funding curve of our financial institution.

the difference between the two is exactly our needed net income, 50 bps (essentially what is stated by Equation 7.14).

We have seen, however, in the previous section that the actual funding level at which we are going to be able to reissue a bond to rebalance our bond/loan portfolio might be equal, higher, or lower than the expected one. Let us try to calculate what the impact is if we are forced to reissue our rebalancing debt at the expected funding level or at a funding level essentially equal to the present short-term one. Let us try to see, in other words using the FX-like terminology of the previous section, what happens if the spot funding spread follows the forward and what if it does not.

The loan and the bonds are floating-rate instruments. Using the six-month LIBOR curve in Figure 7.3 we can calculate forward six-month LIBOR, which gives us, after adding the fixed spread of 30 bps we are charging the borrower, the coupons of the loan. We also know the principal profile of the loan (seen in Figure 7.1), that is, how the outstanding principal changes in time, since we know that every six months there is a repayment of five units of principal. By multiplying the loan coupon for that six-month period times the outstanding principal in that period and dividing by two (the rate is quoted as annualized so we need to divide it by half for a six-month period) we obtain our income for every six-month period.

TABLE 7.11 The income by rate reset period for each instrument in our portfolio.

Years	Loan rate	Loan income	Bond 1 cost	Bond 2 cost	Bond 3 cost	Bond 4 cost	Bond 5 cost
0.5	0.40%	.45	−.08	−.08	−	−	−
1.0	0.47%	.46	−.09	−.09	−	−	−
1.5	0.78%	.44	−.10	−.10	−	−	−
2.0	1.02%	.43	−.11	−.11	−	−	−
2.5	1.34%	.53	−.17	−.17	−	−	−
3.0	1.49%	.56	−.20	−.20	−	−	−
3.5	2.07%	.72	−	−.31	−0.24	−	−
4.0	2.35%	.76	−	−.37	−0.26	−	−
4.5	2.80%	.84	−	−.46	−0.31	−	−
5.0	3.11%	.86	−	−	−0.34	−0.34	−
5.5	3.23%	.81	−	−	−0.35	−0.35	−
6.0	3.50%	.79	−	−	−0.38	−0.38	−
6.5	3.81%	.76	−	−	−0.41	−0.41	−
7.0	4.09%	.72	−	−	−0.44	−0.44	−
7.5	3.55%	.53	−	−	−	−0.38	−
8.0	3.71%	.46	−	−	−	−0.40	−
8.5	3.93%	.39	−	−	−	−0.42	−
9.0	4.11%	.31	−	−	−	−	−0.11
9.5	4.31%	.22	−	−	−	−	−0.12
10.0	4.50%	.11	−	−	−	−	−0.10

We can write it as

$$\text{LoanIncome} = \sum_{i=6M,12M,18M,\dots} \text{OutstandingPrincipal}_i \left(\text{FwdLIBOR}_i + 30bps\right) dt_i \quad (7.17)$$

Which is essentially Equation 7.12. The rate and the income are shown in columns two and three respectively of Table 7.11.

For the bonds it is only slightly more complicated. We assume, for simplicity, that the two bonds that are already in the portfolio (Bond 1 and Bond 2), pay a coupon equal to the spot funding cost of 20 bps below six-month LIBOR. The spread over LIBOR paid by the futures bonds that we need to issue to balance our loan will fix in the future. For example, the spread paid by Bond 3 will fix in three years' time and we shall calculate it in the following way: using the curves shown in Figure 7.3 we calculate, starting in three years' time, the forward four-year (the length of the bond) rate from the LIBOR curve and the forward four-year rate from the funding curve; the difference between funding rate and LIBOR gives us the spread over LIBOR. For Bond 3 this spread is 58 bps. The cost (seen as a negative income) of Bond 3 is given then by the forward LIBOR plus 58 bps multiplied by the bond principal and divided by two. The same calculation can be done for all the other bonds and the result is shown in Table 7.11.

We have calculated the individual income for the loan and each of the bonds, so now we need to see what net result yields our portfolio. To give a meaningful number we need to express it in annualized terms (as it is the standard way of presenting results). We need to calculate the return on the loan and the return on the bonds: since both returns contain the same LIBOR, the difference will give us the return over LIBOR, the number we are interested in.

We are going to take the total income from the loan for each year and we are going to divide it by the average annual principal for the loan (in this simple case the sum of the outstanding principal for each six-month period divided by two). This will give us the loan return (which, by definition of return, is a percentage). The sum of the same calculation for each of the bonds gives us the (negative) return on our bonds. The difference between the two is our net income presented in Table 7.12 in basis points.

The third column shows the net income should the actual funding spread in the future remain constant at the present value. From the table we see that the income we obtain each year is roughly the 50 bps we were aiming for.

The second column shows instead the net income should the funding spread fix according to its expected value as shown in Figure 7.3. We can

TABLE 7.12 Two scenarios for the yearly net income of our portfolio.

Years	Expected net income (bps)	Assumed net income (bps)
1.0	49.67	49.67
2.0	49.72	49.72
3.0	49.57	49.57
4.0	23.22	49.38
5.0	5.20	52.45
6.0	−29.59	49.28
7.0	−29.81	49.12
8.0	−29.88	49.30
9.0	−28.61	54.16
10.0	−49.93	47.10

clearly see that toward the end of the loan, not only we are earning less than the expected spread, but we are actually making a loss.

This is a practical example of refinancing risk, the risk that, because we are forced to refinance the loan with shorter dated debt, we might earn a smaller spread than expected. A possible solution to this risk is to issue variable spread loans in which, as shown in Equation 6.7, the spread over the floating rate paid by the borrower is not fixed but a function of the latest borrowing cost of the lender.

7.4.4 Reset Risk

In the previous section we have made the strong assumption that in the fictitious portfolio of loan(s) and bonds used to understand refinancing risk, the floating rates L_i reset at the same time for bonds and loans. This means that the combined income $I[L \mid B]$ from bonds and loans is given by

$$I[L \mid B] = \sum_i \left(L_i + s_L^{T_0}\right) dt_i - \sum_i \left(L_i + s_A^{T_0}\right) dt_i = \sum_i \left(s_L^{T_0} - s_A^{T_0}\right) dt_i$$

which is essentially the expression given in Equation 7.14 (we have omitted the "$+/-$" since we are combining income and cost).

The reality is often, almost always, different and the situation shown in Figure 7.2 and Table 7.10 follow reality: looking at the issue date of the bonds and loan in Table 7.10 and knowing that all instruments are semiannual in payment frequency, we can see that the loan's LIBOR resets every third of November and May, some bonds' LIBORs reset every October 27 and April 27 and some other bonds' LIBORs reset every December 10 and June 10. This information can be summarized in a more complex form of income

$$I[L \mid B] = \sum_i N_i \left(L_i + s_L^{T_0}\right) dt_i \qquad (7.18)$$

$$- \left[\sum_j N_j \left(L_j + s_A^{T_0}\right) dt_j + \sum_k N_k \left(L_k + s_A^{T_0}\right) dt_k \right]$$

where i follows the resetting of the loan and j and k follow the resetting of the two types of bond (in our example new bonds match the previous debt they are used to repay in terms of dates). In order not to overburden the notation with further suffices for bonds and loan, we hope it is clear enough that N_i, N_j, and N_k are whatever principals applying to the rates L_i, L_j, and L_k respectively.

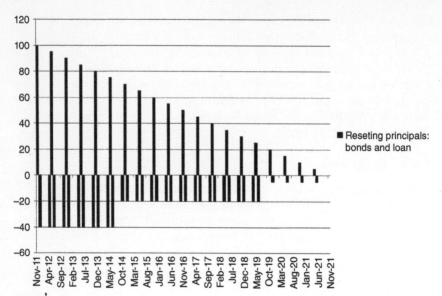

FIGURE 7.4 The net resetting principal of the loan and the bonds in our example.

In Figure 7.4 we display the net resetting principal in time, which is the net amount of principal to which the resetting of a LIBOR applies. In our case the term net is superfluous since in our small portfolio each instrument resets on a different day. In a large pool, however, there could be the situation in which two or more instruments reset on the same day, so in that case we would net their principals. The picture is quite stark in presenting the problem of *reset risk*.

Any financial forecast is by definition hostage to the actual events: whether the actual return on my investment in Ford Motor is similar to my expected forecast depends, of course, on the actual trajectory taken by the share price following its forward value. Whether the share price follows this trajectory in a more or less volatile fashion is of no concern to us. Similarly, the volatility of interest rates has no impact on swap prices.

A picture like the one presented by Figure 7.4 is an example of a situation not involving an option where nevertheless the variance of the underlying matters considerably. It is easy to see how in a time of great volatility, principals that reset even at a time relatively close to each other can do so at very different rates. In particular the greatest risk is rates resetting consistently *against* us, meaning that the floating rate of the loans resets consistently lower than expected, reducing our income, and the floating rate of the debt resets consistently higher than expected, increasing our costs.

A way of gauging the magnitude of this risk is to consider $\mathbf{I}\,[\mathbf{L} \mid \mathbf{B}]$, the value given by Equation 7.18, as the expected income based on the current term structure of interest rates. We then calculate

$$\mathbf{I}_\delta\,[\mathbf{L} \mid \mathbf{B}] = \sum_i N_i \left(L_i - \delta + s_L^{T_0} \right) dt_i \tag{7.19}$$

$$- \left[\sum_j N_j \left(L_j + \delta + s_A^{T_0} \right) dt_j + \sum_k N_k \left(L_k + \delta + s_A^{T_0} \right) dt_k \right]$$

which represents the income in the scenario in which the loan rates L_i reset *always* an amount δ lower than expected and the bonds' rates L_j and L_k reset *always* an amount δ higher than expected. We could set δ equal to 1 bps and define the quantity RV01 as[22]

$$RV01 = \mathbf{I}_\delta\,[\mathbf{L} \mid \mathbf{B}] - \mathbf{I}\,[\mathbf{L} \mid \mathbf{B}]$$

Once we have this amount we can then multiply it by what we think could be the worst movement in interest rates. For example, if the resetting principals are usually spaced by, say, 10 days, we could check historically what has been the greatest ten-day move in LIBOR and multiply it by the calculated value of RV01. This (it is easy to see how RV01 is linear in δ) should give us a rough estimate of the size of our loss due to resetting risk. The size of the loss should be compared with the cost of hedging it, which would be through FRAs: if for every day on which we have some principal resetting we enter into an FRA of equal principal, then our realized income will be equal to our expected income, minus of course the cost of entering into the FRAs. The downside is therefore that this, particularly for a portfolio consisting of a greatly scattered collection of debt and loans, is a very costly strategy.

Resetting risk is a risk that all interest rates traders face and not only those managing a balance of debt and income. The simplest strategy of protection is also the most trivial one: the trader makes sure that the largest amount of instruments is grouped so that the resetting dates occur on the smallest set of different dates.

7.4.5 Numerical Example: Estimating Reset Risk

In the previous section we explained how, in general, although the floating rate indexing our assets (the loans) is the same as the one indexing our

---

[22]The same way as PV01 stand for the present value of 1 bps shift, RV01 could stand for the reset value of 1 bps.

liabilities (the bonds), this rate does not reset on the same date. This could have an adverse effect on our income.

Using as an example our fictitious portfolio of one loan and five bonds and the numerical tools introduced in Section 7.4.3, we are going to try to quantify this risk.

Income shown in Table 7.11 is calculated for every six-month period. In Table 7.12 we express it as a return. In order to calculate the impact of reset risk we need to gauge the sensitivity of *all* the values in Table 7.11 to an adverse resetting of floating interest rates, in our example of six-month LIBOR.

The calculations are exactly the same as the ones carried out for Section 7.4.3, however, as shown in Equation 7.19, we increase by a certain amount the interest rate resetting for bonds and decrease by the same amount the interest rate resetting for loans. This is because we have chosen, somewhat perversely, our portfolio so that the loan rates and the bonds' rates reset, as shown in Figure 7.4, all on different dates. In particular, the loan resets every May 3 and November 3 and the bonds reset every May 10 and November 10, and every April 27 and October 27.

By subtracting the adverse income obtained this way from the income obtained without the extra adverse shift, but simply using the forward rates plus the loan and bond spreads (in practice the income shown in Table 7.11), we gauge the impact of reset risk. This is shown in Table 7.13. In the first column we have the size of the rate shift, in the second the impact, and in the third the actual net income we would earn should the adverse resetting of rates actually take place.

The first line shows what we have defined as RV01, that is, the impact for one basis point. This is the most significant value since, as we have said previously, this type of impact is roughly linear. For example, a useful exercise is to note that our resetting dates are grouped in approximately a 15-day period (from the 27th of one month to the 10th of the following one). This

TABLE 7.13 The effect of floating rates resetting consistently in a way detrimental to the portfolio income.

Size of adverse reset (bps)	Impact on income (absolute value)	Net income after effect (absolute value)
1	−0.10	2.22
5	−0.48	1.84
10	−0.95	1.37
20	−1.91	0.41
30	−2.87	−0.55

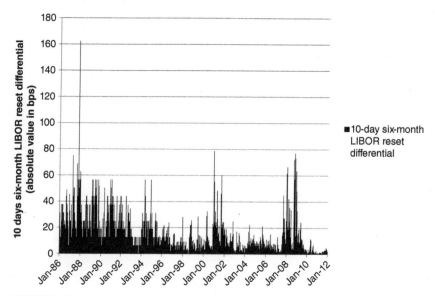

FIGURE 7.5 The absolute value of the 10-day reset differential for USD six-month LIBOR.

means that, considering only working days, we are exposed to rates resetting to roughly 10 days apart. We could ask ourselves what the usual difference is between the values of the same rate resetting 10 days apart. We could refine our question by specifying whether we want a period of high, medium, or low volatility interest rates. Once we have this usual value we can multiply it by the RV01 and obtain the risk we incur due to rate reset.

In our portfolio we are sensitive to the reset of the six-month LIBOR. Imagining that our currency is USD, Figure 7.5 shows the absolute value of the difference between USD six-month LIBOR resetting 10 days apart. We have taken a time series of rates for the past 25 years and we have taken the absolute value of the difference between each rate and the one resetting 10 days earlier.

As we can see, the difference sometimes is very large where one reaches the maximum value of more than 150 bps.[23] From Table 7.13 we see that a consistent adverse setting of the rates equal to 30 bps is enough to produce, as shown in the third column, a net loss.

---

[23]Note that the three large peaks, indicating great rate volatility, correspond to the 1987 crisis, the dot-com crisis, and the 2007 to 2009 financial crisis.

CHAPTER 8

Conclusion

We have reached the end of our discussion and it is probably useful to now draw some conclusions from such a disparate array of topics. These have been multiple and not always connected to each other in an immediately apparent way: We have striven to show, in the introduction and at the beginning of each chapter, the links between them, but it would be important to once more discuss why we have touched upon these concepts.

8.1 CREDIT IS EVERYWHERE

If one and one thing only should have transpired from our discussion, it is that any aspect of any financial activity can be related in some more or less immediate way to the concept of credit. The next tangible step from saying that credit is connected to a financial transaction is to say that credit will affect its value. From what we have learned we can highlight two fundamental ways (two sides of the same phenomenon) in which credit plays a role in the valuation of a financial instrument: one that becomes manifest through ourselves and one through our counterpart.

The first manifestation of credit is the fact that, most of the time, in order to begin any financial activity we need to borrow liquidity, and this funding activity reflects our own credit. We have seen explicitly how this works in Chapter 6 where the funding activity of an institution has been discussed at great length.

The second manifestation of credit is the view we take of our counterpart, and we let the term counterpart take a very general meaning ranging from the issuer of a bond we purchase to the counterpart in a swap transaction or the borrower of a loan we issue. We started discussing credit explicitly in Chapter 3 where we discussed the concept of default and the idea of measuring the probability that it does not happen.

Of course these two aspects are simply the same one seen from two different points of view. Our funding cost is driven by the perception that others have of ourselves, when we are seen by someone else as counterparts, and the possibility that we might default on our obligations. When we assess the creditworthiness of our counterpart we are basically establishing, together with all the other counterparts of our counterpart, our counterpart's funding cost.

These two concepts find the perfect and clearest expression in the idea of assessing the present value of a future cash flow: the value we attribute today to a cash flow in the future has to be closely linked to our belief that the payment will actually take place and the party promising the payment will not default on its obligation to us. We discussed this at great length in Chapter 2. There we have seen that the coming to terms with the crucial role of credit in the action of discounting was an incremental process.

At the beginning it was commonly accepted that to face a counterpart in a swap transaction was as risky as lending a sum of money to a financial institution and therefore the discount rate was driven by the interbank (LIBOR). Then the fact that financial institutions borrow at different levels in different currencies started to play a role. According to whether the currency of a transaction was the institution's native currency, the introduction of a currency basis (which could be positive or negative) on top of the LIBOR took place in the calculation of a discount factor. Under a conceptual (and also mathematical) point of view, this was an important step because it was the first time that one conceived the idea that the index rate to which the cash flows of a swap leg were linked did not represent the same rate used for discounting. From here the next logical step was one involving frequency. If the funding cost of an institution was linked to a specific rate, say the three-month LIBOR, then the difference between this rate and those of other frequencies, represented by the tenor basis swap, should be included in the calculation.

The most recent step is also the most important and the most fundamental under a theoretical point of view. It concerns the introduction of discounting linked to the rate paid by a collateral position. Why is collateral and the concept of collateral itself so important? We have seen in Section 2.4 that collateral can be posted in many ways, but in essence collateral is *real* money. Its reality and its purpose, to mitigate[1] credit risk, mean that by adopting its rate of return as the rate of discounting we are openly acknowledging that discounting is essentially about credit risk.

---

[1] We say mitigate because for practical reasons, as we have mentioned, the presence of collateral does not eliminate credit risk.

None of the preceding is more apparent than in the context of bond pricing. The detailed study of discounting in Chapter 2 and the analysis of the impact of credit in Section 5.3 show, combined, that discounting is the main driver of a bond price. When this is seen in the context of distressed or illiquid bonds as we do in Section 5.4, then we understand how the price of a bond is truly dominated by the credit of the issuer.

We then tried to blend the study of discounting, credit, and bond issuance into the narrative of the day-to-day running of a treasury operation. Crucial to this was the introduction of a financial instrument, the asset swap. The asset swap, as seen in Section 6.1, enabled us to normalize, so to speak, the information contained in a bond price, or its yield, and express it as a spread. The combination of all the asset swap spreads paid by a financial institution on its multiple bonds (all relative to some benchmark floating rate as seen in Section 6.4.1) contribute to the funding curve.

The funding cost of an institution is then the tool to measure its net return and performance. A funding cost expressed as a spread allows itself to be compared to the spread earned on, for example, loans. The difference between the two, simple in principle, is nonetheless a complex measure that forms the core of asset liability management as seen in Section 7.4.

We have thus seen how credit permeates, in a progressively more explicit manner, multiple aspects of the financial landscape, from the simple concept of time value to the measure through which the performance of an entire institution is observed. Let us now proceed from this conceptual summary on the role of credit to a more practical view.

8.2   THE FUNDAMENTAL STEPS TO BORROWING, LENDING, AND INVESTING: A SUMMARY

A useful exercise that will help us put together some of the most important concepts we have discussed is to imagine that we are setting up a brand-new treasury operation.

The first step is to decide how conservative and risk averse we want to be. As mentioned at the very beginning in Sections 1.1 and 1.4 when discussing the origins of capital, in Section 6.4.2 when discussing liquidity, and in Sections 7.1 and 7.3.2 when discussing the capital requirements of a financial institution, we need to decide what leverage we want to apply to our activity. The more aggressive the profile, the greater is the percentage of our lending financed by debt. Whatever level of nondebt we choose to have in our operation we need to obtain it either through donation, personal capital, share issuance, and so on.

We are now in possession of some liquidity, and a principal debt target. We need to make a decision on the type of institution we are trying to build and the relationship we want to establish between our borrowing and lending activities. It is, of course, the case that our lending spread will be greater than our borrowing spread when seen in relation to a similar benchmark: we need to decide conceptually our main reason of business.

Let us try to make this point clearer. In the introductory chapter, in Sections 1.2 and 1.3, we have taken the point of view of a development institution. In that framework the institution's mission is to lend to clients in the developing world. Loans are tailored to specific projects and, in what differentiates this view from that of, say, a small commercial bank, they are not for profit, meaning that the rate paid on the loan is only higher than the rate paid on debt by an amount deemed sufficient to cover operational costs. In this framework, lending is the primary activity and borrowing is carried out in order to fund the lending activity. In other frameworks, as we shall discuss below, lending might not be the driver for the institution and this in turn can have an effect on our borrowing target.

Any debt-issuing business, by mandate, looks for the cheapest possible debt. We have seen in Section 6.2 how this search hinges on the ability of the borrower to issue debt that is attractive to investors. In a sort of manifestation of comparative advantage, we need to ask ourselves what it is that we can offer that would attract investors, ultimately reflecting on our borrowing costs. This might seem, and probably is, a circular argument in the sense that all the special features we can offer in a bond are in the end simply expressions of our credit standing.

If we are a multilateral development bank (MDB) and an investor is attracted to our debt because of this, in the end it is because the investor seeks the good credit of MDBs. If we are a developed country agency or corporate, and we issue an emerging market currency-denominated bond to attract investors, in the end they are attracted to the better credit we can offer compared to local institutions. If investors are attracted to our long-dated debt it is because they believe we are capable of honoring our long-term obligations. Having said that, despite all these features being alternative manifestations of credit standing, it is important to know where to act and to understand some of the challenges, as discussed in Section 6.2.2, involved in issuing simple versus structured debt in the name of ever-smaller funding cost.

In the framework of a development bank, smaller funding level means smaller lending charges for the bank's borrowers. Because of this, our view of the two activities is fairly linked and almost in step. A for-profit institution on the other hand seeks to maximize the net return of its lending activity, that is, the return on its loans once its debt has been repaid. This means that in the case of a traditional financial institution, as we mentioned previously, the lending activity is less of a driving force and it does not necessarily place a cap on the borrowing activity.

If we decide to set up a development institution we shall have a lending target and issue debt to finance it. Once we have achieved the first, our borrowing activity needs to cease, irrespective of how attractive an issuing patch we are crossing. On the contrary, if we decide to set up a traditional financial institution, should we find ourselves in the situation where we can issue at very low funding levels, we might exploit it and, even if we have exhausted our lending scope, try to look for other investment opportunities. This, of course, is a rather forced example since, in general, those who borrow cheaply are those who borrow with restraint.

The type of institution we have decided to set up will dictate our approach to investment (in this context we do not treat loans as investments). We can choose to be conservative and treat our investment portfolio simply as a means of preserving our equity and providing emergency liquidity. In this case we would probably set up a few investment portfolios, each with a specific target and benchmark: a combination of extremely liquid portfolios linked to some overnight rate and other portfolios with a longer dated horizon. The former would be made of assets easy to sell and would help us create an emergency buffer, the latter would increase or maintain a healthy equity position for the institution. We have seen in Sections 6.4.2 and 7.3.1 the types of instruments we can choose to invest in and, in the name of risk aversion, we would try to swap them out in the most conservative way, that is, try to have the least amount of naked exposure to the instruments themselves.

We could choose instead to be more aggressive. We could choose to resemble not a normal fund but rather something more akin to a hedge fund or a (now disappearing) proprietary trading desk of an investment bank. We would choose not to hedge or hedge incompletely and therefore take positions.[2] Alternatively we could hedge in a more innovative way by combining instruments that only we believe are related. This can provide a less expensive form of hedging but at the same time is more risky since it does not offer a guarantee of risk neutrality.

Let us summarize our position. In our decision process we have found the initial capital needed for the leverage profile we have chosen for our

---

[2]As we have seen in Section 7.2, to hedge means to take opposite positions in similar instruments and therefore to be indifferent, that is, risk neutral, to the movement of the underlying. Not to hedge means to be risk partial and therefore take only one open position with respect to some underlying.

institution; we have decided on a strategy to find what it is we can offer, what our comparative advantage is to obtain the cheapest possible funding; we have decided, as far as lending is concerned, whether we want to run a for-profit organization; finally, we have decided on a risk profile for our investments. We now need to decide on a strategy to manage all these different points.

In our analysis we have always tried to observe matters with the widest possible angle. We started stressing the importance of this approach when we said that the nature of our funding (for example, in the context of currency basis) must be taken into account when discounting a cash flow. Often to understand a point one needs to include an array of elements that might not be apparently related but that are nonetheless crucial. In a similar fashion all the activities we have discussed throughout this book represent the necessary core of any banking business. In our mental experiment, the processes that worked toward the building of our treasury operation should all come together in a sound asset liability management.

In Section 7.4.2 we introduced the concept of income,[3] in essence the future, as opposed to the present, value of the sum of payables or receivables. The careful balance of income and cost is essential to the smooth running of our operations. Crucial to achieving this balance is the decision about the level of granularity in the matching of debt and loans. Would a collection, a set, of bonds constitute the funding for a set of loans? Would there be a one-to-one relationship instead where each loan is funded by one specific bond?

Once we have chosen the above we need to choose how to match maturities. We first introduced in Sections 1.2 and 1.3 and then studied in Section 7.4.2 the importance of the relationship between the maturity of a lending instrument and the maturity of a borrowing instrument. When addressing this issue in managing our treasury operation, we need to consider two conflicting issues. On one side there is the almost universal truth that the shorter our borrowing horizon is compared to the lending one, the greater our *potential* profit is going to be. On the other we know that the greater the disparity in maturity between borrowing and lending, the greater the exposure to refinancing risk, that is, the risk of having to issue future debt at a rate considerably higher than the initial one, and even possibly higher than the rate received as income. Since borrowing short and lending long has been the norm since the dawn of banking, refinancing risk has been and is the greatest risk facing any treasury operation. With a wider view one could claim that by being at the center of the careful balance between income and

---

[3] We saw that if we decided that income can only be positive, its negative manifestation is a cost.

cost and therefore of solvency itself, refinancing risk is the greatest risk facing any financial institution or any debt-issuing entity as a whole.

The final decision, after choosing up to which level we want to match the maturities of our cost and income instruments, is more subtle but important nonetheless. We need to consider the frequency of these instruments. In Section 7.4.4 we have seen the important concept of reset risk: cost and income linked to the same floating index, even if matching as far as principal and maturity are concerned, are exposed to the risk that if the index resets on different days it might fix at different levels working against our profit. This apparently small effect, in periods of high interest rate volatility and on portfolios with scattered reset dates, can have very serious consequences not only reducing our profit but even, as seen in the realistic example in Section 7.4.5, generating a loss. Fortunately, since we are starting our operation from the very beginning, the solution can be quite simple and consists of matching the reset frequency of our assets and liabilities at trade inception.

With the ease and speed only possible in the realm of thought experiments, we have laid down the foundations of our treasury operation. By considering issues ranging from the leverage of our institution to the funding target to asset liability management, we have drawn the schematics of our business and in the process we have put together in one picture all that we have learned throughout this book. This, combined with the analysis of credit in its many forms and seen through the example of development banking, has been the core of our discussion.

In the introduction we used the image of a rope. We imagined a rope placed in the hands of the reader/treasurer that would allow us, by pulling on the funding cost of an institution and observing its movement, to see the link between the credit present in the markets and the running of a financial institution's debt management. We hope that at the end of this book, the hold on that rope has tightened to a confident and understanding grip.

Implying Zero Rates from FX Forward Quotes

In Equation 2.3 we have shown how to obtain a discount factor from an FX forward quote. While approximately correct, the issue is a little more complex. FX forwards are not effective immediately in the sense that the real settlement day is not the moment we agree on the price, but a moment $T + n$, that is, a number of days n (usually 1, 2, or 3) later.

If we look at Figure 4.5 we see that next to the FX forward quote there is the actual number of days (e.g., we see that six months is precisely 182 days) for which it is valid; this is to ensure a precise calculation.

If we want to create a discount factor for currency X to *today* (the real definition of present value) we need the combination of USD *forward discount factor* from the effective settlement date to the maturity of the FX forward and the FX forward itself; this will take us to the effective date. Then we need some interest rate instrument in X to discount from the effective date to today.

Let us collect the information we need:

- Now is time T (we usually define now as t but here we try to follow the usual notation)
- The real settlement date $T + n$
- The number of days d determining the length of the FX forward
- The USD forward discount factor (we have usually written a discount factor $D_{i,j}$ without the first suffix denoting the present; here we add it to avoid confusion)

$$D_{T+n,T+n+d}^{USD} = \frac{D_{T,T+n+d}^{USD}}{D_{T,T+n}^{USD}}$$

- The FX forward $FW\,D_{T+n+d}$ itself

- The FX spot FX_{T+n} (we have assumed, which is usually the case, that the effective date for the spot and forwards are the same)
- Some instrument (assume a deposit) with rate R_{T+n}^X to use to discount the short end

Combining all of the above means that if we want to discount a cash flow in currency X taking place at a time $T + n + d$ we need

$$D_{T,T+n+d}^X = \frac{1}{\left(1 + R_{T+n}^X\right)^{T+n-T}} \frac{FX_{T+n}}{FW\ D_{T+n+d}} D_{T+n,T+n+d}^{USD}$$

The main difference from Equation 2.3 is the extra discount in local currency for the first few days immediately after now. Although it might seem a trivial detail when rates are high (which could be the case in emerging markets, which in turn are the markets where we would use FX forwards to imply discount factors)—it could have an impact as large as the bid-offer, the usual measure of relevance.

CDS Spreads and Default Probabilities

In Section 4.2.3 we claimed that

$$1 - S_T \approx \frac{CDS_T}{1 - R} \tag{B.1}$$

That is, the probability of default is roughly equal to the CDS rate divided by one minus recovery. Here is how to get this result. From the definition of CDS we have

$$\frac{CDS_T}{1 - R} = \frac{\sum_i D_i \, [S_{i-1} - S_i]}{\sum_j D_j S_j dt_j}$$

We only want to show that our claim is reasonable for a short-dated T (which is quite normal since when we calculate default probabilities we are gauging something fairly imminent). Equation B.1 is equivalent to showing that

$$\frac{\sum_i D_i \, [S_{i-1} - S_i]}{\sum_j D_j S_j dt_j} \approx 1 - S_T$$

One can assume the special case in which, particularly for a short-dated CDS, all the premium is paid up front, reducing the above to

$$\sum_i D_i \, [S_{i-1} - S_i] \approx 1 - S_T \tag{B.2}$$

From the short-dated assumption it should follow that $D_i \approx 1$ and also $S_{i-1} \approx 1$, in practice approximating the integral to a one-step calculation, which is Equation B.2 itself.

Incidentally since we have (from Equation 3.13) that

$$S_t = e^{-\int_t^T h_s \, ds}$$

using a simple binomial expansion we obtain

$$S_t \approx 1 - h_t$$

from which it follows, combining the above with Equation B.1, that

$$h_t \approx \frac{CDS_t}{1 - R}$$

is often used as the first trial value with which to start the solver algorithm.

Modeling the Credit-Driven Prepayment Option of a Loan

In Section 3.3.2 we mentioned how in almost all cases a loan contains an embedded prepayment option. Here we shall present a simple model on how to value this option; as we mentioned in Section 3.3.2 we shall follow closely Schönbucher [74].

Both interest rate and credit are described by short-rate models, the interest rate by

$$dr = \mu_r dt + \sigma_r d W_1 \tag{C.1}$$

where μ_r and σ_r are the drift and volatility of the interest rate process and the credit by

$$d\lambda = \mu_\lambda dt + \sigma_\lambda \left(\rho d W_1 + \sqrt{1 - \rho^2} d W_2 \right) \tag{C.2}$$

where μ_λ is the drift of the credit process, σ_λ its volatility, and where ρ represents the correlation between the Brownian motion W_1 of the interest rate and the one, W_2, of the credit process. The default time happens at the time of the first jump in a Cox process. For simplicity we assume the recovery rate to be deterministic. Let us imagine that we need to find the price of a security $V(t)$ that is sensitive to credit and interest rate and whose price can be defined as

$$V(t) = v(t, r(t), \lambda(t)) \tag{C.3}$$

Applying Ito's Lemma we obtain

$$dv = \frac{\partial v}{\partial t}dt + \frac{\partial v}{\partial r}dr + \frac{1}{2}\sigma_r^2 \frac{\partial^2 v}{\partial r^2}dt + \frac{\partial v}{\partial \lambda}d\lambda \tag{C.4}$$
$$+ \frac{1}{2}\sigma_\lambda^2 \frac{\partial^2 v}{\partial \lambda^2}dt + \rho\sigma_r\sigma_\lambda \frac{\partial^2 v}{\partial \lambda \partial r}dt + \int_0^1 [g(t, r, \lambda) - v(r, t, \lambda)] m(dt)$$

where $g(t, r, \lambda)$ is the payoff at default and $m(dt)$ is a point process describing default. The application of nonarbitrage conditions leads to

$$\frac{\partial v}{\partial t} + \mathcal{L}v - (\lambda + r)v = -g^e\lambda - f \tag{C.5}$$

where g^e is the expected (deterministic in our case) payoff in case of default and the operator $\mathcal{L}$ is given by

$$\mathcal{L} = \mu_r\frac{\partial}{\partial r} + \frac{1}{2}\sigma_r^2\frac{\partial^2}{\partial r^2} + \mu_\lambda\frac{\partial}{\partial \lambda} + \frac{1}{2}\sigma_\lambda^2\frac{\partial^2}{\partial \lambda^2} + \rho\sigma_r\sigma_\lambda\frac{\partial^2}{\partial \lambda\partial r} \tag{C.6}$$

The above should be solved with the appropriate boundary conditions.

The Relation between Macaulay and Modified Durations

We are going to show, as stated in Section 5.2.3, how the relationship between Macaulay and modified durations are dependent on the type of compounding we choose.

Let us first consider the case of continuous compounding. The modified duration is defined (Equation 5.7) as

$$MD = -\frac{1}{B_t}\frac{\partial B_t}{\partial Y}$$

If we calculate the bond value B_t, assuming continuous compounding, we have

$$B_t = \sum_i^T C_i e^{-YT_i} dt_i$$

where C_T, here and throughout this appendix, includes the principal payment. Taking the derivative of the above and dividing by the bond value we obtain

$$MD = -\frac{1}{B_t}\left[-\sum_i^T T_i C_i e^{-YT_i} dt_i\right] = \sum_i^T \frac{T_i C_i e^{-YT_i} dt_i}{B_t}$$

which is the definition of Macaulay duration given by Equation 5.8.

Let us now consider the situation in which the yield is not continuously compounded, that is,

$$B_t = \sum_i^T \frac{C_i}{(1+Y)^{T_i}} dt_i$$

If we take the derivative and divide by the bond value we obtain

$$
\begin{aligned}
MD &= -\frac{1}{B_t}\left[-\sum_i^T \frac{T_i C_i (1+Y)^{T_i-1}}{(1+Y)^{2T_i}}\right] \\
&= \frac{1}{B_t}\sum_i^T \frac{T_i C_i}{(1+Y)^{1+T_i}} \\
&= \frac{1}{1+Y}\sum_i^T \frac{T_i C_i}{B_t (1+Y)^{T_i}}
\end{aligned}
\tag{D.1}
$$

from which it follows that for noncontinuously compounded yields the relationship between Macaulay duration McD and modified duration is

$$
MD(1+Y) = McD
$$

as given by Equation 5.9.

The Impact of Discounting on an Asset Swap Spread

In this appendix we show that the impact of discounting on an asset swap spread is limited, as discussed in Section 6.1.2.

Let us for simplicity assume (a fairly weak assumption since it would be a common situation) that the fixed and floating legs of the swap have the same frequency. We are going to discount an asset swap with spread s_A with discount factors D_i and then with discount factors $\overline{D_i}$ and see what the difference, if at all, is with the new asset swap spread $\overline{s_A}$. In practice we want to solve

$$\sum_i (L_i + s_A) D_i - \sum_i C D_i = \sum_i (L_i + \overline{s_A}) \overline{D_i} - \sum_i C \overline{D_i} \qquad (E.1)$$

for $\overline{s_A}$, since both sides need to be equal to the bond price because the change in discounting was not applied to the bond.

Grouping the terms in E.1 we obtain

$$\sum_i (L_i + s_A - C) D_i - \sum_i (L_i - C) \overline{D_i} = \overline{s_A} \sum_i \overline{D_i}$$

$$\frac{\sum_i (L_i - C) D_i}{\sum_i \overline{D_i}} + s_A \frac{\sum_i D_i}{\sum_i \overline{D_i}} - \frac{\sum_i (L_i - C)}{\sum_i \overline{D_i}} = \overline{s_A}$$

$$\frac{1}{\sum_i \overline{D_i}} \left(\sum_i L_i D_i - \sum_i L_i \overline{D_i} \right) + \left(C - C \frac{\sum_i D_i}{\sum_i \overline{D_i}} \right) + s_A \frac{\sum_i D_i}{\sum_i \overline{D_i}} = \overline{s_A}$$

Let us imagine that $\sum_i \overline{D_i}$ is slightly greater than $\sum_i D_i$, then the term

$$C - C \frac{\sum_i D_i}{\sum_i \overline{D_i}} \qquad (E.2)$$

will be slightly larger than zero. The term

$$\frac{1}{\sum_i \overline{D_i}} \left(\sum_i L_i D_i - \sum_i L_i \overline{D_i} \right) \tag{E.3}$$

will be slightly less than zero, but smaller in absolute value than the term in Equation E.2. The term

$$s_A \frac{\sum_i D_i}{\sum_i \overline{D_i}} \tag{E.4}$$

will be slightly less than s_A. Combining the three terms in Equations E.2, E.3, and E.4 we can see how

$$s_A \approx \overline{s_A}$$

Of course the same holds if $\sum_i \overline{D_i}$ is slightly smaller than $\sum_i D_i$, in which case each effect would be opposite in sign.

Replication Leading to Risk-Neutral Probabilities

With the idea of stressing the difference between the valuation of financial and nonfinancial instruments as introduced in Section 7.2.1, let us consider a simple example not linked to the financial world. Let us consider an insurance company that pays out $1,000 in case of loss of luggage; statistically it has been found that 10% of the time someone loses a suitcase. A price for this product would then be $100 since it is the probability of the luggage being in the state lost times the payout when this is the case. If the insurance company were to charge $101 to every customer, in the long run they would make a profit: every 10 customers they would collect $1,010, pay out $1,000 to the unfortunate one, and gain $10 profit. The problem is that this is true for a very large number of insurance contracts sold, which realistically will be sold only over time. What if the number of insurance contracts sold is not large enough? What if over two years 2,000 insurance contracts are sold at regular interval and, as expected, 20 suitcases are lost, but all are lost in the first three months? This would create a serious liquidity problem. This approach is based on assigning probabilities based on the distribution of the *real-world measure*; this approach is chosen by insurance companies (which try to protect themselves by being very conservative, that is, pessimistic, about the possible scenarios) but not in finance.

Simplifying what we have said about discounting, let us say that if I were to borrow $1 today for time T, I would expect the lender to want more than $1 in T, say $\exp(rT)$, where r is the cost of borrowing, which we assume to be constant and continuously compounded. Similarly, the present value of $1 in T is given by $\exp(-rT)$. Let us define this simple bond as $B_t = B_0 \exp(rt)$.

Let us imagine a situation in which we have a stock worth S_0 at time $t = 0$ and which after a time step T is equal to either S_u or S_d

$$S_0 \begin{cases} S_u & S_u > S_0 \\ S_d & S_d < S_0 \end{cases}$$

and we need to price a derivative whose payoff is $V(T) = (S_T - S_0)^+$. We could try to price it as in the preceding insurance example, but should we sell it we would be exposed to the return of the stock and hence it would work only on a very large number of options sold. Let us then use a different approach. The payoff of the option can take two values, either $V_u = S_u - S_0$ in case the stock goes up to the value S_u, or $V_d = 0$ if the stock goes down to the value S_d. Let us then construct a portfolio in which we buy α amount of stock S and β amount of bond B_t. With this portfolio we try to simulate the behavior of the option itself, that is, we would like to see

$$\alpha S_u + \beta B_0 \exp(rT) = V_u \quad \text{if} \quad S_T = S_u$$
$$\alpha S_d + \beta B_0 \exp(rT) = V_d \quad \text{if} \quad S_T = S_d$$

Since we have two equations and two unknowns we can easily solve for α and β and find

$$\alpha = \frac{V_u - V_d}{S_u - S_d} \quad \text{and} \quad \beta = \frac{1}{B_0 \exp(rT)} \frac{V_d S_u - V_u S_d}{S_u - S_d} \tag{F.1}$$

If we buy stock and bonds at the beginning in quantities given by α and β, we can say that the price of the derivative is given by

$$V = S_0 \frac{V_u - V_d}{S_u - S_d} + \exp(-rT) \frac{V_d S_u - V_u S_d}{S_u - S_d} \tag{F.2}$$

From the above we can see that we are absolutely indifferent to where the stock goes; in any case we are able to express the value of the derivative, because we have correctly *replicated* it. The concept of replication is fundamental in modern option pricing, but let us first observe another important point. Let us define the quantity

$$q = \frac{S_0 \exp(rt) - S_d}{S_u - S_d}$$

and we can argue that this value has to be between 0 and 1. We can also see that we can rewrite Equation F.2 as

$$V = \exp(-rt) [q V_u + (1 - q) V_d] \tag{F.3}$$

We can safely say that q is some sort of probability and therefore the above equation looks a lot like the type of valuation used in the insurance example before: the probability of the stock going up times the payout in that situation and the probability of the stock going down times what the payout would be in that situation. The crucial difference is that the probabilities are not obtained in the same way: q and $1 - q$ are probabilities in the *risk-neutral measure*. The name is due exactly to the fact that in this type of valuation we are indifferent to the actual behavior of the stock, provided that we can buy it. This small detail is absolutely crucial because, as we said, we have priced the derivative by *replication*: if we cannot buy the stock then the valuation fails. This simple and yet extremely clever strategy is at the center of the revolution brought by Black and Scholes in 1973.

References

1. Viral V. Acharya and Lasse Heje Pedersen. (2005). *Asset pricing with liquidity risk. Journal of Financial Economics*, 77, 375–410.
2. Tobias Adrian and Hyun Song Shin. (2010). *Liquidity and leverage. Journal of Financial Intermediation*, 3, 418–437.
3. Edward I. Altman and Duen Li Kao. (1992). *Rating drift of high yield bonds. Journal of Fixed Income*, 1:4, 15–20.
4. Leif B. G. Andersen and Vladimir V. Piterbarg. (2010). *Interest rate modeling.* London: Atlantic Financial Press.
5. Sarah Babb. (2009). *Behind the development banks: Washington politics, world poverty an the wealth of nations.* Chicago: University of Chicago Press.
6. David K. Backus and Gregor W. Smith. (1992). *Consumption and real exchange rates in dynamic economies with non-traded goods. Journal of International Economics*, 35, 297–316.
7. Eric Banks. (2004). *Liquidity risk: managing asset and funding risks.* London: Palgrave Macmillan.
8. Bank for International Settlements. (2004). *Basel II: international convergence of capital measurement and capital standard: a revised framework.*
9. Ravi M. Bansal and Magnus Dahlquist. (2000). *The forward premium puzzle: different tales from developed and emerging economies. Journal of International Economics*, **51**, 115–144.
10. Martin Baxter and Andrew Rennie. (1996). *Financial calculus: an introduction to derivative pricing.* Cambridge: Cambridge University Press.
11. Eric Benhamou. (2003). *Swaps: basis swaps* article appearing in the forthcoming *Encyclopedia of Financial Engineering and Risk Management.*
12. Arthur M. Berd, Roy Mashal and Peili Wang. (2004). *Defining, estimating and using credit term structures. Part 3: consistent CDS-Bond basis.* Lehman Brothers, Quantitative Credit Research.
13. Bilson, J. F. O. (1981). *The speculative efficiency hypothesis. Journal of Business*, 54, 435.
14. Fischer Black and Myron Scholes. (1973). *The pricing of options and corporate liabilities. Journal of Political Economy*, **81**, 637–654.
15. Carl de Boor. (1978). *A practical guide to splines.* New York: Springer Verlag.
16. Steven M. Bragg. (2010). *Treasury management: the practitioner's guide.* Berlin: Wiley Corporate F & A.
17. Damiano Brigo and Aurelien Alfonsi. (2005). *Credit default swap calibration and derivative pricing with the SSRD stochastic intensity model, Finance and Stochastics.* **9**, 29–42.

18. Damiano Brigo and Agostino Capponi. (2008). *Bilateral counterparty risk valuation with stochastic dynamical models and application to Credit Default Swaps. arXiv.* Available at http://arxiv.org/abs/0812.3705

19. Damiano Brigo and Fabio Mercurio. (2006). *Interest Rate Models—Theory and Practice. With Smile, Inflation and Credit.* Berlin: Springer.

20. Damiano Brigo and Massimo Morini. (2005). *CDS market formulas and models. Proceedings of the 18th annual Warwick options conference.*

21. Damiano Brigo, Andrea Pallavicini, and Vasileios Papatheodorou. (2009). *Bilateral counterparty risk valuation for interest-rate products: impact of volatilities and correlations. arXiv,* **911** 23. Available at http://arxiv.org/abs/0911.3331

22. Markus K. Brunnermeier and Lasse Heje Pedersen. (2008). *Market liquidity and funding liquidity. Review of Financial Studies,* **22,** 2201–2238.

23. Markus K. Brunnermeier, Stefan Nagel, and Lasse Heje Pedersen. (2008). *Carry trades and currency crashes. National Bureau of Economic Research working paper.*

24. Craig Burnside, Martin Eichenbaum, Isaac Kleshchelski, and Sergio Rebelo. (2011). *Do peso problems explain the returns to the carry trade? Review of Financial Studies,* **24,** 853–891.

25. Christopher A. Candelaria, Jose A. Lopez, and Mark M. Spiegel. (2010). *Bond currency denomination and the Yen carry trade. The Federal Reserve Bank of San Francisco working paper.*

26. Chuang-Chang Chang and Yu Jih-Chieh. (2006). *A spread-based model for the valuation of credit derivatives with correlated defaults and counterparty risks. Research in Finance,* **23,** 193–220.

27. Laurie Carver. (2012). *Traders close ranks against FVA critics. Risk, September* 18–22.

28. Robert Cooper. (2004). *Corporate treasury and cash management.* London: Palgrave Macmillan.

29. Sanjiv R. Das and Rangarajan K. Sundaram. (2000). *A discrete-time approach to arbitrage free pricing of credit derivatives. Management Science,* **46,** 46–62.

30. Emanuel Derman and Nassim Nicholas Taleb. (2005). *The illusions of dynamic replication. Quantitative Finance,* **5,** 323–326.

31. Mathias Drehmann and Kleopatra Nikolau. (2008). *Funding liquidity risk: definition and measurements. EFA 2009 Bergen Meetings Paper.*

32. Darrel Duffie and Kenneth Singleton. (1997). *An econometric model of the term structure of interest rate swap yields. Journal of Finance,* **52,** 1287–1323.

33. Darrel Duffie, Jun Pan and Kenneth Singleton. (2000). *Transform analysis and asset pricing for affine jump diffusion. Econometrica,* **68,** 1343–1376.

34. *Gauchos and gadflies.* (2011). *The Economist,* Oct. 22nd.

35. Philippe Ehlers and Philipp Schönbucher. (2006). *The influence of FX risk on credit spreads.* Working paper.

36. Bernd Engelmann. (2011). *A framework for pricing and risk management of loans with embedded options.* SSRN eLibrary.

37. Alison Etheridge. (2002). *A course in financial calculus.* Cambridge: Cambridge University Press.

38. Frank J. Fabozzi. (2005). *The handbook of fixed income securities*. New York: McGraw-Hill.
39. Statement of Financial Accounting Standards No. 133. (1998). *Financial Accounting Standards Board*.
40. Christian P. Fries. (2010). *Discounting Revisited. Valuations under funding costs, counterparty risk and collateralization*. Working paper.
41. Masaaki Fujii, Yasufumi Shimada, and Akihiko Takahashi. (2010). *A note on construction of multiple swap curves with and without collateral*. CARF Working Paper Series No. CARF-F-154.
42. Masaaki Fujii, Yasufumi Shimada and Akihiko Takahashi. (2010). *Collateral posting and choice of collateral currency: implications for derivative pricing and risk management*. CARF Working Paper Series No. CARF-F-216.
43. Yevgeny Goncharov. (2002). *An intensity-based approach for valuation of mortgage contracts subject to prepayment risk*. Working paper.
44. Jon Gregory. (2009). *Being two-faced over counterparty risk. Risk*, **22**, 86–90.
45. Patrick S. Hagan and Graeme West. (2006). *Interpolation methods for curve construction. Applied Mathematical Finance*, **13**, 89–126.
46. Jean Helwege, Samuel Maurer, Asani Sarkar and Yuan Wang. (2009). *Credit Default Swaps Auctions and Price Discovery. The Journal of Fixed Income* **19**, 34–42.
47. Karen A. Horcher. (2005). *Essentials of managing treasury*. Wiley.
48. John Hull and Alan White. (2012). *The FVA debate. Risk Magazine*, July 83–85.
49. John Hull and Alan White. (2012). *The FVA debate continues: Hull and White respond to their critics. Risk Magazine*, October 18–22.
50. John Hull and Alan White. (2012). *LIBOR vs. OIS: The Derivatives Discounting Dilemma*. Working paper, University of Toronto.
51. John Hull, Izzy Nelken, and Alan White. (2004). *Merton's model, credit risk and volatility skews. Journal of Credit Risk*, **1**, 3–28.
52. International Swaps and Derivatives Association, Inc. (1994). ISDA Credit Support Annex.
53. International Swaps and Derivatives Association, Inc. (1999). ISDA 1999 Collateral Review.
54. Craig A. Jeffrey. (2009). *The strategic treasurer: a partnership for corporate growth*. London: Wiley.
55. Michael Johannes and Suresh Sundaresan. (2007). *The impact of collateralization on swap rates. Journal of Finance*, **62**, 383–410.
56. Philippe Jorion. (2000). *Risk management lessons from Long Term Capital Management. European Financial Management*, **6**, 277–300.
57. J. B. Kau, D. C. Keenan, W. J. Muller III, and J. F. Epperson. (1992). *A generalized valuation model for fixed-rate residential mortgages. Journal of Money, Credit and Banking*, **3**, 279–299.
58. Gregory V. Kitter. (1999). *Investment Mathematics for Finance and treasury professionals: a practical approach*. London: Wiley.
59. David Lando and Torben M. Skødeberg. (2002). *Analyzing rating transitions and rating drift with continuous observations. Journal of Banking and Finance*, **26**, 423–444.

60. Stephen Laughton and Aura Vaisbrot. (2012). *In defense of FVA—a response to Hull and White. Risk*, September 23–24.
61. Alexander Lipton and Arthur Sepp. (2009). *Credit value adjustment for credit default swaps via the structural default model. The Journal of Credit Risk*, 5, 123–146.
62. Robert C. Merton. (1974). *On the pricing of corporate debt: the risk structure of interest rates. Journal of Finance*, 29, 449–470.
63. François-Louis Michaud and Christian Upper. (2008). *What drives interbank rates? Evidence from the LIBOR panel. BIS Quarterly Review*, March 2008, 47–58.
64. Massimo Morini and Andrea Prampolini. (2011). *Risky funding with counterparty and liquidity charges. Risk Magazine*, March 70–75.
65. Dominic O'Kane and Stuart Turnbull. (2003). *Valuation of Credit Default Swaps*. Lehman Brothers, Quantitative Credit Research.
66. Dominic O'Kane. (2000). *Introduction to asset swaps*. Lehman Brothers, European Fixed Income Research.
67. Gianluca Oricchio. (2011). *Credit treasury: a credit pricing guide in liquid and non-liquid markets*. London: Palgrave Macmillan.
68. Claus M. Pedersen. (2006). *Explaining the Lehman Brothers option adjusted spread of a corporate bond*. Lehman Brothers, Quantitative Credit Research.
69. Richard Peet. (2009). *Unholy trinity: the IMF, the World Bank and the WTO*. Zed Books.
70. Vladimir V. Piterbarg. (2010). *Funding beyond discounting: collateral agreements and derivatives pricing. Risk Magazine*, February 97–102.
71. Guillaume Plantin and Hyun Song Shin. (2011). *Carry trades, monetary policy and speculative dynamics*. Working paper.
72. William H. Press, Brian P. Flannery, Saul A. Teukolsky, and William T. Vetterling. (1992). *Numerical recipes in C: the art of scientific computing*. Cambridge: Cambridge University Press.
73. Philipp J. Schönbucher. (2000). *Credit risk modeling and credit derivatives*. PhD thesis, Faculty of Economics, Bonn University, January.
74. Philipp J. Schönbucher. (2003). *Credit Derivatives pricing models*. London: Wiley Finance.
75. Krista Schwarz. (2010). *Mind the gap: disentangling credit and liquidity risk in spreads*. Working paper.
76. Donald J. Smith. (2011). *Bond math: the theory behind the formulas*. London: Wiley Finance.
77. Richard Stanton. (1995). *Rational Prepayment and the valuation of Mortgage-Backed Securities. Review of Financial Studies*, 8, 677–708.
78. Nassim N. Taleb. (1997). *Dynamic hedging: managing vanilla and exotic options*. London: John Wiley & Sons.
79. Bruce Tuckman. (2002). *Fixed income securities: tools for today's markets*. 2nd edition. London: John Wiley & Sons.
80. Bruce Tuckman and Jean-Baptiste Homè. (2003). *Consistent Pricing of FX Forwards, Cross-Currency Basis Swaps and Interest Rate Swaps in Several Currencies*. Lehman Brothers internal research paper.

81. Evert B. Vrugt. (2011). *Estimating implied default probabilities and recovery values from sovereign bond prices. The Journal of Fixed Income*, **21**, 5–14.
82. Daniel F. Waggoner. (1997). *Spline Methods for extracting interest rate curves from coupon bond prices. Federal Reserve Bank of Atlanta working paper*.
83. Catherine Weaver. (2008). *Hypocrisy trap: the World Bank and the poverty of reform*. Princeton, NJ: Princeton University Press.
84. Christopher Whittall. (2010). *The price is wrong. Risk Magazine*, March online.

About the Web Site

In order to illustrate some of the more practical points presented in this book, we offer the reader two spreadsheets containing a considerable amount of VBA code that the reader is free to use, copy, or modify. Additional material of potential interest to the reader will be added to the web site in the future. The choice of implementation is given by the fact that most people are familiar with VBA. In order to show the points made, all languages are more or less equivalent and, most important, VBA is available to anyone with an Excel license and does not need compiling. To access the spreadsheets, please visit www.wiley.com/go/treasuryfinance and enter the following password on the sign-in page: treasury789.

THE IMPLEMENTATION OF THE BOOTSTRAPPING OF AN INTEREST RATE CURVE

The spreadsheet "TreasuryFinanceInterestRateCurve.xlsm" contains the implementation of the bootstrapping of an interest rate curve as shown in Section 2.5. As mentioned above, the code is written in VBA so that it can be used in any Excel session. It is probably not the most efficient way of bootstrapping (ideally one would have built an object handle instead of bootstrapping at each interpolation request), but it is extremely easy to understand and to modify if needed.

The spreadsheet is fairly self-explanatory and already contains some realistic input values. We need to stress some constraints needed for the function to work:

- The first column of the input range must contain the type code of the instrument used (D for deposit, F for FRA, and S for swap)
- The second column must contain the maturity code of the instrument (for FRAs it is the beginning): it is given as a number and a letter code (D for day, W for week, M for month, and Y for year)

- The third column must contain the length code for FRAs only
- The fourth column must contain the main quote value (it needs to be input in absolute value, that is, not as percentage or basis points)
- The fifth column must contain the (optional) cross currency basis (this value will be used only for instruments with type code S)
- The first market data entry must be a deposit
- Forward rate agreements need to appear between deposits and swap rates
- Forward rate agreements need to be quoted with the code of the from date in the second column and the code of the length of the instruments in the third column.
- The user should select 1 for exponential interpolation and 0 for linear

THE IMPLEMENTATION OF THE BOOTSTRAPPING OF A HAZARD RATE CURVE

The spreadsheet "TreasuryFinanceHazardRateCurve.xlsm" contains the code that can be used to bootstrap a set of CDS rates in order to obtain the survival probability at a moment in time for a particular entity as of the date on which the market data is taken. The code is written in VBA so that it can be used in any Excel session. As we said previously for the interest rate curve, it is not the most efficient since we are bootstrapping the curve at each request, but it is very easy to understand and to modify if needed.

The spreadsheet is fairly explanatory and already contains some realistic inputs: in particular, the inputs should be given as two separate ranges, one for the CDS rates and one for the Interest Rate inputs. The interest rate inputs are given in the form of zero rates; we assume the user has already constructed the curve separately (for example, using the code contained in the spreadsheet "TreasuryFinanceInterestRateCurve.xlsm").

We also need to stress

- The first line of each range should only include, in the first column, the date to which the data refers (the as of date).
- In the credit range, the first column should be used for the maturity code of the instrument, the second column for the coupon of the CDS, and the third column for the recovery rate assumed for that CDS.

■ In the interest rate range, the first column should be used for the maturity code and the second column for the zero rate input.

Should the optimization process fail, the function returns ZERO NOT FOUND; the number of iterations is kept at the moment to 100. This hard-coded number can be increased or, in a useful modification of the function, can be chosen by the user.

Index